SUBSCRIPTION NOTICE

This Wiley product is updated on a periodic basis with supplements to reflect important changes in the subject matter. If you purchased this product directly from John Wiley & Sons, we have already recorded your subscription for this update service.

If, however, you purchased this product from a bookstore and wish to receive (1) the current update at no additional charge, and (2) future updates and revised or related volumes billed separately with a 30-day examination review, please send your name, company name (if applicable), address, and the title of the product to:

Supplement Department
John Wiley & Sons, Inc.
One Wiley Drive
Somerset, NJ 08875
1-800-225-5945

ENVIRONMENTAL DISPUTE HANDBOOK: LIABILITY AND CLAIMS
VOLUME 2

DAVID A. CARPENTER

ROBERT F. CUSHMAN

BRUCE W. ROZNOWSKI

Editors

Coopers
&Lybrand

Wiley Law Publications
JOHN WILEY & SONS, INC.
New York • Chichester • Brisbane • Toronto • Singapore

Library of Congress Cataloging-in-Publication Data

Environmental dispute handbook : liability and claims / David A.
  Carpenter, Robert F. Cushman, Bruce W. Roznowski, editors.
      p.   cm. — (Environmental law series)
  Includes bibliographical references.
  ISBN 0-471-54863-4 (v. 1). — ISBN 0-471-54865-0 (v. 2). —
  ISBN 0-471-54546-5 (set)
  1. Liability for hazardous substances pollution damages—United
States. 2. Liability for environmental damages—United States.
3. Actions and defenses—United States. I. Carpenter, David A.
(David Allen), 1931–   . II. Cushman, Robert Frank, 1931–
III. Roznowski, Bruce W. IV. Series.
KF1299.M39E575   1991
346.7303′8—dc20
[347.30638]   90-29173
                                    CIP

Printed in the United States of America

10 9 8 7 6 5 4 3 2 1

SUMMARY CONTENTS

SUMMARY CONTENTS

DETAILED CONTENTS

Chapter 2   Liability for Environmental Problems under Federal Statutes

Gail H. Allyn, Esquire
Pitney, Hardin, Kipp & Szuch
Morristown, New Jersey

Paul W. Pocalyko, CPA
Coopers & Lybrand
Philadelphia, Pennsylvania

Edward J. Fitzgerald
Coopers & Lybrand
Philadelphia, Pennsylvania

Henry G. Morgan, Esquire
Morgan, Mehluish, Monaghan, Arvidson, Abrutyn & Lisowski
Livingston, New Jersey

Warren C. Nitti, Esquire
Morgan, Mehluish, Monaghan, Arvidson, Abrutyn & Lisowski
Livingston, New Jersey

William L. Jennings, CPA
Coopers & Lybrand
Atlanta, Georgia

Robert D. Mowrey, Esquire
Alston & Bird
Atlanta, Georgia

R. Wayne Thorpe, Esquire
Alston & Bird
Atlanta, Georgia

Chapter 11   Past Owners

John B. Isbister, Esquire
Tydings & Rosenberg
Baltimore, Maryland

Bruce McCall
Coopers & Lybrand
Baltimore, Maryland

Mark L. Yeager, Esquire
McDermott, Will & Emery
Chicago, Illinois

VOLUME 2

James P. Barber, Esquire
Hancock, Rothert & Bunshoft
San Francisco, California

James A. Robertson, CPA
Coopers & Lybrand
Newport Beach, California

Martin E. Gilmore, CPA
Coopers & Lybrand
San Francisco, California

John E. Schulz, Esquire
Bechtel National, Inc.
San Francisco, California

PART V   PROCEDURAL CONSIDERATIONS

Chapter 24   Disposition of Environmental Disputes Without Litigation

Maureen A. Brennan, Esquire
Baker & Hostetler
Cleveland, Ohio

John E. Frazier
Coopers & Lybrand
Philadelphia, Pennsylvania

Mitchell E. Burack, Esquire
Pepper, Hamilton & Scheetz
Philadelphia, Pennsylvania

Craig M. Jacobsen, CPA
Coopers & Lybrand
Dallas, Texas

David Richman, Esquire
Pepper, Hamilton & Scheetz
Philadelphia, Pennsylvania

SHORT REFERENCE LIST

Short Reference	Full Reference
ARARs	Appropriate, relevant and applicable requirements
CAA	Clean Air Act
CERCLA	Comprehensive Environmental Response, Compensation and Liability Act (also known as Superfund)
CWA	Clean Water Act (also known as the Federal Water Pollution Act)
DOT	Department of Transportation
EPA	Environmental Protection Agency
EPCRA	Emergency Planning and Community Right-to-Know Act
FIFRA	Federal Insecticide, Fungicide and Rodenticide Act
HMTA	Hazardous Materials Transportation Act
NAAQS	National Ambient Air Quality Standards (under the Clean Air Act)
NBAR	Nonbinding preliminary allocation of responsibility
NCP	National Contingency Plan
NEPA	National Environmental Policy Act
NPDES	National Pollution Discharge Elimination System
NPL	National Priorities List
OSHA	Occupational Safety and Health Act
PRP	Potentially responsible party
RCRA	Resource Conservation and Recovery Act

SHORT REFERENCE LIST

Short Reference	*Full Reference*
RI/FS	Remedial investigation/Feasibility study
ROD	Record of Decision
SARA	Superfund Amendments and Reauthorization Act
Superfund	Same as CERCLA
TSCA	Toxic Substances Control Act
T/S/D	Treatment, storage, or disposal
UST	Underground storage tanks

PART III

OTHER POSSIBLE LIABILITY

CHAPTER 15

INSURERS AND INSURANCE COVERAGE ISSUES

James P. Barber
James A. Robertson*

James P. Barber is a partner with Hancock, Rothert & Bunshoft in San Francisco, California. His practice has concentrated on the representation of London market insurers on environmental coverage claims and litigation. He is a graduate of the University of California at Santa Barbara and Hastings College of the Law, where he was an articles editor for the *Hastings Law Journal.* Mr. Barber is a member of the Self Insurers and Risk Managers Committee of the Tort and Insurance Practice Section of the American Bar Association and the Defense Research Institute. He has coauthored materials for several seminars given on the subject of pollution insurance coverage issues. (The views expressed in this chapter are his own and are not necessarily the views of his firm or its clients.)

James A. Robertson is the director of Insurance Litigation and Claims Services with Coopers & Lybrand in Newport Beach, California. He has served as an expert witness for all types of property and casualty insurance coverages and on customs and practices of underwriters, agents, and brokers. During his career he has accumulated extensive experience as an author, insurance and risk management consultant, positions in insurance agency and brokerage administration and management, and supervisory underwriting positions for a major insurer. He is internationally known as an author of more than 40 publications. Mr. Robertson holds the Chartered Property Casualty Underwriter (CPCU) and Associate in Risk Management (ARM) professional designations, a B.A. degree from the University of Iowa and an M.S.A. degree from Pepperdine University.

*The authors gratefully acknowledge Susan Ardisson of Hancock, Rothert & Bunshoft, for her extensive contribution in researching and condensing the legal references in this chapter into manageable form, and in drafting and editing portions of the original manuscript.

INSURANCE POLICY PROVISIONS

§ 15.1   Origins of Environmental Coverage Litigation

Prior to 1980, pollution coverage litigation was virtually nonexistent. However, since the passage of the Comprehensive Environmental Response, Compensation and Liability Act (CERCLA) by Congress in 1980, there has been a dramatic increase in pollution coverage litigation.[1] The

---

[1] Prior to CERCLA, the few reported decisions that dealt with insurance coverage for pollution-related damages arose out of common law nuisance actions. Generally, these courts refused to extend coverage for such activities on the theory that they were intended by the insured and were not the result of an accident. *See, e.g.,* White v. Smith, 440 S.W.2d 497 (Mo. Ct. App. 1969).

magnitude of the problem is also increasing with each passing year. In 1982, there were 419 sites designated by the Environmental Protection Agency (EPA) for inclusion on the National Priorities List (NPL). By 1990, this figure had grown to 1,187 sites, 116 of which are federal facilities.[2] Only 25 sites have been deleted from the NPL, and according to the EPA there are more than 27,000 sites in the United States that "need some degree of . . . cleanup."[3] The cost of cleaning up each site has also greatly increased over the last decade. In 1980, CERCLA was funded at $1.6 billion for five years.[4] In 1985, Congress passed the Superfund Amendments and Reauthorization Act (SARA),[5] which authorized funding of $8.5 billion, a five-fold increase over the initial CERCLA program. The proposed budget for the EPA is $2.7 billion for fiscal year 1991. Most of the EPA's budget is for enforcement efforts and cleanup of the sites themselves. The average cost of a cleanup currently averages between $21 and $30 million.

Federal and state governments are looking to the private sector to pay what by some accounts is expected to be over $300 billion.[6] The private sector is in turn looking to its insurers to pay for the costs of the cleanup. The focus of most of the coverage litigation to date is on the Comprehensive General Liability (CGL) policy, which is the form of insurance that has provided coverage to most businesses in the United States for nearly five decades.[7] This chapter will discuss the major coverage issues which have arisen and are likely to arise in the 1990s.

§ 15.2   Comprehensive General Liability Coverage

The type of insurance most often involved in disputes over insuring environmental claims is the Comprehensive General Liability (CGL) policy. CGL insurance coverage has evolved dramatically over the past five decades, since its origins in antecedent forms that were in use from at least the 1930s.

---

[2] 55 Fed. Reg. 35,502 (Aug. 3, 1990).

[3] 19 Env't Rep. (BNA) 1, 9 (May 6, 1988).

[4] Hazardous Substance Response Trust Fund, 42 U.S.C. § 9631 (1988).

[5] 42 U.S.C. § 9601–9675 (1986) (amending 42 U.S.C. § 9601 (1980)).

[6] 19 Env't Rep. (BNA) 1, 9 (May 6, 1988).

[7] *See generally* J. Long & D. Gregg, Property and Liability Insurance Handbook 492, 510 (1965) [hereinafter Long & Gregg]; Ribner, *Modern Environmental Insurance Law*, 63 St. John's L. Rev. 755 (1989).

§ 15.3 —Policies Issued Before 1955

Before the development and universal acceptance of the CGL form, insureds tended to purchase separate liability policies for various hazards for which the insurance industry had developed specific, limited policy forms.[8] Although there were at least two editions of the CGL policy form before 1955,[9] packaging coverages in one policy was not as common then as it became in the late 1950s and 1960s. Some of the types of policies an insured could purchase were:

1. Owner's, Landlord's & Tenant's Liability (OL&T), for an insured's premises
2. Manufacturer's & Contractor's Liability (M&C), for an insured's operations that usually were conducted away from the insured's own premises, at the premises of another
3. Owner's & Contractor's Protective Liability (O&CP), for liability arising out of the work of independent contractors of the insured
4. Products and Completed Operations Liability (PCO), for injuries or damage caused by an insured's products sold to or work performed for another.[10]

   All of these policy forms, as well as the CGL, could provide insurance for both bodily injury and property damage liability, although sometimes separate policies would be purchased for each. The policies contained insuring agreements describing the scope of risks insured and stating that liability covered by the policy must arise from bodily injury or property damage caused by an accident during the policy period.

The 1955 CGL Form

The third revision by the National Bureau of Casualty Underwriters (NBCU) of the CGL policy form was used after July 1955 in most U.S. jurisdictions.[11] There were no significant changes in this form's insuring

---

[8] Long & Gregg at 462.

[9] According to Fire, Casualty and Surety Bulletins Casualty Surety Volume, Public Liability B-1 (The National Underwriter Co., June, 1985), "[t]he first standard form Comprehensive General Liability insurance was developed jointly by the National Bureau of Casualty and Surety Underwriters and the Mutual Casualty Insurance Rating Bureau and made available to member companies in 1940." Some other authors have claimed that the earliest CGL form dates from about 1935.

[10] Long & Gregg at 461–75. Separate policies to insure OL&T, M&C, and O&CP risks continued to be available until ISO introduced the 1986 CGL forms.

[11] National Bureau of Casualty Underwriters, Circular to All Companies/General Liability Division #751 (Mar. 4, 1955).

agreements with respect to covering bodily injury or property damage caused by accident, except that language was added intending to limit defense coverage only to accidents for which the policy might also provide indemnification; defense obligations were not to continue if the limits of liability of the policy were exhausted. The defense insuring agreement, *Agreement II—Defense, Settlement, Supplementary Payments,* opened with the words "With respect to such insurance as is afforded by this policy" in order to implement this change.

There were no separate definitions of bodily injury, property damage, or accident in the 1955 CGL or related liability forms, and these terms had not been defined separately in the policy in earlier forms. *Insuring Agreement I, Coverage A—Bodily Injury Liability,* was worded:

> To pay on behalf of the insured all sums which the insured shall become legally obligated to pay as damages because of bodily injury, sickness or disease, including death at any time resulting therefrom, sustained by any person and caused by accident.

Insuring Agreement I, Coverage B—Property Damage Liability said: "To pay on behalf of the insured all sums which the insured shall become legally obligated to pay as damages because of injury to or destruction of property, including the loss of use thereof, cause by accident."

As a further limitation of coverage, *Insuring Agreement IV—Policy Period, Territory,* read: "This policy applies only to accidents which occur during the policy period within the United States of America, its territories or possessions, or Canada."

The term *accident* was supposed to connote fortuity, which meant that the insured event was undesigned and unexpected, occurring suddenly.[12] Even if the event could have been anticipated, the time at which it would actually occur could not, and the injurious results of the accident were unintended from the insured's perspective. In most instances, the concept of insuring an accident was thought to preclude covering deliberately intended acts, even if the act had unexpected results.

Interpreting the meaning of *accident* and *caused by accident* created problems for insurers because there was no uniformity in the judicial decisions.[13] One problem developed over coverage for disease under bodily injury. Some courts held that a disease that developed gradually over a lengthy period was not an accident.[14] In cases involving property damage, there were cases finding that there was no coverage for intentional acts

---

[12] Long & Gregg at 466.

[13] *Id.*

[14] *Id.*

that had the unintended result of causing damage.[15] As a result, many insureds began requesting endorsements to the CGL policy, substituting the word "occurrence" for "accident."[16]

§ 15.4   —The 1966 CGL Form

A new version of the CGL policy form was introduced in October 1966, which contained many differences from earlier versions of the form. The insuring agreements were substantially revised, combining bodily injury and property damage in the same agreement, and also including the statement of defense obligations in the insuring agreement. Several terms were defined in the policy for the first time, including *bodily injury, property damage,* and *damages.* One of the most significant revisions for insurers was the change from *accident* to *occurrence* as the principal term triggering the coverage for bodily injury and property damage.

The 1966 CGL insuring agreement, *I. Bodily Injury Liability Coverage/ Property Damage Liability Coverage,* read as follows:

> The company will pay on behalf of the insured all sums which the insured shall become legally obligated to pay as damages because of
>
> bodily injury or
> property damage
>
> to which this insurance applies, caused by an occurrence, and the company shall have the right and duty to defend any suit against the insured seeking damages on account of such bodily injury or property damage, even if any of the allegations of the suit are groundless, false or fraudulent, and may make such investigation and settlement of any claim or suit as it deems expedient, but the company shall not be obligated to pay any claim or judgment or to defend any suit after the applicable limit of the company's liability has been exhausted by payment of judgments or settlements.

Key terms relating to the scope and trigger of coverage were defined as follows:

> "Bodily injury" means bodily injury, sickness or disease sustained by any person.

---

[15] *See* various citations on cases in *Hazardous Waste, Toxic Tort, and Products Liability Insurance Problems 1987,* Commercial Law and Practice Course Handbook No. 419 (Practising Law Inst. 1987). In many cases, early decisions favored insurers by imposing limitations on the types of events covered by the word "accident." Subsequent decisions have been far less favorable to insurers. Most of the early limitations have now been superseded by later cases that extend the coverage in a variety of ways, as will be seen in the discussion of current cases dealing with accident vs. occurrence in § **15.10.**

[16] Long & Gregg at 466.

"Damages" includes damages for death and for care and loss of services resulting from bodily injury and damages for loss of use of property resulting from property damage.

"Occurrence" means an accident, including injurious exposure to conditions, which results, during the policy period, in bodily injury or property damage neither expected nor intended from the standpoint of the insured.

"Property damage" means injury to or destruction of tangible property.

Coverage for bodily injury was unchanged from earlier editions of the CGL form, but the other terms were significantly altered. *Damages* contained essential elements of both the bodily injury and property damage definitions. In the property damage definition, the specific statement that coverage applied only to tangible property appeared for the first time. And finally, the occurrence definition—destined to be the subject of exhaustive litigation to interpret every word and nuance of its meaning—appeared for the first time. As stated by one commentator, "[f]or many years to come, these policies may haunt the insurers who issued them."[17]

Important features of the occurrence definition include its reference to its predecessor trigger, accident, supplemented by the concept of repeated or ongoing happenings in the words "injurious exposure to conditions." In the 1955 CGL form and earlier versions of other liability policies, there was no language suggesting that an accident could be a continuous or ongoing event. In addition, by placement of the words "neither expected nor intended from the standpoint of the insured" in the final phrase, the definition indicated that coverage would apply to acts causing bodily injury or property damage if the resulting injury or damage was unexpected and unintended.

There was one additional, and important, statement in the policy about what constituted an occurrence (thus, presumably a covered occurrence), contained in insuring agreement, *III. Limits of Liability:* "For the purpose of determining the limit of the [insurance] company's liability, all bodily injury and property damage arising out of continuous or repeated exposure to substantially the same general conditions shall be considered as arising out of the same occurrence."

This wording was intended to help define what constituted one occurrence, which later became important in multiple toxic tort claims arising out of the release of substances at indeterminable times in the past. In particular, this policy wording led to litigation over the "stacking" of policy limits, that is, covering many occurrences in policies not subject to an aggregate limit or the same occurrence in many successive policies. If applicable, this could mean that each occurrence had the entire policy limit

---

[17] Hamilton & Routman, *Cleaning Up America: Superfund and Its Impact on the Insurance Industry,* CPCU J. 172 (Society of CPCU, Sept. 1988).

available, even over several different policies, if release of the same substance(s) caused injury to many claimants over several years.

§ 15.5   —Early Pollution Exclusions

One of the earliest pollution exclusions introduced by the United States insurance industry was the 1970 exclusion of the Insurance Rating Board, a predecessor to Insurance Services Office (ISO), which read:

> This insurance does not apply: . . . to bodily injury or property damage arising out of the discharge, dispersal, release or escape of smoke, vapors, soot, fumes, acids, alkalis, toxic chemicals, liquids or gases, waste materials or other irritants, contaminants or pollutants into or upon land, the atmosphere or any watercourse or body of water; but this exclusion does not apply if such discharge, dispersal, release or escape is sudden and accidental.[18]

There were two versions of this exclusion. The one quoted above was intended for use with policies for most types of businesses except for those subject to the risk of releasing oil and gas into the environment. Oil and gas industry versions of the above exclusion applied "whether or not [the event] is sudden and accidental."[19]

§ 15.6   —The 1973 CGL Form and
Pollution Exclusions

The ISO introduced a new edition of the CGL form in January 1973, about the time that publicity for some of the early serious environmental claims, such as Love Canal in New York, was beginning to surface. In some instances, words were simply rearranged in the 1973 form. But in other cases, definitions were changed significantly. Key terms of the 1973 form are requoted here for comparison with the definitions quoted in § 15.4:

> "Bodily injury" means bodily injury, sickness or disease sustained by any person which occurs during the policy period, including death at any time resulting therefrom.
>
> "Occurrence" means an accident, including continuous or repeated exposure to conditions, which results in bodily injury or property damage neither expected nor intended from the standpoint of the insured.
>
> "Property damage" means (1) physical injury to or destruction of tangible property which occurs during the policy period, including the loss of

---

[18] Copyright © 1973, Insurance Services Office, Inc.

[19] Fire, Casualty & Surety Bulletins, Casualty Surety Volume, Public Liability Cop-2 (Nov. 1987).

use thereof at any time resulting therefrom, or (2) loss of use of tangible property which has not been physically injured or destroyed provided such loss of use is caused by an occurrence during the policy period.[20]

The wording in the limits of liability section of the policy stating that continuous and repeated exposure to "substantially the same general conditions" constitutes one occurrence remained unchanged from the 1966 CGL form.

The 1973 CGL form contained a pollution exclusion identified as exclusion (f). Although this exclusion was previously added to 1966 CGL policies by an endorsement, in the 1973 CGL form exclusion (f) was part of the policy.

§ 15.7   Lloyd's Pollution Exclusions

London's Non-Marine Association (N.M.A.) forms for pollution exclusions began evolving with the weakened interpretation of the word *accident* by the American courts in the 1950s. When the requirement of suddenness in the concept of accident was no longer clear, the insurance industry became concerned with not providing insurance coverage for certain types of injuries occurring over a long period of time. Seepage, subsidence, and pollution claims were the chief concerns.

For example, at the Terminal Island Naval Base in California, the Navy sued insured oil companies for subsidence cause by slant drilling.[21] Subsidence was first noticed in 1943 and continued until 1958 when the suit was filed. Two issues concerned insurers when faced with these claims. First, the damage occurred gradually, over a period of 15 to 20 years. Second, the damage was the result of the insured's expected, intended, and ongoing business operations. The Oyster Bed claims were also of concern. These arose out of the gradual discharge over a period of years of polluted water into oyster beds in Louisiana. Again, the cause of the damage was the ongoing discharge of pollutants into the water, which also was ostensibly expected and intended, not accidental, and therefore precluded from coverage.[22]

Like their domestic counterparts, certain London market insurers sought to preclude coverage for these types of gradual and expected or intended harm. At the same time, however, American insureds and brokers were advocating the use of the occurrence concept. Through the use of the

---

[20] Copyright © 1973, Insurance Services Office, Inc.

[21] Cametal Corp. v. National Auto. & Casualty Ins. Co., 189 Cal. App. 2d Supp. 831, 11 Cal. Rptr. 280 (1961).

[22] T. McGeough, *Insurance Coverage of Actions for Environmental Damage,* Def. Res. Inst. (1977).

word *occurrence* insureds were seeking the very coverage insurers sought to avoid: coverage for gradual injury. By the late 1950s, some London market insurers acquiesced in the desires of their American insureds and began offering occurrence-based liability policies, which typically covered injuries caused by "repeated exposure to conditions." Thus, the occurrence policies deleted the temporal (suddeness) requirement that was previously contained in accident policies but retained the fortuity requirement.

§ 15.8 —Development of Seepage and Pollution Clauses

Although some London market insurers agreed to forego the suddeness requirement in accident-based policies and convert to occurrence-based policies, they were not willing to provide coverage for all gradually caused damage. Losses related to seepage, pollution, and subsidence were chief areas that they did not intend to insure. As a result of this concern, in 1960 a N.M.A. subcommittee of London underwriters and brokers was formed for the purpose of developing a seepage and pollution exclusion clause, which resulted in the drafting of N.M.A. 1333 in 1961.[23] N.M.A. 1333 reads as follows:

SEEPAGE AND POLLUTION CLAUSE

This Insurance does not cover any liability for:

(1) Removal of, loss of or damage to subsurface oil or gas or any other natural substance, the property of others,
provided always that this paragraph (1) shall not apply to any liability which would otherwise be covered under this Insurance for such removal, loss or damage directly attributable to blowout, cratering or fire of an oil or gas well owned or operated by, or under the control of, the Assured.

(2) Property damage resulting from subsidence caused by subsurface operations of the Assured.

(3) Property damage caused by seepage, pollution or contamination, unless such seepage, pollution or contamination is caused by a sudden, unintended and unexpected happening during the period of this Insurance,

but this paragraph (3) shall not be construed as excluding any liability which would otherwise be covered under this Insurance for property damage caused by a sudden, unintended and unexpected happening during the period of this Insurance arising out of seepage, pollution or contamination.

---

[23] Transcript of Proceedings, vol. 51 at 9261, Shell Oil Co. v. Accident & Casualty Ins. Co., No. 278953 (Cal. Super. Ct. Feb. 24, 1988).

This Clause shall not extend this Insurance to cover any liability which would not have been covered under this Insurance had this Clause not been attached.

The intent of this clause was, in part, to exclude pollution resulting from gradual intended or expected causes. "Sudden" had its plain, temporal meaning.[24]

§ 15.9   —New Pollution Clauses

A series of expensive pollution losses in the late 1960s caused American and London market insurers to reassess their coverage of oil and chemical companies. In March 1967, an oil tanker grounded off the coast of England, creating an oil slick that spanned both sides of the English Channel.[25] In 1969, an offshore oil well operated by the Union Oil Company blew out in the Santa Barbara Channel, creating a 50-square-mile oil slick.[26]

In response to these new pollution problems, insurers developed revised seepage and pollution exclusion clauses, N.M.A. 1683, 1684, 1685, and 1686.

N.M.A. 1685 provides as follows:

INDUSTRIES, SEEPAGE, POLLUTION AND CONTAMINATION CLAUSE No. 3 (Approved by Lloyd's Underwriters' Non-Marine Association)

This Insurance does not cover any liability for:

(1) Personal Injury or Bodily Injury or loss of, damage to, or loss of use of property directly or indirectly caused by seepage, pollution or contamination, provided always that this paragraph (1) shall not apply to liability for Personal Injury or Bodily Injury or loss of or physical damage to or destruction of tangible property, or loss of use of such property damaged or destroyed, where such seepage, pollution or contamination is caused by a sudden, unintended and unexpected happening during the period of this Insurance.

(2) The cost of removing, nullifying or cleaning-up seeping, polluting or contaminating substances unless the seepage, pollution or contamination is caused by a sudden, unintended and unexpected happening during the period of this Insurance.

---

[24] Judicial Decision re Phrase I Issues at 38, Shell Oil Co. v. Accident & Casualty Ins. Co., No. 278953 (Cal. Super. Ct. Oct. 6, 1988).

[25] *See generally In re* Barracuda Tanker Corp., 281 F. Supp. 228 (S.D.N.Y. 1968) (setting forth history of the spill).

[26] *See generally* Pauley Petroleum, Inc. v. United States, 591 F.2d 1308, 1310–12 (Ct. Cl. 1979) (setting forth history of the spills).

(3) Fines, penalties, punitive or exemplary damages.

This clause shall not extend this Insurance to cover any liability which would not have been covered under this Insurance had this Clause not been attached.

N.M.A. 1686 provides as follows:

INDUSTRIES, SEEPAGE, POLLUTION AND CONTAMINATION EXCLUSION CLAUSE NO. 4

(Approved by Lloyd's Underwriters' Non-Marine Association)

This Insurance does not cover any liability for:

(1) Personal Injury or Bodily Injury or loss of, damage to, or loss of use of property directly or indirectly caused by seepage, pollution or contamination.

(2) The cost of removing, nullifying or cleaning-up seepage, pollution or contaminating substances.

(3) Fines, penalties, punitive or exemplary damages.

N.M.A. 1683 and 1684 parallel 1685 and 1686, although they also contain provisions relating to subsidence and subsurface damage resulting from oil and gas operations. The provisions relating to seepage, pollution, and contamination are identical.

These clauses were intended to limit potential insurance liability to sudden, unexpected, and unintended events. The word *sudden* had its plain, temporal meaning. The concept of fortuity was embodied in the words *unintended and unexpected.* Intentional or expected acts, such as pollution created in the normal course of business, also was not intended to be covered.[27]

OVERVIEW OF COURT DECISIONS

§ 15.10 Accidents and Occurrences

It is no secret that variations in court interpretations of the wording of past CGL policies have caused problems for both insureds and insurers. Because the ISO's most recent CGL forms were not introduced until 1986 (see § 15.17), many of the cases that help to understand the way courts interpret the wording of policies issued by insurers concern the older

---

[27] Judicial Decision re Phrase I Issues at 39–40, Shell Oil Co. v. Accident & Casualty Ins. Co., No. 278953 (Cal. Super. Ct. Oct. 6, 1988).

versions of CGL coverage wording discussed in §§ **15.3** through **15.9**. It is useful to introduce this part of the chapter with the ISO's own words about some of the problems insurers have faced with the 1973 and earlier versions of the CGL:

> Litigation relating to the existing [1973] "occurrence" policy has been costly and time-consuming. For the most part such litigation . . . has centered on latent bodily injury and long-term exposure issues involving substances such as asbestos and DES. A key issue in the dispute is: When did the injury or damage occur? . . . Litigation over that question is likely to affect more and more insureds of all sizes in all types of business.[28]

Most current environmental coverage disputes involve general liability insurance policies written on an occurrence basis.[29] This means that most of the policies involved in disputes were issued after 1966, and contain wordings like the terms quoted in §§ **15.2** through **15.9** for 1966 or 1973 CGL forms. Based on the occurrence definition, one issue that is the focus of litigation is whether the language, "neither expected nor intended from the standpoint of the insured," requires that the insured had the specific intent to inflict the harm or whether this wording requires the insured to prove that it neither knew nor should have known that it was substantially probable that its acts of pollution would result in bodily injury or property damage. As can be expected, the courts have reached differing conclusions.

Several cases illustrate the view that "neither expected nor intended from the standpoint of the insured" requires that the insured had the specific intent to cause the harm. These include *Ray Industries, Inc. v. Liberty Mutual Insurance Co.,*[30] *U.S.F.&G. Co. v. Specialty Coatings, Co.*[31] and *Allstate Insurance Co. v. Freeman.*[32]

In Freeman, the Michigan Supreme Court ruled that a subjective standard of inquiry applied. The court stated, "The finder of fact may exclude coverage either for actions in which the insured subjectively *expected* injury or loss or where the loss is the consequence of the insured's subjective

---

[28] Insurance Services Office, Inc., *New Commercial General Liability Program* 1–2 (2d ed. Apr. 1985) (copyright © 1984, 1985 Insurance Services Office, Inc.).

[29] In the 1950s, cases such as Beryllium Corp. v. American Mut. Liability Ins. Co., 223 F.2d 71 (3d Cir. 1955), and Canadian Radium & Uranium Corp. v. Indemnity Ins. Co., 411 Ill. 325, 104 N.E.2d 250, 254 (1952), extended the term accident to include an event causing harm that was unexpected and unintended, even though it was not sudden. As a result, the insurance industry began to substitute "occurrence" for "accident" and to exclude events of pollution causing harm, unless they were sudden, unexpected, and unintended.

[30] 728 F. Supp. 1310 (E.D. Mich. 1989).

[31] 180 Ill. App. 3d 378, 535 N.E.2d 1071 (1989).

[32] 432 Mich. 656, 443 N.W.2d 734 (1989).

intention both to the act itself, and the resultant harm."[33] The court went on to state that the insured need not have intended the actual injury that occurred but only some type of reasonably foreseeable harm.

In *Ray Industries, Inc. v. Liberty Mutual Insurance Co.,*[34] a federal district court also ruled that courts must apply a subjective standard when interpreting the clause "neither expected nor intended from the standpoint of the insured." According to the court, the definition of an occurrence "focuses on the insured's expectation regarding damage." Again, in *U.S.F.&G. Co. v. Specialty Coatings Co.,*[35] the court ruled that even though the insured may be strictly liable for environmental harm under state law, a subjective standard must be applied to determine whether the insured intended or expected the damage that occurred.

In contrast to the courts in *Ray Industries, Freeman,* and *Specialty Coatings,* several courts have concluded that the proper inquiry is an objective one, requiring the insured to prove that it neither knew nor should have known that it was substantially probable that its pollution activities would result in injury. One of the first cases to reach this conclusion was *City of Carter Lake v. Aetna Casualty & Surety Co.*[36] According to the court, "If the assured knew or should have known that there was a substantial probability that certain results would follow his acts or omissions, then there has not been an occurrence or accident as defined in this type of policy when such results actually come to pass."[37]

An objective inquiry was also applied in *American Universal Insurance Co. v. Whitewood Custom Treaters.*[38] In this case, the insured operated a chemical treatment plant that allegedly leaked hazardous chemicals onto the property of the claimants, who sued the insured for negligence, nuisance, and trespass. The insurers filed a declaratory relief action to establish that they owed neither a defense nor indemnification to the insured. The court determined that there had been no occurrence under the policy, by applying the objective test of *substantial probability.* According to the court:

> Substantial probability is more than reasonably foreseeable. The indications must be strong enough to alert a reasonably prudent man not only to the possibility of the results occurring, but the indications must also be sufficient to forewarn him that the results are highly likely to occur.[39]

---

[33] *Id.* at 731, 443 N.W.2d at 768 (emphasis in original).

[34] 728 F. Supp. 1310, 1314 (E.D. Mich. 1989).

[35] 180 Ill. App. 3d 378, 535 N.E.2d 1071 (1989).

[36] 604 F.2d 1052 (8th Cir. 1979).

[37] *Id.* at 1059.

[38] 707 F. Supp. 1140 (D.S.D. 1989).

[39] *Id.* at 1149.

§ 15.11   Property Damage

There are several cases that held that contamination of the environment constitutes property damage under the standard CGL policy[40] and that property damage extends to the pollution of groundwater and aquifers.[41] What is less clear, and is as yet unresolved, is whether a level of pollution that is less than an unacceptable threshold under current allowable standards constitutes property damage. At this time, there is no authority that addresses this question. Insureds will look back to policies that provided coverage at the time the insured was polluting at levels that have since become unacceptable. Insurers are likely to argue that there is no coverage because there was no property damage until the enactment of new legislation that lowered acceptable levels.

Another issue that has resulted in a split of authority is whether cleanup by the insured of its own property to prevent migration of pollution to third party's property is covered under a CGL policy. Most courts have found that the *owned premises exclusion* is inapplicable and that such mitigation efforts are covered in order to prevent third-party property damage,[42] although this result runs against the whole tenor of third-party property damage.

§ 15.12   Bodily Injury and Other Personal Injuries

If the plaintiff has sustained actual bodily injury due to exposure to a toxic substance, subject to its other terms and conditions, the standard CGL policy expressly covers the bodily injury. Therefore, if an occurrence is found under the policy and no exclusions or conditions apply, the resulting bodily injury is covered.[43]

A more difficult issue arises when the plaintiff seeks compensation for future injuries and risks. A variety of theories have been developed to

---

[40] *See, e.g.,* Continental Ins. v. Northeastern Pharmaceutical & Chem. Co., 842 F.2d 977 (8th Cir.), *cert. denied,* 108 S. Ct. 66 (1988); Mraz v. Canadian Universal Ins. Co., 804 F.2d 1325 (4th Cir. 1986); Upjohn Co. v. New Hampshire Ins. Co, 178 Mich. App. 706, 444 N.W.2d 813 (1989).

[41] Aerojet-General Corp. v. Superior Court, 211 Cal. App. 3d 216, 258 Cal. Rptr. 684 (1989); Upjohn Co. v. New Hampshire Ins. Co., 178 Mich. App. 706, 444 N.W.2d 813 (1989).

[42] *See, e.g.,* Broadwell Realty v. Fidelity & Casualty, 218 N.J. 516, 528 A.2d 76 (1987); W.C. Hayes v. Maryland Casualty, 688 F. Supp. 1513 (N.D. Fla. 1988).

[43] Although elements of proof dealing with causation and damages may pose problems for the claimant-plaintiff, stating a cause of action when actual injury has been sustained is not difficult. *See, e.g.,* Anderson v. W.R. Grace & Co., 628 F. Supp. 1219, 1225 (D. Mass. 1986) ("It is clear that a cause of action occurs when an insidious disease manifests itself.").

address the growing number of claims by individuals exposed to toxic chemicals and other toxic pollution. They include causes of action for cancerphobia, increased risk of cancer, reimbursement of medical surveillance costs, and damage to the immunological system.

Cancerphobia

Cancerphobia is the present anxiety over development of cancer in the future,[44] and it is being claimed increasingly by plaintiffs in toxic tort cases. Several courts have recognized it as a valid cause of action when there is some evidence of physical impact or injury.[45]

A minority of courts, however, have permitted recovery even when there is no evidence that the plaintiff sustained any physical injury or impact from exposure. in *In re Moornevich,*[46] for example, the court ruled that the plaintiff's fear of cancer from exposure to asbestos was reasonable and allowed recovery. The court based its ruling on evidence that asbestos is a known carcinogen, the plaintiff had long-term exposure to asbestos, and many of the plaintiff's coworkers were dying from exposure to asbestos. A Tennessee court also permitted recovery for cancerphobia, ruling that a jury could find the mere ingestion of a carcinogen in water to constitute sufficient "injury, even though subsequent testing showed no physical manifestation," in *Laxton v. Orkin Exterminating Co.*[47] Finally, in *Hagerty v. L&L Marine Services, Inc.,*[48] the Fifth Circuit stated that:

> With or without physical injury or impact, a plaintiff is entitled to recover damages for serious mental distress arising from his fear of developing cancer where his fear is reasonable and causally related to the defendant's negligence. The circumstances surrounding the fear-inducing occurrence may themselves supply sufficient indicia of genuineness.[49]

In *Hagerty,* there was evidence that the plaintiff had suffered a physical impact in the form of dizziness and stinging in his extremities when he was doused with chemicals. Irrespective of the physical impact, the court ruled that there were sufficient indicia of genuineness to warrant rejection of the defendant's summary judgment motion because the plaintiff knew

---

[44] Gale & Goyer, *Recovery for Cancerphobia and Increased Risk of Cancer,* 15 Cumb. L. Rev. 723, 730 (1984–85).

[45] *See, e.g.,* Wetherhill v. University of Chicago, 565 F. Supp. 1553 (N.D. Ill. 1983) (plaintiff's fear of developing cancer because of prenatal exposure to DES was reasonable because scientific studies showed a link between DES and cancer.)

[46] 634 F. Supp. 636 (D. Me. 1986).

[47] 639 S.W.2d 431, 434 (Tenn. 1982).

[48] 788 F.2d 315 (5th Cir. 1986).

[49] *Id.* at 318.

the chemical in which he was doused, dripolene, was a carcinogen, he felt effects at the time of the accident, he saw a doctor for periodic testing, and he subsequently left his job due to fear of similar accidents.

The majority of courts, however, continues to require some evidence of physical injury or impact before permitting a plaintiff to recover for fear of cancer[50] and requires that the fear of contracting cancer be a reasonable fear.[51] Finally, it should be noted that at least one court has imposed one further limitation on plaintiffs' recovery. The *Laxton*[52] court held that the plaintiffs could recover mental distress damages only for the period of time "between discovery of the ingestion and [a] negative medical diagnosis or other information that puts to rest the fear of injury."

Increased Risk of Cancer

A separate claim that often arises in toxic tort cases is a cause of action for increased risk of cancer. In this cause of action, the plaintiff usually alleges that due to exposure to a particular substance, his or her chances of contracting cancer is higher than it was before exposure.

Although some courts have not permitted a claim for increased risk of cancer because a risk does not constitute an injury,[53] the general rule is that the plaintiff may recover damages if he or she can prove to a reasonable medical certainty that the disease will occur. Generally, proof of a reasonable medical certainty requires evidence that the plaintiff has a greater than 50 percent chance of contracting cancer.[54]

---

[50] *See, e.g.,* Deleski v. Raymark Indus., Inc., 819 F.2d 377, 380–81 (3d Cir. 1987) (neither New Jersey nor Pennsylvania law allows recovery for emotional distress for fear of cancer without some proof of physical injury); Jackson v. Johns-Manville Sales Corp., 781 F.2d 394, 414–15 (5th Cir. 1986) (Mississippi law allows recovery for fear of cancer for plaintiff who has present physical injury such as asbestosis); Schweitzer v. Consolidated Rail Corp., 758 F.2d 936, 942 (3d Cir. 1985), *cert. denied,* 474 U.S. 864 (1985) (mere exposure to asbestos does not give rise to a cause of action because it would result in "windfalls for those who never take ill and insufficient compensation for those who do"); Babash v. Philadelphia Elec. Co., 717 F. Supp. 297, 300 (M.D. Pa. 1989) (rejecting plaintiff's emotional distress claim for fear of cancer because there was no present physical injury).

[51] *See, e.g.,* Anderson v. W.R. Grace & Co., 620 F. Supp. 1219, 1228 (D. Mass. 1986); Farrall v. A.C.&S. Co., 558 A.2d 1078 (Del. Super. Ct. 1989); Sterling v. Velsicol Chem. Corp., 647 F. Supp. 303 (W.D. Tenn. 1986), *aff'd in part, rev'd in part on other grounds,* 855 F.2d 1188 (6th Cir. 1988).

[52] Laxton v. Orkin Exterminating Co., 639 S.W.2d at 434.

[53] *See, e.g.,* Deleski v. Raymark Indus., Inc., 819 F.2d 366, 388–81 (3d Cir. 1987); Adams v. Johns-Manville Sales Corp., 727 F.2d 533, 537–38 (5th Cir. 1984); Plummer v. Abbott Laboratories, 568 F. Supp. 920, 922 (D.R.I. 1983).

[54] *See, e.g.,* Jackson v. Johns-Manville Sales Corp., 781 F.2d 394, 412–13 (5th Cir.), *cert. denied,* 478 U.S. 1822 (1986); Ayers v. Township of Jackson, 106 N.J. 557, 525 A.2d 287 (1987).

Medical Surveillance Costs

Although there may be insufficient evidence to support a claim for increased risk of cancer, a court may still award damages for the cost of future medical surveillance and testing to ensure that any disease resulting from exposure will be detected and treated promptly. For example, in *Mauro v. Raymark Industries, Inc.,*[55] the New Jersey Supreme Court denied a claim for increased risk of cancer but permitted the plaintiff to recover future medical surveillance costs because these costs were "specific monetary damages which can be measured by the cost of periodic medical examinations." The *Mauro* court set out the specific factors to be considered in determining an award for surveillance costs:

> [t]he cost of medical surveillance is a compensable item of damages where the proofs demonstrate, through reliable expert testimony predicated upon the significance and extent of exposure to chemicals, the toxicity of the chemicals, the seriousness of the diseases for which individuals are at risk, the relative increase in the chance of onset of disease in those exposed, and the value of early diagnosis, that such surveillance to monitor the effect of exposure to toxic chemicals is reasonable and necessary.[56]

Damage to Immunological System

An increasingly popular type of claim in toxic tort cases is the allegation that chemical exposure has damaged or weakened the plaintiff's immune system, rendering the body more susceptible to disease in general. This type of claim is more far-reaching because it links many common illnesses, such as arthritis, diabetes, and allergies, which are caused by a multitude of different factors, to the one chemical exposure incident.

Several courts have recognized damage to the immune system as a present injury.[57] However, the issue which most plaintiffs usually fail to overcome is causation. For example, in *Stites v. Sudstrand Heat Transfer, Inc.,*[58] the plaintiff alleged damage to the immune system from chronic exposure to TCE. In a motion for summary judgment, the defendant presented affidavits from nine immunology experts who stated that it was impossible to conclude to a reasonable certainty that TCE caused any immunological problems. The court granted summary judgment in favor of the defendant.

---

[55] 116 N.J. 126, 561 A.2d 257 (1989).

[56] *Id.* at 136–137 (quoting Ayers v. Township of Jackson, 106 N.J. 557, 606, 525 A.2d 287 (1987)).

[57] *See, e.g.,* Elam v. Alcoloac, 765 S.W.2d 42 (Mo. Ct. App. 1988); Barton v. Firestone Tire & Rubber Co., 673 F. Supp. 1466, 1469 (N.D. Cal. 1987); Sterling v. Velsicol Chem. Corp., 647 F. Supp. 303, 325 (W.D. Tenn. 1986).

[58] 660 F. Supp. 1516 (W.D. Mich. 1987).

§ 15.13   The Number of Occurrences

Once an occurrence triggers coverage under a policy, it is important to ascertain the number of occurrences in order to determine:

1. The number of deductibles, if any, that must be absorbed by the insured
2. The application of coverage limits under each policy
3. The allocation of potential exposure between primary and excess or umbrella policies.

Courts historically have been divided on whether the number of occurrences is determined by analyzing causes or results. The minority view is to determine the number of occurrences by looking at the number of results or injuries.[59] The majority view is to determine the number of occurrences by examining the number of causes of the property damage.[60]

The question of what is the cause of injury or property damage, however, is a perplexing legal and factual issue. The modern view focuses on the conduct of the insured that proximately caused property damage, but this test has led different courts to reach different conclusions. For example, courts variously have held that the fact that all fungible raw materials were produced at one location and delivered to many fabricating plants was one occurrence;[61] each shipment of a contaminated product was a separate occurence;[62] and each deposit of hazardous material or each failure to abate pollution was a separate occurrence.[63]

An explanation of the inconsistency of the courts probably lies in the inconsistency of the insureds on this issue, advocating a single occurrence when deductibles are high and many occurrences when deductibles are low. If the doctrine of the reasonable expectations of the insured is applied, unreasonable applications sometimes follow.

MANAGING LIABILITY

§ 15.14   Liability for Past Involvement

For insurers, the problem of managing potential liability arising out of events that occurred in the past is almost entirely a legal defense problem.

---

[59] *See, e.g.,* Transamerica Ins. Co. v. Bellefonte Ins. Co., 490 F. Supp. 935 (E.D. Pa. 1980).

[60] *See, e.g.,* Michigan Chem. Corp. v. Midland Ins. Co., 728 F.2d 374 (6th Cir. 1984).

[61] Union Carbide Corp. v. Travelers Indem. Co., 399 F. Supp. 12 (W.D. Pa. 1975).

[62] Michigan Chem. Corp. v. Midland Ins. Co., 728 F.2d 378 (6th Cir. 1984).

[63] Centennial Ins. Co. v. Lumberman's Mut. Casualty Co., 677 F. Supp. 342 (E.D. Pa. 1987).

For most of the years likely to be at issue, there will be few, if any, insurance company records left to identify the insureds, the policies, or the specific insurance forms that were provided. Records identifying which insurer provided coverage for specific years often are discovered late in the litigation, which impedes those insurers' ability to prepare a defense. This delay often prevents insurers from learning (1) whether new hazardous waste actions (including PRP notices) will be filed against former insureds, (2) whether the former insureds have records identifying their past insurers and the insurance provided for specific time periods, (3) the nature of the substances, processes, or sites for which liability insurance may apply, and (4) the nature of the damages or injuries alleged to be covered. These unknowns make it difficult for insurers to assess potential liability for events that already have occurred. At best, insurers can make some preparations by being aware of the allegations and defenses that have been used, with varying success, in past cases in different venues.

§ 15.15   Damages

One of the issues confronted by policyholders and insurers is whether government mandated response costs incurred by the insured are covered damages under comprehensive general liabiltiy policies. Often this question is resolved at the outset of the case by summary judgment or summary adjudication of issues. Generally, CGL policies have provided that the insurer "will pay on behalf of the insured all sums which the insured shall become legally obligated to pay as damages, for bodily injury and property damage." Insurers contend that the term *as damages* is limited to traditional legal claims for damages and does not extend to equitable claims for restitution. Insureds argue, on the other hand, that the plain meaning of damages includes costs incurred by them at the government's demand to remediate contamination and are therefore covered. The courts have ruled inconsistently on this question.

United States Aviex Co. v. Travelers Insurance Co.[64] was one of the first appellate cases to address the equitable nature of a suit to recover cleanup costs. In *Aviex,* the insured brought a declaratory relief action against the insurer, seeking a judgment that the insurer was obligated to pay for the cost of the cleanup mandated by a state injunction. Ruling for the insured, the court held that "damages" included the cost of cleanup, stating that:

> damages include sums which the insured is obligated to pay by reason of liability imposed upon him by law [and] . . . it is merely fortuitous from the standpoint of either plaintiff or defendant that the state has chosen to have

---

[64] 125 Mich. App. 579, 336 N.W.2d 838 (1983).

plaintiff remedy the contamination problem rather than choosing to incur the costs of cleanup itself and then suing plaintiff to recover those costs.[65]

Another view of the issue was offered in *Chesapeake Utilities Corp. v. American Home Assurance,*[66] in which the court found that "damages," which was not defined in the policy, was ambiguous and construed it against the insurers. According to the court, "A reasonable if not the reasonable interpretation of "damages" is that the term includes both equitable as well as legal relief. Accordingly, the insurers' legal, technical definition of damages is rejected."[67] The court denied the insurers' motion for summary judgment on this issue.

The opposite result was reached by the Eighth Circuit Court of Appeals in *Continental Insurance Companies v. Northeastern Pharmaceutical & Chemical Co.*[68] In that case, the Eighth Circuit ruled en banc that cleanup costs are not damages within the meaning of CGL policies. The court found that "damages" is not ambiguous in the insurance context and that the plain meaning of damages used in CGL policies refers to legal damages and does not cover cleanup costs, which it considered equitable monetary relief.

The Fourth Circuit also ruled in favor of insurers on the damages issue in *Maryland Casualty Co. v. Armco, Inc.*[69] In this case, the United States government sued the insured for reimbursement of cleanup costs and for injunctive relief. The insurers brought a declaratory relief action against the insured concerning its liability under a CGL policy. The court ruled that the ordinary meaning of damages is somewhat limited and that damages, as distinguished from claims for injunctive or restitutionary relief, includes "only payments to third persons when those persons have a legal claim for damages."[70] According to the court, the CGL policy did not cover "expenditures which result from complying with the directives of regulatory agencies."[71]

A number of state supreme courts also have considered the damages issues, again reaching conflicting results. The supreme courts of Washington,[72] Minnesota, California, Massachusetts, and North Carolina[73] ruled

---

[65] *Id.* at 590, 336 N.W.2d at 843.

[66] 704 F. Supp. 551 (D. Del. 1989).

[67] *Id.* at 560.

[68] 842 F.2d 977 (8th Cir.) *cert. denied,* 108 S. Ct. 66 (1988).

[69] 822 F.2d 1348 (4th Cir. 1987), *cert. denied,* 108 S. Ct. 703 (1988).

[70] *Id.* at 1352.

[71] *Id.* at 1354.

[72] *See, e.g.,* The Boeing Co. v. Aetna Casualty & Sur. Co., 113 Wash. 2d 869, 784 P.2d 507 (1990).

[73] C.D. Spangler Constr. Co. v. Industrial Crank Shaft & Eng'g Co., 326 N.C. 133, 388 S.E.2d 557 (1990).

in favor of insureds, finding that response costs are covered damages. The supreme courts of Maine[74] and New Hampshire have ruled in favor of insurers and determined that response costs are not covered damages.

§ 15.16   Liability for Future Involvement

Insurers attempting to control their exposure to future claims for pollution claims face an interesting challenge. Some of the factors that will determine how much insurers will pay for hazardous waste claims are:

The type of coverage negotiated and wording of policies issued

The types of events that insurers attempt to exclude in policies

The exposure of the insured's business to hazardous chemicals and waste claims, which may arise from a variety of chemicals and other substances used in the business or manufacturing, byproducts of manufacturing, and the toxicity or other risks of injury or damage inherent in the products manufactured or sold by the business

The success of insurers in defending against attempts to broaden the meaning or erode the effectiveness of the language in the policies issued, especially with respect to exclusions in the policies issued today

Legislation that retroactively creates liability for pollution claims that currently would not be actionable, or related to substances presently not believed to be harmful, especially if such legislation relates to exposures not excluded under present coverage forms.

§ 15.17   Current Insurance Forms

After almost four years of debate and public comment about what revisions should be made, the ISO introduced new versions of the CGL form, renamed Commercial General Liability, in January 1986. The ISO recognized the serious, ongoing litigation problems with earlier CGL forms and hoped to eliminate some future litigation with new lanaguage, and by offering two versions of the 1986 CGL: an occurrence version, triggered similarly to the 1973 CGL form and a claims-made form, applicable only to claims actually made during the policy period arising from occurrences that happened after a retroactive date stated in the policy declarations. The period of time in which to make a covered claim is subject to extension past the expiration date of the policy under certain specific circumstances that may vary in the forms actually issued by different insurers.

---

[74] Patrons Oxford Mut. Ins. Co. v. Marois, 573 A.2d 16 (Me. 1990).

Coverage under a claims-made policy thus is intended to cease after the policy or its extended reporting provisions have expired.

Because ISO adopted a plain language format for all of its new forms starting in the late 1970s, the wording of all policy terms changed, even if there was no intended change in the meaning. The key terms in the 1986 CGL forms have been reworded as follows:

> "Bodily injury" means bodily injury, sickness or disease sustained by a person, including death resulting from any of these at any time.
>
> "Occurrence" means an accident, including continuous or repeated exposure to substantially the same general harmful conditions.
>
> "Property damage" means:
>
> a. Physical injury to tangible property, including all resulting loss of use of that property; or
>
> b. Loss of use of tangible property that is not physically injured.[75]

The statement that formerly appeared in the bodily injury and property damage definitions about when coverage applies now appears in the CGL insuring agreement: "This insurance applies only to 'bodily injury' and 'property damage' which occurs during the policy period." In addition, exclusion 2.a. in both 1986 CGL forms (occurrence and claims-made versions) contains a variant of language previously found in the definition of occurrence, and now reads as follows:

> This insurance does not apply to: . . . "Bodily injury" or "property damage" expected or intended from the standpoint of the insured. This exclusion does not apply to "bodily injury" resulting from the use of reasonable force to protect persons or property.[76]

The 1986 CGL pollution exclusion has the stated purpose of removing from the policy all possible coverage for pollution claims. As a result, the ISO abandoned its attempt to develop wording that would replace the often litigated and maligned wording, "sudden and accidental," which was rooted in the older concepts of liability policies covering accidental, fortuitous events. The new exclusion (f) reads as follows:

> This insurance does not apply to:
>
> (1) "Bodily injury" or "property damage" arising out of the actual, alleged or threatened discharge, dispersal, release or escape of pollutants:

---

[75] Insurance Services Office, Inc., Commercial General Liability Coverage Form, Nos. GL0001 1185 and GL0002 0286, copyright © 1982, 1984, Insurance Services Offices, Inc.

[76] *Id.*

   (a) At or from premises you own, rent or occupy;

   (b) At or from any site or location used by or for you or others for the handling, storage, disposal, processing or treatment of waste;

   (c) Which are at any time transported, handled, stored, treated, disposed of, or processed as waste by or for you or any person or organization for whom you may be legally responsible; or

   (d) At or from any site or location on which you or any contractors or subcontractors working directly or indirectly on your behalf are performing operations;

      (i) if the pollutants are brought on or to the site or location in connection with such operations; or

     (ii) if the operations are to test for, monitor, clean up, remove, contain, treat, detoxify or neutralize pollutants.

(2) Any loss, cost, or expense arising out of any governmental direction or request that you test for, monitor, clean up, remove, contain, treat, detoxify or neutralize pollutants.

Pollutants means any solid, liquid, gaseous or thermal irritant or contaminant, including smoke, vapor, soot, fumes, acids, alkalis, chemicals and waste. Waste includes materials to be recycled, reconditioned or reclaimed.[77]

ISO provided an endorsement, CG0041, that gave back coverage under subparagraphs (a) and (d) (i) above for bodily injury or property damage arising out of heat, smoke, or fumes from a hostile fire. A subsequent change in the CGL form incorporates this change so that it does not have to be requested by insureds.

Although the new pollution exclusion appears to be very broad, there may still be instances when pollution exposures may be insured. These arise out of some types of events that might occur away from premises owned, rented, or occupied by the insured.[78]

§ 15.18   Environmental Impairment Liability Forms

One of the common reasons for exclusions in insurance policies has always been to shift coverage out of one form over to another one designed to provide coverage of the risk. Most types of pollution were recognized as candidates for special coverage forms when insureds and insurers began to recognize the uncertainty (created by inconsistent judicial interpretations of pollution coverage under the 1973 form) about what pollution

---

[77] *Id.*

[78] Some potential exposures are discussed in Fire, Casualty & Surety Bulletins, Casualty Surety Volume, Public Liability Aa-7ff. (Apr. 1985). *See also id.* at Cop-1ff., Copl-1ff., and Copm-1ff.

events were covered under a traditional CGL policy. Insurers, in particular, hoped that introducing special environmental coverage forms would help defuse the public and judicial reaction to removing pollution coverage of all types from the CGL form, whether gradual or sudden and accidental.

In the early 1980s, the ISO began providing a pollution liability policy form, *Environmental Impact Liability,* or EIL, to replace coverage not available under CGL policies. Coverage was for claims made during the policy period for events commencing after the policy's retroactive date (either policy inception or at some earlier date).

Coverage options in the ISO's new EIL forms introduced in 1986 either included or excluded cleanup costs. There are numerous additional features, but because we assume in this chapter that only unintended (by the insurer) coverage for pollution creates a serious litigation problem, we will not dwell on the forms intended by the industry to provide the coverage for a premium, using options the insured can select.

The principal problem with coverage for pollution is its scarcity. Few insurers advertise their willingness to provide the coverage, although it is reported to be available for many businesses that do not handle or discharge known hazardous substances. From an insurer's perspective, the risk of future liability in offering these forms is the uncertainty that courts will consistently enforce wording in the policy as to what was intended to be either covered or excluded. History teaches that such consistency is one of the most unlikely results one can expect, and that some courts will stretch the language of the policy in many unanticipated ways in order to find coverage where none was intended by the insurer.

§ 15.19   Duty to Defend

Environmental coverage litigation has generated a new issue in the often litigated question of an insurer's duty to defend: whether the insured's receipt of a potentially responsible party (PRP) letter from the EPA, or similar notification from a state agency, triggers the insurer's duty to defend. Typically, a primary liability policy requires an insurer to provide the insured with a defense to a "suit for damages from the insured."[79] A PRP letter, although not a suit, asks the insured to investigate and undertake "voluntary" action to remediate the contamination for which it may be responsible. A preliminary review of the decisions by the courts that have considered this issue reveals that the more the agency's action is like a

---

[79] For example, the wording of a standard CGL policy provides that the insurer "shall have the right and duty to defend any suit against the insured seeking damages on account of bodily injury or property damage."

judicial proceeding, in other words adversarial and coercive in nature, the ·more likely a court will regard it as a suit triggering the insurer's duty to defend. While this issue currently affects mostly policies issued before the advent of more restrictive pollution exclusions in the early 1980s, it may have an impact on a variety of other potential liability proceedings that continue to be covered, and that thus may be initiated by regulatory agencies in the future rather than only by injured claimants.

One of the early cases to consider this issue was *Fireman's Fund Insurance Cos. v. Ex-Cell-O Corp.*[80] In *Ex-Cell-O,* the insureds received PRP letters concerning 16 sites, were notified by a state agency that it had initiated cleanup and considered the insured potentially responsible at four sites, and expected immediate agency action at another site. The insurers claimed that they had no duty to defend the environmental claims until the insured became defendants in a "traditional lawsuit for money damages."[81] The court rejected their position, stating that:

> coverage does not hinge on the form of action taken or the nature of relief sought, but on actual or threatened use of legal process to coerce payment or conduct by a policyholder. . . . a "suit" includes any effort to impose on the policyholders a liability ultimately enforceable by a court.[82]

The Second Circuit also found the insurer had a duty to defend in *Avondale Industries, Inc. v. Travelers Indemnity Co.*[83] The insured in *Avondale* was notified by a state agency that it intended to take immediate action to clean up the site and to recover all costs it expended in the cleanup. The letter also requested the insured to provide the agency with information about its disposal activities at the site and demanded that the insured submit a plan for remediation of the site or reimburse the state for remediation. The letter threatened to impose penalties for failure to comply and demanded that the insured attend a meeting with other PRPs or else a suit would be initiated against the insured. In ruling in favor of the insured, the court stated:

> The demand letter commences a formal proceeding against Avondale, advising it that public authority has assumed an adversarial posture toward it, and that disregard of [its] demands may result in the loss of substantial rights by Avondale. These strike us as the hallmarks of litigation and are sufficiently adversarial to constitute a suit under New York law and within the meaning of the policy.[84]

---

[80] 662 F. Supp. 71 (E.D. Mich. 1987).

[81] *Id.* at 75.

[82] *Id.*

[83] 887 F.2d 1200 (2d Cir. 1989).

[84] *Id.* at 1206.

The court also noted that New York had adopted a broad construction of the word suit and that the public interest was better served by prompt cleanup.

In contrast to the *Ex-Cell-O* and *Avondale* courts, the court in *Harter Corp. v. Home Indemnity,*[85] determined that the insurer did not have to defend an insured in an EPA investigation in which the EPA had notified the insured that it was a PRP. According to the court, to construe as a suit the EPA's threat to hold the insured liable for cleanup costs would do violence to the plain and ordinary meaning of the word "suit,"[86] which the court ruled was unambiguous and "plainly means some sort of court proceeding. It is undisputed that a PRP letter is not a court proceeding."[87] Accordingly, the court found that the insurer had no duty to defend at this time.

---

[85] 713 F. Supp. 231 (W.D. Mich. 1989).

[86] *Id.* at 232.

[87] *Id.* at 233.

CHAPTER 16

TITLE INSURANCE AND ENVIRONMENTAL WASTE LIENS

Harold A. Drees
Gary R. Stephani

Harold A. Drees is senior vice president of Attorneys' Title Insurance Fund, Inc., and has been on The Fund's legal staff for 28 years. He has authored articles and lectured throughout Florida on title matters and title insurance claims. He is one of the less than 200 Florida lawyers certified as a "real estate lawyer." Mr. Drees has been very active in local, state, and national bar activities and also serves as regent and treasurer of the American College of Mortgage Attorneys.

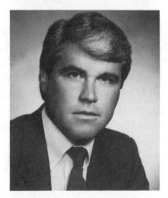

Gary R. Stephani is a partner in the litigation services group of the Washington, D.C., office of Coopers & Lybrand. He is a CPA, specializing in insurance operations, financial, and regulatory aspects. Mr. Stephani has served as a consultant and expert on various business litigation engagements and is a frequent speaker on insurance topics.

§ 16.1   Title Insurance Generally

Title insurance is a rather unique type of insurance. Instead of insuring against possible future events, as do life, fire, casualty, and liability insurance, title insurance insures buyers and mortgage lenders against loss and damages resulting from defects in the title to real property that already existed when the policy was issued, but which were not excluded or excepted from coverage. Title insurance is often compared to boiler insurance; that is, neither is written without an examination that minimizes the probability of a loss's occurring.

The statutory definition of *title insurance* differs slightly from state to state, but basically it is defined as

> "the insuring, guaranteeing or indemnifying of designated owners of real estate or any interest therein against loss or damage which may result by reason of the title being vested in a manner otherwise than as stated in the title insurance policy, or by reason of the title being unmarketable, or by reason of the title being subject to liens, encumbrances or other matters adversely affecting the rights of use, enjoyment or disposition thereof, and not excepted in the policy, all in accordance with the terms of a title insurance policy approved as to substance and form, or doing anything equivalent in substance to any of the foregoing in a manner designed to evade the provisions of this chapter."[1]

Title insurance policies are generally of two basic types. The first type is the *owner policy* that insures a buyer of real property against loss or

---

[1] Mich. Comp. Laws § 500.7301.

damages resulting from title defects that were not picked up by the title examiner, or from matters that cannot usually be discovered by the title examiner. In the category of defects that were not picked up would be matters such as judgment liens, tax liens, missed reservations, omitted mortgages, and similar types of defects. In the category of undiscoverable defects would be matters such as unknown heirs, forgeries, voidable deeds from minors, and fraudulent transactions.

The second type of policy is a *mortgagee* or *loan policy,* which is generally issued to a lender who lends money on a mortgage, deed of trust, or other security instrument from the landowner. In addition to having coverage against defects, as the owner does under an owner policy, the lender has the additional protection under the loan policy of being insured against loss should the security not be of the priority set out in the policy. Not always, but usually, a lender wants assurance that the lien it has is a valid and enforceable first lien on the real estate, subject generally only to governmentally imposed taxes or assessment liens. The lender wants to be assured that in the event the loan goes into default, that title can be acquired through a judicial process that will be free of subordinate liens that might otherwise affect the title.

Therefore, to give this protection, title insurance underwriters and their agents must take extreme care in examining the title to determine the priority of the lien being insured. Because the examiner relies primarily, and sometimes solely, on the recording statutes of the particular state to determine the insurability of title, any provision in any law that allows a lien to arise and attach to real estate without need for its recording in the local land records, to the detriment of buyers and lenders, gives title insurance underwriters serious concern.

§ 16.2   State Superliens

The concern of title insurers over environmental superliens was particularly evident during the early 1980s when some states, particularly in the Northeast,[2] passed environmental superlien statutes that gave the state, or an agency of the state, a lien against all of the real estate that the responsible party owned or may acquire, with the priority of the lien superceding all other liens against the property. This type of superlien statute presented a problem for the title insurers because when a policy was being issued there was no record evidence that such a lien existed. Nor could a title examiner possibly determine if in the future some lien might arise that would take priority over the interest being insured. However, from

---

[2] Some of the states having superliens in the early 1980s were Massachusetts, New Hampshire, New Jersey, and Connecticut.

the few reported cases involving title insurance and superliens the courts have generally held that:

> The fact that there may exist on the property environmental waste at the time the insured acquired title for which the insured is liable for cleanup costs does not give rise to a claim under the title policy based on the unmarketability of title, and
>
> Even if a claim of lien were filed subsequent to the acquiring of title by the insured that takes priority over prior liens and relates back in priority to a time prior to policy issuance, the title insurer is not liable.[3]

An interesting case involving a title insurer and the Connecticut environmental superlien statute is *South Shore Bank v. Stewart Title Guaranty Co.*[4] In this case, South Shore Bank was seeking a declaratory judgment to have Stewart Title held responsible for the expenses of removal, cleanup, and monitoring of hazardous waste on property insured by Stewart Title under a loan policy. The policy contained in it an endorsement by which Stewart Title insured against loss or damages sustained by the insured by reason of a lien that attached to the insured premises pursuant to the Connecticut superlien statute as a result of conditions existing on or at the insured premises as of the date of the policy if such lien claims priority over the lien of the insured mortgage. About a year after the policy was issued it was determined by the state environmental authority that there was hazardous waste on the property. By this time the mortgage was in default. When South Shore Bank was made aware of the hazardous waste problem, it notified Stewart Title that it expected to make a claim against the policy after acquiring title in its foreclosure suit.

On a motion for summary judgment filed by the defendant, Stewart Title, the court held in its favor. The court noted that because no lien had as yet been created under the Connecticut superlien statute, the endorsement coverage had not come into play. The possibility that an environmental lien might arise that would take priority over the prior mortgage lien does not trigger insurance coverage under the endorsement. The court followed the reasoning of *Chicago Title Insurance Co. v. Kumar,*[5] holding that the mere possibility that a future lien may be created is insufficient to create a defect or encumbrance on title. The court also stated that the specific reference to the statutory lien provision of the Connecticut statute in the endorsement is not to ensure an immediate response to environmental pollution but rather to protect the insured from a challenge to

---

[3] Chicago Title Ins. Co. v. Kumar, 24 Mass. App. Ct. 53, 506 N.E.2d 154 (1987).

[4] 688 F. Supp. 803 (D. Mass. 1988).

[5] 24 Mass. App. Ct. 53, 506 N.E.2d 154 (1987).

its title by reason of a lien that would take priority over South Shore Bank's legal rights in the property.

The fact that a title insurer may not be liable under its policy for a superlien recorded after the date of policy issuance does not mean that the lien is ineffective, however. In the New Jersey case of *Kessler v. Tarrats,*[6] the court held that notwithstanding the fact that the original mortgage was even dated and recorded prior to the enactment of the New Jersey superlien statute, the superlien did take priority over that mortgage held by the assignee of the original mortgagee. The superlien law of New Jersey was characterized by one judge in a New Jersey case as being comparable to "a hibernating time bomb."[7]

To a large extent, the states that passed these broad, all-encompassing superlien statutes in the early 1980s have since amended their laws so that in most situations these state superliens no longer affect residential properties, nor do they become liens on lands other than the land being reclaimed and owned by the responsible party. Also, innocent third parties purchasing or taking a security interest in the property are generally not affected unless the state, or the proper agency of the state, has filed evidence of its claim of lien in the land records.[8] No attempt has been made to list or characterize the various state environmental lien laws because of the continuous changes taking place each time state legislators meet. However, real estate lawyers and title insurers in the various states do need to keep abreast of the environmental laws of the state or states wherein they practice or do business.

§ 16.3 Affirmative Coverage and Endorsement

Some lenders, particularly during the 1980s, were demanding of title insurers and their agents that they provide affirmative coverage against loss resulting from hazardous waste's being found on the property. Some title

---

[6] 476 N.J. Super. 326, 476 A. 2d 326 (1984).

[7] Simon v. Oldmans Township, 203 N.J. Super. 365, 497 A.2d 204 (1985).

[8] Massachusetts has revised its superlien statute to exempt property that is single or multi-family housing and limits the lien to the site of the hazard release. The notice of lien must be filed in the proper records. Mass. Ann. Laws ch. 21E. New Hampshire revised its superlien statute to exempt residential property from superlien priority, require recording, and limit superlien priority to the land on which the hazardous waste was located. N.H. Rev. Stat. Ann. § 147-13:10-6(III)(a)(c). New Jersey revised its superlien statute to create a two-tier lien priority. As to property subject to the cleanup, unless it is residential, the lien is a superlien; as to other real property of the discharger of the hazardous waste, it is a nonpriority lien. Notice of lien must also be recorded. N.J. Stat. Ann. 58.10-23.11f. Connecticut revised its superlien statute to exempt residential and certain commercial real property from the superlien priority aspect. Only the waste removal site is subject to the lien. Conn. Gen. Stat. §§ 22a–452a.

insurers, through their agents, were actually giving such coverage based on a personal inspection of the property, some superficial testing, and a review of record title to determine the type of persons or entities that may have had an interest in the property in the past. Some lenders were also asking that the policy set out on its face in affirmative language that the property was free of any hazardous waste. Usually such language was not approved by the title insurance underwriter but was given by an agent who, being familiar with local land use, felt no substantial risk was being created. Probably very little thought was given to the vast number of substances listed by EPA that qualify as hazardous waste materials. Such coverage is far beyond the scope of title insurance, and the insurance departments of several of the states, like Florida, demanded that this practice be stopped.[9] Not only was it far beyond the scope of title insurance to provide this protection but, as compared to the premium a liability company would charge for similar protection, the premium received by a title insurance company for this protection was a very small fraction of what liability actuarials considered it to be worth.[10] It is believed such casualty type coverage previously provided in a few title policies has since been stopped.

Some lenders require an endorsement to mortgagee policies to ensure the lender that the insured loan has priority over any environmental lien. This endorsement, commonly referred to as the *ALTA 8.1 endorsement,*[11] is usually given on a loan policy on residential property based on an examination of the public records that does not disclose any claim of lien filed prior to the interest being insured. Basically, the coverage is given even without the endorsement. A copy of the endorsement and instructions given by one company is set out in §§ **16.9** and **16.10**. This endorsement form is used in practically all the states and was created primarily to satisfy the requirement of the Florida National Mortgage Association (FNMA) and other secondary market lenders.

---

[9] Memorandum of Decision and Declaratory Ruling, *In re* Lawyers Title Ins. Corp. Petition for Declaratory Judgment, No. RD 86-22 (Conn., Jan. 8, 1987); Informal Telephone Notice from Fla. Dept of Ins. (1989) to prohibit assuring in title policy the nonhazardous waste condition of insured title.

[10] The annual premium charged by a casualty insurer for environmental type coverage on a claims-made policy was estimated to be 30 times the one-time premium paid to a title insurer whose agent was exposing the company to a similar risk when insuring against hazardous waste loss.

[11] *ALTA* is the American Land Title Association.

§ 16.4   Environmental Protection Lien Endorsement Form

ENVIRONMENTAL PROTECTION LIEN ENDORSEMENT (ALTA Form 8.1)

Attorneys' Title Insurance Fund, Inc.

ORLANDO, FLORIDA

Endorsement No. _____ to Policy No.:

The insurance afforded by this endorsement is only effective if the land is used or is to be used primarily for residential purposes.

Attorneys' Title Insurance Fund, Inc. insures the insured against loss or damage sustained by reason of lack of priority of the lien of the insured mortgage over:

(a) any environmental protection lien which, at Date of Policy, is recorded in those records established under state statutes at Date of Policy for the purpose of imparting constructive notice of matters relating to real property to purchasers for value and without knowledge, or filed in the records of the clerk of the United States district court for the district in which the land is located, except as set forth in Schedule B; or

(b) any environmental protection lien provided for by any state statute in effect at Date of Policy, except environmental protection liens provided for by the following state statutes:

This endorsement is made a part of the policy and is subject to all of the terms and provisions thereof and of any prior endorsements thereto. Except to the extent expressly stated, it neither modifies any of the terms and provisions of the policy and any prior endorsements, nor does it extend the effective date of the policy and any prior endorsements, nor does it increase the face amount thereof.

In Witness Whereof, Attorneys' Title Insurance Fund, Inc. has caused its name and seal to be hereunto affixed by its duly authorized Agent as of the date shown herein, the effective date of this endorsement.

Name of Fund Agent	Date	Agent No.

Attorneys' Title Insurance Fund, Inc.

By   Charles J. Kovaleski
                      President

_____
Attorney Agent's Signature
ALTA Form 8.1 (6/89) Fund Form EPL1

INSTRUCTIONS FOR PREPARING THE ENVIRONMENTAL
PROTECTION LIEN ENDORSEMENT (ALTA 8.1)

The ALTA 8.1 endorsement is to be issued in conjunction with the mortgagee policy of title insurance form–ALTA loan policy. This endorsement provides for affirmative coverage against loss or damage by reason of a lack of priority of the insured mortgage over any environmental protection lien which is in existence at date of policy. To issue this endorsement, all that is necessary is the determination that there is not of record either notice of a lien or lien for cleanup and removal. If the title examination reveals such a lien, it would be shown as an exception under Schedule B. If the examination does not reveal such a lien, then the endorsement is issued. This endorsement is primarily used in one- to four-family residential transactions and is a requirement of the secondary mortgage market.

Paragraph (a) of the endorsement reflects that there are no liens filed in the records of the clerk of the United States District Court of the district in which the land is located. A check of Federal District Court records is not necessary because federal law provides for the creation of a lien by such recording in a limited situation. Specifically, it is provided "if the state has not by law designated one office for the receipt of such notices of liens, the notice shall be filed in the office of the clerk of the United States District Court for the district in which the real property is located." 42 U.S.C., Sec 9607(1)(3). It is The Fund's opinion that existing Florida law does designate one office for the receipt of notice of liens for hazardous waste cleanup and that this office is the clerk of the circuit court of the county in which the property is located. See Sec. 28.222, F.S. As a result, no check of the Federal District Court records is necessary in order to issue The Fund's 8.1 endorsement in Florida.

The ALTA 8.1 endorsement at paragraph (b) contains space for the insertion of state statutes which may create a 'superlien' to be given priority over earlier recorded interest. There are presently no such statutes in Florida. Consequently 'none' would be typed on the endorsement. Should Florida at some point in the future adopt legislation which would provide for a 'superlien,' then this information will be given to you for inclusion in the endorsement.

Paragraph (a) of the endorsement really provides no coverage greater than that provided by the policy without the endorsement when the ALTA 1987 Loan policy form is used. It may provide a little additional comfort to those insured under the 1970 or 1984 ALTA loan policy forms in that it extends to liens filed in the Federal District Court Clerk's office, if that is the proper place of filing.

Paragraph (b) of the endorsement affords additional post-policy coverage in insuring that there are no environmental protection liens that could attain priority over the lien of the insured mortgage provided by state statutes in effect at date of policy except those stated or generally excepted. This provision in the endorsement, which was requested by FNMA because of its concern about superliens, does not insure against loss by reason of personal liability of the lender; it does not insure against loss by reason of local regulations creating liens; and it does not insure that there are not environmental violations or hazardous materials on the property. It simply insures that there are no state statutes in effect at the date of policy that could cause a later filed environmental protection lien to attain priority over the lien of the insured mortgage.

In addition to state statutes, it may become common for local cities and counties to adopt codes to provide for environmental cleanup cost superliens. Dade County, Florida, for example, adopted such a code,[12] which provides:

(i) Owners of real property shall be liable for the sums expended by the county pursuant to section 24-5(30) when the violation of this chapter occurred or continued to exist or appeared imminent upon the real property aforesaid, regardless of fault and regardless of knowledge of the aforesaid violation. All sums expended by the county pursuant to section 24-5(30) of this Code shall constitute and are hereby imposed as special assessments against the real property aforesaid, and until fully paid and discharged or barred by law, shall remain liens equal in rank and dignity with the lien of county ad valorem taxes and superior in rank and dignity to all other liens, encumbrances, titles and claims in, to or against the real property involved. All such sums shall become immediately due and owing to the county upon expenditure by the county and shall become delinquent if not fully paid within sixty (60) days after the due date. All such delinquent sums shall bear a penalty of fifteen (15) per cent per annum. Unpaid and delinquent sums, together with all penalties imposed thereon, shall remain and constitute special assessment liens against the real property involved for the period of five (5) years from due date thereof. Said special assessment liens may be enforced by the director by any of the methods provided in Chapter 85, Florida Statutes, or, in the alternative, foreclosure proceedings may be instituted and prosecuted by the director pursuant to the provisions of Chapter 173, Florida Statutes, or the collection and enforcement of payment thereof may be accomplished by any other method provided by law. All sums covered by the county pursuant to this provision shall be deposited by the county into the fund from which said sums were expended.

§ 16.5   The CERCLA Lien

Most state environmental lien statutes have some similarity to the federal law insofar as third-party purchasers and holders of security interest are concerned. This federal law is the Comprehensive Environmental

---

[12] Dade County, Fla., Code § 24-57.

Response, Compensation and Liability Act of 1980,[13] commonly known as CERCLA, as amended by the Superfund Amendments and Reauthorization Act of 1986 (SARA).[14]

Until the 1986 amendment to CERCLA, the federal government had no way of reclaiming its loss for the removal of hazardous waste from real property other than to seek a judgment against a responsible person or persons and then attempt to collect on or enforce the judgment as a lien on the judgment debtor's property. The 1986 amendment to CERCLA added language of particular concern to real estate lawyers and title insurers. It provides for a lien in favor of the United States[15] and reads as follows:

(1) In General—All costs and damages for which a person is liable to the United States under subsection (a) of this section (other than the owner or operator of a vessel under paragraph (1) of subsection (a) shall constitute a lien in favor of the United States upon all real property and rights to such property which—

 (A) belong to such person; and

 (B) are subject to or affected by a removal or remedial action.

(2) DURATION—The lien imposed by this subsection shall arise at the later of the following:

 (A) The time costs are first incurred by the United States with respect to a response action under this Act.

 (B) The time that the person referred to in paragraph (1) is provided (by certified or registered mail) written notice of potential liability.

Such lien shall continue until the liability for the costs (or a judgment against the person arising out of such liability) is satisfied or becomes unenforceable through operation of the statute of limitations provided in section 113.

(3) NOTICE AND VALIDITY—The lien imposed by this subsection shall be subject to the rights of any purchaser, holder of a security interest, or judgment lien creditor whose interest is perfected under applicable State law before notice of the lien has been filed in the appropriate office within the State (or county or other governmental subdivision), as designated by State law, in which the real property subject to the lien is located. Any such purchaser, holder of a security interest, or judgment lien creditor shall be afforded the same protections against the lien imposed by this subsection as are afforded under State law against a judgment lien which arises out of an unsecured obligation and which arises as of the time of the filing of the notice of the lien

---

[13] Pub. L. No. 96-510, 94 Stat. 2767 (1980).

[14] Pub. L. No. 99-499, _____ Stat. _____ (198__) (codified at 42 U.S.C. §§ 9601–9675 (1988)).

[15] SARA § 107(l); 42 U.S.C. § 9607(l).

imposed by this subsection. If the State has not by law designated one office for the receipt of such notices of liens, the notice shall be filed in the office of the clerk of the United States district court for the district in which the real property is located. For purposes of this subsection, the terms "purchaser" and "security interest" shall have the definitions provided under section 6323(h) of the Internal Revenue Code of 1954.

(4) ACTION IN REM—The costs constituting the lien may be recovered in an action in rem in the United States district court for the district in which the removal or remedial action is occurring or has occurred. Nothing in this subsection shall affect the right of the United States to bring an action against any person to recover all costs and damages for which such person is liable under subsection (a) of this section.

Although the federal lien provided by SARA has been in effect since 1986, only a few articles have been written in legal, real estate, and banking publications concerning environmental liens,[16] and only a limited number of seminars have been given explaining its ramifications. Surprisingly, even in the 97-page detailed report given by the General Accounting Office of the United States to a Senate Subcommittee on December 14, 1989 on the matter of identifying financially viable parties to hold responsible, and for the recovery of cleanup costs, no mention was made of the availability of CERCLA liens or their enforcement benefits to EPA.[17]

An example somewhat akin to environmental liens under SARA are federal tax liens. Under federal law, if Mr. Jones does not pay his income tax the IRS has a lien on all of his property, both real and personal.[18] This lien arises without the necessity of the IRS filing anything in the land records or under whatever state law might otherwise be required for the creation of a lien against real or personal property. The lien is against all of the property of the taxpayer. This differs slightly from the lien provided by SARA in that the lien under SARA is applicable only to the real property and rights to such property. It is not a lien against the personal property as is a federal tax lien. Persons dealing with Mr. Jones who are

---

[16] Weissman, *Superfund—Lender Liability,* Mortgage Banking (Feb. 1987); Bozarth, *Environmental Liens and Title Insurance,* Lawyers Title News (Jan.–Apr. 1989); O.H. Beasley, Title Insurance 1987: The New Policy Forms ch. 18 (1989); *A Lender's Guide to Environmental Liability Risk Management,* Mortgage Banking (May 1987); ABA Division for Professional Education, Environmental Liabilities, Super Liens & Title Insurance (Video July 6, 1990); Beasley, *Titles, Toxics and Terrible Trouble,* Washington Area Realtor (May 1988).

[17] United States General Accounting Office Report to the Chairman, Subcommittee on Superfund, Ocean and Water Protection, and U.S. Senate Committee on Environmental and Public Works, SUPERFUND—A More Vigorous and Better Managed Enforcement Program Is Needed (Dec. 1989).

[18] 26 U.S.C. § 6321 (1988).

not on actual notice of the IRS's lien can purchase land from Jones free of the lien if the IRS did not first file its claim of lien in the land records in accordance with the laws of the state where the land is situated. Obviously, if the IRS does file its claim of lien in the proper land records, then all third parties are on constructive notice of the lien, and anyone purchasing land from Jones or accepting a security interest from Jones thereafter would take subject to the IRS tax lien.

Another difference between the federal tax lien and the SARA environmental lien is that if a third person has actual knowledge of the federal tax lien, even though the claim of lien is not recorded, the third person purchaser or lender takes subject to it. There is some question whether actual knowledge of costs incurred or notification to the potentially responsible party under CERCLA, without the recording of the claim of lien, would be a lien to the detriment of the third party. It is generally believed that it would not.[19]

Also, unlike the federal tax lien, which is for an amount certain and ascertainable, the environmental lien for cleanup costs is as of the time of filing not certain as to the amount. The ultimate extent of the lien will be for an amount that is not ascertainable until long afterward. The lien is said to arise at the time the person is provided written notice of potential liability by certified or registered mail or at the time costs are first incurred, whichever is later, and will continue until satisfied or becoming unenforceable through operation of the statute of limitation provided in § 113 of CERCLA.[20]

§ 16.6   Liability of the Title Insurer

Unless a title insurer has gone beyond the regular policy coverage in providing some affirmative environmental type coverage, or unless the title insurer has failed in its search or examination of the title to pick up a recorded notice of lien filed under some environmental law, it is unlikely a title insurer will suffer any claim loss under its policy coverage. Although the approved ALTA policy forms are not used in all the states or by all title insurance underwriters, undoubtedly all forms do contain in them coverage exclusion language similar, if not identical, to that in the ALTA owner and loan policy forms.

When CERCLA was enacted in 1980, the ALTA forms in general use were those identified as ALTA-1970. The ALTA forms were revised in 1984 to specifically exclude environmental type liens and again in 1987 to

---

[19] Memorandum by Asst. Administrator for EPA, Guidance on Federal Superfund Liens (Sept. 22, 1987).

[20] 42 U.S.C. § 9613.

refine the exclusion language and add, among other things, a more definite definition of *public records*. The exclusionary language within these three forms follows:

1970 ALTA FORM

1. Any law, ordinance or governmental regulation (including but not limited to building and zoning ordinances) restricting or regulating or prohibiting the occupancy, use or enjoyment of the land, or regulating the character, dimensions or location of any improvement now or hereafter erected on the land, or prohibiting a separation in ownership or a reduction in the dimensions or area of the land, or the effect of any violation of any such law, ordinance or governmental regulation.

2. Rights of eminent domain or governmental rights of police power unless notice of the exercise of such rights appears in the public records at date of policy.

1984 ALTA FORM

1. (a) Governmental police power.
   (b) Any law, ordinance or governmental regulation relating to environmental protection.
   (c) Any law, ordinance or governmental regulation (including but not limited to building and zoning ordinances) restricting or regulating or prohibiting the occupancy, use or enjoyment of the land, or regulating the character, dimensions or location of any improvement now or hereafter erected on the land, or prohibiting a separation in ownership or a change in the dimensions or area of the land or any parcel of which the land is or was a part.
   (d) The effect of any violation of the matters excluded under (a), (b) or (c) above, unless notice of a defect, lien or encumbrance resulting from a violation has been recorded at date of policy in those records in which under state statutes deeds, mortgages, lis pendens, liens or other title encumbrances must be recorded in order to impart constructive notice to purchasers of the land for value and without knowledge; provided, however, that without limitation, such records shall not be construed to include records in any of the offices of federal, state or local environmental protection, zoning, building, health or public safety authorities.

2. Rights of eminent domain unless notice of the exercise of such rights appears in the public records at date of policy.

1987 ALTA FORM

1. (a) Any law, ordinance or governmental regulation (including but not limited to building and zoning laws, ordinances, or regulations)

restricting, regulating, prohibiting or relating to (i) the occupancy, use or enjoyment of the land; (ii) the character, dimensions or location of any improvement now or hereafter erected on the land; (iii) a separation in ownership or a change in the dimensions or area of the land or any parcel of which the land is or was a part; or (iv) environmental protection, or the effect of any violation of these laws, ordinances or governmental regulations, except to the extent that a notice of the enforcement thereof or a notice of a defect, lien or encumbrance resulting from a violation or alleged violation affecting the land has been recorded in the public records at Date of Policy.

(b) Any governmental police power not excluded by (a) above, except to the extent that a notice of the exercise thereof or a notice of a defect, lien or encumbrance resulting from a violation or alleged violation affecting the land has been recorded in the public records at Date of Policy.

2. Rights of eminent domain unless notice of the exercise thereof has been recorded in the public records at Date of Policy, but not excluding from coverage any taking which has occurred prior to Date of Policy which would be binding on the rights of a purchaser for value without knowledge.

As was stated in § 16.2, the courts have held that title policies insure neither the salability of the land nor against environmental liens that relate back in time but which are not discoverable to a title examiner through search of the public records at the date of the policy.[21] In the New Jersey case of *Simon v. Oldmans Township,*[22] involving an action filed by a purchaser of a tax certificate to have the purchase rescinded because the land might become subject to an environmental state superlien that would take priority over the tax certificate holder's rights, the court stated:

Seen, not from the clinical viewpoint of an environmentalist but from the coldly practical position of those whose interests involve the status of land titles in New Jersey, this statute, (superlien) is a hibernating time bomb. Our whole system of recordation of land titles depends upon the ability of one who seeks to acquire an interest in real property to ascertain beyond peradventure the true state of the title. The entire industry of title insurance depends on this. The willingness of lending institutions to finance the acquisition of real estate depends on it. The financial safety of myriad numbers of owners of real property depends on it. It is probably an understatement that the financial health of a great portion of our economy depends on the simple fact that anyone wishing to invest in real estate, or finance such investment, is able to go to the proper recording officer and be assured of the posture of the title, saving only forgery.[23]

---

[21] *See* Chicago Title Ins. Co. v. Kumar, 24 Mass. App. Ct. 53, 506 N.E.2d 154 (1987).

[22] *See* Simon v. Oldmans Township, 203 N.J. Super. 365, 497 A.2d 204 (1985).

[23] 497 A.2d at 209.

Although no title insurer was a party to this case, the language of the court provides some comfort to the title insurer.

§ 16.7 Tort Liability of Title Insurer

Although CERCLA has not presented any real problems to title insurers that are unique from other types of liens, title insurers are nevertheless quite interested in the subject and realize that the potential liability for missing a recorded environmental lien, as compared to missing a judgment or mortgage, could well result in a claim for a much larger amount than the usual missed judgment or omitted mortgage. Claims for omitted judgments, mortgages, and other liens are generally for amounts far less than the face amount of the policy upon which a claim is made. In a situation of an omitted environmental lien, however, it would be rather common for the lien to be in an amount in excess of the policy limits. Another concern of the title insurers is that their liability might not be limited to the face amount of the policy in the event that an omitted environmental lien is in excess of that amount.

During recent years the courts of various states have taken the position that a title insurer's liability is not limited to the face amount of the policy if the title insurer, through its negligence, fails to note as an exception some title defect of record that results in a loss greater than the policy amount. In other words, an insurer may be sued in tort by the insured because of the negligence of the insurer in failing to fulfill its duty to have properly examined the title. A title insurance company has a duty to exercise reasonable care when it issues a title binder or commitment, and its failure to do may subject it to liability in either contract or tort.[24] Not all states, however, are in accord that a title insurer's liability goes beyond the policy contract. Some courts have taken the position that the insurer has no duty under the policy to search the records and that any search it may actually have undertaken was done solely for its protection as indemnitor against losses covered by the policy.[25]

Even in those jurisdictions in which the court has found the title insurer liable in tort for defects omitted in its policy, it is probable that the court would not have gone beyond policy contract coverage if the policy had been issued by an agent of the insurer based on the agent's negligent examination of title. In the cases reviewed, it was situations in which the title insurer issued directly and not through an agent, that is, the title insurer examined its own title information in a negligent manner, that the

---

[24] Shada v. Title & Trust Co., 457 So. 2d 553 (Fla. 4th Dist. Ct. App. 1984); Jarchow v. Transamerica Title Ins. Co., 48 Cal. App. 3d 917, 122 Cal. Rptr. 470 (1975).

[25] Horn v. Lawyers' Title Ins. Corp., 89 N.M. 709, 557 P.2d 206 (1976); Anderson v. Title Ins. Co., 655 P.2d 82 (ID. 1982).

title insurer was ordered to pay a sum greater than the policy contract amount.[26]

§ 16.8   Filed CERCLA Liens

The number of notices of liens filed by the EPA under CERCLA as of August 1990 is still manageable. For the benefit of title insurers as well as for the benefit of purchasers and lenders in real estate, the EPA does periodically provide the American Land Title Association (ALTA) on an informal basis a listing of the various properties in the states on which notices of liens have been filed. This listing may not be 100 percent accurate, but it does give title insurers and others routinely dealing primarily with vacant and commercial properties a warning of the lien's existence in addition to the notices of liens filed in the public records of the various states. A listing of the lands upon which notices of liens have been filed as of March 9, 1990, as reported by EPA to ALTA, is included in § **16.12**. You will note from the list that some of the properties have already been released, undoubtedly upon some settlement agreement between the EPA and the landowner. Although this list contains only 101 sites, it has been estimated that there may be as high as 60,000 sites in the country that could be subject to waste cleanups and therefore subject to the lien provisions of CERCLA and various state laws.[27]

Based on a telephone conversation on August 13, 1990, with personnel in the office of Enforcement and Compliance Monitoring in EPA's Washington, D.C., offices, there apparently has been no attempt as of that date to enforce any of the nearly 100 liens, although some of them have been of record for several years. This failure to enforce the liens however could be for many reasons. For instance, the United States may not wish to become the owner of the property; settlement negotiations may be underway; recovery from other sources is more likely; or perhaps in many instances the final tab for the total cost involved in the remedial action has not been calculated.

Sections 16.13 through **16.15** contain examples of the letters to property owners advising of potential liability, a notice of federal lien, and a release of lien filed by the EPA. These forms used by the EPA do differ considerably in style and format, depending to a large extent on which of the 10 regional offices of EPA issued the document. As a minimum, the notice of lien should include:

---

[26] Jarchow v. TransAmerica Title Ins. Co., 48 Cal. App. 3d 917, 122 Cal. Rptr. 470 (1975).

[27] Sources of information provided by Coopers & Lybrand state that the probable number of contaminated land sites varies from 25,000 identified sources to 60,000 potential sites.

1. The name of the property owner
2. An adequate legal description of the property subject to the lien
3. An explanation of the basis for the lien
4. The address of the official having the authority to sign the notice of lien
5. A provision that the lien shall remain until all liability is satisfied or becomes unenforceable under the statute of limitations.[28]

§ 16.9   The Landowner's Dilemma

The owner of land upon which a CERCLA notice of lien (see § 16.14) has been filed is pretty much at the mercy of the EPA. If the EPA does not commence an action of cost recovery or enforcement, the landowner is not in a position to contest the validity of the lien. Thus, to free the property of the lien the landowner must either settle with the EPA or await termination of the lien in accordance with the limitation statute.

In the case of *Reardon v. United States,*[29] the Reardons sought injunctive relief against the United States and EPA involving a notice of lien that EPA had filed against the Reardons' property during March 1989. The Reardons claimed that they were innocent landowners and consequently not liable to the EPA for the cost of soil contamination removal and, also, that the lien placed on the property by the EPA was in violation of their constitutional rights under the Fifth Amendment because it deprived them of their property without due process.

With regard to their claim as innocent landowner, the court held that there was no constitutional or statutory authority for the Reardons in such a situation to challenge the CERCLA lien because no action had been commenced by the EPA to compel them to pay for the cleanup costs.

With regard to the Reardons' claim that the filing of the notice of lien deprived them of their property without due process of law, and therefore was in violation of the Fifth Amendment to the United States Constitution, the court compared such a lien to a mechanics' lien and determined that the Reardons had not been deprived of their property by the filing of the notice of lien. The court cited a Supreme Court decision[30] that affirmed an Arizona case in which it was held that restrictions imposed on the alienation of property by the mechanics' lien was not a significant

---

[28] Memorandum by Asst. Administrator for EPA, Guidance on Federal Superfund Liens (Sept. 22, 1987).

[29] 731 F. Supp. 558 (D. Mass. 1990).

[30] Speilman-Fond, Inc. v. Hanson's Inc., 379 F. Supp. 997 (D. Ariz.) (three-judge panel), *aff'd,* 417 U.S. 901 (1973).

property interest protected by the due process clause. The court in the Arizona case stated:

> Here, a lien is filed against the property and clouds title. It cannot be denied that the effect of such lien may make it difficult to alienate the property. If the plaintiffs can find a willing buyer, however, there is nothing in the statues or the liens which prohibits the consummation of the transaction. Even though a willing buyer may be more difficult to find, once he is found there is nothing to prevent plaintiffs from making the sale to him. The liens do nothing more than impinge upon economic interests in the property owner. The right to alienate has not been harmed, and the difficulties which the lien creates may be ameliorated through the use of bonding or title insurance.[31]

The federal district court in the *Reardon* case stated that the CERCLA lien appears analogous to a mechanics' lien and did not interfere with the Reardons' ability to use or possess the property. The CERCLA lien does act as a cloud on the title and may impinge the right to alienate the property, just like the mechanics' lien; it does not, however, bar the subsequent transfer of the Reardons' property, and the CERCLA lien only affects the Reardons' economic interest in the property. Therefore, the court held that the CERCLA lien did not deprive the Reardons of any property interest protected by the Fifth Amendment.

Not considered by the court in the *Reardon* case was the fact that many mechanic's lien statutes throughout the country do differ substantially from a CERCLA lien in that (1) the limitation statute for the enforcement of a mechanics' lien is ordinarily of a much shorter duration than for the in rem enforcement of a CERCLA lien; (2) there are usually provisions under the mechanics' lien statute for transferring the lien to bond and therefore relieving the property of the encumbrance; and (3) it is common for mechanics' lien statutes to provide for a method (usually referred to as the notice of contest of lien) by which the liened property owner can require the lienor to file an action to enforce the lien within a given period of time or otherwise lose his rights to enforce.

§ 16.10 Title Insurer As Title Information Provider

Because subsequent buyers and lenders may have liability for hazardous waste removal aside from the lien aspect, buyers and lenders should be counselled to take all precautions to eliminate this liability. The one precaution is to put the buyer or lender in the position of a good faith

---

[31] Reardon v. United States, 731 F. Supp. at 572.

purchaser in order to enable the party to assert the innocent purchaser defense.[32] One of the requirements in asserting this defense is that the purchaser must show that it investigated to determine the existence or nonexistence of waste hazard pollution because of past usage. To do this, one of the factors to be considered is a review of past ownership of the property and a review of any third party who may have had a record interest in the property. Many title insurers and agents have and operate title information providers through which they sell title information going back many years, disclosing the names of the various parties who have had an interest in the property. To the purchaser or lender this can be important in determining if any of the owners had business names that would indicate usage of the property that might have created environmental problems. For instance, if in the chain of title were found owners such as dry cleaning establishments, filling stations, chemical manufacturers, or perhaps a dumping company with an easement across the property, a buyer would be put on notice of the potential hazardous waste problem and could not later assert a defense against a claim by the government based on the innocent party defense. These reports sold by title information providers go by different names, but generally they show the names of all parties over a period of 40 years or more who have or had some record claim or interest in the property. Some title information providers require that the buyer or lender who is relying on this information sign the order for the title information and recognize various disclaimers of the title information provider. The American Land Title Association is in the process of preparing an Application for the Issuance of a Recorded Document Guaranty. Other companies have their own terminology and forms for ordering such information.

§ 16.11   Unresolved Issues

The state superlien statutes and the CERCLA lien present many interesting questions that the various appellate courts will undoubtedly have to decide in the future. Some of the more interesting are listed here.

Priority of state superlien over local tax lien.   If a state superlien statute provides that the lien will take priority over all other liens, will this be interpreted to mean that it will prime a local tax or assessment lien? Also, would a superlien prime a prior recorded federal tax lien? Will the courts give consideration to the fact that the recorded superlien is a lien on

---

[32] 42 U.S.C. §§ 9601(35)(A), 9607(b)(4).

specific real property while a federal tax lien is a general lien on all of the property of the taxpayer?

Protection of purchaser. CERCLA § 107(l)(3) provides that any purchaser, holder of a security interest, or judgment lien creditor whose interest is perfected under state law prior to the filing of the CERCLA notice of lien shall be afforded the same protections against the CERCLA lien as are afforded under state law against a judgment lien arising out of an unsecured obligation. Does this mean that, if a purchaser is protected under the state law from the enforcement of a judgment lien against the purchased property because it is exempt under state law, the purchaser will have the same protection as against the enforcement of a CERCLA lien?

Redemption rights. The United States and federal agencies, when made parties to a foreclosure of a superior mortgage, have 120 days or one year from the foreclosure sale[33] (time depends on type lien held by the government) within which to exercise its right of redemption. In the foreclosure of a mortgage against the United States as an inferior CERCLA lienholder, it would appear that the United States would have a year within which to redeem. The 120 days is limited to liens under the Internal Revenue Laws. If the United States had an inferior tax lien and an inferior CERCLA lien, the United States as a tax lienholder would have 120 days' right of redemption, and as a CERCLA lienholder would have a year's right of redemption.

Buyer's knowledge of lien. If a purchaser of property upon which the owner has been advised by EPA of potential liability by certified mail knows about this notice to owner but at the time of purchase the notice of lien has not been filed, will the property be encumbered by the lien in the hands of the purchaser? Because CERCLA does not speak to the issue of whether the buyer's knowledge of the lien is equivalent to notice of tax lien, it would seem that a purchaser with actual knowledge of the lien should take free of the lien. But until an appellate court so holds it is doubtful that any title insurer would knowingly insure the title without exception for the CERCLA lien.

Position of former mortgagee. What is the position of a superior mortgagee who forecloses against the CERCLA lienor after the mortgagee acquires title at the foreclosure sale? Under some case law it would seem that although the CERCLA lien would have been eliminated, in addition

---

[33] 42 U.S.C. § 2410(c).

to the EPA's right to redeem the EPA could still look to the former mort-gagee as a title holder to the same extent as anyone else who may have purchased contaminated property, and now the former mortgagee may have personal liability for the cleanup costs.[34]

Lien against security interest.   Is the CERCLA lien also a lien against the security interest of a mortgagee? Does it differ in a lien state as com-pared to a title state? The lien is against all the real property and the rights to such property.

Lien filed after deed recorded.   Because in most jurisdictions possession of real property is equivalent to constructive notice under the recording acts, would a purchaser of contaminated property upon which there was a CERCLA lien but no notice of lien filed when the purchaser went into possession, hold title free of the lien, even though the purchaser's deed was recorded after the notice of lien? There are some cases involving federal tax liens in which the courts have held the property to be free of the tax lien.[35] Further, will the United States always have priority over a pur-chaser or holder of a security interest if the notice of lien is recorded prior to the deed or the instrument creating the security interest? In states in which the recording acts are not based strictly on who gets to the court-house first, it would seem that if A purchases from B property upon which there is a CERCLA lien but the notice of lien has not yet been recorded, then B would take free of the CERCLA lien notwithstanding the fact that the CERCLA lien is filed prior to the filing of the deed to B.[36]

The future should produce some interesting law through the courts' inter-pretations of the CERCLA lien provisions and similar state statutes.

§ 16.12   Federal Superfund Liens as of March 1990

Table 16.1 is compiled by the Office of Enforcement and Compliance Monitoring (OECM), EPA, Washington, D.C., based upon information submitted by EPA's 10 regional offices. By compiling and making this list available to the public, OECM and EPA make no representations regard-ing the accuracy or completeness of the list.

---

[34] 42 U.S.C. § 9607(l)(4).

[35] Niagara County Sav. Bank v. Reese, 12 Misc. 2d 489, 179 N.Y.S.2d 453 (1958); State Fidelity Fed. Sav. & Loan Ass'n v. Wehrly, 263 N.E.2d 801 (Ohio Ct. App. 1970).

[36] Van Eepoel Real Estate Co. v. Sarasota Milk Co., 100 Fla. 438, 129 So. 892 (1930).

Table 16–1

List of Federal Superfund Liens

Last Update: March 9, 1990

	Date Lien Filed or Signed by RA	Site	Region	Location	Estimated Value
1.	Dec. 10, 1986	Tinkham	I	Londonderry, NH	Released 10/4/89
2.	Dec. 26, 1986	Tinkham	I	Londonderry, NH	Released 10/4/89
3.	Jan. 23, 1987	Western Processing	X	Kent, WA	$ 6,500,000
4.	Jan. 30, 1987	Auburn Rd. Landfill	I	Londonderry, NH	
5.	Jan. 30, 1987	Salem Acres	I	Salem, MA	
6.	Feb. 2, 1987	Printed Circuits	III	Levittown, PA	$ 245,211
7.	Feb. 11, 1987	Zenith Chemical Co.	IV	Whitfield City, GA	
8.	Feb. 12, 1987	Nicolet, Inc.	III	Ambler, PA	
9.	Feb. 25, 1987	Renora, Inc.	II	Edison Township, NJ	
10.	May 25, 1987	Gary Heldt	VIII	Brookings, SD	
11.	May 19, 1987	Tower Chemical Co.	IV	Clermont, FL	$ 1,200,000
12.	June 24, 1987	American Environmental Energy Corp.	IV	Duval County, FL	$ 777,000
13.	Aug. 9, 1987	Printed Circuits	III	Bucks County, PA	$ 750,000
14.	Aug. 19, 1987	Northernaire Plating	V	Cadillac, MI	
15.	Aug. 21, 1987	Indiana Jones	V	Fort Wayne, IN	$ 225,000
16.	Sept. 11, 1987	E.C. Kramer	IX	Anaheim, CA	
17.	Sept. 21, 1987	Rigel Street Drum	IX	San Diego, CA	Released 5/10/89
18.	Sept. 30, 1987	ROIC	IX	Sun Valley, CA	
19.	Oct. 7, 1987	ABCO	IX	Monrovia, CA	Released 5/10/89
20.	Oct. 8, 1987	Rolfite Company	I	Shelton, CT	$ 1,500,000
21.	Oct. 22, 1987	Ellisville/Rosalie	VII	Ellisville, MO	$ 177,000
22.	Oct. 22, 1987	Ellisville/Callahan	VII	Ellisville, MO	$ 886,000
23.	Oct. 22, 1987	Aidex	VII	Mills County, IA	$10,000,000
24.	Nov. 4, 1987	Metcoa, Inc., Pesses Company	VI	Fort Worth, TX	$ 332,759

No.	Date	Name		Location	Amount/Status
25.	Nov. 18, 1987	Peter Gull	IX	Norco, CA	
26.	Nov. 18, 1987	Martin Woods	IX	Norco, CA	$ 400,000
27.	Nov. 19, 1987	Mowbray Engineering	IV	Greenville, AL	
28.	Nov. 19, 1987	Coleman Evans	IV	Duval Co., FL	
29.	Jan. 8, 1988	Conservation Chemical Company	V	Gary, IN	$ 5,800,000
30.	Feb. 8, 1988	Cam-or	V	Indiana	
31.	Feb. 16, 1988	Middletown Road	III	Annapolis, MD	$25,000,000
32.	Feb. 18, 1988	Lackawanna Refuse	III	Old Forge, PA	Released approx. 5/10/89
33.	Feb. 22, 1988	Rigel Street Drum (amended See #17, above)	IX	San Diego, CA	
34.	Feb. 19, 1988	Whittier Propel	IX	Whittier, CA	Released 6/2/89
35.	Feb. 19, 1988	Greencastle	IX	Los Angeles, CA	
36.	Mar. 10, 1988	DiCello	IX	San Diego, CA	
37.	Mar. 21, 1988	Western Carolina Smelting	IV	Madison Co., NC	Released Dec. 20, 1988
38.	Mar. 21, 1988	Bishop Frank Green	IV	Fayetteville, NC	Released 1/27/89
39.	Apr. 11, 1988	Clothier	II	Granby, NY	
40.	Apr. 22, 1988	Westfir Energy Company	X	Westfir, OR	
41.	Apr. 25, 1988	Whitmoyer Laboratories Inc.	III	Myerstown, PA	$ 147,756+
42.	Apr. 25, 1988	Lehigh Electric and Engineering Company	III	Old Forge, PA	$ 5,034,406
43.	Apr. 26, 1988	Apache Power Company	IX	Cochise County, AZ	
44.	May 19, 1988	A.H.A.S.	IX	Monterey Park, CA	
45.	May 19, 1988	OII	IX	Monterey Park, CA	
46.	May 25, 1988	Chem Science	V	Wisconsin	$ 500,000
47.	May 27, 1988	International Disk	V	Michigan	$ 500,000
48.	May 31, 1988	Pallister Paint	X	Everett, WA	
49.	June 14, 1988	Lee's Lane Landfill	IV	Jefferson Co., KY	
50.	June 17, 1988	Herman	IX	Los Angeles, CA	
51.	June 28, 1988	Eager Beaver	III	Townville, PA	
52.	June 30, 1988	Northside Sanitary Landfill (3 liens)	V	Indiana	$ 1,600,000
53.	July 11, 1988	Reliable Plating	V	Ohio	$ 520,000

	Date Lien Filed or Signed by RA	Site	Region	Location	Estimated Value
54.	July 13, 1988	Accra-Pac	V	Indiana	$ 317,000
55.	July 19, 1988	Pristine	V	Ohio	$13,000,000
56.	July 25, 1988	Stamina Mills	I	North Smithfield, RI	$30,000,000+
57.	Aug. 1, 1988	Kane & Lombard	III	Baltimore City, MD	
58.	Aug. 2, 1988	Shaffer Equip. Co. (2 liens)	III	Fayette City, WVA	$ 4,000,000
59.	Aug. 11, 1988	General Laminates	IV	Hamilton Co., FL	
60.	Aug. 12, 1988	Mattiache	II	Glen Cove, NY	$ 1,000,000+
61.	Aug. 15, 1988	John & Mary Miletich (Midco Site)	V	Gary, IN	
62.	Aug. 22, 1988	Interstate Transformer	III	Ellwood City, PA	$ 700,000
63.	Aug. 24, 1988	Midco II	V	Indiana	$ 200,000
64.	Aug. 29, 1988	Summit National	V	Ohio	$47,500,000
65.	Aug. 30, 1988	Waste Disposal Engineering	V	Indiana	$14,000,000
66.	Sept. 12, 1988	Garvey Avenue	IX	Baldwin Park, CA	
67.	Sept. 26, 1988	Oconomowoc	V	Wisconsin	$ 1,100,000
68.	Sept. 27, 1988	Southern Crop Svcs.	IV	Delray Beach, FL	
69.	Sept. 29, 1988	Bergeron Marine	IV	Hancock Co., MS	
70.	Oct. 4, 1988	Liquid Waste Mgmt.	V	Ohio	$ 200,000
71.	Oct. 11, 1988	Rome Coal Tar	IV	Rome, GA	
72.	Oct. 21, 1988	Spectra-Chem	V	Wisconsin	$ 108,342+
73.	Nov. 1, 1988	Bruin Lagoon	III	Butler County, PA	$10,000,000
74.	Nov. 4, 1988	Burrows LF	V	Michigan	$ 3,600,000
75.	Nov. 9, 1988	Priority Finishing	I	Putnam, CN	$ 900,000
76.	Nov. 9, 1988	Aerolite Chrome Corp.	IX	Washoe City, Reno, NV	
77.	Nov. 10, 1988	Newport Dump	IV	Wilder, KY	
78.	Nov. 15, 1988	Jasco Chemical	IX	Santa Clara, CA	
79.	Dec. 7, 1988	Tyler Drum	V	Lake County, IN	
79.	Jan. 9, 1989	Michael Battery	VII	Bettendorf, IA	$ 311,000
80.	Jan. 30, 1989	Season-All Industries	III	Jefferson City, PA	$ 500,000
81.	Feb. 13, 1989	Oak Grove Landfill	V	Michigan	$13,000,000

82.	Mar. 2, 1989	Milbar Boulevard	II	New York	
83.	Mar. 8, 1989	Chadbourne Tire Fire	IV	Columbus City, NC	
84.	Mar. 14, 1989	Norwood PCB site	I	Norwood, MA	
85.	Apr. 3, 1989	Hebelka Auto Salvage Yard	III	Lehigh City, PA	$ 5,500,000
86.	Apr. 29, 1989	Amtreco Corp.	IV	Clinch Co., GA	
87.	May 15, 1989	Stasburg Landfill	III	Chester Co., PA	
88.	May 17, 1989	Michael T. Chovanak	VIII	Helena, MT	
89.	June 1, 1989	Marianne Canny	II	Binghamton, NY	
90.	June 1, 1989	Lawrence J. Pizer	VIII	Adams County, CO	
91.	June 15, 1989	A.I.W. Frank Site (Continental Refrig. Co.)	III	Exton, PA	$ 8,000,000
92.	June 14, 1989	East Quincy Ave.	VIII	Arapahoe Co., CO	
93.	July 5, 1989	Skippers III	IV	Brevard City, FL	
94.	Aug. 21, 1989	Silver Bow/ARCO	VIII	Silver Bow City, MT	
95.	Aug. 21, 1989	Valley Wood Preserving	IX	Stanislaus City, CA	
96.	Aug. 21, 1989	Lorentz Barrel & Drum	IX	Santa Clara City, CA	
97.	Sept. 18, 1989	Indiana Refining Inc.	V	Princeton, IN	
98.	Sept. 1989	Bliss Tank Site (3 liens)	VII	, MO	
99.	Oct. 10, 1989	Aerovox/New Bedford	I	New Bedford, MA	$20,000,000+
100.	Nov. 14, 1989	Avtex Fibers/Front Royal, Inc.	III	Front Royal, VA	$40,000,000
101.	Dec. 4, 1989	Interchem	VII	Sioux City, IA	

§ 16.13   Sample EPA Letter Asserting
Notice of Lien

UNITED STATES ENVIRONMENTAL PROTECTION AGENCY
REGION I
J.F. KENNEDY FEDERAL BUILDING, BOSTON, MASSACHUSETTS 02203–2211

BY CERTIFIED MAIL — RETURN RECEIPT REQUESTED

October 20, 1987

Mr. Stephen Read
The Rolfite Company
1221 Brickell Avenue
Miami, Florida 33131

Re: *Notice of Federal Lien on The Rolfite Company property in Shelton, CT*

Dear Mr. Read:

By this letter, EPA informs you that a lien has been perfected on the property owned by The Rolfite Company (Rolfite) in Shelton, CT. In particular, on or about October 15, 1987, EPA perfected a lien on property that was conveyed to The Rolfite Company and that is described in the deed set forth on pages 199 through 203 of Book Volume 444 of the Town Clerk of Shelton, by filing notice of that lien with the Town Clerk of Shelton, as provided under Section 107(l) of the Comprehensive Environmental Response, Compensation and Liability Act (CERCLA), 42 U.S.C. § 9607(l), as amended by the Superfund Amendment and Reauthorization Act (SARA), Pub.L. 99-499, and Connecticut state law. A copy of the Notice of Federal Lien is attached hereto.

Under Section 107(l) of CERCLA, all costs and damages for which a person is liable under Section 107(a) of CERCLA constitute a lien in favor of the United States upon all real property and rights to such property which belong to such persons and are subject to, or affected by, a removal or remedial action. As indicated in EPA's letter to you dated May 14, 1987, Rolfite, as the owner and operator of the facility, is a potentially responsible party under Section 107(a) of CERCLA. In addition, EPA has expended and anticipates continuing to expend monies for response actions at the facility. Thus, a lien arose in favor of the United States on all of Rolfite's property affected by or subject to the removal and remedial actions at the Rolfite facility. At present, the amount of this lien is estimated at one million five hundred thousand dollars ($1,500,000). However, due to the fact that EPA response actions are ongoing, final actual costs are not known and may be significantly higher. This lien will continue until the liability for the costs incurred by the United States is satisfied or becomes unenforceable through the operation of the statute of limitations as provided by Section 113 of SARA.

By perfecting this lien it is the EPA's intent to protect its right to recover all costs and damages for which Rolfite is liable to the United States by securing EPA's priority within the hierarchy of all known and potential purchasers, holders of security interests, and judgment lien creditors of Rolfite.

If you have any questions about the matters discussed herein, please call me at (617) 565-3440.

Yours truly,

Linda L. Ujifusa
Assistant Regional Counsel

attachments

§ 16.14   Notice of Lien

UNITED STATES ENVIRONMENTAL PROTECTION AGENCY
REGION V

NOTICE OF A FEDERAL LIEN UNDER
THE SUPERFUND AMENDMENTS
AND REAUTHORIZATION ACT OF 1986

As provided by Section 107(f) of the Superfund Amendments and Reauthorization Act of 1986 (SARA), Pub. L. No. 99-499, 100 Stat. 1613, amending the Comprehensive Environmental Response, Compensation, and Liability Act of 1980 (CERCLA), 42 U.S.C. Section 9601 *et seq.*, notice is hereby given that the costs and damages plus interest and administrative costs for which Oconomowoc Electroplating Co., Inc., is liable under Section 107(a) of CERCLA, as amended by SARA, constitute a lien in favor of the United States upon all real property and rights to such property which belong to said persons and are, have been, or will be subject to or affected by removal and remedial actions at or near 2573 W. Oak Street in the City of Ashippun, County of Dodge, State of Wisconsin, including the real property described as follows: in Subdivision of Lots Eight (8) and Nineteen (19), Block Ten (10) of the Plat of Ashippun Village.

This lien shall continue until liability for the costs (or a judgment against such persons arising out of such liability) is satisfied or becomes unenforceable through the operation of the statute of limitations as provided by Section 113 of SARA.

IN WITNESS WHEREOF, the United States has caused this instrument to be executed through the United States Environmental Protection Agency, and its agent in his official capacity as Regional Administrator of the United States Environmental Protection Agency, Region V.

Dated at Chicago, Illinois, this <u>26th</u> day of <u>September</u>, 1988.

_____
Valdas V. Adamkus
Regional Administrator
U.S. EPA, Region V
230 S. Dearborn St.
Chicago, Il 60604

United States of America   )
State of Illinois   )   SS
County of Cook   )

On this <u>26th</u> day of <u>September</u>, 1988, there appeared personally before me, the undersigned Notary, _Valdas V. Adamkus_ known to me to be the Regional Administrator of the United States Environmental Protection Agency, Region V, and he acknowledged that he signed the foregoing NOTICE OF FEDERAL LIEN in a representative capacity as the free and voluntary act and deed of the United States and its said Agency for the uses and purposes therein mentioned. Given under my hand and official seal and year first stated above.

_____
NOTARY PUBLIC in and for
the State of Illinois

My Commission Expires: <u>September 18, 1991</u>

§ 16.15   Release of Lien

U.S ENVIRONMENTAL PROTECTION AGENCY
REGION I
J.F.K. FEDERAL BUILDING, Boston, MA 02203

NOTICE AND CERTIFICATION OF RELEASE OF LIEN UNDER SECTION 107(l) OF THE COMPREHENSIVE ENVIRONMENTAL RESPONSE, COMPENSATION, AND LIABILITY ACT (CERCLA), 42 U.S.C. § 9607(l)

RELEASE OF LIEN RECORDED AT BOOK 2647, PAGE 2237
ROCKINGHAM COUNTY REGISTRY OF DEEDS, NEW HAMPSHIRE

The lien for costs and damages provided by Section 107 of CERCLA for which Judy M. Tinkham, Fred S. Tinkham, and Tinkham Investments are liable under 42 U.S.C. § 9607 is hereby released. This Certificate of Release authorizes the proper officer in the office where the Notice of Lien was filed and recorded at Book 2647, Page 2237, to record in the records the release of this lien.

Dated at Boston, Massachusetts, this 4th day of October, 1989.

UNITED STATES OF AMERICA and
UNITED STATES ENVIRONMENTAL PROTECTION AGENCY

By: _____

    Paul Keough
    Acting Regional Administrator
    U.S. EPA Region I

Subscribed and sworn before me on this, the 4th day of October, 1989.

_____

Notary Public
My Commission expires: July 19, 1996

CHAPTER 17

LIABILITY OF ARCHITECTS AND ENGINEERS

Vincent J. Kiernan
Joseph S. Moran
Christopher A. Myers

Vincent J. Kiernan is a manager in Coopers & Lybrand's Washington, D.C., Business Investigation Services Group. His primary responsibilities involve claim analysis on environmental, construction, and real estate matters. He has been involved with several environmental projects around the country analyzing alternative remediation options, trust arrangements, and financial reporting requirements. Mr. Kiernan received his B.S. in Business from Wake Forest University and his M.B.A. from the College of William & Mary.

Joseph S. Moran is an attorney in the Washington, D.C., office of Rivkin, Radler, Bayh, Hart & Kremer. As head of the environmental section, he provides representation in complex environmental enforcement and permitting litigation, and counsels industries, financial institutions, and developers on transactional environmental due diligence requirements. Mr. Moran was formerly a senior attorney-advisor in United States EPA's enforcement division and earlier served as the secretary of the Metropolitan District Commission, a large multi-service environmental agency.

Mr. Moran received his J.D. degree from Suffolk Law School and his B.A. from Pace College. He frequently writes and lectures on environmental enforcement and regulatory issues.

Christopher A. Myers is a partner in the Washington, D.C., office of Rivkin, Radler, Bayh, Hart & Kremer and is a member of the firm's litigation practice group. His practice focuses primarily in the field of complex litigation, including construction, products liability, professional malpractice, and fraud. In addition to his trial practice, he has taught trial advocacy at George Washington University Law School and in CLE courses around the country. Mr. Myers is a member of the bars of the District of Columbia, Virginia, and Maryland.

§ 17.1   Introduction

The enactment of environmental statutes over the past twenty years has resulted in significant changes in the way people make, use and dispose of a wide variety of products. These statutes require industry and, to a lesser extent, government entities to acquire pollution control technology to treat waste water, remove pollutants from air emissions, and take steps to ensure that hazardous waste does not escape into the environment. Once pollutants have been released into the environment, Superfund mandates that those responsible pay. Additional legislation is continually being offered, designed to impose new and more stringent requirements to control pollution.

This environmental legislation has created and will continue to create exciting new opportunities for architects and engineers. The demand for design professionals with environmental training and experience is growing.[1] This demand is not limited to the United States; other regions of the world are also starting to tackle their huge environmental problems. In Europe alone, the opportunities for design professionals are tremendous. Analysts predict that between $30 to 120 billion will be spent on environment-related projects during the 1990s alone.[2] The growth that design professionals expect to see will most likely be focused on waste water treatment plants, resource recovery facilities, hazardous waste site remediations, and Clean Air Act retrofit work. These types of projects may create a new boom area for design professionals in the 1990s.

With these new opportunities, however, come new responsibilities and a greater potential for risk exposure for design professionals. Courts have consistently expanded the web of liability created by the Comprehensive Environmental Response Compensation and Liability Act (CERCLA or Superfund).[3] Some of the traditional safeguards that protected architects and engineers in the past have been challenged, and more challenges can be expected in the future. Thus, in order to minimize their potential liability, it is important that architects and engineers be aware of the risks in dealing with environmental issues, particularly those involving the cleanup of hazardous substances.

It is difficult to provide a general description of the liability of design professionals in every situation. The relationships among the architect or engineer and clients, construction managers, contractors, subcontractors, construction workers, and other parties not involved in design or construction vary with the nature of the project being built. As a general rule, however, architects and engineers are subject to three types of common law liability: breach of contract or warranty, negligence in design, and negligence in supervision.[4] In addition, a small number of cases have held design professionals to be strictly liable in tort.[5]

---

[1] *Environmental Wages Soaring,* Engineering News Rec. 9 (Nov. 30, 1989).

[2] *Making the World a Cleaner Place,* Engineering News Rec. 30 (Oct. 29, 1989).

[3] 42 U.S.C. §§ 9601–9626 (1988).

[4] *See* Farrug, *The Necessity of Expert Testimony in Establishing the Standard of Care For Design Professionals,* 38 DePaul L. Rev. 873, 876 (1989) [hereinafter Farrug, *The Standard of Care*]; *see also* 5 Am. Jur. 2d *Architects* § 23 (discussing liabilities of architects generally, citing cases).

[5] Note also that an architect or engineer who commits a fraud upon his or her employer also will be liable for any resulting injury. See § **17.2.**

Finally, and perhaps most troubling to design professionals, recent interpretations of CERCLA have resulted in liability findings against parties who, in the past, were thought to be outside the reach of Superfund. As EPA and the courts begin to look harder for the deep pockets to pay for hazardous waste cleanups, it is conceivable that liability could be extended to affect design professionals.

The following sections review traditional theories of architect and engineer liability in an environmental context. They also examine how courts have applied existing environmental laws to design professionals and assess some of the possible directions judicial decisions may take in the future.

§ 17.2   Contract Actions Against Design Professionals

Until the late 1950s, the doctrine of privity of contract held that the duty of care of an architect or other design professional was only to those parties with whom he had contracted. Because contractual relationships usually existed only between the architect and the owner, the architect was insulated from liability to virtually anyone else.[6] In addition to the privity requirement, a general judicial deference to professionals further protected architects and engineers.[7] However, as the law has evolved in recent years, the areas of potential liability for design professionals have increased significantly.

Traditionally, owners brought suits against architects and engineers in tort for negligence or for breach of contract. However, many of the tort suits were barred on the basis of the shorter statute of limitations, which began to run on the date of the negligent act and not when the injury was

---

[6] A few exceptions were made to the privity requirement for circumstances involving fraud, misrepresentation, or third-party beneficiaries. The fraud/misrepresentation exception has limited application to design professionals. To show misrepresentation, the injured party must have reasonably relied on misrepresentations made by the design professional. *See generally* Prosser, *Misrepresentations and Third Persons,* 19 Vand. L. Rev. 231 (1966). Generally, the injury is an economic one, such as when a bidder relies on information from an architect and then suffers an economic loss. *See, e.g.,* United States v. Rogers & Rogers, 161 F. Supp. 132 (S.D. Cal. 1958). When personal injuries to third parties are alleged, the third party usually had not received any information from the architect. Thus, the misrepresentation exception seems to be limited to third parties who are somehow involved in the construction process. *See* Note, *The Crumbling Tower of Architectural Immunity: Evolution and Expansion of the Liability to Third Parties,* 45 Ohio St. L.J. 217, 219 at n.29 (1984) [hereinafter Note, *Architectural Immunity*].

[7] Note, *Architectural Malpractice: A Contract-Based Approach,* 92 Harv. L. Rev. 1075, 1078 (1979) [hereinafter Note, *A Contract-Based Approach*].

discovered.[8] The protection afforded to design professionals by the privity doctrine and by a deferential judiciary was so effective that professional liability insurance was not considered necessary.[9]

The historical protection from liability provided to design professionals has eroded substantially during the last thirty years. This erosion began with the demise of the privity doctrine. The end of the privity requirement began as long ago as 1916 with the famous case of *MacPherson v. Buick Motor Co.*[10] In that case, the court eliminated the privity of contract requirement in suits against a manufacturer for negligent design of a product. The court permitted recovery for faulty design by anyone who might foreseeably use the product.

In 1957, the foreseeability test was applied for the first time to a design professional's liability for negligent design. In *Inman v. Binghamton Housing Authority,*[11] the New York Court of Appeals held that the foreseeability test of *MacPherson* was applicable to architects, and that privity of contract was no longer required in order for an injured party to recover for negligent design. Later decisions have been nearly unanimous in extending the architect's duty beyond the limits of the privity of contract doctrine, and the general rule today is that a lack of privity of contract is no longer a bar to a negligence action against a design professional.[12]

The expansion of liability of architects and engineers occasioned by the fall of the privity doctrine has occurred primarily in the tort area. See § 17.5. Liability under contract theories has remained much the same as it had been before the *Inman* case.

§ 17.3 —Standards for Determining Contract Liability

In many respects an action for breach of contract against a design professional is almost identical to one for negligence. That is because a contract

---

[8] *See, e.g.,* Board of Educ. v. Joseph J. Duffy Co., 97 Ill. App. 2d 158, 240 N.E.2d 5 (1968). *See also* Sosnow v. Paud, 43 A.D.2d 978, 352 N.Y.S.2d 502 (1974), *aff'd mem.,* 36 N.Y.2d 780, 330 N.E.2d 643, 369 N.Y.S.2d 693 (1975); Note, *A Contract-Based Approach* at 1078.

[9] Note, *Liability of Architects and Engineers to Third Parties: A New Approach,* 53 Notre Dame L. Rev. 306, 307 n.7 (1977).

[10] 217 N.Y. 382, 111 N.E. 1050 (1916).

[11] 3 N.Y.2d 137, 143 N.E.2d 895, 164 N.Y.S.2d 699 (1957).

[12] *See, e.g.,* Montijo v. Swift, 219 Cal. App. 2d 351, 33 Cal. Rptr. 133 (1963); Miller v. DeWitt, 37 Ill. 2d 273, 226 N.E.2d 630 (1967); Laukkanen v. Jewel Tea Co., 78 Ill. App. 2d 153, 222 N.E.2d 584 (1966); Simon v. Omaha Pub. Power Dist., 189 Neb. 183, 202 N.W.2d 157 (1972); *but see* Peyronnin Constr. Co. v. Weiss, 137 Ind. App. 417, 208 N.E.2d 489 (1965); *see also* Note, *Architectural Immunity* at 220–221.

for design services contains a duty based in tort law. Typically, a design contract does not guarantee a specific result, nor does it normally specify the standard of care to which the design professional will be held. In the absence of any special agreement written into the contract, therefore, the law imposes an implied promise to exercise the ordinary and reasonable skill of the design profession. This is virtually identical to the negligence standard.[13] In either a negligence or a breach of contract action against a design professional, "the professional is held to a standard which comports with the learning, skill and care ordinarily associated with and practiced by those professionals who practice in the same region as the defendant professional at the time of the alleged negligence."[14]

In recent years, with the increasing size and complexity of modern buildings and engineering projects, the work of design professionals frequently falls outside the traditional concept of the "master builder," in which an architect or engineer designs all aspects of the project and then supervises and manages its construction on behalf of the owner. Design professionals must be careful that their contracts describe with precision the services they will provide on a given project. It is the contract provisions that will create the duties of care to which the architect or engineer will be held. Duties should be imposed only if their performance could be reasonably expected of the professional under the particular circumstances of the contract.

For example, if an engineer's contract requires her to design a waste water treatment facility but provides for no role whatsoever in supervising its construction, and she does not assume such a role, then she should have no liability in either contract or tort if a contractor's failure to follow the design caused economic damage to the owner or injury to a third party.

---

[13] *See, e.g.,* Mississippi Meadows, Inc. v. Hodson, 13 Ill. App. 3d 24, 26, 299 N.E.2d 359, 361 (1973) ("the duty of an architect depends upon the particular agreement he has entered with the person who employs him and in the absence of a special agreement . . . he is only liable if he fails to exercise reasonable care and skill."), *appeal denied,* 54 Ill. 2d 597 (1973); Miller v. DeWitt, 59 Ill. App. 2d 38, 208 N.E.2d 249, 284 (1965), *aff'd in part, rev'd in part on other grounds,* 37 Ill. 2d 273, 226 N.E.2d 630 (1967) ("The architects in contracting for their services implied . . . that they would exercise and apply in the case their skill, ability and judgment reasonably and without neglect."). *See also* J. Sweet, Legal Aspects of Architecture, Engineering and the Construction Process 838–39 (2d ed. 1977) (because the professional standard is one of reasonableness, client may treat contract breach as a tort); Note, *A Contract-Based Approach* at 1089 (suit in contract is similar to one in tort because contract interpretation is infected with tort standard of reasonable care).

[14] Farrug, *The Standard of Care* at 879.

§ 17.4   —Breach of Implied Warranty Claims

In addition to claims for breach of contract, a number of design professionals have also been sued for breach of implied warranties. The basic premise of such suits is that when a design professional contracts to design a structure, she should be deemed to impliedly warrant that, if the structure is completed in accordance with her plans, it will be fit for its intended purpose.[15] However, the majority rule is that architects and engineers, like other professionals, should not be subject to such suits, and that they do not guarantee or warrant a satisfactory result.[16] The rationale for this rule was stated by the Minnesota Supreme Court in *City of Mounds View v. Walijarvi:*

> Architects, doctors, engineers, attorneys, and others deal in somewhat inexact sciences and are continually called upon to exercise their skilled judgment in order to anticipate and provide for random factors which are incapable of precise measurement. The indeterminate nature of these factors makes it impossible for professional service people to gauge them with complete accuracy in every instance. Thus, doctors cannot promise that every operation will be successful; a lawyer can never be certain that a contract he drafts is without latent ambiguity; and an architect cannot be certain that a structural design will interact with natural forces as anticipated. Because of the inescapable possibility of error which inheres in these services, the law has traditionally required, not perfect results, but rather the exercise of that skill and judgment which can be reasonably expected from similarly situated professionals.

> * * * *

> [Further], while it is undoubtedly fair to impose strict liability on manufacturers who have ample opportunity to test their products for defects before marketing them, the same cannot be said of architects. Normally, an architect has but a single chance to create a design for a client which produces a defect-free structure. Accordingly, we do not think it just that architects should be forced to bear the same burden of liability for their products as that which has been imposed on manufacturers generally.[17]

---

[15] *See* City of Mounds View v. Walijarvi, 263 N.W.2d 420, 423 (Minn. 1978).

[16] *Id. See also* Gravely v. Providence Partnership, 549 F.2d 958, 960 (4th Cir. 1977); Note, *Architectural Immunity* at 250–51. There are a few courts, however, that have held that by undertaking to furnish plans and specifications, a design professional warrants their sufficiency for the intended purpose. *See* Broyles v. Brown Eng'g Co., 275 Ala. 35, 151 So. 2d 767 (1963); Hill v. Ploar Pantries, 219 S.C. 263, 64 S.E.2d 885 (1951); Niver v. Nash, 7 Wash. 558, 35 P. 380 (1893).

[17] City of Mounds View v. Walijarvi, 263 N.W.2d at 424–25.

When a design professional steps outside his traditional role as the agent or advisor of the owner, however, a number of courts have held that implied warranty theories may apply. For example, if an architect or engineer becomes allied with the contractor, either through a joint venture or as part of a single organization that combines the design and construction functions, his economic interests may potentially conflict with the owner's. Under such circumstances, several courts have found that the organization impliedly warrants the fitness of its product for the client's purpose, as long as the client does not furnish the plans and relies on the organization's expertise.[18] In *Robertson Lumber Co. v. Stephen Farmers Co-op Elevator Co.,*[19] the court affirmed an award of damages for a defectively constructed grain storage facility on a theory of implied warranty, distinguishing the provision of purely design services from a combination of services that included construction of the building.[20]

It is also possible for a design professional to obligate herself by contract to a higher standard of care or to warrant a particular result. For example, in *Arkansas Rice Growers Cooperative Association v. Alchemy Industries,*[21] a design firm was held liable for breaching an express warranty in a contract that called for it to provide:

> the necessary engineering plant layout and equipment design and the on-site engineering supervision and start-up engineering services necessary for the construction of a hull by-product facility capable of reducing a minimum of seven and one-half tons of rice hulls per hour to ash and producing a minimum of 48 million BTU's per hour of steam at 200 lbs. pressure.[22]

The court found that this provision was an express warranty of the design. Therefore, proof that the facility failed to perform as promised under certain conditions was sufficient to establish the designer's liability for breach.[23]

The holding in *Arkansas Rice Growers* could be applied in an environmental context. For example, if an engineering firm contracted to provide plant design and construction engineering supervision for a waste water treatment plant intended to treat a specific volume of waste water to a certain level, a court could find an express warranty in such a contract. To

---

[18] *See, e.g.,* Robertson Lumber Co. v. Stephen Farmers Coop. Elevator Co., 274 Minn. 17, 24, 143 N.W.2d 622, 626 (1966); Prier v. Refrigeration Eng'r Co., 74 Wash. 2d 25, 29, 442 P.2d 621, 624 (1968); Note, *A Contract-Based Approach* at 1093–94.

[19] 274 Minn. 17, 143 N.W.2d 622 (1966).

[20] *Id.; see also* City of Mounds View v. Walijarvi, 263 N.W.2d at 424 n.4.

[21] 797 F.2d 565 (8th Cir. 1986).

[22] *Id.* at 566.

[23] *Id.* at 569–570.

avoid this kind of liability, design professionals, whenever possible, should explicitly exclude warranties in their contracts.[24]

§ 17.5   Tort Actions Against Architects and Engineers

As outlined in §§ 17.3 and 17.4, architects and engineers have a duty to conform their conduct to a standard of reasonable care.[25] Like other professionals, such as physicians and attorneys, they are expected to possess a minimum level of special knowledge and ability and must exercise skilled judgment because of the complex nature of the profession.[26] The standard of reasonable care for design professionals is often traced to the early case of *Coombs v. Beede:*

> The responsibility resting on an architect is essentially the same as that which rests upon the lawyer to his client, or upon the physician to his patient, or which rests upon anyone to another where such person pretends to possess some special skill and ability in some special employment, and offers his services to the public on account of his fitness to act in the line of business for which he may be employed. The undertaking of an architect implies that he possesses skill and ability, including taste, sufficient enough to enable him to perform the required services at least ordinarily and reasonably well; and that he will exercise and apply, in the given case, his skill and ability, his judgement and taste reasonably and without neglect.[27]

When an architect or engineer fails to meet this standard, she may be liable in tort for professional negligence. An action will lie against an engineer and architect for professional negligence if it can be shown that: 1) the architect or engineer breached her duty of care; 2) the breach was the proximate cause of an injury that resulted in actual damages; and 3) the plaintiff and the risk were reasonably foreseeable.[28]

---

[24] Decisions like *Arkansas Rice Growers* might induce owners to press design professionals to include similar specific warranties in their contracts. The benefit of such provisions may prove illusory, however, because a special warranty may impair or exceed the scope of coverage afforded by the design professional's malpractice insurance policy.

[25] Restatement (Second) of Torts § 324A (1965).

[26] Rosos Litho Supply Corp. v. Hansen, 123 Ill. App. 3d 290, 462 N.E.2d 566 (1984); Swarthout v. Beard, 33 Mich. App. 395, 190 N.W.2d 373 (1971); *see also* Block, *As The Walls Came Tumbling Down: Expanded Liability Under Design-Build Construction Contracting,* 17 J. Marshall L. Rev. 1, 19 (1984).

[27] 89 Me. 187, 188, 36 A. 104 (1896).

[28] *See* R. Cushman & D. Carpenter, Proving and Pricing Construction Claims 377–78 (John Wiley & Sons 1990) (citing Donnelly Constr. Co. v. Oberg/Hunt/Gilleland, 139 Ariz. 184, 677 P.2d 1292, 1295 (1984)).

There are countless situations in which an architect's or engineer's conduct can constitute professional negligence. Generally, however, a design professional is charged with negligence either in the design and preparation of plans and specifications,[29] or in the administration or inspection of the construction of the project.[30] With respect to the design function, the failure of an architect or engineer to draft plans and specifications with an adequate degree of precision and specificity may constitute professional negligence. Areas in which malpractice may occur in contract administration typically include inspection, supervision, review of shop drawings, and approval or acceptance of work.

Frequently, one of the key issues in architect/engineer malpractice cases is foreseeability, that is, whether the injured party and the claimed harm could have been reasonably anticipated.[31] In *Inman v. Binghamton Housing Authority,*[32] the court held that the design professional owes a duty to those members of the public who can be reasonably anticipated to be present or to use the structure.[33] Thus, an architect or engineer may become liable to anyone who is lawfully present on or who uses a structure of her design, and who is injured due to the failure of the architect or engineer to exercise the proper level of skills.

In the environmental field, both the design and administration of construction of pollution control facilities provide significant danger of malpractice liability for an architect or engineer. Consider this hypothetical: An engineering firm is hired to design and implement a specific plan to remediate a hazardous waste disposal site. Preliminary investigations by another firm indicate a particular kind of remedial plan for the site, based on previous experience with sites containing similar hazardous wastes and similar site conditions. Actual site conditions differ from those indicated in the preliminary investigation. As a result, when the remedial plan is designed and implemented, it does not remediate the site to the levels required by law. The owner of the facility is required by governmental

---

[29] *See, e.g.,* Inman v. Binghamton Hous. Auth., 3 N.Y.2d 137, 143 N.E.2d 895 (1957) (architect liable for having designed an apartment house porch without a protective railing); Donnelly Constr. Co. v. Oberg/Hunt/Gilleland, 139 Ariz. 184, 677 P.2d 1292 (1984) (contractor's action against architect sustained for negligent preparation of plans and specifications).

[30] *See, e.g.,* City of Columbus v. Clark-Dietz & Assocs. Eng'rs, 550 F. Supp. 610 (N.D. Miss. 1982) (architect/engineer liable for negligent supervision in construction of a protective levee surrounding construction site for a waste water treatment plant).

[31] *See* Stewart v. Jefferson Plywood Co., 255 Or. 603, 469 P.2d 783, 786, (1970) ("foreseeability is an element of fault; the community deems a person to be at fault only when the injury caused by him is one which could have been anticipated because there was a reasonable likelihood that it could happen").

[32] 3 N.Y.2d 137, 143 N.E.2d 895 (1957).

[33] *Id.* at 143–146; *see also* Laukkanen v. Jewel Tea Co., 78 Ill. App. 2d 153, 222 N.E.2d 584 (1966).

agencies to perform additional remedial investigations. Those investigations reveal that the contamination of the site is far more extensive than the previous investigation showed and contains additional hazardous constituents that are not susceptible to treatment under the original plan. The cost for additional remediation is more than double the original estimate. The owner sues both the original engineering firm as well as the engineering firm which designed and implemented the selected remedial plan. The potential for liability of both of the professional design firms is great.

Consider also another hypothetical situation which deals with construction of a waste water treatment plant: An architectural/engineering firm is retained to design and implement a waste water treatment system at a large manufacturing facility. The manufacturing facility is subject to certain standards contained in its National Pollutant Discharge Elimination System (NPDES) permit issued by EPA and the state. The architectural/engineering firm bases its design on manufacturing processes it found at the site during its preliminary evaluation. It does not make inquiry about seasonal fluctuations or variations in production processes, nor does it inquire about any proposed changes in production in response to new product needs or regulatory changes. When the waste water treatment plant is constructed, it does not consistently treat the waste waters to the required levels due to seasonal fluctuations and changes in production. The result is frequent violations of the discharge limits contained in the NPDES permit. The manufacturer could then sue the architect/engineering firm, claiming professional negligence. The potential damages are significant.

Also consider in each hypothetical the potential harm to third parties due to the acts or omissions of the design professional. The failure to properly remediate in the first example could result in toxics migrating onto adjacent land. In the second hypothetical, the discharge of improperly treated waste water could contaminate a downstream drinking water supply. In both situations the design professional could be held liable.

There are countless other possible situations involving the design and construction supervision of pollution control facilities. Because of the complexity of these projects, the potential for allegations of negligence in the design and construction administration of pollution control systems is high.

§ 17.6 Tort Liability of Design Professionals to Third Persons

Given the fall of the privity doctrine,[34] the potential liability of a design professional currently extends beyond just the owner; it is not even limited

---

[34] See § 17.2.

to those involved in the construction process. In brief, any person who might, with reasonable foreseeability, sustain an injury due to the acts or omissions of the designer of a building or facility could maintain an action against the designer.[35] In the area of professional negligence, courts have consistently held that the law imposes certain expectations that the design professional's actions will not cause foreseeable injury to others. These societal expectations serve to define the scope of a design professional's duty of care.[36]

Liability to third parties may be for negligence in failing to exercise the ordinary skill of the design profession, which results in the erection of an unsafe structure, which, in turn, results in an injury to someone lawfully on the premises. Liability exists whether the negligence consists of defects in the plan or a failure to properly supervise construction.[37] For example, in *Caldwell v. Bechtel,*[38] injuries to construction workers sustained during the construction of subway tunnels were found to be within the "range of apprehension" as envisioned by the court, and the engineering construction firm, which had general oversight and contract administration responsibilities, could be held liable for the injuries.[39]

Thus, an architectural or engineering firm must take reasonable precautions pursuant to its duty of care to protect any party from any foreseeable risk of injury. In situations involving the remediation of hazardous waste sites, in which a design professional may be involved in arranging for the transport of hazardous waste or participating in the management of a site, the risk of injury to foreseeable third parties is high, and extra precaution must be taken.

§ 17.7   Strict Liability Theories

Although the general rule is that design professionals are not liable under strict liability theories, there may be exceptions if they are involved in certain hazardous activities or if they perform activities beyond traditional design science. This is especially true in the environmental context, when both the government and private plaintiffs are devising imaginative new theories to get at deep pockets to pay for remediating environmental disasters.

---

[35] See § 17.2.

[36] *See* Caldwell v. Bechtel, Inc., 631 F.2d 989, 997 (D.C. Cir. 1980); *see generally* McDonald, *Common Law Liability of Architects and Engineers for Negligence to Non-Contractual Parties,* The Construction Law. vol. 9 (1989).

[37] Fox v. Stanley J. Howell & Assocs., Inc., 309 N.W.2d 520 (Iowa Ct. App. 1981).

[38] 631 F.2d 989 (D.C. Cir. 1980).

[39] *Id.* at 1001.

Under strict liability theory, a defendant can be held liable without a showing that the defendant acted negligently, so long as the plaintiff shows a causal connection between his or her injury and the defendant's conduct.[40] Common law claims based in strict liability are brought in at least two circumstances: (1) when a plaintiff suffers injury from the defendant's abnormally dangerous or ultrahazardous activity,[41] or (2) when a plaintiff suffers injury from the defendant's allegedly defective and unreasonably dangerous product.[42] Design professionals have been named as defendants in both circumstances, although as a general rule courts refuse to apply principles of strict liability to architects and engineers.[43]

§ 17.8   —Abnormally Dangerous Activities

The beginning of strict liability for damages from abnormally dangerous activity is often traced to the nineteenth century English case of *Rylands*

---

[40] *See* Prosser and Keeton on Torts § 75, at 534 (5th ed. 1984); Bagley v. Controlled Env't Corp., 127 N.H. 556, 503 A.2d 823, 825 (1986) ("legal liability is said to be strict when it is imposed even though the defendant has committed no legal fault consisting of a common law or statutory duty") (citation omitted).

[41] *See* Restatement (Second) of Torts § 519 (1977) ("One who carries on an abnormally dangerous activity is subject to liability for harm to the person, land or chattels of another resulting from the activity, although he has exercised the utmost care to prevent the harm").

[42] *See* Restatement (Second) of Torts § 402(a) (1965) (seller of product liable for subsequent injury caused by that product when product defective and unreasonably dangerous to consumer) [hereinafter § 402A]. Most states have adopted some form of strict products liability. § 402A is the common thread in most jurisdictions. It provides:

(1) One who sells any product in a defective condition unreasonably dangerous to the user or consumer or to his property is subject to liability for physical harm thereby caused to the ultimate user or consumer, or to his property, if

(a) the seller is engaged in the business of selling such a product, and

(b) it is expected to and does reach the user or consumer without substantial change in the condition in which it is sold.

(2) The rule stated in Subsection (1) applies although

(a) the seller has experienced all possible care in the preparation and sale of his product, and

(b) the user or consumer has not bought the product from or entered into any contractual relation with the seller.

See also **Ch. 7.**

[43] *See, e.g.,* City of Mounds View v. Walijarvi, 263 N.W.2d 420, 424–425 (Minn. 1978) (strict liability not applicable to architectural services); Cincinnati Gas & Elec. Co. v. General Elec. Co., 656 F. Supp. 67 (S.D. Ohio 1986) (strict liability not applicable to design engineering services); *see also* Note, *Architectural Immunity* at 246–250 (discussing cases ruling strict liability not applicable to design professionals); *see also* Note, *Liability of Design Professionals — The Necessity of Fault,* 58 Iowa L. Rev. 1221 (1973).

v. Fletcher,[44] which, coincidentally, has relevance to environmental issues today. In *Rylands,* a group of mill owners built a reservoir on their property, which, unknown to them, had abandoned coal mines beneath its surface. Subsequently, water from the reservoir burst into the abandoned mines, flooding neighboring mines operated by the plaintiff. In allowing the plaintiff to recover in strict liability, the court reasoned that "if a person brings . . . on his land anything which, if it should escape, may cause damage to his neighbor, he does so at his own peril. . . . the question is not whether the defendant has acted with due care and caution, but whether his acts have [caused] . . . damage."[45] In recent years, a number of plaintiffs, having suffered damage from environmental waste, have asserted *Rylands'* strict liability principles as a basis for recovery. Courts have responded differently.

In *New Jersey Department of Environmental Protection v. Ventron,*[46] the New Jersey Supreme Court, citing *Rylands,* held that "a landowner is strictly liable to others for harm caused by toxic wastes that are stored on his property and flow onto the property of others."[47] The court ruled that dumping toxic mercury adjacent to a creek is an "abnormally dangerous activity" sufficient to justify strict liability.[48] Other courts have ruled that the burying of radioactive waste,[49] the dumping of hazardous waste in a landfill,[50] and the recycling of oil[51] each constitute an "abnormally dangerous activity" sufficient to invoke strict liability.

In contrast to these decisions, other courts have been less willing to impose common law strict liability in the context of environmental litigation. For example, the New Hampshire Supreme Court, in *Bagley v. Environment Corp.,*[52] "decline[d] to impose strict liability . . . [w]ith respect to the dumping of . . . waste products."[53] In *Cincinnati Gas & Electric Co.*

---

[44] L.R. 1 Ex. 265 (1866), *aff'd,* L.R. 3 H.L. 330 (1868). *See generally* Prosser & Keeton on Torts § 78, at 545–549 (5th ed. 1984). Note that the phrase "abnormally dangerous" is sometimes referred to as "ultrahazardous" or "extra-hazardous."

[45] Rylands v. Fletcher, L.R. 1 Ex. 265.

[46] 94 N.J. 473, 468 A.2d 150 (1983).

[47] *Id.,* 468 A.2d at 157.

[48] *Id.*

[49] *See* T&E Indus., Inc. v. Safety Light Corp., 227 N.J. Super. 228, 546 A.2d 570 (N.J. Super. Ct. App. Div. 1988).

[50] *See* Kenney v. Scientific, Inc., 204 N.J. Super. 228, 497 A.2d 1310 (N.J. Super. Ct. Law Div. 1985).

[51] Allied Corp. v. Frola, 730 F. Supp. 626 (D.N.J. 1990).

[52] 127 N.H. 556, 503 A.2d 823 (1986).

[53] 502 A.2d at 826 (expressly rejecting doctrine of *Rylands v. Fletcher,* unless plaintiff demonstrates that "requirement to prove legal fault" would act as a "practical barrier to an otherwise meritorious claim") (per Souter, J.).

v. General Electric Co.,[54] a utility company sued the designer of a nuclear power plant in strict liability, alleging that the plant's containment facility was unable to withstand forces generated or contain the radioactive steam. Millions of dollars in damages were claimed. The court dismissed the claim, holding that strict liability is not applicable to the provision of professional services:

> The doctrine of strict liability is primarily intended to impose special liability on those who market defective products to the general public in a mass-production context. . . . Even if the . . . design could somehow be construed as a product for purposes of [Restatement (Second) of Torts] section 402A, the design was specially tailored to the . . . plant and was not mass-produced.[55]

It is expected, however, that plaintiffs will continue to look for ways to try to impose strict liability on design professionals who work in the environmental area.

§ 17.9   —Injuries from Defective Products

The concept of strict products liability reflects a public policy decision that injuries caused by defective products should be borne by the manufacturer rather than injured persons who are considered "powerless" to protect themselves.[56]

Should the policy reasons for imposing strict products liability on product manufacturers apply to the architect-client or engineer-client relationship? As a general rule, courts have said no, mainly because design professionals are deemed to provide services, not "products."[57] For example, in *Lowrie v. City of Evanston,*[58] an Illinois court held that strict liability was not applicable to a municipal parking building designed and built

---

[54] 656 F. Supp. 49 (S.D. Ohio 1986).

[55] *Id.* at 66.

[56] Greenman v. Yuba Power Prods., Inc., 59 Cal. 2d 57, 377 P.2d 897, 901, 27 Cal. Rptr. 697 (1963); *see generally* Henderson, *Coping with the Time Dimension in Products Liability,* 69 Calif. L. Rev. 919, 931–939 (1981) (summarizing policy reasons underlying concept of strict products liability). See also **Ch. 7.**

[57] *See* 63 Am. Jur. 2d *Products Liability* §§ 219, 221 ("principles of products liability, particularly strict liability in tort . . . have generally not been applied to the rendition of professional services, such as . . . professional engineer . . . or architect") (citing, inter alia, Stuart v. Crestview Mut. Water Co., 34 Cal. App. 3d 802, 110 Cal. Rptr. 543 (1973) (engineering firm rendering professional services not analogous to manufacturers who place products on market; strict liability not applicable)).

[58] 50 Ill. App. 3d 376, 365 N.E.2d 923, 928 (1977).

by a group of architects and engineers, because the building was not a
"product" within the meaning of strict products liability. In *Hall v.
State*,[59] a New York court ruled that designs for a highway and bridge,
provided by State Department of Transportation engineers, were not
"products" within the concept of strict products liability, but rather were
a "provision of professional services."[60]

In essence, courts refuse to equate a single construction project designed for a specific client, with a mass-produced product sold on the
open market.[61] The Third Circuit's decision in *LaRosa v. Scientific Design
Co.*[62] highlights this important distinction:

> Professional services do not ordinarily lend themselves to the doctrine of
> tort liability without fault because they lack the elements which gave rise to
> the doctrine. There is no mass production of goods or a large body of
> distant consumers whom it would be unfair to require to trace the article
> they used along the channels of trade to the original manufacturer and
> there to pinpoint an act of negligence remote from their ability to inquire.
> Thus, professional services form a marked contrast to consumer product
> cases.[63]

Subsequent court decisions generally have been consistent with *LaRosa*.
For example, in *Chubb Group of Insurance Companies v. C.F. Murphy &
Associates*,[64] the court found that "[t]he underlying consumer protection
principles of strict [products] liability simply do not appear to be applicable to the constructors of a large commercial building built for a particular
client."[65]

---

[59] 106 Misc. 2d 860, 435 N.Y.S.2d 663 (1981).

[60] 435 N.Y.S.2d at 666 (citing Fisher v. Morrison Homes, Inc., 109 Cal. App. 3d 131, 167
Cal. Rptr. 133 (1980)); *see also* K-Mart Corp. v. Midcon Realty Group, 489 F. Supp.
813 (D. Conn. 1980) (architect's building plans not found to be a product within meaning of Restatement § 402A).

[61] *See* Hall v. State, 106 Misc. 2d 860, 435 N.Y.S.2d 663 (1981) ("a provider of services is
not subject to suit on grounds of strict products liability . . . [explicitly noting a]
. . . services versus chattels distinction"). *See also* Counts v. MK-Ferguson Co., 862
F.2d 1338 (8th Cir. 1988) (supplier of engineering services in construction of grain
storage building not subject to strict liability).

[62] 402 F.2d 937 (3d Cir. 1968).

[63] *Id.* at 942–43 (citing Gagne v. Bertran, 43 Cal. 2d 481, 275 P.2d 15, 20–21 (1954)
("those who sell their services for the guidance of others in their economic, financial,
and personal affairs are not liable in the absence of negligence or intentional misconduct. . . . Those who hire experts . . . are not justified in expecting infallibility, but
can only expect reasonable care and competence. They purchase service, not insurance.") (Traynor, J.).

[64] 656 S.W.2d 766 (Mo. Ct. App. 1983).

[65] *Id.* at 780. This lawsuit involved claims against several different parties associated with
the design and construction of Kemper Arena, whose roof had collapsed. *See also*

Because professional design services are not mass-produced or mass-marketed, courts for the most part will not subject architects or engineers to suits based on strict products liability.[66] However, if design professionals *do* take on characteristics of a mass-manufacturer, judges may respond by adopting an expansive notion of strict liability. For example, at least one court has imposed strict liability upon a builder-vendor of mass-produced homes.[67]

It is unclear how courts will draw the line in this area. If a designer/builder of mass-produced homes can be strictly liable, what about a designer of treatment systems or technology, who sells the same design to different customers? How many sales are necessary before a court will consider something to have been mass-produced? How much importance will courts in the future place on the ability to test a design before it is sold? Will courts consider the ability to test a design on a computer to be the equivalent of a manufacturer's premarketing testing? These questions are likely to be faced by future courts, and the results will have serious implications for design professionals.

Another grey area which sometimes confronts courts in determining whether strict products liability should apply to design professionals is that design services may be arguably a "hybrid-transaction,"[68] hybrid in the sense that, on the one hand, the architect/engineer is in effect selling a product (such as a building or a bridge); but, on the other hand, is also providing a service (and thus the transmitted product is simply incidental).

If the essence of the transaction is the rendition of services, and such services are not mass-produced, strict liability should not be available to the plaintiff. However, when the thrust of the transaction is the transfer of a product and the product is, in fact, mass-produced, strict liability may be available to the plaintiff. The design of pollution control facilities or the provision and implementation of site remediation plans have the potential for being viewed as a product or hybrid. Thus far, however, courts have not addressed the issue of whether specific treatment technologies are products.

Queenbury Union Free School Dist. v. Jim Walter Corp., 91 Misc. 2d 804, 398 N.Y.S.2d 832 (1977) (strict liability not applicable to architect for professional services rendered in preparing school plans).

[66] Some courts base this distinction, in part, on the fact that manufacturers of mass-produced products have an opportunity to test and evaluate those products to eliminate defects before marketing, whereas the providers of design services generally do not. Design professionals are usually dealing with a unique building or facility that cannot be tested in a factory before being built. *See, e.g.,* City of Mounds View v. Walijarvi, 263 N.W.2d 420, 424–25 (Minn. 1978).

[67] *See* Schipper v. Levitt & Sons, Inc., 44 N.J. 70, 207 A.2d 314 (1965) (strict liability applies to design professional engaged in mass production of homes).

[68] *See* Prosser and Keeton on Torts § 104, at 719–721 (5th ed. 1984) (discussing notion of hybrid-transaction with respect to health care services).

§ 17.10   Potential Liability of Architects and
Engineers under Superfund

Recent court interpretations of CERCLA[69] have created the spectre of massive liability for design professionals under that statute. It is conceivable that the activities of architects and engineers may in certain circumstances be viewed as participation in the management or operations of a facility to an extent necessary to establish liability under CERCLA § 101(20)(A). Although architects and engineers are principally involved in the design of a facility or building, as the owner's "representative" they may become directly involved in the management and direction of the construction effort. Architects and engineers also may specify materials and methods of installation in the project. All of these activities create the potential for liability.

CERCLA was enacted to address "hazardous substances released into the environment and the cleanup of inactive hazardous waste disposal sites."[70] Its passage (and subsequent amendments and reauthorization) has resulted in a massive nationwide effort to clean up abandoned hazardous waste sites. Under the statute, EPA will remediate a site where hazardous substances have been released and attempt to find the parties who were responsible for the release. Various potentially responsible parties (PRPs) may be liable to the government for its cleanup costs at a site, including generators of the hazardous substances released at the site, transporters who actually delivered the substances to the site, the site owner, and the site operator.[71] Under Superfund's strict liability standard, these parties are all responsible for the government's cleanup costs without regard to fault.

CERCLA imposes strict and joint and several liability on owners and operators of sites where there has been a release of hazardous substances. Strict liability means that a person is liable without proving his or her negligence in the release of hazardous substances. Joint and several liability means that each person who contributed hazardous substances to a site at which there was a release is liable for the cost of the entire cleanup, regardless of the quantity of hazardous substances that person contributed.

The liability provisions of CERCLA generally provide that generators, past or present owners and operators, and transporters of hazardous substances who selected the disposal site are all liable under CERCLA[72] for remediating the site in question or reimbursing the Superfund trust fund in the event the United States undertakes the cleanup using Superfund

---

[69] 42 U.S.C. §§ 9601–9626 (also referred to as Superfund).

[70] S. Rep. No. 848, 96th Cong., 2d Sess. 1 (1980).

[71] 42 U.S.C. § 9607(a).

[72] *Id.*

monies. However, federal court decisions have expanded the scope of liability to affect an even broader group of persons with a far less direct connection with the site or the release.

In *United States v. Mirabile,*[73] an official of a bank which had loaned money to a treatment company sat on an oversight board which had responsibility for the day-to-day operations of the company's facility. The operation of the facility resulted in a release of hazardous substances. The court found that the bank official and the bank were potentially liable because of the extent of participation of the bank official in the business operations of the facility. The decision supports a finding of liability if a party was sufficiently involved in the operations of the site that it should have known of waste disposal problems and should have taken steps to prevent such problems, without regard to the party's actual knowledge of them.[74]

Other courts have interpreted CERCLA liberally in order to extend liability to deep pockets whose connection to a site is not direct.[75] In *United States v. Fleet Factors Corp.,*[76] the court found liable a party who was not even participating in operational decisions but was merely involved in financial decisions. The *Fleet Factors* decision indicates a significantly lower threshold for liability than the day-to-day control required under the *Mirabile* interpretation of operator liability. The court in *Fleet Factors* found that:

> participating in the financial management of the facility to a degree indicating a capacity to influence the corporation's treatment of hazardous waste may result in 'owner' liability. It is not necessary for the [party] actually to involve itself in the day-to-day operations of the facility in order to be liable . . . nor is it necessary for the [party] to participate in management decisions relating to hazardous waste. Rather, a [party] will be liable if its involvement with the management of the facility is sufficiently broad to support the inference that it could affect hazardous waste disposal decisions if it so chose.[77]

Under the Eleventh Circuit's interpretation, there is no need to show any involvement with hazardous waste decisions. Although the court was dealing with a lender who held a security interest in the assets of the operator, the theory embraced by the court—that involvement in the management of

---

[73] 23 Env't Rep. Cas. (BNA) 1511 (E.D. Pa. 1985).

[74] *Id.* at 1513.

[75] *See* United States v. Northeastern Pharmaceutical & Chem. Co., 579 F. Supp. 823 (W.D. Mo. 1984), *aff'd in part, rev'd in part,* 810 F.2d 726 (8th Cir. 1986), *cert. den'd,* 484 U.S. 848 (1988) (NEPACCO).

[76] 31 Env't Rep. Cas. (BNA) 1465 (11th Cir. 1990).

[77] *Id.*

an entity unrelated to its hazardous waste operations can result in liability—has serious implications for design professionals.

Any activity that may be viewed as participation in the management of operations of a facility could potentially result in CERCLA liability for the design professional. For example, design configurations or materials specifications could be viewed as management decisions. Design professionals may also have a role in oversight of the actual construction process, such as movement of earth, the construction of structures and building components, and the supervision of the construction site. Such activities could conceivably be considered participation in the management of a facility under the *Fleet Factors* rationale or, in a slightly different scenario, may be viewed as operating a facility.

In *Tanglewood East Homeowners v. Charles Thomas, Inc.,*[78] the court recognized the possibility that persons who disturbed preexisting contamination in the process of readying property for a construction project could be held liable under CERCLA. The court theorized that developers, construction companies, and real estate agents and agencies who were involved with the site and arranged or helped to arrange for construction activities could be deemed generators of hazardous substances under CERCLA if they were, in part, responsible for activities that disturbed preexisting contamination. It is just a small additional step to include design professionals in this web of liability.

Given the courts' broad interpretations of potential liability in order that the remedial goals of CERCLA be achieved,[79] it is not hard to conceive of a court's finding design professionals liable. Consider the following hypothetical: A site was formerly occupied by an industrial facility whose operations, unbeknownst to its current owner, had resulted in the release of hazardous substances into the soil and groundwater. The new owner retains an architect and a construction engineering firm to design and construct a new building on the site. In the course of design and construction, the architect becomes involved in the efforts of the construction engineering firm. The construction engineering firm oversees the excavation and construction of the building. The excavation requires the removal of a substantial quantity of soil, which is transported from one part of the site to another. It is subsequently determined that the site is contaminated and that the soil that had been removed contains substantial levels of hazardous substances. Under the *Tanglewood* court's theory, the disturbance of preexisting contamination could render the construction engineering firm, as well as the architect, liable as generators of hazardous substances. The architect and the engineering firm might also be considered

---

[78] 849 F.2d 1568 (5th Cir. 1988).

[79] *See* United States v. New Castle County, 727 F. Supp. 854, 859 (D. Del. 1989); United States v. Aceto Agricultural Chem. Corp., 872 F.2d 1373, 1380 (8th Cir. 1989).

site operators, or as having arranged for the transport of hazardous substances under CERCLA. Consequently, the architect and engineering firm could be jointly and severally liable for the entire cost of the cleanup of the contamination at the site, and for any private actions that may have arisen because of exposure to toxics resulting from the movement of the contaminated soil from one part of the site to the other.

This hypothetical indicates that architects and engineers may be exposed to liability under CERCLA, but one case that dealt specifically with potential liability for an engineering design firm found that CERCLA did not apply. In *Edward Hines Lumber Co. v. Vulcan Materials Co.,*[80] the court held that a firm that designed and built a portion of a plant that generated a hazardous substance that was released was not liable under CERCLA. The court found that:

> the statute does not fix liability on slipshod architects, clumsy engineers, poor construction contractors, or negligent suppliers of on-the-job training. . . . The liability falls on owners and operators; architects, engineers, construction contractors and instructors must chip in only to the extent that they have agreed to do so by contract.[81]

While this deference to design professionals has been relied on in several subsequent cases,[82] given the contrary trend culminating in the *Fleet Factors* decision, other courts may choose to follow the Eleventh Circuit rather than the Seventh Circuit on this issue. Thus, architects and engineers should consider taking steps to minimize potential liability under CERCLA.

§ 17.11   Potential Liability under Other Environmental Statutes

Other environmental regulatory statutes, including the Clean Air Act, Clean Water Act, Resource Conservation Recovery Act, and Safe Drinking Water Act all require design, installation, or construction of pollution control facilities in order for regulated companies to comply with emissions standards, waste water discharge standards, or treatment standards. In order to meet these standards, the companies must rely on design professionals to develop the technology and put it in place. Obviously, the potential for negligence claims for poorly designed, poorly installed, or

---

[80] 685 F. Supp. 651 (N.D. Ill.), *aff'd,* 861 F.2d 155 (7th Cir. 1988).

[81] *Id.,* 861 F.2d at 157.

[82] *See, e.g.,* United States v. New Castle County, 727 F. Supp. 854, 866 (D. Del. 1989); United States v. Consolidated Rail Corp., 729 F. Supp. 1461, 1468 (D. Del. 1990).

ineffective pollution control facilities may arise. Also, innovative technologies that attempt to meet the standards of environmental laws through new and different approaches may expose design professionals involved in developing and implementing such technologies to liability under negligence or strict liability theories.

Additionally, under § 404 of the Clean Water Act,[83] persons who fill wetlands without first obtaining a permit from the Army Corps of Engineers are liable for restoration and penalties. If an owner relied on a design professional to handle all aspects of a construction project, and that design professional failed to obtain the requisite permits, she might be liable to the owner in tort or contract, or to the government for restitution and civil penalties.

§ 17.12   Environmental Tort Liability to Third Persons

Environmental tort lawsuits have increased significantly over the past decade. Exposure to toxic or hazardous substances in the workplace, or due to an accidental release, or because of proximity to manufacturing or waste disposal facilities has resulted in numerous lawsuits under various theories of liability. Exposure to asbestos alone has prompted thousands of individual lawsuits and forced most major asbestos product companies into bankruptcy. Because of dwindling resources of asbestos product manufacturers and their insurers, litigants may look to design professionals as an alternative source of recovery. If it could be shown that an architect or engineer specified an asbestos product and an action were not time-barred, a viable theory of liability could be developed.

Environmental tort actions against architects and engineers most likely would be based on theories of negligence or strict liability. Other theories for environmental torts, such as nuisance and trespass, would more likely be brought against actual owners and operators[84] of facilities for property damage rather than physical injury.[85] In addition, courts have shown a willingness to ease the burden of plaintiffs' proofs by adopting evidentiary doctrines such as negligence per se or res ipsa loquitur in environmental tort actions.[86]

In addition to the traditional toxic tort lawsuits based on exposure to industrial toxic chemicals, there is a growing number of successful

---

[83] 33 U.S.C. § 1344.

[84] As distinguished from the expansive definition of owner/operator under CERCLA (see **Chs. 9** through **11**).

[85] *See generally Developments in the Law of Toxic Waste Litigation,* 99 Harv. L. Rev. 1458 (1986).

[86] *See, e.g.,* Reynolds Metals Co. v. Yturbide, 258 F.2d 321 (9th Cir. 1958), *cert. den'd,* 358 U.S. 840, 79 S. Ct. 66 (1958).

lawsuits based on exposure to indoor air pollution. In indoor facilities, injuries can arise from both man-made products and from naturally occurring materials like radon. Radon is an odorless and colorless gas that EPA believes poses a serious threat of cancer. Indoor air pollution is becoming increasingly recognized as a source of injury to persons exposed.[87] Architects and engineers, as well as manufacturers and builders, may face significant exposure in this area.

Most indoor environments have some level of hazardous pollutants. Various causes, including defective design or inappropriate building materials, may result in hazardous fumes being emitted into the indoor air. Combined with inadequate or poorly designed ventilation systems, such hazardous pollutants may expose persons to a serious risk of illness. Liability may arise when a pollutant is present in a concentration that may be injurious to an individual exposed over a period of time. If an architect or engineer improperly designed a ventilation system or specified the use of pollution-causing building materials, such as plywood with formaldehyde or carpets that have glues that give off toxic emissions, the design professional might be found liable. In these situations, the theories of recovery could include breach of contract, breach of express or implied warranty, or negligence. Strict liability would also be possible if a designer specified the use of a hazardous substance that escaped and caused harm.

§ 17.13   Damages Against Design Professionals Generally

Once it has been determined that an architect or engineer is liable, the issue of damages must be addressed. The most common types of claims for damages against architects and engineers related to environmental work include damages resulting from breach of contract or warranty and from negligent design or supervision of construction. This section reviews the cost components included within each type of claim.

The two basic types of damages that arise in contract actions against design professionals are *direct damages,* which are damages arising directly from the breach of a contract, and *consequential damages,* which are those that may be reasonably held to have been within the contemplation of the parties at the time of contract.[88] Direct damages include the cost of correcting or completing work called for in the contract. If this

---

[87] *See* Zimmerman, *Indoor Issues—Pollution Liability Increasing,* Nat'l L. J. (July 23, 1990).

[88] Roanoke Hosp. Assoc. v. Doyle & Russell, Inc., 215 Va. 796, 214 S.E.2d 155, 160 (1975). *See also* R. Cushman & K. Cushman, Construction Litigation: Representing The Owner § 12.3 (2d ed. 1990).

is not feasible, then the amount by which the value of the project has diminished as a result of the defective or incomplete work must be calculated. Consequential damages arise as an indirect result of the architect or engineer's acts. Lost profits are the most common form of consequential damages.[89]

From an accounting and financial perspective, there are generally accepted methods of calculating damages but no set formulas. Depending on the type of case, different methodologies may be used. The simplest method, calculation of damages based on actual costs, requires an accountant or financial analyst to compare what should have been incurred to what was actually incurred. This method, commonly known as the *three column approach*, computes the difference between the expected and the actual. The result is the third column or damage calculation. In seeking damages resulting from an architect's or engineer's acts, breaches, or omissions, the plaintiff typically seeks damages that restore the plaintiff to the position it would have been in had the architect's or engineer's actions not occurred.

The challenge arises in environmental disputes when remedial action has not yet taken place and no actual damage amounts or costs have been incurred. In such cases, the forecasting of costs is required. Such calculations often require developing economic models capable of predicting a damage amount.

There are several keys to calculating proper damages. First, the expert must have all appropriate documents and other sources of information. Second, the expert must evaluate not only the obvious economic losses but also those less apparent losses that may not directly flow from the acts or omissions of the architect or engineer. The third step requires that the expert factor in any mitigating impacts that might reduce the damage total.

Typical damages arising in environmental actions include cleanup and corrective costs and lost opportunity costs. Cleanup and corrective costs are those incurred or expected to be incurred to remove contamination and to restore a facility to its precontaminated status. These costs may also arise in capital construction projects for the design and installation of pollution control facilities.

Consider this hypothetical: An engineer is hired by a municipality to design and oversee the expansion of a waste water treatment facility. Upon completion, the facility is not treating the waste water to the contractually agreed level. It is determined that the engineer had undersized both the pumps and the discharge lines; as a result, the pumps and lines have to be replaced. The corrective costs would include the expense of removing the pumps and lines and the costs of replacing them with new

---

[89] *See generally* R. Dunn, Recovery of Damages for Lost Profits, (1989).

pumps and lines. In analyzing a damage claim, an accounting or financial expert requests all relevant documents, including redesign costs, contractor cost reports, labor distribution reports, material summaries, equipment charges, subcontractor invoices, and overhead summaries.

Lost opportunity costs, as they relate to damage claims against architects and engineers, can arise as a result of a facility owner's or user's not having access to it when expected, usually because of late completion or interruption of normal operations. For example, suppose a used oil recycler contracts with an engineering design firm to develop a more efficient extraction system. In anticipation of the system's coming on-line, the recycler contracts with a large number of new clients. The system fails and results in a major release of used oil. In addition to incurring cleanup costs, the recycler is not able to service the new accounts. The recycler could claim damages not only for the cost of cleanup but also for the unrealized revenues from the lost accounts.

§ 17.14   Damages under CERCLA

The cost and accounting process for remediation of major Superfund sites is usually far more complex due to the scale of the cleanup effort. Once a site has been identified by the government for cleanup, a multi-step process goes into action, and the cost meter is turned on. Included in this process are the preliminary assessment/site investigation, remedial investigation/feasibility study, record of decision, remedial design, and, finally, the remedial action.[90] Throughout each of these steps the government, through the EPA and the Department of Justice, incurs costs that can be significant. The government will be looking to the responsible parties to recover these costs in full.

There are two basic analyses typically performed on the government's claims for charges under CERCLA. These analyses are (1) the government's incurred cost claims, and (2) the alternative remediation plans. The *incurred cost claims* include components for items such as personnel, outside contractors, and overhead. The personnel components are varied and include government technicians and attorneys. The outside contractors include firms hired by EPA to provide various services to the site, including soil sampling, chemical analysis, groundwater monitoring, and security. The overheads include all indirect costs incurred by EPA, such as support personnel, buildings and facilities, training, public affairs, and computers. The government pools these overhead costs and performs various allocation steps in determining what is charged to the site and what the responsible parties should pay.

---

[90] Variations may be found under state cleanup programs.

Incurred cost claims have been challenged by defendants, with mixed results. However, reviews should be performed on the claims to assure they are reasonable. The government must be able to provide sufficient cost documentation to verify that all costs included in the claims were in fact incurred and provided some benefit to the site in question.[91] This support should include at least the following: cost reports; time cards detailing technicians' and attorneys' time, specifically identifying the hours incurred for the site; payroll; outside contractor contracts and invoices detailing services provided, as well as verification of payment; cost reports detailing all the costs included in the overhead pools that have been allocated to the site; and documents detailing the allocation process.

Once this documentation has been gathered, it should be reviewed for the appropriateness of costs included and purged of any types of costs that were either not incurred or provided no benefit to the site. The claim also should be reviewed for the layering of overheads resulting from the use of several contractors. A common occurrence in the award of contract work is EPA overhead's being added to both contractor and subcontractor overheads. The result is that multiple layers of the same overheads are included improperly in the claim.

The second major area for damage review is the evaluation of *alternative remediation plans* considered by the government. As part of the cleanup process, the government develops several remedial alternatives before deciding on the appropriate plan. The responsible parties can have a role in the selection of the final plan. Therefore, it is prudent to review these alternatives for accuracy and reasonableness. This review should include the tests and verification procedures that compare industry estimates and quotes. For example, a proposed remediation plan may call for neutralizing contaminated soil with a mixing soil. The quantities and cost of mix material, equipment rates, and manpower estimates (both hours and wage scales) should be compared to prevailing market rates and site-specific design parameters. Another test would compare the estimates to actual costs incurred at a similar site. Finally, the estimates can be entered into financial models and analyzed. Use of modeling would allow the reviewer to change key underlying assumptions and determine the accuracy of the estimate.

Although the review and verification process of CERCLA claims may be unwieldly, time-consuming, and expensive, the cleanup costs are usually so enormous and the liability to responsible parties so substantial that it is usually justified.

---

[91] The government may recover costs associated with the cleanup of a site "not inconsistent with the National Contingency Plan" (NCP), the government's blueprint for Superfund cleanups. *See* CERCLA § 107(a)(4)(A).

§ 17.15   Environmental Indemnification
Provisions to Protect Against Liability

It has become standard operating procedure for purchasers of real estate, or for financial institutions loaning money for the purchase of real estate, to perform *environmental due diligence* prior to concluding a transaction. It may be prudent for architects and engineers who will be involved in the type of activity that theoretically could result in liability to perform at least a minimal environmental due diligence assessment. Such an effort might include inquiring into the type of activities previously occurring at the property and determining whether there have been previous investigations of the property. Obviously, any blatant signs of toxic contamination (such as stressed vegetation, oozing drums, or above- or below-ground storage tanks surrounded by stained soil) should prompt concern. However, even if a site does not appear to present any environmental concerns, a design professional should avoid signing any acknowledgment that he or she has inspected the site and found no problems.

When reviewing elements of the work required under a contract, design professionals should identify those tasks that could involve contact with hazardous substances, pollutants, or contaminants and have liability issues addressed specifically in their contract. Obtaining representations and indemnification from the property owner or contracting party specifically to cover any liability arising from any release or threatened release of hazardous substances is advisable. Although such an agreement may not bar an action by the government to hold an architect or engineer liable, it would at least provide an opportunity for recovery from the property owner or contracting party.

§ 17.16   Indemnification of Design
Professionals Acting As Response Action
Contractors under CERCLA

CERCLA contains provisions that limit the liability and allow for limited indemnification of contractors hired to help clean up Superfund sites. First, under § 119 of CERCLA, adopted as part of the Superfund amendments of 1986, a response action contractor[92] retained to address a release or threatened release of a hazardous substance from a facility:

---

[92] § 119(e)(2) defines a *response action contractor* as

    A) any—

        (i)   person who enters into a response action contract with respect to any release or threatened release of a hazardous substance or pollutant or contaminant from a facility and is carrying out such contracts; and shall not be liable to any person for injuries, cost, damages and expenses or other liability (including but not limited to claims for indemnification or contribution and claims by third parties for death, personal injury, illness or loss of or damage to property or economical loss) which results from a release or threatened release.[93]

This limitation of liability protects response action contractors hired by EPA, other federal agencies, states, and persons undertaking cleanup of their own sites. It applies to both Superfund liability and third-party liability under federal laws.[94]

This limitation on liability, however, has some important exceptions. It does not apply when a release is caused by negligent acts or intentional misconduct of the response action contractor.[95] It also does not apply to the liability of an employer who is a response action contractor for any claims by an employee seeking workers' compensation.[96]

In addition to the limitations on liability, EPA is authorized to indemnify response action contractors against negligence, but not gross negligence or intentional misconduct.[97] This authorization is subject to certain requirements, chief among them being an obligation on the part of the contractor to make "diligent efforts" to obtain insurance. Since 1988, EPA has been attempting to establish regulations which implement these indemnification provisions. However, a disagreement between EPA and the contracting community on the availability of insurance for contractors and what constitutes diligent efforts to obtain such insurance has delayed promulgation. Recently, EPA has come to recognize that the availability of insurance for response action contractors is limited at best. Revised regulations are now expected to be proposed in 1990.[98]

    (ii)   person, public or non-profit private entity, conducting a field demonstration pursuant to § 311(b); and

    (iii)   recipients of grants (including subgrantees) under § 126 for the training and education of workers who are or may be engaged in activities related to hazardous removal, containment or emergency response under this chapter; and

  B) any person who is retained or hired by a person described in subparagraph A to provide any of the services related to a response action.

[93] CERCLA § 119(a)(1).

[94] *Id.*

[95] *Id.* § 119(a)(2).

[96] *Id.* § 119(a)(3).

[97] *Id.* § 119(c)(1).

[98] Under the Clean Water Act, 33 U.S.C. §§ 1251–1376, EPA also provides immunity from negligence (other than gross negligence) for design professionals if innovative processes or techniques are used in the design of sewage treatment facilities. 40 C.F.R. § 35.908 app. C-1 (1989).

Clearly, given the high risks for design firms associated with remedial activities at contaminated sites, design professionals need to take every precaution to ensure that their exposure to liability is minimized. The traditional means of protecting against such risks through insurance has become prohibitively expensive in many areas or simply unavailable. This makes the inclusion of clear, broad indemnification and limitation of liability language important in any contract. Various groups, including the American Consulting Engineers Council, have developed checklists and sample contract language that may be a valuable resource for design professionals.[99]

---

[99] *See Commentary on Indemnification and Limitation of Liability Clauses,* Business Practices Committee, Hazardous Waste Action Coalition, American Consulting Engineers Council, a paper distributed at the Fifth Annual Construction Litigation Superconference (May 22–23, 1990).

CHAPTER 18

ACCOUNTANT AND ATTORNEY LIABILITY

Theodore F. Martens
Kevin J. Walsh*

Theodore F. Martens is an audit partner and the partner in charge of the Litigation Services practice in the New York Metropolitan Region of Coopers & Lybrand. His litigation experience includes a broad range of commercial and environmental matters. He has had extensive experience with accountant's and auditor's liability as a member of Coopers & Lybrand's Office of General Counsel. Mr. Martens is a CPA with over twelve years of experience and is also a chartered life underwriter (CLU).

Kevin J. Walsh is a litigation partner at Kelley Drye & Warren in New York, New York. He has represented major United States and European chemical companies in groundwater contamination litigation resulting from widely used pesticides. Kelley Drye and Warren has represented land owners, financial institutions, and insurers in litigation arising from hazardous waste disposal. Mr. Walsh received his undergraduate degree from Fordham University in New York City and his J.D. degree from the University of Virginia.

*Mr. Walsh gratefully acknowledges the assistance of Cynthia S. Papsdorf, Robert J. Bergson, and John Harris, associates in the New York office of Kelley Drye & Warren.

§ 18.1   Introduction

Other chapters in this book deal with the liability of parties in the manufacturing phase (manufacturers, producers, and transporters of hazardous
waste), owners and operators, lenders, insurers, or professionals directly
involved in planning or designing the facility in question. This chapter is
unique in that it focuses on the potential liability of parties who are more
commonly seen as professional advisors removed from direct responsibility for planning, designing, or operating facilities, that is, attorneys and
accountants.

Perhaps consistent with that distance from environmentally significant
waste producing activities, the authors have found no decision imposing
liability for environmental damages pursuant to the Comprehensive

Environmental Response, Compensation and Liability Act (CERCLA)[1] upon such professionals for acts in their professional capacity. Obviously, like any employee, in-house lawyers and accountants who function as business executives or who are intimately involved in a company's waste disposal decisions may become personally liable, either civilly or criminally, for environmental contamination occurring during the course of their employment. Similarly, attorneys or accountants who serve as directors of companies accept the risks of liability attendant upon such office should they fail to take action sufficient to prevent contamination. Lenders, who are also one step removed from the actual contamination process, may be found to be owners or operators[2] and hence liable under CERCLA.

It is also possible to imagine an outside law or accounting firm supervising the dismantling of the assets of a discontinued operation and actively conducting sales of assets, hence becoming an operator with CERCLA liability, but as yet such cases have not been reported.

In the absence of specific cases holding attorneys or accountants liable for environmental damages, the present sources of possible liability appear to be traditional common law claims and statutory remedies such as securities laws, which have been utilized to impose liability on professionals. Accordingly, discussed in this chapter are (1) the sources for professionals' liability, and (2) steps professionals can take to prevent future liability and/or minimize past liability and hence protect themselves by protecting their clients.

BASIS OF LIABILITY

§ 18.2 Common Law Negligence Liability to Client

Of course, the classic basis for professional liability is the common law malpractice claim brought by the client for damages and grounded in principles of negligence. With respect to attorney malpractice, the elements of the action are that an attorney-client relationship existed,[3] giving

---

[1] 42 U.S.C. §§ 9601–9675 (1988 & Supp. 1990).

[2] See United States v. Fleet Factors Corp., 901 F.2d 1550 (11th Cir. 1990).

[3] Snyder v. Baumecker, 708 F. Supp. 1451, 1462 (D.N.J. 1989); Lorraine v. Grover, Cimet, Weinstein & Stauber, P.A., 467 So. 2d 315, 317 (Fla. Ct. App. 1985). A formal or lengthy relationship is not necessary. In Togstad v. Vesely, Otto, Miller, & Keefe, 291 N.W.2d 686 (Minn. 1980) the client consulted with the attorney for approximately one hour regarding a potential medical malpractice claim, at the end of which she was told that she had no case. No fee arrangements were discussed, nor was she billed for the interview. The court held that the requirement of an attorney-client relationship was satisfied.

rise to a duty by the attorney, and a breach of that duty[4] proximately causing damages to the client.[5]

When the conduct under scrutiny is that of a professional, the standard of care is framed in terms of the skill and knowledge possessed by members of that profession. "The standard of care to which an attorney must adhere is measured by the skill generally possessed and employed by practitioners of the profession."[6] Many courts have held that the defendant attorney's knowledge, skill, and care will be judged in relation to the knowledge, skill, and care of attorneys in the state, some expressly holding that these standards are the same throughout the state and do not differ among the various communities.[7] Some jurisdictions, including California,[8] Kansas,[9] and Louisiana,[10] have held that an attorney is only obligated to exercise that degree of care "which is exercised by prudent practicing attorneys in his locality."[11]

Similarly, an accountant has a duty to perform services with professional due care, which requires that work be done by someone with adequate knowledge and necessary experience, and to stay within the provisions of the Code of Professional Conduct and other professional standards of the American Institute of Certified Public Accountants

---

[4] Jordan v. Lipsig, Sullivan, Mollen & Liapakis, 689 F. Supp. 192 (S.D.N.Y. 1988).

[5] Stewart v. Hall, 770 F.2d 1267, 1269 (4th Cir. 1985). In determining proximate causation it is not necessary that the attorney's negligence be the sole cause of client's loss. *See, e.g.,* Cline v. Watkins, 66 Cal. App. 3d 174, 135 Cal. Rptr. 838, 840 (1977) ("'[A]n attorney's negligence need not be the *sole* cause of his client's loss in order to subject him to liability. This is to say, where there is causation in fact it need not be the sole proximate cause'") (quoting Starr v. Mooslin, 14 Cal. App. 3d 988, 1002, 92 Cal. Rptr. 583, 590 (1971)). Many courts have adopted a *but for test. See, e.g.,* Hanlin v. Mitchelson, 794 F.2d 834, 838 (2d Cir. 1986) (under New York law, "proof that but for the alleged malpractice the plaintiff would have been successful in the underlying action" is a required element of legal malpractice); Stewart v. Hall, 770 F.2d at 1270 (alleged negligence is actionable only upon determination that underlying claim would have been resolved differently but for attorney's negligence).

In the context of environmental advice this will likely mean that the client must establish that, had the attorney's advice been different, not only would the client have acted differently, but these different actions would have prevented or obviated the damages. When the actions relate to an existing but stable problem it is difficult to fashion a scenario in which the attorney's advice would be the proximate cause of the client's damages.

[6] Gans v. Mundy, 762 F.2d 338, 341 (3d Cir.), *cert. denied,* 474 U.S. 1010 (1985) (Pennsylvania law). *See generally* 7A C.J.S. *Attorney and Client* § 254 at 458–60 (1980).

[7] Kellos v. Sawilowsky, 254 Ga. 4, 325 S.E.2d 757 (1985); Cook, Flanagan & Berst v. Clausing, 73 Wash. 2d 393, 438 P.2d 865, 866–67 (1968).

[8] Lipscomb v. Krause, 87 Cal. App. 3d 970, 151 Cal. Rptr. 465 (1978).

[9] Bowman v. Doherty, 235 Kan. 870, 686 P.2d 112 (1984).

[10] Montgomery v. Jack, 556 So. 2d 267 (La. Ct. App. 1990).

[11] *Id.* at 271.

(AICPA). The failure of an accountant to apply the usual standard of due care in an engagement results in a potential liability to the client on the basis of negligence.

If the professional is a specialist, the standard becomes the knowledge and skill generally possessed and exercised by specialists within the profession. Although certain jurisdictions have established statutory or regulatory procedures by which an attorney may be certified as a specialist in certain designated areas, it is not necessary for a recognized specialty to exist before a lawyer's conduct is subjected to a heightened scrutiny.[12]

Whether or not the particular jurisdiction recognizes environmental law as a legal specialty, given the general awareness of environmental issues, when an attorney represents clients in commercial real estate transactions or business acquisitions, expertise in environmental law may be assumed to be part of the normal skills. Counsel must either meet the standards, obtain expert assistance, or risk exposure to malpractice liability if, for example, he or she fails to recommend an environmental audit on properties or business operations that may have engaged in conduct resulting in hazardous waste. In *Horne v. Peckham*,[13] the court approved the following jury instruction:

> It is the duty of an attorney who is a general practitioner to refer his client to a specialist or recommend the assistance of a specialist if under the circumstances a reasonably careful and skillful practitioner would do so.
>
> If he fails to perform that duty and undertakes to perform professional services without the aid of a specialist, it is his further duty to have the knowledge and skill ordinarily possessed, and exercise the care and skill ordinarily used by specialists in good standing in the same or similar locality and under the same circumstances.
>
> A failure to perform any such duty is negligence.[14]

The speciality in question was taxation, but the case indicates that the general practitioner facing a possible contamination problem ought to

---

[12] In Wright v. Williams, 47 Cal. App. 3d 802, 810, 121 Cal. Rptr. 194, 199 (1975), the court restated the long-standing California rule that "[t]he standard is that of members of the profession 'in the same or a similar locality *under similar circumstances.*'" It went on to hold that the fact that one holds himself out as a legal specialist (in this case a specialist in maritime law) is one of those "circumstances" that must be considered.

We thus conclude that a lawyer holding himself out to the public and the profession as specializing in an area of the law must exercise the skill, prudence, and diligence exercised by other specialists of ordinary skill and capacity specializing in the same field.

See also Bowman v. Doherty, 235 Kan. 870, 686 P.2d 112, 120 (1984) (court held that because defendant was "involved in the practice of criminal law" he will be judged by the professional standards of that particular area of law).

[13] 97 Cal. App. 3d 404, 158 Cal. Rptr. 714 (1979).

[14] *Id.* at 414, 158 Cal. Rptr. at 720.

consider calling in environmental specialists in order to avoid potential liability.

§ 18.3   Other Common Law Theories for Professionals' Liability to Clients

For statute of limitation reasons, courts have on occasion analyzed attorney liability on a contractual basis, so that whether the case proceeds under a tort or contract theory is not of substantive significance, because the duty owed under either theory is to perform reasonably, according to the standard of care applicable to attorneys in the state or locality.[15]

Although there are cases with language to the effect that "an attorney does not ordinarily guarantee the soundness of his opinions and, accordingly, is not liable for every mistake he may make in his practice,"[16] those decisions often arise in the context of an attorney's estimate or prediction of the outcome of a litigation. In the context of an opinion letter, it can be asserted that the attorney or accountant may be held to a higher standard. It is not undisputed whether, absent a relevant statutory provision, reliance on an expert will provide protection to the lawyer rendering an opinion. At least one commentator has suggested that it would.[17]

Similarly, the accountant can be liable for breach of contract if he or she fails to meet the terms of the engagement, fails to perform the engagement in accordance with generally accepted auditing standards (GAAS), does not deliver the opinion on the agreed-upon date, or breaches client confidentiality.

Clients utilizing common law theories for claims against professionals have also used theories of negligent misrepresentation. Although formulations differ, it is generally held that the representation must be made within the context of a relationship that gives rise to the right of the plaintiff to rely upon the utterances of the defendant;[18] the defendant must

---

[15] *See* Lucas v. Hamm, 56 Cal. 2d 583, 364 P.2d 685, 15 Cal. Rptr. 821 (1961), *cert. denied,* 368 U.S. 987 (1962). *See also* Note, *Malpractice Suits Against Local Counsel or Specialists,* 68 Va. L. Rev. 571, 577 (1982) ("the decision to proceed under tort or contract principles will not vary significantly the substantive standards for liability").

[16] Helmbrecht v. St. Paul Ins. Co., 122 Wis. 2d 94, 362 N.W.2d 118, 129 (1985). *See also* Lundy, Butler & Lundy v. Bierman, 398 N.W.2d 212 (Iowa Ct. App. 1986) ("An attorney is not an insurer of successful outcome of litigation unless he makes a special contract to that effect").

[17] Fuld, *Lawyers' Standards and Responsibilities in Rendering Opinions,* 33 Bus. Law. 1295 (1978).

[18] "The long-standing rule is that recovery may be had for pecuniary loss arising from negligent representations where there is actual privity of contract between the parties or a relationship so close as to approach that of privity." Ossining Union Free School Dist. v. Anderson, 73 N.Y.2d 417, 424, 539 N.E.2d 91, 94, 541 N.Y.S.2d 335, 338 (1989).

know that the plaintiff will so rely and that if the utterance is false injury will result; the plaintiff must show reliance and damages proximately caused by the representation.[19] Accounting malpractice actions typically involve allegations that an accountant failed to comply with one or more of the GAAS. Most of these allegations focus on the accountant's negligence in performing the audit; however, fraud allegations are prevalent in those situations in which the plaintiff alleges that the accountant knowingly and intentionally failed to follow GAAS.

Along the same lines, theories of fraud, fraudulent misrepresentation, and fraudulent concealment can of course be asserted against professionals who are guilty of misrepresentations to clients. Common law fraudulent misrepresentation is generally comprised of a false representation of a material fact, scienter, reliance, and damages.[20] A cause of action for fraudulent concealment generally requires: a relationship between the parties, which gives rise to a duty to disclose; knowledge of the material facts by the party bound to disclose; nondisclosure; scienter; reliance; and damages.[21] The misrepresentation or omission must be the proximate cause of the injury; that is, the injury must be a natural and probable consequence thereof, or the defrauder ought to have foreseen that the injury was such a probable consequence.[22]

Again, a claim arising in the environmental context on these theories would differ only in subject matter, not legal theory. Thus, for example, an attorney or accountant who misrepresented to a client what due diligence work had been done to protect against possible environmental liabilities would face the possibility of liability under such theories.

It should be noted that the Superfund Amendments and Reauthorization Act of 1986 (SARA)[23] has created an innocent landowner defense, which provides that a purchaser who undertakes "all appropriate inquiry into the previous ownership and uses of the property consistent with good commercial or customary practice" will not be held liable.[24] Presumably, if counsel, on behalf of the client in the transaction, has undertaken sufficient due

---

[19] *See* Somarelf v. American Bureau of Shipping, 704 F. Supp. 59 (D.N.J. 1988); *In re* Worlds of Wonder Sec. Litig., 694 F. Supp. 1427 (N.D. Cal. 1988). In the environmental area it is difficult to see how such a claim would arise, short of an attorney's representing to his client that he had undertaken environmental due diligence efforts which, in fact, had not been done.

[20] *See* West v. Western Casualty & Sur. Co., 846 F.2d 387 (7th Cir. 1988); Murray v. Xerox Corp., 811 F.2d 118 (2d Cir. 1987); Garcia v. Williams, 704 F. Supp. 984 (N.D. Cal. 1988).

[21] *See, e.g.,* Leasing Serv. Corp. v. Broetje, 545 F. Supp. 362 (S.D.N.Y. 1982).

[22] *See* Cable v. Hechler, 532 F. Supp. 239 (E.D.N.Y. 1981), aff'd, 685 F.2d 423 (2d Cir. 1982).

[23] 42 U.S.C. §§ 9601–9675 (1983 & Supp. 1990).

[24] *Id.* § 9601(35)(B).

diligence inquiry to establish the defense for the client, there would be no damage to the client and hence no claim against the attorney.

§ 18.4   Liability to Third Parties

Of course, in addition to claims from clients, professionals may be faced with claims from third parties who may have been injured by the client's environmental contamination. Although there exists substantial judicial authority for the proposition that only a client can sue the attorney for malpractice because of traditional rules of privity, one commentator has noted that "[g]eneralizations concerning the state of the law are not accurate or reliable. The rules concerning the requirement of privity have been in a state of transition for over two decades."[25] With that caveat, we note that although the attorney's duty extends beyond those privy to the attorney-client contract, there must nonetheless be a basis for a duty between the plaintiff and the attorney. The commentators have identified two principal theories under which the attorney has been held to have a duty to parties other than the client. The more traditional approach is based on the concept of a third-party beneficiary contract to allow anticipated beneficiaries of the attorney's work to sue for negligent performance thereof, such as "claims by a would-be beneficiary of a will."[26] California has applied a balancing test to determine when liability will be imposed on the basis of a duty owed to non-clients:

> [A]n attorney may owe a duty to a third person, and may be liable if the third person who was intended to be benefitted by his performance is injured by his negligent execution of that duty. "An attorney may be liable for damage caused by his negligence to a person intended to be benefitted by his performance irrespective of any lack of privity of contract between the attorney and the party to be benefitted. . . . The liability sounds in tort. . . . The determination of whether the duty undertaken by an attorney extends to a third party not in privity 'involves the balancing of various factors, among which are the extent to which the transaction was intended to affect the plaintiff, the foreseeability of harm to him, the degree of certainty that the plaintiff suffered injury, the closeness of the connection between the defendant's conduct and the injury suffered, the moral blame attached to the defendant's conduct, and the policy of preventing future harm.'"[27]

---

[25] R. Mallen & J. Smith, Legal Malpractice § 7.10 at 379–80 (3d ed. 1989).

[26] *Id.* at 379.

[27] Roberts v. Ball, Hunt, Hart, Brown & Baerwitz, 57 Cal. App. 3d 104, 110, 128 Cal. Rptr. 901, 905–06 (1976) (quoting Donald v. Garry, 19 Cal. App. 3d 769, 771–72, 97 Cal. Rptr. 191, 192 (1971)).

Consistent with the general policy of spreading the costs of environmental damages over all responsible parties, it is entirely conceivable that this rationale could be used to hold an attorney liable to, for example, homeowners who claim damages as a result of a corporation's failure to provide statutorily required notification of the use of hazardous substances and seek redress against counsel who failed to advise the company of its obligations under the law. The *Restatement (Second) of Torts* specifically recognizes liability to third parties if the professional has a public duty to disclose information and the plaintiff is one of the class of persons for whose benefit the duty was created.[28]

The possible liability of accountants to third parties has evolved dramatically.[29] The older and more restrictive standard was exemplified by cases such as *Ultrameres Corp. v. Touche,*[30] in which a plaintiff's cause of action was disallowed due to lack of contractual privity or a relationship that would "approach that of privity."[31] An emerging trend has been to hold accountants liable for negligent misrepresentations "by actually foreseen and limited classes of persons." This trend was started in *Rusch Factors, Inc. v. Levin,*[32] in which the plaintiff loaned $337,000 to the accountant's client based on negligently prepared financial statements and successfully sought damages from the accountant. The *Rusch* approach is based on *Restatement (Second) of Torts* § 522. The dramatic

---

[28] Restatement (Second) of Torts § 552 (1981) defines and limits the cause as follows:

Information Negligently Supplied for the Guidance of Others

(1) One who, in the course of his business, profession or employment, or in any other transaction in which he has a pecuniary interest, supplies false information for the guidance of others in their business transactions, is subject to liability for pecuniary loss caused to them by their justifiable reliance upon the information, if he fails to exercise reasonable care or competence in obtaining or communicating the information.

(2) Except as stated in Subsection (3), the liability stated in Subsection (1) is limited to loss suffered

(a) by the person or one of a limited group of persons for whose benefit and guidance he intends to supply the information or knows that the recipient intends to supply it; and

(b) through reliance upon it in a transaction that he intends the information to influence or knows that the recipient so intends or in a substantially similar transaction.

(3) The liability of one who is under a public duty to give the information extends to loss suffered by any of the class of persons for whose benefit the duty is created, in any of the transactions in which it is intended to protect them.

[29] *See* R. Mallen & J. Smith, Legal Malpractice §§ 7.9–7.12 (3d ed. 1989).

[30] 255 N.Y. 170, 174 N.E. 441 (1931).

[31] *Id.* at 183, 174 N.E. at 445.

[32] 284 F. Supp. 85 (D.R.I. 1968).

departure from an *Ultrameres* type standard was evidenced by *H. Rosenblum, Inc. v. Adler,*[33] in which it was held that an independent auditor "has a duty to all those whom that auditor should reasonably foresee as recipients from the company of the [financial] statements."[34] Similarly, a later case, *Citizens State Bank v. Timm, Schmidt & Co., S.C.,*[35] explicitly rejected the "Restatement's [standard] of limiting liability to certain third parties [as] too restrictive."

More recently, in *International Mortgage Co. v. John P. Butler Accountancy Corp.,*[36] a California appellate court used the *Rosenblum* and *Timm* standards of liability. The *Butler* court cited the changing role of the accountant and supported "a financial disincentive for negligent conduct [which] . . . will heighten the profession's cautionary techniques."[37] The trend toward expanding the scope and enforcement of environmental laws along with the increased acceptance of accountant's liability to third parties will in all probability result in future liability of accountants if financial statements do not accurately reflect costs related to environmental issues.

§ 18.5   Liability under Federal Securities Laws

Perhaps the most likely statutory basis for liability to third parties of attorneys and/or accountants is the federal securities laws regarding disclosures in the context of sales of securities. It is easy to conceive of a situation in which a publicly held company announces massive anticipated environmental cleanup costs and is then subject to claims from disgruntled investors asserting that the company and its counsel and accountants should have disclosed such liabilities at an earlier date. At least one case asserting such a theory is presently pending in a federal district court, *Steiner v. Baxter,*[38] but the complaint in that case names neither lawyers or accountants. Under standard theories of securities law, attorneys and accountants have often been held liable when material facts are not adequately disclosed. Again, the theories are already in place and the environmental context amounts only to a difference in the subject matter of the material facts, nondisclosure of which could result in liability.

---

[33] 93 N.J. 324, 461 A.2d 138 (1983).

[34] *Id.* at 352, 461 A.2d at 153.

[35] 113 Wis. 2d 376, 335 N.W.2d 361, 366 (1983).

[36] 177 Cal. App. 3d 806, 223 Cal. Rptr. 218 (1986).

[37] *Id.* at 820, 223 Cal. Rptr. at 227.

[38] Civil Action No. 89-M-809 (D. Colo.), as reported in N.Y. Times, June 24, 1990, at F10.

Section 10(b) of the 1934 Securities Exchange Act[39] and Rule 10b-5 promulgated thereunder[40] provides a cause of action for a misstatement or omission of a material fact in connection with the sale of a security, made with scienter, on which plaintiff relied, proximately resulting in plaintiff's injury.[41] Under § 11 of the Securities Act of 1933, a purchaser of a registered security has a right of action when the registration statement contains untrue statements of, or omissions of, a material fact.[42] Similarly, under § 12(2) of the Act,[43] the plaintiff must allege that the defendant, as a seller of a security, "misrepresented or failed to state material facts to the plaintiff in connection with the sale" and that the plaintiff "had no knowledge of the untruth or omission."[44] However, under § 12(2) the plaintiff need not establish that the defendant acted with scienter or that the plaintiff relied in any way on the defendant's misrepresentations or omissions.

In addition to being primarily liable for their own direct violations of these statutes, lawyers and accountants can also be secondarily liable as *control persons* under the securities laws or as aiders and abettors, and it is under these secondary liability theories that most claims against attorneys and accountants have been brought.

Under § 77(o) of the 1933 Securities Act and § 78(t) of the 1934 Securities Exchange Act any person who controls a person found liable under, inter alia, § 12(2) and/or § 10(b) can be held jointly and severally liable with the person so controlled.[45] The SEC definition of control is "the possession, direct or indirect, of the power to direct or cause the direction of the management and policies of a person, whether through the ownership of voting securities, by contract, or otherwise."[46]

Outside counsel and accountants have been held liable on theories of aiding and abetting securities violations. A prima facie case of aiding and abetting a violation of § 10(b) is established when the plaintiff shows that:

1. There is an independent wrong (a violation of the securities laws)
2. The aider and abettor knows of that wrong's existence

---

[39] 15 U.S.C. § 78j(b).

[40] 17 C.F.R. § 240.10b-5.

[41] *See, e.g.,* Froid v. Barner, 649 F. Supp. 1418, 1421 (D.N.J. 1986).

[42] 15 U.S.C. § 77(k).

[43] *Id.* § 77(l).

[44] Junker v. Crory, 650 F.2d 1349, 1359 (5th Cir. 1981).

[45] 15 U.S.C. §§ 77(o), 78(t) (1981).

[46] 17 C.F.R. § 230.45 (1988).

3. Substantial assistance has been given by the aider/abettor in effecting that wrong.[47]

There are, of course, numerous issues as to the degree of participation required of outside counsel or accountants before they become control persons or aiders or abettors. The requirement for active participation sufficient to find that the lawyer or accountant actively assisted a 10b-5 violation, as well as the need to show that the lawyer or accountant is a seller under § 12(2), and the availability of certain good-faith defenses for control persons,[48] all create issues that are intensely litigated. However, the theories for liability of lawyers and accountants in connection with alleged failures to disclose are well established and would certainly be applicable to a claim of failure to adequately disclose potential environmental liabilities.

Thus, while there is a dearth of case law specifically imposing liability on attorneys and accountants in connection with environmental damages, it is clear that existing theories provide many bases upon which clients and third parties may attempt to assert liability against lawyers and accountants. Accordingly, we now examine steps which attorneys and accountants can take to protect themselves and their clients from such potential liabilities.

USE OF ACCOUNTANTS AND ATTORNEYS TO MINIMIZE FUTURE RISKS

§ 18.6   Counselling Clients to Avoid Environmental Liability

In opining as to how accountants and lawyers can help their clients avoid potential liability for environmental injury, the simplistic answer is, of course, counsel the client to comply with all applicable laws. Given the explosion in federal and state environmental legislation and regulation, however, such advice is more easily given than followed. Indeed, the New Jersey Supreme Court, in a recent review of that state's much expanded environmental statutes, noted that the statutory scheme was "extraordinarily complex" but concluded that "[g]iven the realities of our world, such complexity is unavoidable if the very real problems addressed by this

---

[47] Kronfeld v. First Jersey Nat'l Bank, 638 F. Supp. 1454, 1469 (D.N.J. 1986); Walck v. American Stock Exch., Inc., 687 F.2d 778, 790–91 (3d Cir. 1982), *cert. denied,* 461 U.S. 942, *reh'g denied,* 463 U.S. 1236 (1983); ITT, An Int'l Inv. Trust v. Cornfeld, 619 F.2d 909, 922 (2d Cir. 1980).

[48] *See, e.g.,* 15 U.S.C. §§ 77(o), 78(t) (1981).

body of law are to be confronted."[49] In light of the web of federal statutes and the state-to-state variations, clearly this chapter cannot provide detailed guidance on every situation to the attorney or accountant. Accordingly, we have concentrated herein on practices and procedures that are particularly helpful in the environmental area and hence should be considered by practitioners. These are the general blueprints rather than specific tools.

§ 18.7   Environmental Due Diligence Audits

The use of title insurance and title searches in a purchase of real estate is of course standard practice for any attorney. An accountant's review of reserves, contingent liabilities, and accounts receivable is similarly de rigueur in the acquisition of a commercial enterprise. To this list must now be added the environmental due diligence assessment or environmental audit, whenever the transaction involves a business or property that may have been used in a way that potential environmental claims may result.[50] An environmental assessment or audit can disclose the existence of actual and potential environmental liabilities and toxic tort claims, provide estimates for remediation costs, and ascertain compliance with applicable regulations and permit requirements.[51]

Underscoring the significance of environmental audits, one court, in considering whether a bank had "owned or operated" a facility at which hazardous substances were disposed, specifically noted that banks could protect themselves by requiring borrowers to "submit to periodic environmental audits,"[52] and cited another case in which the court viewed such research as "routine."[53] Given these views by the courts, it is clear that counsel who proceeds with a major transaction without recommending an environmental audit runs a grave risk of being found to have failed to provide the client with services on a level expected from the normally competent professional.[54] Understandably, the client would be disturbed

---

[49] *Report of Supreme Court Committee on Environmental Litigation,* 125 N.J.L.J. 1413, 1417 (May 24, 1990).

[50] For a good general review of the use of environmental audits, *see* Cogen, *What You Need to Know About Environmental Audits,* 35 The Practical Lawyer 17 (Oct. 1989); Myers, *The Goals and Techniques of Environmental Audits,* 30 The Practical Lawyer 41 (Jan. 1984).

[51] *See* Vanderveer, *Environmental Auditing* in Environmental Law Handbook (J. Arbuch, ed. 1983).

[52] United States v. Fleet Factors Corp., 901 F.2d 1550, 1559 (11th Cir. 1990).

[53] United States v. Maryland Bank & Trust Co., 632 F. Supp. 573 (D. Md. 1986).

[54] *See* Newman, *How to Counsel the Land Developer on Superfund and Superliens,* 34 The Practical Lawyer 13 (Oct. 1988) (in depth discussion of factors to be considered

to learn, for example, that *after* the acquisition, the property for which he just paid $1 million requires $10 million in cleanup costs.[55] In such a scenario, it can be expected that the client will look to his legal and/or financial advisors to help make up the unexpected loss and, accordingly, a preacquisition audit is virtually a requirement if an attorney or accountant is to avoid malpractice liability.

As the terminology suggests, the intent of an acquisition audit is to penetrate behind the paper trail of the target company or property and determine the facts that may result in possible future liabilities, much the way an accountant's audit seeks to verify the facts against the company's balance sheets. The environmental auditor would investigate whether present and past uses of the property and surrounding areas create the potential for contamination. The environmental auditors would consider such things as: the use of hazardous substances; air emissions; storm water run-off practices; waste storage and disposal practices; prior releases of hazardous substances; and past remedial action (if any). Special problem areas, such as the use of underground storage tanks or PCB and asbestos containing equipment, would also warrant attention. In addition, because liability can extend to waste generators,[56] off-site releases and disposal of hazardous materials should also be included in the study.

§ 18.8 —What the Audit Entails

It cannot be expected that every environmental auditor will utilize the same means of evaluating potential problems, but a comprehensive

---

and steps to be taken in minimizing liability arising from the acquisition and development of land).

[55] *Cf.,* United States v. Price, 523 F. Supp. 1055 (D.N.J. 1981), *aff'd,* 688 F. 2d 204 (3d Cir. 1982). In *Price,* the United States brought suit against the current owners of property formerly used as a landfill, as well as the former owners/landfill operators, to compel cleanup of the site under the Safe Drinking Water Act (42 U.S.C. § 300i) and the Resource Conservation and Recovery Act (42 U.S.C. § 6973). Although the current owners argued that the disposal of any hazardous substances had ceased before they purchased the property, the court ruled that they could be held liable under the Safe Water Drinking Act because their actions "contributed to" the disposal. Among the factors cited by the court were the fact that the owners were aware that the property had been used for a landfill; that, as sophisticated buyers (real estate brokers and investors), the owners had an obligation to investigate the condition of the property prior to closing but deliberately chose not to; and that subsequent to the purchase the owners became aware that toxic chemicals were buried at the site but took no steps to alleviate the condition.

[56] *See, e.g.,* CERCLA, 42 U.S.C. § 9607(a).

acquisition audit[57] will most likely include the following (although not necessarily exclusively or in the order set forth):

1. A site visit for obvious signs of contamination or activities and equipment associated with environmental contamination on the site *and* contiguous property. The visit may include photographs of the site as well as samplings of the air, soil, surface waters, and groundwater.

2. A chain of title and tax record search to determine prior owners, the nature of their use of the property, and whether any representations, covenants, or indemnification agreements pertaining to the condition of the property were made.

3. Testing of pollution control devices and review of prior inspection records and test results.

4. Consultation with applicable federal and state agencies and review of agency files for current compliance and past noncompliance problems, as revealed by notice letters, release reports, inspection and monitoring records, remediation studies, complaints, judgments, and consent orders.

5. Review of local zoning, land use, and permit requirements, as well as copies of all current permits and permit applications held and submitted by the seller.

6. Meetings with the local health, building, and fire departments and review of files for reports of violations, complaints, etc.

7. Review of court records for complaints, judgments, or settlement agreements pertaining to the property.

8. Review of past environmental inspection reports and audits conducted by or in the possession of the seller.

9. Review of data regarding the seller's waste management and disposal practices.

10. Review of SEC mandated filings and disclosures.

11. Review of the seller's environmental budgets and expenditure reports.

Numerous engineering and consulting services now provide environmental audits. Although the specific qualifications of the professionals involved in any environmental audit will vary, one firm offering such services advertises that it employs professionals qualified in environmental management, hydrogeology, geology and geochemistry, chemical, civil

---

[57] For a thorough discussion of audit considerations in the context of the merger or acquisition of a business, *see* Bernstein, *Environmental Due Diligence Reviews in the Merger and Acquisition Context,* in The Impact of Environmental Regulations on Business Transaction (Practicing Law Institute 1988).

and environmental engineering, environmental and analytical toxicology and epidemiology, and hazard modeling.[58] Counsel should structure the team to include the expertise likely to be required for evaluation of the particular business or property.

§ 18.9   —Buyer's Need for Environmental Audit

Significantly, a properly conducted environmental audit can provide the purchaser with the groundwork necessary to establish defenses to future claims for antecedent environmental liability, and is essentially a prerequisite to establishing the innocent purchaser defense to a CERCLA claim.[59] Under the Superfund Amendments and Reauthorization Act of 1986 (SARA), an innocent landowner may avoid CERCLA liability if, at the time the property was acquired, he "did not know and *had no reason to know* that any hazardous substance which is the subject of the release or threatened release [for which liability is alleged] was disposed of on, in, or at the facility."[60] The statute further provides that in order to establish that the defendant property owner "had no reason to know" of the disposal of hazardous waste, he

> must have undertaken, at the time of acquisition, all appropriate inquiry into the previous ownership and uses of the property consistent with good commercial or customary practice in an effort to minimize liability. For purposes of the preceding sentence the court shall take into account any specialized knowledge or experience on the part of the defendant, the relationship of the purchase price to the value of the property if uncontaminated, commonly known or reasonably ascertainable information about the property, the obviousness of the presence or likely presence of contamination at the property, and the ability to detect such contamination by appropriate inspection.[61]

Of course, if contamination is discovered and the transaction is nevertheless consummated the defense will no longer be available.[62]

---

[58] Arthur D. Little, Inc., Cambridge, Massachusetts.

[59] 42 U.S.C. § 9601(35).

[60] *Id.* § 9601(35)(A)(i) (emphasis added).

[61] *Id.* § 9601(35)(B).

[62] It should be noted that CERCLA imposes a greater standard of liability upon current owners or operators of property than on former owners or operators. A former owner or operator can be liable only if there is a release or threatened release of a hazardous substance which was disposed of during its period of ownership or use. *See* 42 U.S.C. § 9607(a)(2). A current owner or operator, on the other hand, can be liable for *any* release of a hazardous substance, *See id.* § 9607(a)(i).

In addition to addressing concerns of liability for contamination, the environmental audit can be employed to determine whether the business or property being acquired currently complies with applicable regulatory requirements and, equally as important, whether the business or property can be operated or used in the manner intended by the buyer or tenant. Again, the client would legitimately look to hold his attorney liable if he is fined for the seller's noncompliance or he is unable to use the property as he had intended because of an inability to transfer necessary permits. Even though contractual representations of the seller may enable the buyer or lessee to rescind the contract under such circumstances, a preacquisition audit would eliminate the problem.

§ 18.10   —Seller's Need for Environmental Audit

Most of the foregoing sections address concerns of the buyer of a business or land, but the seller should also consider conducting its own environmental audit, because inattention to environmental concerns can be extremely costly to the seller as well. First, the transaction may be governed by divestiture statutes such as New Jersey's Environmental Cleanup Responsibility Act (ECRA),[63] which requires the seller to demonstrate that prior to sale that there has been no release of hazardous substances on its property or, if there was, either that it has been cleaned up or a cleanup plan with adequate financial security has been approved by the Department of Environmental Protection (DEP).[64] In the event of noncompliance, the buyer may recover from the seller the costs of remediation and both DEP and the buyer may rescind the sale.[65]

However, even if an environmental audit is not mandatory, it is nevertheless advisable, especially if the purchaser intends to continue to operate the same business or make a similar use of the property. A thorough environmental audit can create a record that the property conveyed was "clean" at the time of conveyance, and hence the burden for subsequent environmental liability shifts to the purchaser and its successors. For instance, under CERCLA, a former property owner or operator is liable only if there is a release or threatened release of a hazardous substance which was disposed on the property during the period of that party's ownership or use of the property.[66] By establishing an environmental benchmark as of the time possession is relinquished, the environmental

---

[63] *See* N.J. Stat. Ann. §§ 13:1K-6 to -14; *see also* Conn. Gen Stat. title 22a; Cal. Health & Safety Code § 25359.7(a).

[64] N.J. Stat. Ann. § 13:1K-6 to -14.

[65] *Id.* § 13:1K-13(a).

[66] 42 U.S.C. § 9607(a)(2).

audit forms the predicate for the defense. This not only benefits the seller but helps the attorney to avoid liability to his client. Like the buyer who sues his attorney after learning that he unknowingly purchased environmental liability, the disgruntled seller who learned that he retained environmental liability following his sale is likely to look to his attorney for relief.

Another advantage to the seller is that by conducting its own environmental audit, it can possibly limit the scope of the buyer's audit and the degree of disruption of the seller's operations. The seller who conducts a presale environmental audit will also be in a better position to decide upon the representations and warranties it is willing to give. If environmental liability or potential liability is discovered, the seller may wish to correct the problem itself (hopefully without the need for government oversight) or reduce the asking price proportionally. Finally, the completed environmental audit may be a useful selling tool.

Thus, the earlier in the transaction the environmental audit is conducted, the better for both the buyer and the seller. It must be kept in mind that one of the paramount purposes of an environmental audit is to ascertain potential liability so that the risk of loss may be allocated among the parties.[67] If the environmental audit is conducted during, or prior to, the contract negotiation phase, the agreement can then be drafted based upon concrete facts rather than conjecture and surmise, and the parties will be better protected.

Although some sellers may believe it is contrary to their best interests to, in effect, trigger reporting or cleanup obligations that may not otherwise have been required, it can reasonably be expected that the buyer will conduct his own environmental audit, thereby rendering the issue moot.

§ 18.11   —Property Owner's Need for Environmental Audit

Even if no acquisition or sale is contemplated, the property or business owner may nonetheless find an environmental audit is warranted. For instance, the environmental regulations in effect may already impose an

---

[67] Liability for CERCLA and RCRA claims, however, is absolute, and the seller's transfer of liability to the buyer is ineffective against third parties or the EPA. *See, e.g.,* Lyncott Corp. v. Chemical Waste Management Co., 690 F. Supp. 1409 (E.D. Pa. 1988); Chemical Waste Management, Inc. v. Armstrong World Industries, Inc. 669 F. Supp. 1285 (E.D. Pa. 1987). Nevertheless, the courts will enforce releases or indemnification agreements entered into between the parties. *See, e.g.,* Mardan Corp. v. C.G.C. Music, Ltd., 804 F.2d 1454 (9th Cir. 1986).

affirmative obligation to monitor and report environmental activities.[68] An environmental self-assessment can ensure compliance with the various federal, state, and local environmental regulations and ordinances, including right to know laws,[69] and hence prevent fines or penalties for noncompliance. A compliance audit could also investigate whether all conditions and requirements for the issuance and maintenance of necessary permits have been satisfied. Another type of audit may have as its goal compliance with SEC disclosure requirements, with the focus on potential litigation, remediation, and compliance costs.

§ 18.12   The Role of the Accountant in the Environmental Audit Process

In connection with evaluation of an environmental audit conducted by legal counsel, an accountant is typically utilized to analyze the financial consequences associated with the investment in new equipment or the commencement of cleanup activities.

An accountant can determine the accuracy and reasonableness of estimated costs of remedial solutions proposed by the government and potentially responsible parties. This task can be accomplished by reviewing the engineers' cost estimates and comparing these anticipated costs to industry standard costs. An accountant can also compare the EPA's estimated costs for remedial solutions at a site to EPA's estimated or actual costs of similar recommended solutions at other sites. Additionally, the accountant can develop financial models to provide what-if analyses to key assumptions underlying the cost estimates for various recommended remedial solutions.

The accountant can establish systems and controls to substantiate costs for allocation to appropriate sites and potentially responsible parties. It is also important to establish a system to capture the necessary information and documentation so that claims for potential reimbursement of costs can be completed accurately.

---

[68] For example, New Jersey's statutory scheme includes the Worker and Community Right to Know Act, N.J. Stat. Ann. §§ 34:5A-1 to -31, which requires the disclosure of information about hazardous substances used in the workplace; the Toxic Catastrophe Prevention Act, N.J. Stat. Ann. §§ 13:1K-15 to -32, which requires companies handling certain specified hazardous substances to prepare and submit plans to assess, manage and reduce the risk of the release of such substances; and the Comprehensive Regulated Medical Waste Management Act, N.J. Stat. Ann. §§ 13:1E-48.1 to -48.25, which requires registration and record keeping by generators, haulers and operators of facilities disposing of medical waste.

[69] *See, e.g.,* N.J. Stat. Ann. § 34:5A-1 to -31. (Worker and Community Right to Know Act).

A cost allocation system should incorporate the relevant information to produce a meaningful analysis and equitable cost distribution. This procedure usually commences with the identification of potentially responsible parties for allocation purposes and the establishment of key allocation factors, such as toxicity, volume, and mobility. Expenses are identified and categorized as either fixed or variable prior to the allocation of the applicable factors. After the costs have been allocated to the potentially responsible parties, a cost report is then issued to each respective party.

An accountant can be retained to analyze the EPA's penalty determination for violations. The EPA's penalty policy is based upon the economic benefit derived by an entity due to its failure to comply with an EPA regulation. A computerized financial model can be created for such penalty determination in order to enable companies to analyze the sensitivity of various underlying assumptions. This type of information can be extremely useful to a company during the negotiation process.

§ 18.13 The Role of the Attorney in the Environmental Audit Process

It is advisable to have an attorney on the audit team, because one of the primary goals of most environmental audits is to provide the client with a legal analysis of potential liability. Obviously, the attorney's expertise is required to evaluate the facts disclosed by the audit in view of the applicable statutes, regulations, and permit requirements. The attorney is in the best position to communicate with the regulatory agencies and prepare the applications necessary for the issuance or transfer of any required permits. In addition, the information obtained from the audit must be evaluated from a legal perspective in order to determine whether disclosure must be made to regulatory authorities, to the other party to the transaction, or, in the case of a publicly held company, to the public via SEC mandated financial disclosure.

If the attorney participates in the planning and implementation of the audit, he can ensure that the investigation generates only the information needed to satisfy the purpose of the audit. More importantly, counsel can ensure that the audit is conducted in a manner that best preserves the benefits of the attorney-client and attorney work-product privileges.

Under the rationale espoused by the Supreme Court in *Upjohn Co. v. United States*,[70] the *facts* that are uncovered during the course of the

---

[70] 449 U.S. 383 (1981). In *Upjohn*, after independent accountants discovered during an audit that one of its foreign subsidiaries had made questionable payments to foreign officials, Upjohn conducted an internal investigation. Questionnaires were sent to

environmental audit would not be exempt from disclosure, but *communications* made by the client or the client's employees during the course of the audit (so long as they are necessary for the client to receive legal advice and are kept confidential) would be privileged, provided:

1. An attorney has been retained to render legal advice
2. The communications were made to the attorney to enable the attorney to render legal advice
3. The communications are kept confidential
4. There has not been a waiver of the privilege.

The attorney's notes and memoranda concerning the audit would likewise be exempt from disclosure under the *Upjohn* case, as attorney work-product. In addition, under certain circumstances, it may even be possible to shield the audit itself from disclosure pursuant to the work-product doctrine, provided that:

1. The audit was conducted under the supervision of an attorney
2. It was prepared in anticipation of litigation[71]
3. It contains the "mental impressions, conclusions, opinions or legal theories" of the attorney
4. The protection has not been waived.[72]

§ 18.14   Contractual Considerations

Certainly the primary area in which counsel must protect the client (and, by definition, protect himself by fulfilling his obligations to the client) is in drafting the agreement to provide whatever protection may be possible in light of potential environmental liabilities disclosed in the environmental audit.

---

managers of Upjohn's foreign affiliates requesting that details of any such payments be sent to the company's counsel. In addition, counsel questioned the foreign managers and certain of Upjohn's officers and employees. Following the submission to the SEC of reports disclosing the payments, the IRS demanded production of all files regarding the investigation, including the questionnaires and any notes or memoranda.

The Supreme Court held that the questionnaires and any responses to interview questions were protected from disclosure by the attorney-client privilege because the communications were made to an attorney to secure legal advice. The Court also held that the attorney's notes and memoranda were protected as attorney work-product.

[71] In order to establish that the audit was prepared in anticipation of litigation, the attorney and his client should document potential litigation and enforcement proceedings prior to the auditing process.

[72] *See, e.g.,* Hickman v. Taylor, 329 U.S. 495 (1947); Fed. R. Civ. P. 26(b)(3).

For example, the contract may provide that if significant potential environmental liability is revealed, the buyer has the right to rescind the contract. Another option may be a provision to carve geographically or departmentally the environmentally problematic areas from the deal. Alternatively, the seller himself may elect to take the steps necessary to clean up the site and/or bring it into compliance. Other possibilities would be provisions to reduce the purchase price by the amount of estimated remediation or compliance costs, or to have a portion of the purchase price deposited in escrow to fund the remediation or compliance process. This is an area in which the accountant's estimate of costs will be crucial.

Regardless of the means chosen, it is essential that the contract expressly make clear the nature and extent of each party's liability. Any conditions precedent, and the remedy for breach thereof, should be clearly spelled out. Conditions may include the right to conduct an audit, with details as to the degree of access and cooperation from the other party; the absence of environmental contamination (with specific standards as to what constitutes contamination); the seller's compliance with all applicable statutes and regulations (except as specifically excluded); and the ability to transfer and/or obtain all necessary permits for the intended use. If the seller is to take steps to remediate contamination or to bring the property into compliance, definite timetables and objectively quantifiable standards should be recited.

The buyer will want the contract to include representations and warranties from the seller specifically providing that, except as explicitly set forth in the contract itself or schedules appended thereto, no environmental problems exist at the site; the seller has not used, generated, or disposed of hazardous wastes on the property; the property is and was at all times during seller's possession in compliance with all environmental laws; there are no pending or threatened environmental claims or enforcement actions; and the seller is in possession of all required permits.

The contract should set forth in detail the terms of any indemnification[73] or escrow agreements with respect to any past, present, and future environmental liabilities. CERCLA expressly provides that a private indemnity agreement cannot affect the liability of an otherwise responsible party, but it also provides that nothing in CERCLA prohibits a purchaser or anyone else from securing an indemnity.[74] Any known environmental problems which are to be included or excluded should be expressly stated.

---

[73] In order to avoid excessive or unwarranted claims for indemnification, the seller may insist that the buyer agree to share the costs on a percentage basis or to expend a specified dollar amount before the obligation to indemnify arises. An example of a "shared liability" clause is included in § **18.15**.

[74] 42 U.S.C. § 9607(e).

Section 18.15 hereto contains provisions from a contract for the purchase of a company in the chemical manufacturing business. While the sample contains only suggested provisions, which must of course be modified to the facts and circumstances of the specific transaction, the provisions are indicators of items to be considered in such a context.[75]

§ 18.15 Sample Provisions from Purchase Contract

The following is an example of the types of clauses that should be included in a typical purchase agreement for an environmentally sensitive business, in this case a chemical manufacturer.

3.16 *Contracts*. Schedule 3.16 is a list of all written contracts, commitments, personal property leases, and other written agreements to which any of the Corporations [being conveyed by seller] is a party and which meet the criteria set forth in paragraphs (a) through (k) below, true and complete copies of which have been made available to Buyer:

* * *

(f) involve the handling, treatment, storage, transportation, recycling, reclamation, or disposal of hazardous wastes or substances generated by or related to the Business;

3.17 *Health and Safety Conditions*. Schedule 3.17 sets forth the following:

(i)   current Material Safety Data Sheets for the current products of the Business;

(ii)   product labels for the current products of the Business;

(iii) internal health and safety audits of the Corporations with respect to the properties or assets of the Business from January 1, 1983;

(iv)   a summary of epidemiological data since January 1, 1981 possessed by the Corporations and related to the Business;

(v)   a summary of toxicological studies conducted by or on behalf of the Corporations and related to the Business;

(vi)   industrial hygiene surveys of the Corporations with respect to the properties or assets of the Business for the years 1984, 1985 and 1986;

(vii)   a summary of personnel safety statistics of the Corporations with respect to the properties or assets of the Business for each year since January, 1981;

---

[75] *See also* Newman, *How to Counsel the Land Developer on Superfund and Superliens,* 34 The Practical Lawyer 13, (Oct. 1988), which provides sample clauses dealing with the issue of hazardous substances in sales and leases of real property.

(viii) all annual summaries of workers' compensation liabilities relating to the Business prepared by . . . [or] for the Corporations from January 1, 1983 through December 31, 1985; and

(ix)   a history of Toxic Substances Control Act and Occupational Safety and Health Act actions with respect to facilities of the Business since January 1, 1981.

To Seller's knowledge, the information contained in the documents listed in this Section 3.17 is true, correct, and complete in all material respects. To Seller's knowledge, except as set forth on Schedules 3.17 and 3.21, each of the Corporations, in connection with their operation of the Business, is in substantial compliance with all applicable foreign, federal, state, and local occupational health and safety laws, rules, and regulations.

3.18   *Environmental Conditions.*
Schedule 3.18 sets forth the following:

(i)   all facilities for the treatment, storage, and disposal of wastes and waste products currently owned or used in the Business and located on the Real Property; all waste disposal sites on the Real Property which are or have been owned or used by the Corporations (or their predecessors in interest); and all underground storage tanks, as defined in 40 C.F.R. § 260.10, located on the Real Property which are or were owned or used by the Corporations (or their predecessors in interest). As to each facility, site, or underground storage tank, Schedule 3.18 describes the time period used and the type of waste treated, stored, or disposed, or, in the case of underground storage tanks, the type of material stored;

(ii)   all spills, leaks, or losses of hazardous or other similar substances occurring on or from the Real Property since January 1, 1984 and reported to foreign, federal, state, or local authorities pursuant to requirements of RCRA, CERCLA, or similar foreign, federal, state, and local statutes, laws, ordinances, rules, or regulations;

(iii)   all internal environmental audits conducted by the Corporations since January 1, 1985, relating to the Business;

(iv)   and other environmental conditions on the Real Property, including treatment, storage or disposal of waste products.

To Seller's knowledge, the information contained in the documents listed in this Section is true, correct, and complete in all material respects. Except as set forth on Schedules 3.18 and 3.21, there is not pending, nor, to Seller's knowledge, is there now threatened, any suit, complaint, or administrative action alleging that any of the Corporations in connection with their operations of the Business on the Real Property is in violation of Environmental Laws (as defined in Section 13.2(a)(ii)) or that any of the Corporations in connection with their operations of the Business on the Real Property is a party responsible for remedial action pursuant to RCRA, CERCLA, FIFRA, or similar foreign, federal, state, and local statutes, laws, ordinances, rules, and regulations, or otherwise relating to the treatment, storage, or disposal of waste or waste products or spills, leaks, or losses of hazardous or other similar substances occurring on or from the Real Property with respect to the Business, that if decided adversely would have a material adverse effect on the assets, properties, business, prospects, or condition of the Business (financial or otherwise). Except as disclosed on Schedule 3.18, none of the Corporations is in default under or in violation of any Environmental Laws, judgments, orders, or decrees with respect to the Business, except for such defaults or violations, if any, that in the aggregate do not and will not materially adversely affect the property, operations, financial condition, or prospects of the Business. Except as disclosed on Schedule 3.18, the Business is in substantial compliance with all applicable Environmental Laws.

3.19   *Permits, Registrations, Licenses, etc.*
(a) Schedule 3.19 sets forth the following: . . .

   (iv)   All other governmental permits, licenses, approvals, certificates of inspection, filings, and registrations issued to or held by the Corporations with respect to the Business and material to the conduct of the Business. To Seller's knowledge, none of the governmental permits, licenses, approvals, certificates of inspection, filings, or registrations listed on Schedule 3.19, except as may be set forth therein, will terminate or lapse by reason of the consummation of the transactions contemplated hereby or by the Supplemental Agreements. Except as set forth on Schedule 3.19, to Seller's knowledge there are no other material governmental licenses, permits, franchises, registrations, and other governmental authorizations that are currently required for the lawful operation of the Business and that are material to the Business.

USE OF ACCOUNTANTS AND ATTORNEYS TO MINIMIZE PAST LIABILITY

§ 18.16   Counselling Clients Once Environmental Damage Occurs

Of course, the accountant and attorney can best reduce potential liability to their clients and third parties for past incidents by ensuring that the client's liability is either eliminated or reduced to the maximum extent legally permissible. Other chapters in this book deal with specific types of clients, such as property owners, lenders, waste generators, and waste haulers, and specific types of liability, such as those under CERCLA, state environmental statutes, and common law. Once an environmental damage has occurred, the role of the attorney or accountant in minimizing damages is not dissimilar from the roles played by such professionals in any civil/criminal litigation in which a client faces a substantial exposure. Counsel must, with the assistance of company personnel and retained experts, conduct an investigation into the underlying events, identify potential plaintiffs and codefendants, and begin to structure the litigation response. Accountants are involved in estimating remediation costs, the financing for them, and estimating the impact on the business. These are standard roles for these professionals, and it is beyond the scope of this single chapter to discuss the general response of the attorney or accountant in the aftermath of environmental contamination. However, an environmental problem does involve specific issues that must be considered by the professional. The following sections focus briefly on some of these issues of special concern.

§ 18.17   Creating the Insurance Profile and Ensuring Notice to All Possibly Liable Insurers

In nearly all situations involving potential liability for the release of a hazardous substance, one of the first and most important tasks the attorney should perform is to obtain the client's insurance policies and ascertain the client's environmental liability insurance coverage. Specific exclusions and disclaimers for environmental claims are discussed more fully in **Chapter 15**. If the client has not already done so, an insurance profile should be prepared identifying, inter alia, the names of the carriers, coverage periods, policy limits, and exclusions. The client's insurance broker may be able to provide missing policies or information to fill in any gaps. In certain circumstances, the existence and scope of coverage can be established through the use of correspondence and claim files if the policies themselves are unavailable.

Once the insurance profile has been prepared, the attorney should confirm that notification has been given to all carriers from the date on which the substance was first disposed on the property (whether such disposal was intentional or not) to the date of the release or the date on which notice of the release was given to the insured.[76] Attention should also be given to notifying a third party's insurers if, by virtue of a contractual relationship or otherwise, the client may be an additional insured or beneficiary under the third party's policy.

§ 18.18   Damage Control by Public Relations Response

Environmental contamination events involving issues of public health and safety are often the focus of intense publicity and demand an orchestrated

---

[76] Untimely notice to insurance carriers could result in denial of coverage. *See, e.g.,* Olin Corp. v. Insurance Co. of N. Am., No. 84-1968 (S.D.N.Y. Aug. 2, 1990) (WESTLAW, Allfeds library).

public relations response by the company involved. We would suggest the lawyer or accountant not serve as the public spokesman; unfortunately, professionals are often not considered credible by the general public.

The focus of the company's public comments should be on what is being done to remedy the situation. Rather than blanket statements of responsibility, specific acts undertaken by the company and plans for further action should be stressed. Obviously, counsel should advise the client to avoid damaging admissions regarding the cause of the accident. On the other hand, for goodwill reasons, the company will be under considerable pressure to make public information regarding the cause of the problem.

Clearly, this is a case-by-case decision based on the particular circumstances, and no hard and fast guidelines are available. Nevertheless, following Johnson & Johnson's success in responding to the Tylenol tamperings and Union Carbide's prompt response to the Bhopal, India gas leak, substantial literature has been written on the issue of public relations/damage control response, and should be consulted.[77] The critical lesson to be learned, however, is that a crisis management plan should be prepared well before anything goes wrong.

§ 18.19   Using the Accountant in Superfund Litigation

The EPA ranks waste sites according to the severity of the waste problem. Hazardous wastes and toxic materials are the focus of legislation and regulations dedicated to managing and enforcing cleanup of the environment. The complex task of identifying the required cost and financial responsibility for the cleanup of a site often results in litigation.

The accountant can be engaged to perform a review on the allocation of costs and expenses among the parties responsible for the cleanup of a contaminated site. This review includes such items as the appropriateness of cost allocations, the adequacy of the incurred cost determination, and additional cost resulting from multiple layers of contractors. The EPA, Department of Justice, and their contractors allocate their indirect costs to individual sites; each one of them in all likelihood utilizes a different cost allocation method. The method currently used by the EPA allocates indirect costs based on direct labor hours incurred at individual sites by regional EPA personnel. This allocation method should be analyzed to determine whether the inclusion of certain costs is appropriate and

---

[77] *See, e.g.,* Ruskin, *The Threat of Toxic Torts,* Management Review 50 (June 1990); Yagoda, *Cleaning Up a Dirty Image,* Business Month 58 (April 1990); Stanton, *Crisis 89: Lessons Learned,* Public Relations Journal 15 (Sept. 1989).

whether the mathematical computation of their cost component is valid and accurate.

The EPA typically prepares a summary cost documentation package to support its incurred cost claim for a particular site. This documentation would normally include bid records, contract/statement of work, work orders, invoices, payment vouchers, program reports, stop work orders, and the like. The EPA has contracted with several companies to perform cleanup procedures at numerous Superfund sites throughout the United States and will bill its contractors based on a single monthly invoice for work at all sites. The report by the Office of Technical Assessment, entitled *Assessing Contractor Use in Superfund,* stated:

> Redundant contractor work, poorly defined work by the government, greater use of less experienced people, poorly supervised work that leads to late recognition of problems, greater concerns about being criticized which lead to unnecessary, defensive work, and changing agency policies and personnel all probably contribute to high government cleanup costs. From looking at actual costs and speaking to contractors and PRPs, we find it plausible that the government may spend from 100 to 500 percent more than a private client would spend to accomplish essentially the same site study or cleanup.[78]

The accountant would review the propriety of the proportion used by the contractor in detailing expenditures at each site. Additionally, the allocation of expense analysis would involve other factors such as each party's financial resources and insurance coverages. An accountant can analyze alternative compliance practices and prioritize the cost/benefit of certain procedures and methods by utilizing computer technology.

The accountant also can be involved in the formulation of various financial models to determine which particular cleanup strategy would be the most cost effective.

The government seeks reimbursement for funds expended by the EPA for cleanup of the hazardous site as well as for funds expended by the U.S. Department of Justice in enforcement activities. Besides cleanup costs, the government and its contractors may incur and seek reimbursement for costs in preremedial activities, such as costs to secure the site, costs to determine the nature and extent of contamination, and costs incurred to perform feasibility studies prior to the selection of a cleanup remedy. A Government Accounting Office (GAO) Report, entitled *Superfund Contracts—EPA Needs to Control Contractor Costs,* found that:

> [The] EPA has not sufficiently monitored, controlled, and challenged contractor expenditures and professional hour usage for remedial studies.

---

[78] Office of Technical Assessment (OTA) Report, *Assessing Contractor Use in Superfund* (Jan. 1989).

. . . In over 50 percent of the 43 sites GAO reviewed, inadequate contractor or subcontractor performance, as determined by EPA, increased the cost of performing the remedial studies. EPA did not, however, challenge questionable costs for most of these increased although it has options for doing so. By not consistently and fully challenging questionable contractor costs, EPA could be conveying a message to contractors that it is willing to accept all costs regardless of the level of performance provided, thereby lessening the contractor's incentives to control costs. As a result, EPA may be paying more than needed for remedial studies.[79]

In cases in which the EPA has expended funds to clean up a hazardous waste site and seeks to recover the costs and damages incurred, the accountant can be engaged to review, analyze, and question the validity of such costs. Additionally, companies may be required to pay fines or penalties, or to reimburse expenses and costs. An accountant can review the financial and tax consequences of certain accounting approaches, such as capitalization versus expensing of such costs. Ideally, settlements should be structured to derive the most advantageous economic solution by minimizing the adverse effect on the company's cash flow.

Further, the accountant can establish systems and controls to substantiate costs for allocation to appropriate sites and potentially responsible parties. Another important tactic that should be considered is the establishment of a system to capture the necessary information and documentation so that claims for potential reimbursement of costs can be accurately computed.

A cost allocation system should incorporate the relevant information to produce a meaningful analysis and equitable cost distribution. This procedure usually commences with the identification of potentially responsible parties for allocation purposes and the establishment of key allocation factors (toxicity, volume, and mobility). Expenses are subsequently identified and categorized as either fixed or variable before allocating the applicable factors. After the costs have been assigned to the potentially responsible parties, a cost report is then issued to each respective party.

An accountant can be retained to analyze the EPA's penalty determination for violations. This EPA policy is based upon the economic benefit derived by an entity due to its failure to comply with an EPA regulation. A computerized financial model can be created for such penalty determination in order to enable companies to analyze the sensitivity of various underlying assumptions. This type of information can be extremely useful to a company during the negotiation process.

---

[79] GAO Report, *Superfund Contracts—EPA Needs to Controi Contractor Costs* (July 1988).

PART IV

REMEDYING THE SITUATION

CHAPTER 19

REMEDIES FOR ENVIRONMENTAL PROBLEMS

Martin E. Gilmore
John E. Schulz

Martin E. Gilmore is a managing associate in the San Francisco, California, office of Coopers & Lybrand and is the director of the Engineering and Construction/Hazardous Waste Practice. He consults with owners of hazardous waste sites concerning organization and execution of remediation projects. His previous experience includes fifteen years as a design manager and project manager for industrial process plant design and construction. Prior to joining Coopers & Lybrand, Mr. Gilmore was a project manager for Bechtel Environmental, Inc., planning and managing environmental remediation projects and chemical waste treatment plant design. He is a registered professional engineer, and holds an M.S. in chemical engineering from Stanford University.

John E. Schulz is senior environmental counsel for Bechtel National, Inc. and Bechtel Environmental, Inc., San Francisco, California. He joined Bechtel in May 1988 after prosecuting superfund litigation for the U.S. Department of Justice. Mr. Schulz, who specializes in environmental compliance counseling, government affairs work, and environmental risk evaluation, is one of the few specialty lawyers at Bechtel. Formerly editor in chief of the *Environmental Law Reporter,* Mr. Schulz is a member of the ABA's Natural Resources Section, the California bar and the Federal Action Committee of the Hazardous Waste Action Coalition. He received his bachelor's degree from Princeton and his J.D. from Yale Law School.

§ 19.1   Introduction

This chapter addresses both the legal and technical aspects of remedying environmental contamination by hazardous materials. The legal aspects include identification of hazardous materials, cleanup standards and procedures, and treatment/disposal requirements. The technical aspects include sources of contaminants, treatment methods, disposal and containment, waste reduction/recycling/reuse, and handling of asbestos.

LEGAL ASPECTS

§ 19.2   Statutory Basis

Depending primarily on the substances involved and the characteristics of the contaminated site, one of three federal (and any comparable state) statutory schemes governs environmental cleanups. The federal laws are the Comprehensive Environmental Response, Compensation and Liability Act (CERCLA or Superfund);[1] the Solid Waste Disposal Act, as amended by the Resource Conservation and Recovery Act (RCRA);[2] for PCBs only, the Toxic Substances Control Act (TSCA);[3] and for asbestos only, the Clean Air Act (CAA)[4] or the Asbestos Hazard Emergency Response Act (AHERA).[5]

§ 19.3   CERCLA Cleanups

Sites subject to CERCLA are primarily those that do not presently receive waste shipments. In other words, CERCLA focuses on former dumpsites. Frequently, but not invariably, CERCLA sites are abandoned. This contrasts with the active disposal facilities regulated under RCRA with its elaborate system of permits and regulations. Again in contrast to RCRA facilities, which usually have one owner, many firms are associated with the typical CERCLA site: all those that previously disposed of hazardous materials there, certain firms that transported wastes there, and all or most owners and operators over the history of the site. Such CERCLA-liable parties are known as potentially responsible parties, or PRPs.

The foregoing does not mean that abandoned sites are not also subject to RCRA. Indeed, EPA relied on RCRA to secure cleanups of such facilities before the enactment of CERCLA in 1980. Even now, some facilities are subject to both laws, and their owners may within limits have the power to determine which law they must obey. See **§§ 19.10 and 19.11** for discussion of this situation and the pros and cons of each law.

The substances subject to CERCLA are called *hazardous substances* and *pollutants or contaminants*. They are defined in CERCLA §§ 101(14) (42 U.S.C. § 9601(14) and 101(33) (42 U.S.C. § 9601(33)). The hazardous

---

[1] 42 U.S.C. §§ 9601–9675 (1988).

[2] 42 U.S.C. §§ 6901–6992.

[3] 15 U.S.C. §§ 2601–2629.

[4] 42 U.S.C. §§ 7401–7626.

[5] 20 U.S.C. §§ 4014, 4021.

substance definition primarily references the toxics provisions of RCRA, CAA, the Federal Water Pollution Control Act, and other federal laws. A complete list of the more than 1,300 CERCLA hazardous substances is set forth in 40 C.F.R. part 302. It includes all radionuclides, which are also governed by the Atomic Energy Act, and many chemical substances also covered by RCRA.

Under CERCLA, *pollutant or contaminant* includes any material that, upon release into the environment, may cause disease, death, behavioral abnormalities, cancer, genetic mutation, physiological malfunctions (including malfunctions in reproduction), or physical deformations in any organism or its offspring.

Some major categories of toxic chemicals are excluded from CERCLA, although they often are within the coverage of state laws otherwise resembling CERCLA. Most prominently, the terms hazardous substance and pollutant or contaminant do not include "petroleum, including crude oil or any fraction thereof which is not otherwise specifically listed or designated as a hazardous substance under subparagraphs (A) through (F) of this paragraph [RCRA, CAA, FWPCA, etc.]."[6] There is also an exclusion for "natural gas, natural gas liquids, liquefied natural gas, or synthetic gas usable for fuel (or mixtures of natural gas and such synthetic gas)."[7]

§ 19.4 —Stages, Standards, and Procedures in Cleanup Process

The following discussion generally refers to the "lead agency" as carrying out cleanups. The term usually means the Environmental Protection Agency (EPA), but it also refers to other federal agencies in cases in which federal facilities are contaminated and must carry out cleanups under CERCLA.

CERCLA also authorizes private parties to carry out cleanups. If they do so in a manner "consistent with CERCLA," they may recover their costs from other PRPs under CERCLA § 107(a)(4)(B). The 1990 revision of the National Contingency Plan (NCP), EPA's blueprint for the conduct of hazardous materials cleanups, eased the required showing for consistency with the NCP. Previously, the private party who cleaned up had to demonstrate compliance with specific NCP provisions. Under the new NCP, consistency with the NCP requires only a showing that the cleanup, when evaluated as a whole, achieved "substantial compliance" with generally applicable NCP requirements and resulted in a CERCLA-quality cleanup.[8]

---

[6] CERCLA §§ 101(14), (33), 42 U.S.C. §§ 9601(14), (33).

[7] *Id.*

[8] 40 C.F.R. § 300.700(c)(3) (1990).

The March 1990 NCP, 40 CFR part 300, specifies the following stages for such work:

1. Removal site evaluation (possibly followed by one or more removals)
2. Remedial site evaluation, including a preliminary assessment (PA) and a site inspection (SI)
3. Remedial investigation (RI), followed by feasibility study (FS)
4. Remedial design (RD)
5. Remedial action (RA).

In this list, removals and RAs are classes of remedies. The procedures for and constraints on remedy selection vary dramatically according to which of them is involved. *Removals* are early, emergency actions designed to cope with urgent risks to the public or the environment. As such, they are relatively unencumbered with procedural requirements. By contrast, *RAs* must meet often stringent cleanup standards and comply with frequently onerous procedures for state and public involvement.

CERCLA and the NCP require immediate reporting of spills or releases of hazardous materials. Upon receipt, the National Response Center (NRC) must notify the On Scene Coordinator (OSC) and, if radioactive materials are present, the EPA Radiological Response Coordinator. The OSC or a private party conducting the response, then immediately determines whether a removal or RA should be undertaken.

§ 19.5 —Removals

The procedures for determining the need for and conducting of removals are in subpart E of the NCP at 40 C.F.R. §§ 300.410 and .415. They mandate prompt action to eliminate the release and include expedited assessment of site hazards and prompt selection and implementation of the removal action.

Specifically, the lead agency must undertake a *removal site evaluation* as promptly as possible. This includes a removal preliminary assessment, based on readily available information, which may, among other things, addresses

1. Identification of the source and nature of the release or threat of release
2. Evaluation by EPA's Agency for Toxic Substances and Disease Registry (ATSDR) or by others, such as state public health agencies, of the threat to public health
3. Evaluation of the magnitude of the threat

4. Evaluation of factors necessary to make the decision as to whether a removal is necessary
5. Determination of whether a nonfederal party is undertaking proper response.

At the same time, the agency must make an effort to locate PRPs and determine whether they will conduct the removal.

The NCP lists the following factors as related to determining the need for a removal:

1. Exposure to nearby human populations, animals, or the food chain from hazardous substances, pollutants, or contaminants (*hazardous materials*)
2. Contamination of drinking water supplies or sensitive ecosystems
3. Hazardous materials in drums, barrels, tanks, or other bulk storage containers, that may pose a threat of release
4. High levels of hazardous materials in soils, largely at or near the surface, that may migrate
5. Weather conditions that may cause hazardous materials to migrate or be released
6. Threat of fire or explosion
7. Availability of other federal or state mechanisms to respond to the release
8. Other situations or factors that may pose threats to public health or welfare or the environment.

If the lead agency determines that a removal is appropriate, it must begin as soon as possible to abate, prevent, minimize, stabilize, mitigate, or eliminate the threat. The agency must, in addition, determine whether or not it has at least six months to plan the removal before on-site activities must begin. If it does have six months, the agency must conduct an engineering evaluation/cost analysis (EE/CA) to evaluate removal alternatives for the site. Also, it must follow prescribed procedures if environmental samples are to be collected. Actually, very few removals involve such a six-month planning period.

The NCP includes a nonexhaustive list of "typical" removals that may be undertaken if needed to control releases. These include:

1. Site control methods such as fences, warning signs
2. Drainage controls, such as run-off or run-on diversion
3. Stabilization of berms, dikes, or impoundments, or drainage or closing of lagoons

4. Capping contaminated soils/sludges, in order to reduce migration

5. Use of chemicals or other means to retard spread of release or mitigate its effects

6. Excavation, consolidation, or removal of highly contaminated soils from drainage or other areas

7. Removal of drums, barrels, tanks, or other bulk containers thought to contain hazardous materials

8. Containment, treatment, disposal, or incineration of hazardous materials

9. Provision of alternate water supplies.

A removal may be funded by the Superfund whether or not the site involved is on the National Priorities List (NPL). For non-NPL sites, however, such funding must terminate after $2 million has been obligated or 12 months have elapsed since the commencement of on-site activities. This ceiling is waived if the lead agency determines that (1) continuation is immediately needed to prevent, limit, or mitigate an emergency involving an immediate risk to public health or welfare or to the environment; and (2) such continuation is consistent with the long-term RA to be taken at the site. The NCP also stipulates that, to the extent practicable prior to commencing a Fund-financed removal, the lead agency must make provision for post-removal site control to insure the integrity of the removal. Such control may be conducted by PRPs, the affected state or subdivision, or EPA for Fund-financed RAs (at NPL sites only).

There are Community Relations (CR) requirements for removals, including compilation and public opportunity to scrutinize the administrative record. The extent of the required CR procedures turns on the same distinction referenced above, that is, whether a planning period of at least six months exists prior to required initiation of on-site removal activities.

To the extent practicable considering the exigencies of the situation, Fund-financed removals must attain stringent applicable or relevant and appropriate requirements (ARARs) for cleanup standards under federal environmental laws or state environmental or facility siting laws. However, in contrast with RAs, the "practicability" limitation excludes many ARARs, particularly when there is not sufficient time to identify them before the removal must commence. Waivers of ARARs are also more likely to be available in removal situations than in the case of RAs. In this regard, the preamble to the new NCP emphasizes that removals are intended to be responses to near-term threats, and that if attainment of ARARs might delay rapid response, or cause the response to exceed removal goals, ARARs may be waived as impracticable.[9] The same discussion reports

---

[9] 55 Fed. Reg. 8696 (1990).

that EPA is developing guidance on the process of complying with ARARs during removals.

If the lead agency determines that the removal will not fully address the threat posed by the release, and the release may require RA, the lead agency must assure an orderly transition from removal to RA activities. We now turn to RAs and the more elaborate procedural requirements and standards governing them.

§ 19.6 —Remedial Actions

In the words of the new NCP,[10] RAs are

> actions consistent with [a] permanent remedy taken instead of or in addition to, removal action in the event of a release or threatened release of a hazardous substance into the environment, to prevent or minimize the release of hazardous substances so that they do not migrate to cause substantial danger to present or future public health or welfare or the environment.

The definition concludes with a long but nonexclusive list of specific actions that may be RAs, including storage, perimeter protection using dikes and the like, clay cover, neutralization, cleanup of released hazardous materials, dredging or excavations, on-site treatment or incineration, provision of alternative water supplies, any reasonably required monitoring, permanent relocation of residents, businesses, and community facilities, off-site transport, storage, treatment, and enforcement activities.

For large or varied sites, the RA may be divided into a number of discrete steps; these are called *operable units* (OUs). The same NCP section defines an OU as

> a discrete action that comprises an incremental step toward comprehensively addressing site problems. This discrete portion of a remedial response manages migration, or eliminates or mitigates a release, threat of a release, or pathway of exposure. The cleanup of a site can be divided into a number of operable units, depending on the complexity of the problems associated with the site. Operable units may address geographical portions of a site, specific site problems, or initial phases of an action, or may consist of any set of actions performed over time or any actions that are concurrent but located in different parts of a site.

The 1986 SARA amendments and the 1990 NCP made important changes in the procedures and standards for selecting RAs, including OUs. The overall goals—remedying contaminated sites so that human health and

---

[10] 40 C.F.R. § 300.5.

the environment are protected—remain the same. The revised procedures attempt to ensure that remedies emphasize treatment and destruction of contamination and that affected parties and institutions, including individuals, states, municipalities, and Indian tribes, have a full opportunity to participate in remedy selection.

The major phases of an RA are grouped and described in detail in **§§ 19.7** through **19.9**.

§ 19.7   —Remedial Site Evaluation

This stage involves data gathering and analysis for purposes of evaluating releases of hazardous materials. The preliminary assessment (PA) is an initial review to determine the need for a removal, set priorities for site inspections, and gather data for later evaluation of the release under the EPA's hazard ranking system (HRS). Sites scoring above a threshold figure in the HRS are added to the NPL. The lead agency must perform a PA on all sites in the CERCLA Information System (CERCLIS), EPA's data base of about 30,000 contaminated sites. Affected persons may petition the EPA regional administrator (or other federal agency, for releases on federal facilities) to conduct PAs on other sites.

After conducting the PA, the lead agency completes a PA report, which includes a description of the release and a recommendation regarding further action, including a removal or a site inspection.

The site inspection (SI) aims to (1) eliminate from further consideration releases that pose no significant threat to public health or the environment, (2) determine the need for removals, and (3) collect or develop additional data to evaluate the release pursuant to the HRS and collect yet additional data to better characterize the release for rapid initiation of the RI/FS or other response. If the SI includes field sampling, a two-part sampling and analysis plan is required, containing both the actual number, type, and location of samples and type of analyses, and a separate quality assurance project plan (QAPP).

Upon completion of the SI, the field agency must prepare an SI report.

§ 19.8   —Remedial Investigation/Feasibility Study/Remedy Selection

The core of the remedy selection process is the RI/FS. Its purpose is to assess site conditions and evaluate alternatives to the extent necessary to select a remedy. The activities involved in developing and conducting an RI/FS are (1) project scoping, (2) data collection, including treatability studies, (3) risk assessment, and (4) analysis of alternative remedies.

Scoping

Scoping requires the lead agency to confer with support agencies and specifically to:

1. Assemble and evaluate existing data on the site, including the results of any removals, PAs and SIs, and the National Priorities List listing process

2. Based on the foregoing evaluation, develop a conceptual understanding of the site

3. Identify likely response scenarios and potentially applicable technologies and operable units that may address site problems

4. Undertake limited data collection efforts or studies when such information will assist in scoping the RI/FS or accelerate response actions, and begin to identify the need for treatability studies, as appropriate

5. Identify the type, quality, and quantity of the data that will be collected during the RI/FS to support decisions regarding remedial response activities

6. Prepare site-specific health and safety plans, specifying at a minimum employee training and protective equipment, medical surveillance requirements, standard operating procedures, and a contingency plan that conforms with 29 C.F.R. 1910.120(1)(1) and (1)(2)

7. Notify state and federal trustees of any natural resources injured by the release

8. Develop sampling and analysis plans, with the same two parts described above, for review by EPA

9. Identify potential federal and state ARARs and other guidance to be considered as appropriate.

Data Collection

Data collection involves two activities: community relations (CR) and the RI. The lead agency must, prior to commencing field work for the RI, conduct interviews with local people, officials and groups, prepare a written CR plan, establish one or more local information repositories at or near the location of the RA, and inform the community of the availability of technical assistance grants. If PRPs are participating in the cleanup, they may participate in the CR program to the extent determined by the lead agency in its discretion, and under agency oversight.

The RI, which aims to collect data necessary to characterize the site adequately for purposes of developing and evaluating remedial alternatives, includes conducting field investigations, treatability studies, and baseline risk assessments. It also involves identifying potential ARARs related to the location and contamination at the site. The field investigation assesses

1. The physical characteristics of the site (surface features, soils, geology, hydrogeology, meteorology, ecology)
2. Characteristics or classifications of air, surface water and ground water
3. General characteristics of the waste (quantities, state, concentration, toxicity, propensity to bioaccumulate, persistence, and mobility)
4. Source identification and characterization
5. Actual and potential exposure pathways (through environmental media) and exposure routes (for example, inhalation or ingestion).

Risk Assessment

Risk assessment uses the data developed through field investigation to characterize current and potential threats to human health and the environment posed by contaminants at the site through migration to ground or surface water, releases to air, leaching through soil, and bioaccumulation in the food chain. The results of the baseline risk assessment help establish acceptable exposure levels for use in developing remedial alternatives in the FS.

Analysis of Alternatives

Analysis of alternatives is the domain of the feasibility study (FS). The main purpose of the FS is to ensure that appropriate remedial alternatives are developed and evaluated such that pertinent information concerning the remedial action options can be presented to a decision maker and an appropriate remedy selected. In outline, the lead agency selects a preliminary goal, then generates and screens a large range of alternatives, with the more extreme or impracticable options being eliminated, based on lack of effectiveness or implementability or on grossly excessive cost. The lead agency then conducts a detailed analysis of the advantages and disadvantages of the remaining three to nine alternatives, using nine remedy selection criteria:

1. Overall protection of human health and the environment
2. Compliance with or waiver of the ARARs of other federal and state laws
3. Long-term effectiveness and permanence
4. Reduction of toxicity, mobility, or volume through treatment

5. Short-term effectiveness
6. Implementability
7. Cost
8. State acceptance
9. Community acceptance.

The lead agency then groups these criteria in three categories and uses them to evaluate the remedial alternatives. Numbers (1) and (2) are threshold criteria; alternatives that do not meet them are dropped. Criteria (3) through (7) and, insofar as known, (8) and (9) are then used to evaluate the remaining alternatives, and the lead agency attempts to select the remedial alternative that "utilizes permanent solutions and alternative treatment technologies . . . to the maximum extent practicable" and is "cost-effective" based on a comparison of all the criteria.[11] An alternative is considered cost-effective if its costs are in proportion to its overall effectiveness. An alternative is considered to use maximum practicable permanence and treatment if it scores well under criteria (3) and (4).

Next, working with the state, the lead agency issues a proposed plan setting forth the recommended alternative. Then the public has an opportunity to review and comment on the alternatives studied in the FS and the one offered in the proposed plan. After reviewing and responding to public comments and formally considering criteria (8) and (9), EPA selects and documents the final remedy in a Record of Decision (ROD).

These elaborate procedures and standards for evaluating alternatives reflect the potentially conflicting demands that Congress imposed on EPA in enacting SARA in 1986. For instance, Congress directed EPA to maximize permanent treatment yet also to ensure cost-effective remedies. The EPA was also directed to take into account the preferences of the public and states in selecting remedies, yet those preferences could result in a divergence from other requirements (for example, the public might oppose incineration even though it would constitute permanent treatment).

§ 19.9 —Remedial Design/Remedial Action, Operation, and Maintenance

This stage involves engineering and related work to develop the actual design of the selected remedy and construction work to implement the remedy. In carrying out these activities, the lead agency must assure compliance with all applicable ARARs and with the conditions of any

---

[11] *Id.* § 300.430(e)(5)(iii)(E), (D).

ARAR waivers. The agency also must satisfy CR requirements, including publishing an explanation of significant differences if the remedial action taken, or any settlement or consent decree entered into, differs significantly in scope, performance, or cost from the one set forth in the ROD. Remedy modifications often occur during the RD phase because more is learned about the nature and extent of subterranean contamination. If the change is so extensive that it "fundamentally alters" the ROD remedy, the lead agency must propose and solicit comments on a ROD amendment.

Once the remedy is operational, or, for ground or surface water restoration, once water quality is restored, the state must take over responsibility for funding and performing operation and maintenance (O&M) of the remedy. This is an important issue for states, because the United States generally funds 90 percent of the RA but only 50 percent or less of O&M activities.

Once the lead agency is satisfied that no further response action is necessary, whether or not O&M is continuing, a site may be proposed for deletion from or recategorization on the NPL. Sites at which hazardous substances remain at levels above what would permit unrestricted exposure must be reviewed every five years after remedy initiation; generally, EPA will not delete a site from the NPL until at least one five-year review has occurred following the completion of the RA for the site.

§ 19.10   Corrective Action under RCRA

RCRA governs currently active hazardous waste transport, treatment, storage, and disposal (T/S/D) sites. Transporters are not involved in this discussion. See **Chapter 8**. As noted in § **19.3**, most such facilities have a single owner and/or operator, who will be referred to as an operator for purposes of this chapter. Such sites are required to have a RCRA permit and to comply with literally scores of RCRA regulations. The RCRA corrective action (CA) requirements were added to RCRA by the Hazardous and Solid Waste Amendments (HSWA) of 1984.

RCRA (HSWA) § 3004(u) empowers EPA to require an operator to carry out CA for releases of hazardous wastes/constituents from solid waste management units (SWMUs) of a permitted facility. Under § 3004(v), EPA can require CA for off-site contamination unless the off-site landowner refuses access. According to the EPA, CA requirements also apply under § 3008(h) to facilities that now have interim status or that ever had interim status, and under § 3005(i) to any "regulated unit," that is, any impoundment, waste pile, or land treatment unit that received hazardous waste after July 26, 1982.[12]

---

[12] *Id.* § 264.90(a).

Chemicals subject to regulation under RCRA, and thus to CA requirements, are hazardous wastes and hazardous constituents. *Hazardous wastes* are RCRA solid wastes (solids, liquids, and contained gasses as defined at 40 C.F.R. § 261.2) that exhibit one or more hazardous characteristics (ignitability, corrosivity, reactivity, and TLP toxicity) or are listed in subpart D of 40 C.F.R. part 261. *Constituents* include breakdown and related compounds of hazardous wastes. A waste is listed as hazardous if

1. It is ignitible (has a flash point below 140°F)
2. It is corrosive (has a pH ≤2.0 or ≥12.5)
3. It is reactive
4. It is chemically unstable (can change violently without being detonated, reacts violently with water, or produces toxic emissions when exposed to water or noncorrosive-pH substances)
5. It exhibits TC toxicity, that is, when tested under EPA's Toxicity Characteristic Leaching Procedure (TCLP), it shows greater than the established threshold concentrations of 33 organic chemicals and pesticides and eight metals[13]
6. It has proved fatal in low doses to humans or has a LD-50 or LC-50 figure (lowest dose or concentration fatal to 50 percent of tested laboratory animals) below the regulatory ceiling
7. It contains a toxic constituent listed in Appendix VIII to 40 C.F.R. Part 261
8. It is a waste listed generically by industrial classification.

The wastes that EPA has determined to be hazardous are listed in 40 C.F.R. § 261 part D. Other wastes are also deemed hazardous under RCRA if they exhibit the characteristics listed above. Generators are responsible for testing nonlisted wastes for characteristics. The criteria for testing are set forth in 40 C.F.R. §§ 261.20–.24.

RCRA, like CERCLA, exempts from regulation important categories of materials that are obviously hazardous. For RCRA, the exclusions include domestic sewage and industrial point source discharges regulated under the § 402 of the CWA, many agricultural wastes (irrigation return flows, wastes used as fertilizers, residues of pesticide containers if they are triple-rinsed), most radioactive wastes (source, special nuclear, or byproduct material regulated by the Nuclear Regulatory Commission under the Atomic Energy Act, but *not* mixed wastes, which are radioactive wastes mixed with other RCRA wastes), many mining wastes, several wastes under study,

---

[13] The TCLP test is new; it replaced EPA's Extraction Procedure (EP) toxicity test for large waste generators on Sept. 25, 1990; small quantity generators—those which produce less than 1000 kilograms of hazardous waste in a calendar month and store no more than 6000 kilos—must comply by March 29, 1991.

wastewater treatment sludges, household wastes, incinerator and resource-recovery residues, some reused/recycled materials, and PCBs (regulated only under TSCA).

§ 19.11   —Stages, Standards, and Procedures in Cleanup Process

Partly under the compulsion of the 1984 HSWA, EPA has promulgated CA requirements for T/S/D facility operators, both those in interim status and those with final RCRA permits, and these extend to SWMUs in addition to hazardous waste T/S/D units. The rules are set forth in subpart F of 40 C.F.R. parts 264 (permitted facilities) and 265 (interim status facilities).

All T/S/D facilities, including SWMUs, have substantial groundwater monitoring obligations, because groundwater contamination is the most serious problem with them. EPA requires CA for releases of hazardous wastes or constituents discovered through groundwater monitoring or independently by EPA. For purposes of CA, *hazardous waste* means any substance listed or identified under 40 C.F.R. part 261. EPA interprets the term *constituents* to include all substances that appear in appendix VIII of part 261 and appendix IX of part 264.

The stages in a cleanup under RCRA resemble those involved under CERCLA, but the names are different. RCRA directives specify five major stages:

1. RCRA facility assessment (RFA)
2. RCRA facility investigation (RFI)/Interim measures (IMs)
3. Corrective measures study (CMS)
4. Selection of remedy
5. Implementation of remedy: the corrective action (CA).[14]

IMs are somewhat analogous to removals under CERCLA. RFIs are comparable to Superfund RI/FSs and are governed by EPA's four-volume RCRA Facility Investigation (RFI) Guidance.[15] The RCRA Corrective Action Plan addresses RFIs, CMSs, and CM implementation.

Until recently, the procedures and standards for carrying out the various phases of a RCRA corrective action (CA) were set forth not in regulations but rather in EPA directives, standard RCRA T/S/D facility permit clauses, or enforcement orders under RCRA §§ 3008(h), 7003 and/or 3013. This practice partially reflects the fact that RCRA procedures are

---

[14] The terms are set forth in EPA's OSWER Directive 9902.3, RCRA Corrective Action Plan, EPA/530-SW-88-028 (June 1988) (Interim Final).

[15] EPA OSWER Directive 9502.00-6D (EPA 530/SW-89-031 (May 1989) (Interim Final)).

less formal and more flexible than their counterparts under CERCLA. Also, EPA has tended to shy away from promulgating RCRA regulations partly because most proposed regulations to date were greeted by substantial litigation as soon as they were proposed.[16]

The EPA recently proposed a major regulation in the CA area, the RCRA Corrective Action Rule (CA Rule),[17] which, along with its preamble, covers the entire CA area, addressing the procedures and standards for the phases of CA work. The CA Rule and Preamble also expressly preserve the flexibility typical of EPA's prior CA guidance and incorporate by reference several of the existing guidance documents. Although formally only a proposal, the CA Rule and, more particularly, its Preamble generally reflect current policy in the eyes of EPA Headquarters. In other words, many parts of the proposal as discussed in the CA Preamble are currently in effect. Accordingly, the following discussion incorporates information from the CA Preamble but not the proposed CA Rule itself.

The CA Preamble expressly analogizes CA activities to CERCLA cleanups, stating: "One of the Agency's primary objectives in development of the RCRA corrective action regulations is to achieve substantive consistency with the policies and procedures of the remedial action program under [CERCLA]."[18] It further says that the RCRA CA Rule will normally be an important source of ARARs for CERCLA cleanups. However, it also points up a major difference between the two programs: the facility operator must implement CA under RCRA, whereas many CERCLA cleanups are carried out by the EPA. The stages of RCRA cleanups are also analogous to CERCLA, but unlike the CERCLA NCP, the CA Preamble also stresses that each RCRA stage "serves as a screen, sending forward to the next step those facilities or units at a facility which the Agency has found to be a potential problem, and eliminating from further consideration units and facilities where the Agency has discovered no current environmental problem."[19]

§ 19.12   —Facility Assessment

Generally, the first step in the RCRA process is the RCRA facility assessment (RFA), "which is analogous to the Superfund Preliminary

---

[16] EPA's avoidance of regulations has not escaped criticism. *See, e.g.,* B. Tabler and M. Shere, *EPA's Practice of Regulation-by-Memo,* in 5 Natural Resources and Environment 3 (ABA Section of Natural Resources, Energy and Environmental Law, Fall 1990).

[17] To be codified primarily as subpart S of 40 C.F.R. pt. 264. The proposed CA Rule and an extensive preamble (CA Preamble) are published at 55 Fed. Reg. 30,798–30,884 (July 27, 1990).

[18] 55 Fed. Reg. 30,852 (July 27, 1990).

[19] *Id.* at 30,803.

Assessment/Site Investigation [PA/SI]."[20] Like CERCLA projects, but unlike most CA steps, the RFA is conducted by the agency in charge. In the CA Preamble, *agency* means the EPA regional administrator or, for RCRA/authorized states, the appropriate state environmental agency.

The RFA includes:

1. A review of available information about the site
2. A visual site inspection to confirm information on SWMUs at the site and to note any visual evidence of releases
3. In some cases, a sampling visit to confirm or disprove suspected releases.

§ 19.13   —Facility Investigation

The RCRA Facility Investigation (RFI) is the second CA stage.[21] The purpose of the RFI, which is conducted by the operator but overseen and subject to approval by the agency, is to characterize the nature and extent of contamination at the operator's RCRA facility. Often, as with the CERCLA RI/FS, the corrective measures study (CMS), the third RCRA CA step, is conducted simultaneously with the RFI.[22]

The RFI is frequently narrower in scope as well as more procedurally flexible than its CERCLA counterparts. Whereas the CERCLA RI/FS examines three to nine alternatives (see § **19.8**), a RCRA RFI may evaluate only one or two alternatives. In terms of flexibility, the RFI generally involves phasing, and there is usually a high level of interaction between the operator and the agency.

The types of information that may be required in an RFI include:

1. Characterization of the environmental setting (including information on hydrogeologic conditions, climatological conditions, soil characteristics, surface water characteristics like sediment quality, and air quality and meteorological conditions)
2. Characterization of solid waste management units involved (including their construction, age and type of liner, and chemical and physical analyses of wastes, constituent breakdown products, volumes, and concentrations)
3. Description of the humans and environmental systems that are, have been, or may potentially be exposed to the release (including human

---

[20] *Id.* at 30,801.

[21] The CA Preamble analogizes it to the CERCLA RI and even uses the term *remedial investigation* throughout the RFI discussion. *Id.* at 30,810.

[22] The CA Preamble recognizes this similarity as well. *Id.* at 30,814.

populations and sensitive environmental systems such as wetlands, estuaries, and habitats of endangered or threatened species, some of which information may have previously been developed as part of the operator's RCRA permit application process)

4. Information that will assist the agency in assessing the risk posed to humans and environmental systems by the release (the agency will perform a risk assessment to help determine a final remedy and also the need for IMs before the final remedy is carried out)

5. Extrapolations of future contaminant movement (to help to determine the need for IMs)

6. Laboratory, bench-scale, or pilot-scale tests or studies to determine the feasibility or effectiveness of treatment or other technologies that may be appropriate in implementing remedies at the facility (these measures, more typical of the CMS, may be carried out during the RFI in order to save time)

7. Statistical analyses to aid in the interpretation of data required in the investigation (to determine whether action levels have been exceeded, which normally triggers the corrective measures study (CMS) requirement).

The CA Preamble authorizes the agency to require the operator to develop a work plan for the RFI. Although not always required, RFI work plans will, in the agency's view, need to be submitted by operators "[i]n the great majority of cases."[23]

RFI work plans generally include a description of overall approach (including objectives and schedule of compliance), technical and analytical approaches and methods (including specifications for location, construction, and frequency of sampling monitoring wells), quality assurance procedures (as specified in the RCRA facility investigation guidance document), and data management procedures and formats to document and track the results of investigations and enhance proper interpretation of the data. The agency may also require other elements as needed to support decisions in later stages of the CA process.

Final RFI Reports are required in all cases, as well as periodic interim RFI reports in most cases. The agency reviews and may require modification or correction of these reports. The operator must also prepare a summary of the final report and mail it to all individuals on its facility mailing list.[24]

If the RFI shows that suspected releases are nonexistent or do not pose a threat to human health or the environment, the operator may, on

---

[23] *Id.* at 30,812.

[24] 55 Fed. Reg. 30,813 (July 27, 1990).

request, obtain a permit or compliance schedule modification to delete any further remediation requirements. The operator's request for such a modification triggers several permit modification procedures, including notifying all persons on the facility mailing list of the proposed change, publishing a newspaper notice, and holding a 90-day public comment period. Continuing monitoring and air monitoring may continue even if the CA investigation terminates.[25]

§ 19.14   —Interim Measures

At the other extreme, if the RFI leads the agency to determine that a release or threatened release from a SWMU poses a threat to human health or the environment, the agency may require the operator to conduct interim measures (IMs) at the facility. In making this determination, the agency considers factors related to the immediacy and magnitude of the health/environmental threat, including:

1. The time required to develop and implement a final remedy
2. Actual or potential exposures of nearby human or animal populations to hazardous constituents
3. Actual or potential contamination of drinking water supplies or sensitive ecosystems
4. Further degradation of the medium that may occur if remedial action is not initiated expeditiously
5. Presence of hazardous wastes or hazardous constituents in drums, barrels, or other bulk storage containers that may pose a threat of release
6. Presence in soils at or near the surface of hazardous wastes or constituents that may migrate
7. Weather conditions that may cause releases of hazardous constituents or migration of existing contamination
8. Risks of fire or explosion or the potential for exposure to hazardous constituents as a result of an accident or failure of a container or handling system
9. Any other situations that may pose threats to human health or the environment.

The CA Preamble lists[26] several examples of typical IMs, including making available an alternate supply of drinking water if the operator was

---

[25] *Id.*

[26] *Id.* at 30,839.

responsible for contaminating a public drinking water supply; initiating a groundwater pump and treatment system to control further migration of contamination or to prevent further contamination of an aquifer; fencing off an area of contaminated soil to prevent public access; or overpacking drums in poor condition to prevent possible leakage.

The agency notifies the operator in writing of required IMs and requires the operator to initiate them as soon as practicable or, in emergency situations, immediately. Except in the latter situation, the agency, if necessary, initiates a RCRA permit modification to specify the required IM. In many situations however, the agency assumes that the operator will undertake IMs voluntarily. If rapid initiation is needed and the operator is not cooperative, however, the agency may resort to RCRA § 7003 or CERCLA removal authorities.

As the CA Preamble notes,[27] RCRA Corrective action IMs resemble removals under the CERCLA program. Like their CERCLA counterparts, IMs are required to be consistent with the long-term remedy at the facility. IMs are also one kind of corrective measure (CM). The agency, on a case by case basis, requires operators to demonstrate financial assurances for carrying out IMs and other CMs.

§ 19.15   —Corrective Measures Studies

If contamination is found that could threaten health or the environment, but no immediate response is required, the next CA step (sometimes conducted simultaneous with the RFI, as noted in § 19.14) is the corrective measures study (CMS). The CMS aims to identify and evaluate potential remedial alternatives for the releases that have been identified at the facility. The usual trigger for a CMS is a finding that contamination concentrations exceed applicable action levels (ALs). AL exceedence, however, does not always require a CMS, and a CMS may be required even if ALs are not exceeded.

ALs are health- and environment-based levels determined by the agency to be indicators for protection of human health and the environment. The CA Preamble contains a detailed discussion of the criteria for determining action levels for both carcinogens/mutagens and for systemic toxicants (chemicals causing other toxic effects).[28] The CA Preamble also includes appendixes that list numerous examples of concentrations of specific hazardous constituents that constitute ALs in air, water, and soil.[29]

The scope of a CMS will vary greatly, due to the diversity of the RCRA facility universe. At many facilities, a streamlined CMS will

---

[27] *Id.*

[28] *Id.* at 30,815–20.

[29] *Id.* at 30,865–73.

suffice, addressing only one or two alternatives. In contrast, RCRA facilities that have very extensive or highly complex environmental contamination problems will require a more elaborate CMS that assesses a larger number of alternative remedial technologies or approaches. Yet other facilities will fall in the middle range; the agency will attempt to limit the CMS for them to a short list of plausible remedies.[30]

For each potential remedy selected, the operator must evaluate performance, reliability, ease of implementation, and impacts (including safety, cross-media contaminant transfer, and control of exposures to residual contamination). To evaluate these factors for one or more specific remedies, the operator may be required to develop specific data such as general site conditions, waste characteristics, site geology, soil and surface and groundwater characteristics, and climate. Much of this information may, of course, already be available from the RFI.

The agency often specifies, prior to or during the CMS, target cleanup levels for specific contaminants. The operator should use these in evaluating specific remedial technologies. The agency may regulate the timing of the CMS according to the urgency of the situation; low priority cleanups may be phased.[31]

As with the RFI, the agency normally requires the operator to develop a plan for the CMS and to prepare interim and final reports on the CMS.[32]

§ 19.16   —Selection of Remedy

Generally, all RCRA CA remedies must satisfy four basic standards. They must:

1. Be protective of human health and the environment (including the protective measures, such as provision of alternate water supplies and erection of fences and barriers to shield the public from SWMUs)

2. Attain media cleanup standards specified in the proposed CA Rule

3. Control the sources of releases so as to reduce or eliminate, to the extent practicable, further releases that could pose a threat to human health and the environment (with strong preference given to treatment technologies rather than containment systems)

4. Comply with standards for management of the wastes generated by the remedial activity, as set forth in the proposed CA Rule.[33]

---

[30] 55 Fed. Reg. 30,821 (July 27, 1990).

[31] *Id.* at 30,822–23.

[32] *Id.* at 30,823.

[33] *Id.*

Five decision factors are used to select one of the remedies that meet the four general standards. They are:

1. Long-term reliability and effectiveness
2. Reduction of toxicity, mobility, or volume of wastes
3. Short-term effectiveness
4. Implementability
5. Cost.[34]

This list implies no ranking; indeed, a different factor or factors will predominate in different specific settings. Cost will control only if all remedies achieve the necessary cleanup standards.[35]

The agency specifies a schedule for initiating and completing remedial activities, based on factors such as:

1. Extent and nature of contamination at the facility
2. Practical capabilities of remedial technologies as assessed against cleanup standards and other remedial objectives
3. Availability of treatment or disposal capacity for wastes to be managed as part of the remedy
4. Desirability of utilizing emerging technologies not yet widely available that may offer significant advantages over currently available technologies
5. Potential risks to human health and the environment from exposure to contamination prior to remedy completion.[36]

§ 19.17   —Media Cleanup Standards

Media Cleanup Standards (MCS) are hazardous constituent concentrations in groundwater, surface water, soils, and air that CA remedies must achieve in order to ensure adequate protection of human health and the environment. The CA Preamble discusses MCS at length.[37] The discussion includes the establishment of MCS, determinations that a cleanup to MCS is not required, and the demonstration of compliance with MCS.

Establishment of MCS

If media-specific cleanup standards exist, such as maximum contaminant levels (MCL) under the Safe Drinking Water Act, the agency normally

---

[34] *Id.* at 30,824.

[35] *Id.* at 30,825.

[36] 55 Fed. Reg. 30,825 (July 27, 1990).

[37] *Id.* at 30,825–33.

uses them.[38] In most cases, however, no such specific standards are available, so the agency will then use a two-step approach. First, it sets a starting point. For carcinogens, this is 10^{-6} for lifetime excess cancer risk. Then, however, the agency evaluates a variety of site- and remedy-specific factors, including uncertainty, exposure, technical limitations, water use, cumulative effects of multiple contaminants, and sensitive populations/receptors. The final goal may be 10^{-4} to 10^{-6} or even more protective.[39]

For all contaminants, the following general factors related to remedy protectiveness influence MCS determination:

Multiple contaminants in a medium.   If multiple contaminants are present in a single environmental medium, the agency evaluates the cumulative health risk posed by all, using *Guidelines for the Health Risk Assessment of Chemical Mixtures.*[40] Thus, the protective MCS for each constituent involved is likely to be at a lower concentration than if no other constituents were present.

Sensitive environmental receptors.   The agency considers protection of sensitive environmental receptors such as wetlands and endangered species habitat, although less information is often available about these than about human or laboratory health effects. Sensitive environmental receptors may require lower MCS concentrations than would be necessary to protect human health alone. The agency intends to issue further guidance on evaluating such ecological impacts.

Remedy-specific factors.   The agency, on a case-by-case basis, considers the reliability, effectiveness, practicability, and other remedy-related protectiveness factors in establishing an MCS. For example, a demonstrated technology capable of cleaning up to a concentration posing a 1×10^{-5} level may be selected instead of an unproven technology theoretically capable of a 1×10^{-6} cleanup. MCSs may also vary according to likely pathways of exposure. For instance, if children are not likely to be present or there is no surface exposure, the MCS for contaminated soil would not be based on direct ingestion.

Determination that Cleanup Need Not Meet an MCS

If the agency determines that (1) there is no threat of exposure to releases from a SWMU, (2) cleanup to the MCS will not result in any significant reduction in risk to human or the environment, or (3) cleanup is technically impractical, the agency may decide not to require cleanup to the

---

[38] *Id.* at 30,826.

[39] *Id.*

[40] Published at 51 Fed. Reg. 34,014 (1990).

otherwise applicable MCS. This decision, however, would not relieve an operator from the obligation to prevent further releases; thus, source control measure or measures to protect against exposure to contamination may well be required.

The CA Preamble gives examples of typical situations potentially meeting one or more of these three standards:

1. Areas of broad contamination (the operator may be able to convince the agency that MCS cleanup would not appreciably reduce the existing risks to health or environment)
2. Unusable groundwater (the agency determines that the groundwater is not a present or potential drinking water source and is not hydraulically connected with waters to which the hazardous constituents could migrate)
3. Technical impracticability of remediation (relating both to engineering feasibility and reliability, such as, for instance dense, immiscible contaminants in mature Karst formations or highly fractured bedrock).

Demonstrating Compliance with MCS

To demonstrate compliance with established MCSs or alternative cleanup levels approved by the agency, the operator must show compliance for each medium contaminated; use particular sampling, analytical, and statistical methods; and show no exceedances for an established period of time.

For groundwater, the operator must ordinarily demonstrate compliance throughout the entire area of contaminated groundwater. The agency, however, has flexibility to establish more limited compliance areas and points when necessary.

For air, the compliance point generally would be outside the facility, at the location of the most exposed individual, usually not including employees. This contrasts with the *action level determination point,* which is normally the facility boundary.

For surface water, compliance will be checked at the point at which releases enter the surface water, except for contaminated sediments in surface water bodies.

For soils, the compliance point will be at any point at which direct contact exposure to the soil may occur. This is usually at or near the surface.

The agency specifies compliance methods, including sampling, analytical, and statistical measures, in the operator's permit. The permit will also set forth the frequency of required sampling or monitoring. In many cases, the operator's CMS will have proposed appropriate methods, and the agency may consider and adopt these. The permits also specify the length of time during which the operator must demonstrate that hazardous constituent concentrations have not exceeded specified limits, and they also contain cost estimates and a schedule of compliance for carrying out the remedy. The CA Preamble prescribes no uniform figure for the time during which compliance must be demonstrated, leaving the decision up to the regional administrator, who is to use five factors:

1. Extent and concentration of the release
2. Behavior characteristics of the hazardous constituents in the affected medium
3. Accuracy of monitoring techniques
4. Characteristics of the affected media
5. Any seasonal, meteorological, or other environmental variables that may affect the accuracy of monitoring results.[41]

The agency approves the foregoing CA measures by incorporating them in the operator's RCRA permit. The CA Preamble[42] discusses technical aspects of the required permit modification procedures, which are largely standard RCRA permit modification procedures.[43]

§ 19.18 —Implementation of Remedy

This phase, like its CERCLA counterpart (see § 19.9), comprises remedy design, remedy implementation with progress reports and oversight, and remedy completion, all of which is the responsibility of the operator with agency approval. As with other CA stages, these features are more flexibly administered than their CERCLA counterparts.

Remedy Design

The EPA-approved modified permit usually requires the facility operator to develop a remedial design (RD), including preparing detailed construction plans and specifications for implementing the approved remedy. Such plans must include specifications that demonstrate the RD's compliance with applicable standards for managing hazardous and/or solid wastes during implementation of the remedy, including temporary on-site waste storage in corrective action management units (CAMUs).[44]

---

[41] 55 Fed. Reg. 30,832–33 (July 27, 1990).

[42] *Id.* at 30,834–35.

[43] *See also id.* at 30,846–49.

[44] The waste management standards are discussed in detail at 55 Fed. Reg. 30,840–45 (July 27, 1990).

The operator also must develop implementation and long-term operation, monitoring, and maintenance plans, and a program to maintain quality assurance (QA) during the construction phase of remedy implementation.

The operator must submit all the foregoing RD plans to the agency (regional administrator or the state equivalent) for review and approval. Approval includes appropriate amendments and additions to the permit schedule of compliance. When necessary, the operator will have to amend its CA cost estimate and adjust its financial assurance amount in light of improved cost estimates based on the RD.

Upon approval of the RD, the operator generally is required to place a copy of the RD plans and specifications in the facility's information repository and to give written notice of approval and availability for review of the RD to all persons on the facility's mailing list.

Remedy Implementation

The operator is required to implement the remedy according to the approved RD plans and the revised permit schedule of compliance, and in a manner consistent with the objectives specified for the CM during remedy selection. The agency generally requires the operator to prepare and submit periodic progress reports containing information on construction, operation, and maintenance of the selected remedy. The agency specifies the progress report format and frequency in the compliance schedule, based on factors such as the complexity of the site's waste mixture, complexity of the remedy, hydrogeologic and climatic conditions, and potential for exposure.

All raw data and information developed or submitted during remedy implementation must be maintained in the operating record of the facility as long as the facility operates under a RCRA permit, including the CA permit.

The agency periodically reviews remedy implementation activities throughout the design, construction, operation, and maintenance phases, concentrating most on sites posing the greatest risks to human health. The monitoring includes on-site inspections and oversight as well as review of progress reports. The agency works closely with the operator in overseeing remedy implementation and addressing any problems in a timely manner. If necessary to ensure prompt resolution of problems, the agency may initiate an enforcement action or a public permit modification proceeding or may submit the matter to alternative dispute resolution.[45]

---

[45] The procedures for resorting to alternative dispute resolution are discussed at 55 Fed. Reg. 30,850–51 (July 27, 1990).

Remedy Completion

Standards and procedures for the operator's demonstration that the remedy is complete are discussed at in the CA Rule.[46] Remedies are considered complete when the operator demonstrates its satisfaction of three standards:

1. Media cleanup standards (MCS) must be met for all contaminated media—air, groundwater, soil, and so forth—and for the period required by the agency
2. All permit-required actions to address the source(s) of contamination must be completed
3. All procedures must be satisfied for removal and decontamination of equipment, devices, structures, or units (including CAMUs such as temporary waste piles) that were required to implement the remedy.

As for procedures, on completion of remedy the operator must submit a written certification to the agency by registered mail stating that the remedy has been completed in accordance with the requirements of the CA permit. The certification must be signed by both the operator and by an independent professional skilled in the appropriate technical discipline (such as a hydrogeologist or engineer, depending on the nature of the remedy). The agency reviews the certification to determine whether the remedy has been completed. If an operator is implementing several different remedies, as at different SWMUs at the facility, the agency will not confirm remedy completion until all discrete remedies are complete.

If the agency concludes that the remedy is not complete, it normally notifies the operator of the steps that it must take to complete the remedy. The operator must submit a new certification upon completion of these tasks. Once the agency is satisfied that all remedies are complete, the agency releases the operator from financial assurance requirements and modifies the permit to terminate the permit schedule of compliance.

In some cases, it may become apparent that the selected remedy cannot satisfy performance requirements even after the operator makes active and reasonable efforts to do so. For example, hydrogeologic and geochemical factors at a particular site may not be fully understood, with the result that the remedy fails to achieve the required MCS for groundwater. In this kind of situation, the agency requires the operator to examine available alternative remedies that may be able to achieve applicable MCSs. The agency modifies the permit to require the operator to implement an alternative remedy if one appears feasible and consistent with overall remedial objectives (that is, it would not cause undue cross-media impacts). If no

---

[46] 55 Fed. Reg. 30,837–38 (July 27, 1990).

workable alternative appears, the agency must determine what alternative or additional requirements will be needed to ensure that the remedy adequately protects human health and the environment. For instance, if treatment of contaminated soils to specified levels was not technically feasible, the soils may need to be covered or disposed of in a treatment unit with upgraded engineering controls for release prevention. In other words, a determination of technical impracticability does not relieve the operator of its ultimate responsibility to achieve specified remedy requirements.

§ 19.19   CERCLA Cleanups versus RCRA Cleanups

The foregoing discussion of RCRA corrective actions repeatedly noted similarities between that program and cleanups under CERCLA. The CA Preamble contains a separate discussion of the relationship of these two programs.[47] It begins by stating that "[o]ne of the Agency's primary objectives in development of the RCRA corrective action regulations is to achieve substantive consistency with the policies and procedures of the remedial action program under . . . CERCLA, as amended by . . . SARA." The discussion goes on to point out that if there is contamination related to hazardous waste activities at facilities that conducted treatment, storage, or disposal of hazardous waste "at any time since November 19, 1980, *both RCRA and CERCLA potentially apply.*"[48] The agency aims to maximize consistency in the two programs and thereby "help to ensure that the regulated industry can gain no advantage by proceeding under one program rather than the other."[49] The last point will be true in many respects. The CA Preamble states that similar remedies will be selected under both programs. The cleanup stages are similar, as we have seen.

But there are differences, which may be beneficial or harmful from the point of view of the responsible party (operator). For one thing, as repeatedly underscored in the CA discussion, CA is much more flexible than NCP remedial action. The CA program has few strict requirements. Due to the great variety of RCRA facilities, CA procedures will be required in most but not all cases. This flexibility will probably be helpful from the operator's perspective. Another difference is that CA is almost entirely carried out by the operator, whereas many CERCLA cleanups are conducted by the agency. Here again, the CA approach is probably generally favorable to the operator, because cleanups conducted by the government are more costly than those performed by private parties. The range of potential remedies to be evaluated also is significantly narrower in most CA

---

[47] *Id.* at 30,852–56.

[48] *Id.* at 30,852 (emphasis added).

[49] *Id.*

situations, which again should favor the operator of the contaminated site. And finally, the involvement of the public is less pervasive under RCRA corrective actions, which probably simplifies the process of selecting a remedy as compared with CERCLA.

TECHNICAL ASPECTS

§ 19.20   Overview of Technical Remedies

A nonspecialist who is faced with environmental contamination or environmental remediation problems will benefit from a basic understanding of the technical choices that can be made, or should have been considered, for the containment or remediation effort. The environmental field is continually developing, driven both by legislation and by technological developments. However, the broad outlines are now well established in terms of the choices available and constraints imposed on generators or owners of hazardous wastes. Familiarity with these choices and constraints will provide assistance to those without specialized knowledge, but who still are required to deal with regulatory agencies, technical consultants, or their own companies.

§ 19.21   Sources and Types of Hazardous Wastes

On a detailed level, the list of sources and types of hazardous waste is almost endless. However, two broad categories cover virtually all of the options for legal and technical treatment. Hazardous wastes will either be generated by an ongoing operation, or will be in an inactive or abandoned dump site.

A substance is classed as a hazardous waste by legislation or by regulatory agencies. Hazardous wastes can be solid, sludge, liquid, or contained gas. The definition required by RCRA[50] developed by the EPA states that a waste may be deemed hazardous either because of its general characteristics, or because the EPA has determined that the specific substance is hazardous and has listed it as such.

Wastes are known as *characteristic wastes* if they exhibit one or more of the following characteristics:

1. Ignitable, such as many solvents
2. Corrosive, such as acids

---

[50] Resource Conservation and Recovery Act of 1976, Pub. L. 94-580 (Oct. 21, 1976).

3. Reactive, including substances that tend to explode or create toxic fumes

4. Toxic, meaning harmful or fatal when ingested or absorbed.

The EPA has also determined that certain specific wastes are hazardous. These wastes are *listed wastes* if they fall into the ranges described in § **19.10** through **19.11** and have been categorized and listed by the EPA. As of June, 1990, EPA had listed 349 wastes under RCRA regulation.[51] Listed wastes can be *source-specific,* such as wastewater from petroleum refining or wood preserving; *generic,* such as wastes from processes such as industrial degreasing; or *named chemical products,* such as benzene. The EPA list is dynamic and is periodically updated and modified. The EPA should be contacted if the latest list is needed.

Hazardous waste from ongoing operations is generally covered by RCRA legislation, and ownership and responsibility for the waste is generally well defined. Owners/generators of the waste have more treatment and disposal options because they can modify the production processes as well as treat the waste stream, and because they are handling a waste stream that can be tested and accurately characterized. The RCRA legal requirements are described in §§ **19.10** and **19.11**, and technical options are outlined in §§ **19.20** through **19.28**. If an emergency response to a hazardous substance release is needed, however, Superfund rules and responses will apply instead of RCRA.

Hazardous waste that has been produced in the past and discarded is still the responsibility of the generator to remediate or contain. If the waste has been segregated from others and is still controlled by the generator, remediation may be relatively straightforward. However, exercising cleanup responsibility is frequently more difficult for wastes disposed of in the past because wastes usually have been mixed with those of others at a dump site, or have deteriorated, or the responsibility for them may be difficult to determine. Governing legislation under CERCLA[52] (Superfund) is described in §§ **19.3** through **19.9.**

Technical methods for remediation are generally the same under CERCLA and RCRA. As sites are cleaned up or wastes contained under Superfund rules, the trend will be for more RCRA-governed sites and fewer Superfund sites. If RCRA is successful, it should eventually eliminate the need for Superfund sites.

---

[51] *EPA Issues "Land Ban" Rules for Hazardous Wastes,* Chemical Engineering 21 (June 1990).

[52] Comprehensive Environmental Response, Compensation and Liability Act of 1980, Pub. L. 96-510 (Dec. 11, 1980).

§ 19.22   Treatment of Hazardous Wastes

Hazardous wastes are treated in order to alter their character or composition. Treatment can have various goals, including destruction of the hazardous substance, conversion of a hazardous waste to a nonhazardous material, reduction of waste volume, recovery and reuse of waste stream components, reduction of toxicity, and stabilization to reduce mobility. Under certain conditions, regulators may mandate a treatment technology.

As land disposal methods such as land fill become increasingly scarce, expensive, or illegal, treatment of hazardous wastes is becoming more common. Treatment (as opposed to containment) is most likely[53] to be used on highly toxic waste, highly mobile waste, waste that is several orders of magnitude above health-based levels, and liquids.

Treatment falls into the broad categories of thermal, biological, physical/chemical, and solidification/stabilization technologies. Some of these technologies are undergoing rapid development. Each has advantages and disadvantages. Sections **19.23** through **19.26** describe briefly the applications and constraints of the various treatment methods.

§ 19.23   —Thermal Treatment

Thermal treatment is used on organic wastes either to destroy or concentrate them. The most common thermal method is incineration. Other thermal methods are pyrolysis and thermal desorption.

Incineration destroys organic compounds by burning them at high temperatures. It is a permanent solution and has well-developed technology available for use. It is more commonly used in Europe than in the United States. Incineration systems can sometimes be installed to produce steam or power as usable or saleable byproducts. Incineration is usually an expensive option, both in terms of the initial investment and during continued operation. Disadvantages of incineration include the production of two regulated hazardous byproduct side streams: the exhaust from combustion and the ash consisting of unburned material. Exhaust is usually scrubbed with conventional systems; however, the wide range of hazardous substances that are usually fed to hazardous waste incinerators add more trace pollutants and therefore many complications to scrubbing the exhaust. Ash from incinerators, or soil from which the volatile organic compounds have been removed, usually contains heavy metals that are toxic and must be stabilized before disposal. Regulations governing ash are not yet well established.[54]

---

[53] EPA, Superfund Selection of Remedy (June 1989).
[54] *Governors Turn to Ash,* Engineering News-Record 24 (Aug. 9, 1990).

Experimental thermal techniques being developed include plasma incineration, which uses a plasma arc to burn volatile components at higher temperatures than conventional incineration while transforming the noncombustable components into a glass-like, nonleachable slag.

Thermal desorption is a concentration technique that heats contaminated soils and drives off the volatile organic compounds so that they can be treated separately, so the remaining soil is nonhazardous. Thermal desorption can also be used to separate and concentrate volatile metals such as mercury. Pyrolysis converts hazardous wastes into other products in an oxygen-deficient atmosphere to avoid oxygen-containing exhaust byproducts. Both thermal desorption and pyrolysis are capital-intensive treatments, although desorption is done at lower temperatures with less costly equipment than incineration.

§ 19.24   —Biological Treatment

Biological treatment uses microorganisms such as bacteria to degrade hazardous substances. It is primarily used for organic compounds. It is a permanent solution, because the organic compounds are destroyed. Bioremediation is not yet widely accepted, but its use is growing, and various methods are undergoing development and testing to improve performance and to determine where it is most effective. EPA restrictions on land disposal, under review at this writing, also limit some applications.

A collection of case histories compiled by an industry association[55] indicates that the primary successful, full-scale applications of bioremediation have been for contamination of soils by petroleum products or solvents. The primary advantages are low cost and minimal equipment requirements. The disadvantages have been slow treatment times and difficulty in obtaining uniform reductions to low levels of contamination.

§ 19.25   —Physical/Chemical Treatment

Chemical treatment is targeted at specific, usually inorganic wastes and is used to render the substances nonhazardous. Physical treatment is used to separate and concentrate hazardous substances so they can either be treated further or reused. Types of chemical treatment include neutralization, oxidation, reduction, and dechlorination.

Neutralization decreases acidity or alkalinity, usually by mixing acidic and basic wastes together, then further adjusting the acidity of the mixed

---

[55] *Using Bioremediation—Industry Group Targets Best Applications,* Superfund Report (Dec. 6, 1989).

stream. Neutralized streams are usually nonhazardous and can be disposed to a conventional water treatment plant. *Oxidation* detoxifies specific wastes such as cyanide, phenol, and sulfur compounds, producing other nonhazardous compounds. *Reduction* is used similarly for chromates. *Dechlorination* replaces chlorine with hydrogen and hydroxide ions to detoxify chlorinated substances, which are among the most persistent hazardous substances.

Physical treatment involves separation of toxic or hazardous substances from nonhazardous material. Examples include *precipitation* to remove hazardous solids from water. Heavy metals such as zinc or copper in water can be treated to form insoluble metal salts, which are then precipitated, concentrated, and reused. *Adsorption* is used primarily to remove organic compounds from waste liquid by absorbing them on the surface of specially activated carbon. Adsorption is not a permanent solution, because the carbon with organics will still be hazardous. However, the hazardous substance will be easier to treat because it is now concentrated. Contaminated soils are often *stripped* using steam or air to vaporize volatile compounds, thus separating them for treatment in a much more concentrated, economical form. The remaining soil, which is most of the volume, is rendered nonhazardous.

§ 19.26 —Stabilization/Solidification

Wastes that are partially treated or are slightly hazardous may still be disposed of in landfills or other storage. However, the problems of volume and water-borne transport of hazardous materials must be addressed. *Solidification* is removal of waste water from soils and sludges and reducing the volume, thus making disposal easier and less costly because of the much smaller hazardous volume. Waste water can be removed from sludge by evaporation or filtration, leaving a semi-solid cake for disposal and water that is either nonhazardous or easier to treat.

Sludges or dewatered filter cake solids still contain hazardous substances that are mobile and thus can be leached out of the solid by water and transported via water. This is particularly a problem in landfills because groundwater contamination is possible. The solution is *stabilization,* using substances such as cement, lime, incinerator fly ash, or other substances to chemically react and bind the hazardous substances, thus making the solid less permeable and the hazardous substance less susceptible to transport.

§ 19.27 Containment and Disposal of Wastes

The traditional methods of hazardous waste disposal in unprotected landfills are no longer legal. Both wastes and land disposal are now regulated for future disposal, old landfills are being closed and remediated, and few new land disposal sites are being opened. The graph in **Figure 19–1**, published by the EPA, illustrates the trend since passage of RCRA.

This section discusses the current technology for new land disposal sites and for remediation of existing landfill sites.

Land Disposal

In May 1990, EPA promulgated regulations governing the disposal of hazardous wastes in landfills. These regulations were required under the 1984 amendments of RCRA, or wastes would have been banned from disposal under the land ban provisions of the 1984 RCRA amendments. Under these regulations, prior to disposal all listed wastes and most characterized wastes must be treated in order to reduce their toxicity and mobility and to meet specified performance standards. Land disposal of untreated wastes is prohibited unless the EPA finds that there will be "no migration

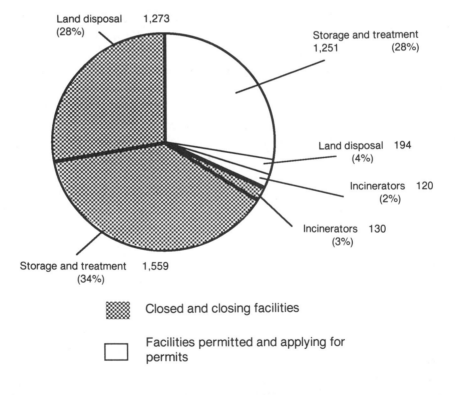

Source: Summary report on RCRA Permit Activities—
January 1990

Figure 19–1. Trends in methods of hazardous waste disposal in landfills.

of hazardous constituents . . . for as long as the wastes remain hazardous." Land disposal includes placement of hazardous waste in landfills, surface impoundments, waste piles, injection wells, land treatment facilities, vaults or bunkers, underground mines, caves, or salt domes. In other words, all hazardous waste disposal is covered.

Under the 1984 HSWA amendments to RCRA, the EPA has established other rules to govern generators of hazardous wastes.[56] Under these rules the generator must determine whether the waste is subject to the rules governing land disposal, what hazardous constituent levels are in the waste, which treatment standards or prohibition levels apply, and whether the waste must be treated or already meets the applicable treatment standard or prohibition level upon generation. Further, the land disposal site itself must have record keeping and testing facilities to record wastes and to confirm that hazardous components are not migrating away from the disposal site.

Existing Landfill Sites

Existing landfill or other land disposal sites that contain hazardous materials are generally being closed and remediated under the Superfund program. Separation and treatment of waste is preferred, using the technologies described in §§ 19.22 through 19.26. Generally, because of the large volumes involved, hazardous substances are stripped or separated from nonhazardous components prior to treatment. Bioremediation without separation is also having success in closed landfills.

In some cases, containment of wastes in place in landfill sites is allowed by the EPA. Containment is more likely to be used when:

1.   Sites are of extraordinary size
2.   Waste material is near health-based levels
3.   Treatment technologies are not feasible or available
4.   Treatment would result in greater risk
5.   Waste is especially difficult to handle or treat.

Containment avoids remediation cost. However, the site will continue to require monitoring, and future legislation may change requirements.

Several methods of immobilizing hazardous wastes in place in landfill sites are being developed. In-situ solidification with substances such as cement and ash has shown promise in reducing leaching and subsequent groundwater contamination. In-situ vitrification uses electrodes placed around contaminated soil to heat and melt the soil. Some organics are

---

[56] EPA, Land Disposal Restrictions, Summary of Requirements (June 1989).

pyrolyzed and destroyed, whereas inorganics such as heavy metals are immobilized once the melted soil freezes into a glass-like block.

§ 19.28   Waste Reduction, Recycling, and Reuse

Generators of wastes will benefit by knowing future trends in regulation, as well as by knowing methods for dealing with past and present regulations. The trend in hazardous waste regulation is toward reduction or elimination of wastes. This is exemplified by the 1984 amendments to RCRA, which require generators of hazardous wastes to certify that they have taken steps to reduce the volume of hazardous waste they generate. California's Department of Health Services has reached agreement with several large chemical and other industrial firms to reduce generation and off-site disposal of incinerable wastes by 50 percent between 1990 and 1992. In addition to meeting legal requirements, however, waste reduction frequently has beneficial economic results for the generator, because an operating cost is reduced or eliminated when waste disposal is reduced.

Several avenues are available for waste reduction and are being actively promoted by regulatory authorities such as the EPA.[57] *Source separation* keeps hazardous waste from contaminating nonhazardous material. It is the easiest and cheapest method of reducing the volume of hazardous material, and it reduces waste disposal costs as well as waste handling and transportation costs.

Changes to internal operations may be required. *Recovery and reuse,* or recycling, captures all or part of a waste stream and feeds it back into an industrial process, thus reducing disposal volume and also reducing costs of raw materials. *Process changes* can be made to substitute feed materials or alter process conditions to produce less of an undesirable waste. Finally, *substitution of products* can eliminate hazardous materials completely. The construction industry is changing from creosote-preserved posts to concrete posts, thus eliminating the possibility of creosote-contaminated soils.

The regulatory trends are clear. Waste elimination or reduction are the priorities. Waste disposal requirements are becoming more stringent, and waste treatment is becoming more expensive. An understanding of the current methods and future trends will assist anyone who is involved with the generation or treatment of hazardous wastes.

---

[57] EPA, Solving the Hazardous Waste Problem (Nov. 1986).

CHAPTER 20

CERCLA REMEDIAL COSTS

Theodore L. Garrett
Frederic R. Miller

Theodore L. Garrett is a partner in the law firm Covington & Burling in Washington, D.C. He coordinates the firm's environmental practice and has been extensively involved in litigation and administrative proceedings. A former law clerk to Chief Justice Burger, he has served as a featured speaker at numerous environmental law and litigation programs and has written widely in the environmental area. Mr. Garrett is vice chairman of the Solid and Hazardous Waste Committee of the ABA Section of Natural Resources, Energy and Environmental Law, a member of the editorial board of the *Environmental Law Reporter,* and a member of the Advisory Committee on Hazardous Waste of the Center for Public Resources.

Frederic R. Miller is the partner in charge of Coopers & Lybrand's Business Investigation Services practice in Washington, D.C. He has significant experience in the cost aspects of environmental litigation, particularly hazardous waste sites. He has appeared as an expert witness in such matters in Federal Court. He has nationwide superfund site experience, including the Chem-Dyne Site, the Hardage Site, the Western Processing Site, the French Limited Site and others. Mr. Miller is a frequent speaker and writer on environmental and construction litigation cost issues. He is a CPA in Washington, D.C. and a member of the American and District of Columbia Institutes of CPAs. He holds an M.B.A. from Cornell University and an A.B. degree from Rutgers College.

§ 20.1   Introduction

Under the CERCLA statute, response actions may either be taken by responsible parties or by the Environmental Protection Agency (EPA) or a state. If the federal government undertakes the response action, expenditures are made from the Hazardous Substances Superfund. In turn, EPA is authorized to recover fund expenditures from responsible parties. Section 107 of CERCLA provides for the recovery of response costs through judicial actions.[1] The recovery of Superfund expenditures through the cost recovery program has been a high EPA priority. The objectives of the program are to maximize the return of revenue to the fund and to encourage settlement without unnecessary recourse to litigation.

Private parties responding to a request by the government for reimbursement of response costs must consider a number of factors. First of all, are the response actions reasonable and cost-effective? If not, there may be a basis for contesting the request. Second, are the particular categories of costs reimbursable? For example, to what extent may medical monitoring costs be recovered? Other issues may arise concerning whether the project has been mismanaged, particularly in light of indications that EPA's oversight of its contractors has been inadequate. Finally, questions may arise as to whether the government or a private party can adequately document the costs claimed. In this connection, basic principles of accounting as well as federal regulations governing government contracts provide a guide as to the kind of documentation that may be expected to support a claim for response costs.

§ 20.2   General Legal Principles

Section 121(b) of CERCLA[2] directs the EPA to "select a remedial action that is protective of human health and the environment, that is cost-effective, and that utilizes permanent solutions and alternative treatment technologies" to the extent practicable. Under CERCLA § 107(a), the

---

[1] 42 U.S.C. § 9607 (1988).

[2] *Id.* § 9621(b).

government may only recover those costs incurred that are "not incon-sistent with the National Contingency Plan" (NCP).[3] The NCP, in turn, must include "means of assuring that remedial action measures are cost-effective."[4] This means that the remedial action selected by the EPA must be the "lowest cost alternative that is technologically feasible,"[5] and must provide adequate protection of public health or the environment.

In view of these requirements, courts have recognized that a cost recov-ery trial under § 107 "will not be a pro forma proceeding but will permit presentation of adequate evidence for careful and exacting study by the court."[6] In *Lone Pine,* the Third Circuit further noted that "[t]he courts are not unaware of bureaucratic excesses and will undoubtedly look care-fully at the claims made by the government when a suit for reimburse-ments is brought under § 9607."[7]

The Sixth Circuit adopted a similar approach in *J.V. Peters & Co. v. EPA.*[8] The court noted that a potentially responsible party (PRP) would have ample opportunity in a cost recovery action to contest whether EPA's actions were inconsistent with the NCP. The court believed that "[t]he pos-sibility of failing to recoup expenditures in a cost-recovery action operates as an effective constraint upon EPA's decision to itself undertake a cleanup under Section 104."[9]

Other judicial decisions have adopted a narrower scope of review of gov-ernment costs. In *United States v. Bell Petroleum Services,*[10] the court took notice of the fact that the government often runs inefficiently but held that it is nonetheless entitled to reimbursement.

Although courts have been somewhat reluctant to second-guess the gov-ernment's response costs, a focused challenge to specific instances of un-necessary or improperly performed work or an arbitrary response action may meet with success.[11]

---

[3] *Id.* § 9607(a)(4)(A).

[4] 42 U.S.C. § 9605(a)(7). *See also* H.R. Res. No. 253, 99th Cong., 1st Sess., pt. 1, at 57 (1985), *reprinted in* 1986 U.S. Cong. & Admin. News 2,835, 2,839 (requiring that all cleanup "must be cost-effective"); 55 Fed. Reg. 8,666, 8,850 (Mar. 8, 1990) (to be codified at 40 C.F.R. § 300.430(f)(1)(ii)(D)).

[5] United States v. NEPACCO, 810 F.2d 726, 748 (8th Cir. 1986), *cert. denied,* 484 U.S. 848 (1987).

[6] Lone Pine Steering Comm. v. EPA, 777 F.2d 882, 887 (3d Cir. 1985), *cert. denied,* 476 U.S. 115 (1986).

[7] *Id.* at 887.

[8] 767 F.2d 263 (6th Cir. 1985).

[9] *Id.* at 266.

[10] 734 F. Supp. 771 (W.D. Tex. 1990).

[11] *See* United States v. Ottati & Goss, Inc., 900 F.2d 429 (1st Cir. 1990); Colorado v. Idarado Mining Co., 707 F. Supp. 1227 (D. Colo. 1989); Amoco Oil Co. v. Borden, Inc., 889 F.2d 664 (5th Cir. 1989).

§ 20.3   Selection of the Remedy

The law concerning EPA's selection of the remedy is not well developed. The government takes the position that the courts have a very narrow scope of review, and that EPA's decision in selecting the remedy must be upheld except in unusual circumstances. Private parties, on the other hand, have been skeptical of EPA's claim for deference, and in some cases they have maintained that the government's selection of the remedy was, in whole or in part, fundamentally flawed and therefore that the government should not be entitled to all of the response costs claimed. In cases in which the remedy is very expensive and appears to be novel or unjustified, responsible parties may well refuse to perform the remedy and challenge the government's selection of the remedy in court.

Section 107 of CERCLA provides that the government may be awarded "all costs of removal action or remedial action . . . not inconsistent with the National Contingency Plan."[12] Thus, responsible parties should carefully review the remedy to determine its consistency with the NCP. For example, the following aspects of the NCP should be considered in detail:

1.   Limitations on response (40 C.F.R. § 300.400(b))
2.   Identification of ARARs (§ 300.400(g))
3.   Appropriateness of removal action (§ 300.415(b)(2))
4.   Developing and screening remedial alternatives (§ 300.430(e))
5.   Selection of remedy (§ 300.430(f)(1))
6.   Documentation of the remedial decision (§ 300.430(f)(5)).

Section 113(j) of CERCLA, 42 U.S.C. § 9613(j), provides that in any judicial action under CERCLA, the government's decision in selecting the response action shall be upheld unless the objecting party can demonstrate on the administrative record that the decision was arbitrary and capricious or otherwise not in accordance with law. Although judicial review is normally limited to the administrative record, § 113(j) provides further that otherwise applicable principles of administrative law shall govern whether any supplemental material may be considered by the courts.

These principles indicate that evidence outside the record may be introduced when the record does not contain all of the information considered by the decision maker, or the record reveals that the agency failed to consider relevant factors or failed adequately to explain its decision making.[13]

---

[12] 42 U.S.C. § 9607(a)(4)(A).

[13] See, e.g., Citizens to Preserve Overton Park, Inc. v. Volpe, 401 U.S. 402, 419–20 (1971); Animal Defense Council v. Hodel, 840 F.2d 1432, 1436 (9th Cir. 1988); Norwich Eaton Pharmaceuticals, Inc. v. Bowen, 808 F.2d 486, 489 (6th Cir.), cert. denied, 484 U.S. 816 (1987).

In addition, it should be noted that under § 7003 of RCRA, judicial review is not confined to the administrative record but must be decided in traditional trials after full discovery.[14]

§ 20.4   Nature of Recoverable Costs

As noted in § 20.3, the government's recoverable costs are limited to "removal action" and "remedial action."[15] The terms *removal* and *remedial action* are further defined in § 101 of CERCLA.[16] The following are key categories of costs that the government has claimed under CERCLA.

Security Measures

Response costs include "security fencing or other measures to limit access."[17] In a private cost recovery suit, however, a district court held that although the costs of erecting a fence were clearly within the definition of reimbursable response costs, they were not recoverable under Superfund because the evidence showed that the plaintiff had taken these actions before it became aware of the presence of contamination on its property.[18]

Investigation, Monitoring, and Evaluation

The term *removal* includes "such actions as may be necessary to monitor, assess, and evaluate the release or threat of release of hazardous substances."[19] A number of decisions have held that recoverable costs of response include costs of investigating, monitoring, testing, and evaluating a site.[20]

---

[14] United States v. Conservation Chem. Co. (II), 661 F. Supp. 1416, 1425 n.16 (W.D. Mo. 1987); United States v. Hardage, 663 F. Supp. 1280, 1286 (W.D. Okla. 1987). The legislative history states that this section "provides for the awarding of equitable relief and, as with any equitable remedy, requires the court to consider all circumstances of the case and to carefully balance all relevant factors." S. Res. No. 284, 98th Cong., 1st Sess. 59 (1983).

[15] 42 U.S.C. § 9607(a)(4)(A).

[16] *Id.* § 9601(23), (24).

[17] *Id.* § 9601(23). *See* Cadillac Fairview/California, Inc. v. Dow Chem. Co., 840 F.2d 691, 695 (9th Cir. 1988); Amoco Oil Co. v. Borden, Inc., 889 F.2d 664, 672 (5th Cir. 1989).

[18] Amland Properties Corp. v. Aluminum Co. of Am., 711 F. Supp. 784, 795 (D.N.J. 1989).

[19] 42 U.S.C. § 9601(23).

[20] *See* United States v. Wade, 577 F. Supp. 1326, 1333 n.4 (E.D. Pa. 1983); United States v. NEPACCO, 579 F. Supp. 823, 850 (W.D. Mo. 1984); City of New York v. Exxon Corp., 633 F. Supp. 609, 617 (S.D.N.Y. 1986).

Alternative Water Supplies, Temporary Evacuation, and Medical Tests

The term *removal* includes "provision of alternative water supplies, temporary evacuation and housing of threatened individuals not otherwise provided for," as well as emergency assistance that may be provided under the disaster relief act.[21] *Remedial action* also includes the cost of permanent relocation if the government determines that such relocation is more cost effective and environmentally preferable to the cleanup of the site itself.[22]

The costs of providing an alternative water supply are recoverable if the existing water supply is contaminated or is threatened with contamination.[23]

There is a split of authority on medical screening or monitoring costs.[24] Courts have held that the costs of medical testing and screening to assess the effect of a release or discharge on public health are recoverable.[25] In *Hopkins v. Elano Corp.,*[26] for example, the court held that Congress did not intend to create a federal toxic tort action or to allow third parties to recover damages caused by the release of hazardous substances, but the court indicated that medical screening may be an appropriate response cost under Superfund. However, several decisions have held that the costs of medical monitoring for personal health reasons are not recoverable.[27]

Cleanup Costs

Removal actions include the cleanup or removal of hazardous substances, the disposal of removed material, or the taking of such other measures as may be necessary to prevent, minimize, or mitigate damage to the public health or welfare or to the environment.[28] Remedial actions include storage, confinement, perimeter protection using dikes, trenches, or ditches, clay cover, neutralization, cleanup of released hazardous substances, recycling or reuse, diversion, destruction, dredging or excavation, repair or

---

[21] 42 U.S.C. § 9601(23).

[22] *Id.* § 9601(24).

[23] Artesian Water Co. v. New Castle County, 659 F. Supp. 1269, 1287–88 (D. Del. 1987).

[24] For a general discussion of this split of authority, *see* Coburn v. Sun Chem. Corp., 17 Chem. Waste Litig. Rep. 106, 109–113 (E.D. Pa. 1988).

[25] Brewer v. Ravan, 680 F. Supp. 1176, 1179 (M.D. Tenn. 1988).

[26] 30 Env't Rep. Cas. (BNA) 1782, 1786 (S.D. Ohio 1989).

[27] Chaplin v. Exxon Co., 25 Env't Rep. Cas. (BNA) 2009, 2011–12 (S.D. Tex. 1987); Wehner v. Syntex, 15 (Computer L. Rep., Inc.) 540, 541 (N.D. Cal. 1987).

[28] 42 U.S.C. § 9601(23).

replacement of leaking containers, collection of leachate or runoff, and on-site treatment or incineration.[29]

Oversight Costs

CERCLA by its terms does not refer expressly to oversight costs. EPA takes the position that it may recover the costs of supervising its contractors, and judicial decisions have allowed such costs.[30]

Prejudgment Interest

CERCLA states that the amounts recoverable "shall include interest."[31] The courts have accordingly held that the government may recover prejudgment interest.[32]

Enforcement Costs

As originally enacted, CERCLA did not define removal or remedial action to include internal agency costs. However, the SARA amendments of 1986 expanded the definition of the term respond or response to "include enforcement activities related thereto."[33] This amendment appears to have settled the question of whether the government can recover the costs of its attorneys and other employees when it files a cost recovery action.[34]

Although courts have indicated that government enforcement costs may be recovered, there remain issues as to particular categories of costs and how they are computed. In *United States v. Ottati & Goss, Inc.,*[35] the court reduced certain costs claimed by the government for lack of sufficient evidence that the costs could be attributed directly to the site in question.[36] The court also discounted certain costs and fees due to "untoward conduct" of the government in handling its lawsuit.[37]

---

[29] *Id.* § 9601(24).

[30] New York v. Shore Realty Corp., 759 F.2d 1032, 1042–43 (2d Cir. 1985); United States v. Ottati & Goss, Inc., 694 F. Supp. 977, 996 (D.N.H. 1988).

[31] 42 U.S.C. § 9607(a).

[32] United States v. Mexico Feed & Seed Co., 729 F. Supp. 1250, 1253–54 (E.D. Mo. 1990).

[33] 42 U.S.C. § 9601(25).

[34] *See* United States v. NEPACCO, 579 F. Supp. at 85; United States v. Mottolo, 695 F. Supp. 615, 631 (D.N.H. 1988); General Elec. Co. v. Litton Business Sys., 715 F. Supp. 949, 958–59 (W.D. Mo. 1989).

[35] 694 F. Supp. 977 (D.N.H. 1988).

[36] *Id.* at 995.

[37] *Id.* at 997. *See also* United States v. Hardage, 733 F. Supp. 1424, 1435 (W.D. Okla. 1989) (holding that there was a genuine issue of material fact as to whether particular indirect costs were excessive).

There is a split in authority on the question of whether attorneys' fees are recoverable as response costs in private cost recovery actions. Several decisions have held that they are not recoverable.[38]

Private Economic or Personal Injury Losses

The courts have held that CERCLA does not provide a remedy for personal injury or for economic losses resulting from the release of hazardous substances.[39]

§ 20.5   Incurred Cost Claims

The March 1990 NCP provides that response actions shall be conducted under existing programs and authority.[40] It also provides that the lead agency shall complete and maintain documentation taken to form the basis for cost recovery, including "accurate accounting" of costs incurred for response actions.[41] EPA's Superfund Cost Recovery Strategy Directive emphasizes that quality record keeping "is essential since the Agency must be able to substantiate the amount of money demanded and what activities were performed for that amount."[42]

Federal government contracts must comply with the Federal Acquisition Regulations (FAR). These regulations address contract methods and types, contract requirements, and contract management.[43] EPA's own regulations provide that the FAR are applicable to all EPA contracts except when excluded.[44] All cooperative agreements require the states to comply with the procurement regulations in 40 C.F.R. part 33 as well as other program provisions. In addition, EPA has issued several directives and memos concerning appropriate contract procedures and cost documentation under

---

[38] Regan v. Cherry Corp., 706 F. Supp. 145, 149 (D.R.I. 1989); T&E Indus., Inc. v. Safety Light Corp., 680 F. Supp. 696, 707–08 (D.N.J. 1988); *In re* Hemingway Transp., Inc., 108 Bankr. 378, 383 (Bankr. D. Mass. 1989). *But see* International Clinical Laboratories, Inc. v. Stevens, 710 F. Supp. 466, 30 Env't Rep. Cas. (BNA) 2067, 2069 (E.D.N.Y. 1990); General Elec. Co. v. Litton Business Sys., Inc., 715 F. Supp. 949, 958–59 (W.D. Mo. 1989).

[39] Allied Towing v. Great E. Petroleum Corp., 642 F. Supp. 1339, 1348 (E.D. Va. 1986); Artesian Water Co. v. New Castle County, 659 F. Supp. at 1285–86; Brewer v. Ravan, 680 F. Supp. 1176, 1179 (M.D. Tenn. 1988); Piccolini v. Simon's Wrecking, 686 F. Supp. 1063, 1068 (M.D. Pa. 1988); Regan v. Cherry Corp., 706 F. Supp. at 151–52.

[40] 40 C.F.R. § 300.160(c) (1990).

[41] *Id.* § 300.160(a)(1).

[42] EPA, Superfund Cost Recovery Strategy, OSWER Directive No. 9832.13 at 36 (July 29, 1988).

[43] *See* 48 C.F.R. §§ 13.000, 27.000, 42.100.

[44] *Id.* § 1501.103.

CERCLA. Taken together, these requirements constitute a significant body of law relating to EPA's recovery of response costs under CERCLA. EPA's contracting and accounting procedures are likely to receive increasing scrutiny as a result of recent investigations and critiques.[45]

The costs associated with the government's *incurred cost claims* typically include all the various costs that governmental agencies claim to have incurred as a result of studying, planning, or performing a site cleanup. The typical type of costs included are:

1. EPA payroll costs
2. EPA indirect costs
3. EPA travel costs
4. Other EPA costs
5. EPA contractor/subcontractor costs
    –Remedial planning contracts
    –Field investigation contracts
    –Technical assistance contracts
    –Contract lab program
    –Enforcement investigation contracts
6. Interagency agreement costs
    –Department of the Interior
    –Department of Justice
    –Direct costs
    –Indirect costs
    –Contractor/subcontractor costs
7. Other federal government agencies.

These claims typically include cost components such as personnel, outside contractors, and overhead. The personnel components usually include expenses for government technicians and attorneys. The majority of these costs usually consist of salaries, benefits, and travel expenses. Outside contractor costs include specialty firms hired by EPA to provide various services to the site, including soil sampling, chemical analysis, groundwater monitoring, and security. The overheads are multi-faceted and include all indirect costs incurred by EPA, such as support personnel, buildings and facilities, training, public affairs, and computers. The government pools these overhead costs and performs various allocation steps in determining

---

[45] *See* General Accounting Office, Superfund Contracts, EPA Needs to Control Contractor Costs (July 1988) [hereinafter GAO Report]; Office of Technology Assessment (U.S. Congress), Assessing Contractor Use in Superfund (January 1989) [hereinafter OTA Report].

what is charged to the site. An indirect rate is developed from this allocation process and applied to the site, using the direct labor hours charged to the site. These direct labor hours are usually for the same attorneys and technicians mentioned.

The incurred cost claim contains many components, which together can add up to a sizeable financial liability for PRPs. At the very least there are several reviews that should be performed on the government's claim to assure that it is justifiable and reasonable. The government must be able to provide sufficient cost documentation to verify that all costs included in the claim were in fact incurred and provided some benefit to the site in question. In many instances, the government has submitted limited documentation summarizing total costs incurred but failed to provide any detail. As EPA Administrator William Reilly reported, "To support cost recovery actions, EPA has to be able to show that its remedy selection decision was neither arbitrary nor capricious, and it must be able to provide adequate documentation of costs related to the site."[46] Additionally, the EPA's Financial Management Division/Office of the Comptroller has issued directives detailing exactly what costs and types of documents should be maintained. EPA policy is to reconcile all documentation with the Financial Management System (FMS), to review all documentation to assure that it is complete and properly chargeable to the specific site, and to assure that records are maintained consistent with the OSWER Directives System.[47] Thus, a review can and should be performed by the PRPs, or their representative, on the costs incurred and included in the government's claims. The following sections elaborate on the documentation appropriate for particular categories of costs.

§ 20.6   —Direct Costs

Direct costs basically consist of payroll, travel, and other costs identifiable to a specific site. The type of documentation that can be requested would include:

Payroll

1. All timesheets and timecards for both EPA Regional and headquarters personnel for whom costs have been charged to the site
2. Pay rate documentation for all applicable personnel in all appropriate time periods

---

[46] EPA, A Management Review of the Superfund Program, William K. Reilly, Administrator, at 3–8 (1989).

[47] Office of the Comptroller, EPA Resources Management Directives System, Financial Management of the Superfund Program, chapter 2550D-6 at 12-1 (1988).

3. Documentation on the types of tasks performed by all appropriate personnel
4. Documentation on the types and amount of employee benefits included.

Travel

1. Regional and headquarters travel summaries listing each trip made by the appropriate personnel. Information should include employee name, dates of travel, travel authorization number, cost amount, and paid treasury schedule number and transaction date.
2. Receipts, including travel and payment vouchers, "Schedule of Expenses and Amount Claimed," travel authorization forms, and documentation regarding the purpose and results of the trip.
3. Invoices supporting multiple site trips should include the basis used for the allocation used.

Other Costs

1. Documentation supporting the purchase of any equipment, materials, or supplies
2. Property inventory listing of all nonexpendable property with a unit acquisition cost of $1,000 or more, and with a life expectancy of one year or more
3. Any other direct costs not included in the above categories.

§ 20.7   —Indirect Costs

Indirect costs are those which cannot be readily identifiable to any one site but which add incremental cost to the cleanup program. The standards relating to indirect costs require that any indirect cost included in billings to EPA represent, in accordance with GAO principles, indirect costs that would not have been otherwise incurred by the agency, or for which explicit congressional authority exists for charging other than the incremental costs of performance.[48]

With that in mind, the type of documentation supporting the indirect costs should include:

1. Summaries of indirect costs for the specific site by fiscal year. This should include program hours, indirect cost rates per hour, and total indirect costs by fiscal year.

---

[48] *Id.*

2. EPA indirect cost "Stand-Alone Document" and all other EPA manuals relating to indirect costs.

3. Superfund Appropriation Trust Fund audit reports (entitled *Auditors' Reports on Financial and Compliance Audit of Obligations and Disbursements Under CERCLA*) for underlying audit workpapers for all applicable fiscal years.

In addition to the necessary documentation review, there should be a review of how the costs incrementally benefitted the site. This review often focuses on the reasonableness of including certain costs within the overhead pools. For example, an argument can be made that many of the ongoing costs of operating the government are fixed; in other words, the government is going to incur the costs regardless of whether the site was identified by EPA or CERCLA was ever passed. A second issue relates to the actual incurrence of the costs. The Government Services Agency (GSA) issues an interagency charge for rent commonly known as SLUC (Standard Level User Charge). This charge is simply an accounting transfer. No actual payments are made by any agency to GSA. However, agencies like EPA often include this charge in its overhead pools, resulting in higher indirect rates. Finally, there is the question of government efficiency. Many parties have questioned the amount of government overhead compared to that of private industry.

§ 20.8   —Interagency Agreements

Interagency Agreements (IAG) are written agreements between Federal agencies to provide goods and services. The EPA has IAGs for Superfund that are designed to provide support in the cleanup effort. Included within the government's claims are the costs associated with IAGs. However, not all of the costs are recovered by the agencies. Depending on the arrangement between the agencies, there may not be an actual transfer of funds for services provided. For example, in 1987 the EPA and the Department of Justice (DOJ) signed two agreements that provided DOJ recovery of only direct charges for services it provided to EPA. Thus, when the DOJ performs enforcement activities on a site using EPA assistance, it can only recover EPA's direct costs in its claims. EPA's indirect costs are not passed on through DOJ to the claim.

PRPs should request documentation for IAGs. This documentation should include:

1. IAG cost summaries listing each Federal agency for which costs are claimed. This information should also list the federal agency by name and interagency agreement number.

2. Employee information, including payroll cost summaries, time-sheets, pay rate documentation for all applicable pay periods, and detailed information on all tasks performed by each employee.

3. Travel vouchers and receipts, "Schedule of Expenses and Amounts Claimed," travel authorization forms, details on all tasks performed by each employee, and the results of each trip.

§ 20.9 —Contractor Costs

A major component of the costs incurred in both removal and remedial actions are contractor costs. Due to EPA staffing limitations and the lack of certain qualified personnel, nearly all Superfund activities are performed by contractors.[49] As such, the impact they exert on the cleanup process and the resulting costs associated therewith are substantial.

Recent reports issued by Congress and other governmental agencies have noted that these contractors have been engaged not merely for carrying out engineering and construction, but also for the technical expertise, information, and analysis that form the backbone of Superfund policies, programs, and decisions. Obviously, with contractors playing such an influential role in the Superfund decision making processes, potential problems can exist, including how contracts are awarded, conflicts of interest, and, of course, cost controls.

The EPA has taken a considerable amount of criticism over the contract award process. Under government contracting requirements, EPA must maintain as competitive a bidding process as possible and cannot limit qualification or award. To promote competition and allow as many contractors to be involved in cleanups as possible, EPA is held to the Federal Acquisition Register (FAR) regulations. These regulations state that:

a) The recipient [EPA] shall conduct all procurement transactions in a manner that provides maximum open and free competition.

b) Procurement practices shall not unduly restrict or eliminate competition.

c) The recipient may use a prequalified list(s) of persons, firms or products if it:

1. Updates its prequalified list(s) at least every six months;

2. Reviews and acts on each request for prequalification made more than 30 days before the closing date for receipt of proposals or bid opening; and

3. Gives adequate public notice of its prequalification procedure in accordance with public notice procedures.

---

[49] OTA Report at 11.

d) A recipient may not use a prequalified list(s) of persons or firms if the procedure unnecessarily restricts competition.[50]

Although the code itself appears clear on what is required, EPA actions have in some cases raised the attention of the General Accounting Office (GAO). Despite these regulations, EPA has had problems with maintaining competition in the award process. This has been especially evident in the Emergency Response Contracting System (ERCS). However, EPA has taken some steps to improve this award procedure to increase competition and lower removal contract prices.[51]

Because of the nature and broad base of services provided by contractors, conflicts of interest are possible. Contractors have not only been awarded removal and remedial work, but also policy and regulatory responsibility. The EPA recognizes that:

> This has been most problematic in the Superfund Program when a firm is awarded a contract for a cleanup program that they also helped design. A real potential for conflict arises if the firm recommends using cleanup technologies or methods offered by its subsidiaries or is charged with implementing in the field the very policies or regulations it developed for EPA in Washington.[52]

The EPA maintains procedures that should identify, review, and, where appropriate, respond to contractor conflicts. However, many contend that not enough has been done. A Senate subcommittee has noted that there are many opportunities to strengthen such procedures.[53]

Since Superfund's original enactment in 1980, Congress and the general public have placed emphasis on getting sites cleaned up as soon as possible. As a result, the EPA's emphasis has been on site remediation with little regard for the costs involved. A General Accounting Office report issued in 1988 stated that "[W]e found that EPA monitoring and control efforts focus on the timeliness and quality of the contractor's work rather than cost . . . we identified cost as the greatest point of risk under remedial contracts."[54] Additionally, it was found that "EPA was emphasizing the accomplishment of program goals and objectives at the expense of sound contract management."[55]

---

[50] 40 C.F.R. § 33.230.

[51] Durenberger and Lautenberg, Report on Superfund Implementation: Cleaning Up The Nation's Clean Up Program 177 [hereinafter Durenberger & Lautenberg].

[52] EPA, A Management Review of the Superfund Program, William K. Reilly, Administrator at 6–9 (1989).

[53] Durenberger & Lautenberg at 181.

[54] GAO Report at 16.

[55] *Id.* at 15.

The EPA awards contract work using cost-plus-fee-award contracts. These agreements pay contractors based on actual hours and expenses incurred. Contractors simply submit their total recorded hours, which are then multiplied by a weighted average hourly rate. Cost-plus-fee-award contracts have been justified on grounds of the uncertainty of project scope. However, the cost-plus arrangement gives the contractors no incentive to control the hours and expenses charged. Additionally, contractors frequently are not required to meet specified results. Thus, contractor performance must be carefully monitored and reviewed by the government.

A GAO review found that many of the management controls available to EPA for contractor review are not fully utilized. EPA has thus failed to question many of the cost increases sought by contractors. As expected, some of the increases were due to expanded scope of work, but it was noted that in many cases the increases were due to poor contractor performance. This poor performance results from a myriad of causes. "For example, contractors placed groundwater monitoring wells in inappropriate locations, made errors in preparing groundwater samples, and inadequately supported remedial study reports and submitted the reports late."[56] Further, GAO found that there was no indication that EPA even challenged the payment of additional costs associated with solving the errors and tardiness. As one EPA official said, "We have to pay no matter how many drafts the contractor has to write to get an acceptable contract" and "I am powerless to do anything about costs associated with poor performance under a level of contract effort."[57]

The bottom line is that PRPs are going to feel the impact of these contracting problems. EPA's failure to get competitive pricing, eliminate conflicts of interest, and, most important, to control contractor costs, will ultimately lead to larger claims. Therefore, it is recommended that as part of any claim review, PRPs analyze contractor costs. In many cases, this component can often be as large, if not larger, than the government's costs. The request for supporting documentation should include:

1. Contractors' cost summaries, including voucher numbers, dates of service, work authorization numbers, national voucher numbers, site specific vouchers, and subsite-specific voucher amounts.

2. Contractors' direct costs, including payroll cost summaries, timesheets for each employee, applicable pay rates, and information detailing all tasks performed by employees

3. Contractors' rate structures, detailing allocation percentage of actual overhead, general and administrative costs, any other indirect costs,

---

[56] *Id.* at 24.

[57] *Id.*

and Defense Contract Audit Administration or other Federal government agency documentation of final audited overhead, general, and administrative costs.

Payments to contractors make up a sizeable portion of Superfund expenditures. As such, any problems arising from the use of contractors ultimately impact the costs included in claims made against PRPs. EPA, to its credit, has recognized this problem and is attempting to develop suitable solutions. However, until viable solutions are found, PRPs must understand that these problems and lack of controls can adversely impact the quality, timeliness, and total costs of removal and remediation.

The passage of CERCLA (and the subsequent passage of SARA) underscores the need for the government and companies across the country to tackle waste site remediation issues. While the potential management problems and financial liabilities seem staggering, they are not hopeless. The solution is not to throw money at the problem. Costs can and should be contained. By improving the efficiency of the cleanup program and holding all participants accountable for the monies spent, costs can be reduced. Additionally, as new approaches are developed, allowing for greater flexibility, costs will decrease.

Although the number of sites actually cleaned up is relatively small,[58] much has been learned by both the government and responsible parties on how to control costs. This knowledge, combined with continued emphasis on the cost effectiveness of the cleanup program, should in turn help EPA become more efficient in managing this effort.

---

[58] As of 1989, only 26 sites had been removed from the National Priorities list, leaving the total at approximately 1200.

CHAPTER 21

CONSEQUENTIAL COSTS

Brad P. Keller
Knute P. Kurtz
Melvin S. Schulze

Brad P. Keller is a manager in the Business Investigation Services Group in the Atlanta, Georgia, office of Coopers & Lybrand. He specializes in providing litigation and reorganization services on real estate and environmental issues. He has also an extensive background in providing litigation and management services to troubled financial institutions. Mr. Keller is a member of the American, Oklahoma, and Georgia Bar Associations. He is a cum laude graduate of the St. Louis University School of Law and a cum laude graduate of the University of Missouri with a B.S. degree in finance and economics.

Knute P. Kurtz is a partner in the Business Investigation Services Group in the Atlanta, Georgia, office of Coopers & Lybrand. He has extensive experience in the construction and real estate industries. The major focus of his practice is providing business and financial advice to attorneys throughout the litigation process, including providing expert testimony. He also advises lenders and owners on restructuring troubled real estate and construction projects. Mr. Kurtz has a B.S. in accounting and is a certified public accountant.

Melvin S. Schulze is an attorney with Hunton & Williams' Energy and Environmental Team in Atlanta, Georgia, where his practice covers a broad range of environmental law issues involving proceedings before state and federal agencies and courts. Mr. Schulze received his B.S. from the University of the South (Sewanee), his M.S. from the University of Michigan, and his J.D. from George Washington University. He is a member of the ABA Administrative Law and Natural Resources Law Sections, the State Bar of Georgia, and the District of Columbia Bar. He currently serves as an assistant editor for *Natural Resources and Environment,* the Natural Resources Law Section's quarterly publication.

§ 21.1   The Concept of Economic Loss

The purpose of the judicial system in resolving disputes is to return the injured party to the position he would have been in had the injury not occurred. The same is equally true of an action that arises out of environmental contamination. One difficult question presented by such an action is how to determine the full extent of the economic loss suffered by a party as the result of the environmental contamination.

Chapter 20 discussed the cleanup costs that may be recoverable as the result of a remediation effort. However, in many instances the economic loss suffered by a party required to engage in a remediation effort may be far greater than simply the cost of the cleanup itself. This chapter focuses on the full extent of the economic loss that may be suffered by a party to an environmental cleanup effort and how a party may attempt to recover that loss.

The direct and immediate damages incurred by a party arising out of environmental contamination are obviously the costs to "clean" the site. There may also be additional costs that are not the direct and immediate result of the contamination but which flow from and are the result of the contamination itself. These other costs are known as the consequential costs or damages.[1]

---

[1] Black's Law Dictionary 352 (5th ed. 1983). The terms *consequential costs* and *consequential damages* are used interchangeably in this chapter.

The one area in which consequential costs from environmental contamination have seen a great deal of development is in the area of personal injury litigation. The concept that an injured party must receive a recovery of consequential damages for lost wages, diminished earning capacity, pain and suffering, emotional distress, and the like in order to be made whole for his or her loss is well developed in our current personal injury jurisprudence. Not as apparently well developed is the concept of making a business enterprise whole for the full extent of its economic loss as the result of environmental contamination. This is perhaps owed to the fact that environmental response costs can quickly reach the million dollar mark in even a relatively small cleanup effort. In addition, these cleanup costs are out-of-pocket expenses that directly impact the bottom line of a business. Consequential costs also impact the bottom line but, because they are seldom viewed as direct out-of-pocket expenses, they tend to be less apparent without a thorough examination of the business and the market in which it functions.

The recovery of these consequential costs may be vital to the continued economic viability of a business. The expenses incurred in cleaning up an environmentally contaminated site may most properly be viewed as no more than the diversion of funds by a business to a non-income producing asset. Any business that diverts hundreds of thousands of dollars a year for a number of years from ongoing operations to a non-income producing asset suffers a loss far greater than merely the dollars diverted to that cleanup effort. Thus, it is the loss suffered by the business from this diversion of assets that conceptually defines the potentially recoverable consequential costs.

§ 21.2   Legal Prerequisites for the Recovery of Consequential Costs

The Comprehensive Environmental Response, Compensation, and Liability Act (CERCLA),[2] as amended, sets forth the types of damages that may be recovered in a private enforcement action. However, this law falls far short in allowing injured parties to seek compensation for the full extent of their economic loss from environmental contamination.[3] Costs not directly related to the cleanup efforts or otherwise deemed not to be "response costs" under CERCLA are not recoverable in a private

---

[2] 42 U.S.C. §§ 9601–9675 (1988).

[3] For a good overview of the present inadequacy in this area of existing federal law, *see* Straube, *Is Full Compensation Possible for the Damage Resulting from the Exxon Valdez Oil Spill,* 19 Envtl. L. Rep. 10338 (1989); Buchele, *State Common Law Actions and Federal Pollution Control Statutes: Can They Work Together?* 1986 U. Ill. L. Rev. 1013 (1986); and Babich, *Restructuring Environmental Law,* 19 Envtl. L. Rep. (Envtl. L. Inst.) 10057 (1989).

enforcement action.[4] Most courts have strictly construed items that may be recovered as response costs. Indeed, even the costs incurred to provide for future medical screening and monitoring costs have been held by some courts not to be response costs and therefore not recoverable under CERCLA.[5] Accordingly, consequential costs are generally not recoverable in an action under the federal Superfund statute.

There are, however, a number of common law theories that may be utilized as part of a private enforcement action that might permit the recovery of consequential costs. The common law theories of trespass, nuisance, strict liability for abnormally dangerous activity, breach of contract, and breach of warranty all represent possible theories of liability that might permit the recovery of consequential costs. These actions are discussed at length in **Chapter 4**. Thus, although CERCLA does not provide for the recovery of consequential costs, there are other avenues available to permit their recovery in an action for environmental contamination.

Regardless of the theory of liability pled in any particular case, there is a factual prerequisite that must be met as a prima facie matter in almost every instance. As a threshold matter it must be shown that there has been physical damage to a proprietary interest of the plaintiff in order to maintain an action for economic loss from environmental contamination.[6] Courts have been extremely reluctant to recognize claims based solely upon economic loss absent such an injury. The principle which underlies this rule is well settled and traces its roots to English common law. This limitation on recovery is best explained as a pragmatic one: the repercussions from permitting recovery for economic loss by those who have at best an indirect relationship to the negligent or tortious conduct would leave damage recovery virtually open-ended.[7] Therefore, actual damage to a proprietary interest must be established. The test utilized by the courts to determine the presence of a proprietary interest focuses on the character of the interest harmed.[8] Such a focus somewhat lessens the impact of the damage to a proprietary interest test and appears to extend the scope of permitted actions. Thus, actions have been permitted when a party has established a course of business conduct that makes commercial use of a public right.[9]

---

[4] Mesiti v. Microdot, Inc., Civil No. 89-321-D, slip op. (D.N.H., June 8, 1990).

[5] Coburn v. San Chem. Corp., 19 Envtl. L. Rep. (Envtl. L. Inst.) 20256 (E.D. Pa. 1989).

[6] Robins Dry Dock v. Flint, 275 U.S. 303 (1927); Louisiana *ex rel.* Guste v. M/V Testbank, 752 F.2d 1019 (5th Cir. 1985) (en banc).

[7] Louisiana *ex rel.* Guste v. M/V Testbank, 752 F.2d 1019.

[8] Louisiana *ex rel.* Guste v. M/V Testbank, 524 F. Supp. 1170 (E.D. La. 1981), *aff'd,* 752 F.2d (5th Cir. 1985) (en banc).

[9] This focus has permitted fisherman and clammers to pursue actions for tortious invasion of commercial fishing areas even though they have no individual property rights

It is also important to note that in certain instances a party's ability to establish liability relies upon its ability to prove damages. For example, it has been held that proof of lowered property values as the result of environmental contamination was sufficient to establish liability under theories of both nuisance and abnormally dangerous activity.[10] Accordingly, a party's focus at the early stages of litigation on the identification and subsequent proof of its full economic loss as consequential costs should not be overlooked.

§ 21.3 Consequential Costs

What then are the consequential costs that may be recovered in a suit arising out of the environmental contamination of another's property? The answer to that question is as broad and far-reaching as are the different types of possible litigants to such an action, the different types of environmental contamination, and the difficulty, extent, and cost of the cleanup effort itself. Accordingly, consequential damages are to a large extent unique to each individual action. Indeed, it has been held that the best way to define consequential costs in the context of environmental contamination is to exclude any notion that it is limited to recovery for either personal injury or physical damage to property.[11]

Consequential costs arising out of environmental contamination fall primarily into three areas:

1. Additional expenses that would not have been incurred, but for the contamination
2. Loss of revenues that could have been realized, but for the contamination
3. The impact of these expenses and revenues on corporate value.

The following discussion examines two different classes of potential plaintiffs most likely to be involved in commercial disputes arising out of environmental contamination. The first category of potential plaintiffs is businesses involved in a manufacturing process. The second category is entities or individuals owning an interest in real property.

It is important to note that due to the unique nature of consequential costs in the context of environmental litigation, this chapter does not

---

with respect to the aquatic life harmed by the contamination. *See generally* Louisiana *ex rel.* Guste v. M/V Testbank, 524 F. Supp. 1170 (E.D. La. 1981); *In re Exxon Valdez,* No. A89-095 Civil (D. Alaska Apr. 25, 1989).

[10] Crawford v. National Lead Co., 19 Envtl. L. Rep. (Envtl. L. Inst.) 21174 (S.D. Ohio 1989).

[11] Sanco, Inc. v. Ford Motor Co., 579 F. Supp. 893 (D. Ind. 1984).

attempt to provide an all-inclusive list of potentially recoverable consequential costs. What follows is an overview of the consequential costs that may be incurred by these two different categories of potential plaintiffs.

§ 21.4 —Manufacturing Businesses

The consequential costs incurred by a manufacturing concern as the result of environmental contamination fall primarily into the three areas previously mentioned: (a) additional expenses that would not have been incurred, but for the contamination; (b) loss of revenues that could have been realized, but for the contamination; and (c) the impact of these expenses and revenues on corporate value.

Additional Expenses

This category consists of all of the expenses incurred by the company due to the presence of environmentally hazardous substances. Included in this category are the costs related to environmental services, building maintenance, interest expense, and increased manufacturing costs.

Any company involved in the cleanup of environmental contamination could incur costs for environmental services that are not recoverable under CERCLA. Such costs might include professional and consulting fees, costs of medical screening and future medical monitoring, and other related expenses. Costs excluded from this category are costs incurred for environmental services determined to be related to cleanup efforts and those costs that were incurred expressly for, or in anticipation of, litigation.[12]

Building maintenance costs include all ongoing operating costs incurred in connection with the maintenance of the facility during the time that detection and remediation efforts took place. Thus, expenses for insurance, repairs and maintenance, security, taxes, utilities, and other related miscellaneous items all fall into this category. However, it is important to note that the cost components in this category necessarily vary to some extent depending upon the extent to which the company is required to cease operations during the cleanup effort.

Often, a company is only required to cease a portion of its operations as the result of the environmental contamination. When this occurs an investigation must be made to determine if the discontinuance of that portion of its operations has resulted in the increase of other manufacturing costs. This may be best described by way of example. One of the products Company A manufactures is remote control, battery-operated model cars. As

---

[12] See § 21.2.

the result of environmental contamination, seepage from an adjoining property, the operating division that produces the motor for these cars is forced to shut down. Rather than quit production of an entire product line, Company A procures motors for its model cars from an alternate source at a higher cost. The increased cost of the motors obviously increases the total cost of production of the model cars. It is the increase in the cost of production that will be included as a consequential cost arising out of the environmental contamination.

Therefore, an analysis of the impact on manufacturing costs from the suspension of operations should be performed any time a company is required to procure products and services that it would have otherwise provided for itself if it were not for the environmental contamination. This is the case whether an entire facility is closed or only a portion of its operations is suspended if that facility provides goods to another part of the company's operations.

Interest expense consists of all interest that has been paid or accrued during the period when the facility's operation is affected by the environmental contamination. Therefore, interest on debt secured by the property, plant, and/or equipment at the facility actually paid as well as accrued interest payable is included in this category.

Other additional expenses arising out of the environmental contamination that may be recoverable as consequential costs include items such as increased maintenance and repair of equipment and special, periodic cleaning procedures or other increased janitorial costs. Indeed, as previously mentioned, the identification of all of the consequential costs incurred by a manufacturing concern from environmental contamination is for the most part dependent on an analysis of the full impact the contamination has on the company's operations.

Loss of Revenues

The most obvious revenue loss that will be sustained by a company is the reduction in sales of goods in the normal course of business resulting from the suspension of operations during cleanup efforts. Obviously, this revenue loss will be net of expenses, and care must be taken to insure that any increase in expenses is not included in this calculation.

Not so obvious, but a potentially substantial revenue loss nonetheless, is any reduction in sales as the result of the company's inability to expand its production. This includes any revenue loss resulting from delays in bringing new products to market in addition to the inability to increase the production of existing goods.

Delays in bringing new products to market may result in a significant revenue loss to a company, particularly when the delay is substantial. A substantial delay in introducing a new product can, and often does, result in a permanent loss of market share for that product. Thus, the company loses not only revenues from the delay in sales but a permanent revenue loss as the direct result of the inability to introduce the product in a timely fashion. Indeed, should the loss of market share be significant, the company may find that the manufacture of the product is not profitable, thereby preventing it from being able to recover its research, development, and production costs, all as a result of the environmental contamination. If this occurs, these costs should also be included in a calculation of consequential costs. Because these losses may be too speculative, however, courts may be reluctant to award damages based upon lost market shares or loss of future sales.

Another source of lost revenue is any reduction in the salvage value of plant equipment due to the environmental contamination. If the anticipated value of the equipment at the end of its useful life has been so reduced, the company sustains a loss equal to the present value as compared to the previously anticipated sales value of that equipment.

Impairment of Corporate Value

Perhaps the most significant and most often overlooked consequential cost to a company is the loss of corporate value as a result of environmental contamination. A company required to divert funds to a non-income producing asset while contemporaneously suffering a loss of revenues will sustain an impairment of its corporate value. In order to ascertain the impairment of value suffered by the company, it is necessary to perform two different corporate valuation analyses. One analysis values the company at the present time. The second analysis values the company as if the environmental contamination had not occurred.

Basically stated, loss of corporate value represents the incremental difference in corporate worth that would have been realized had the above-stated expenditures not been incurred and had the above-stated revenue been realized. To determine the net impairment of corporate value, the total loss of corporate value must, however, be adjusted for the other items of expense and revenue separately claimed in the suit.

The primary assumptions that underlie this analysis are that, had the contamination not occurred:

1. No environmental expenses would have been incurred
2. All applicable revenues would have been realized in applicable years
3. The company would have instead used these funds as well as the costs spent to clean up the facility as capital available to fund ongoing operations of the business.

Therefore, the consequential cost identified as the impairment of corporate value is represented by the difference between the fair market value of the company had the environmental contamination not occurred and the present fair market value of the company.

Indeed, the consequential cost to a company represented by the impairment of its corporate value can be a very significant amount. In one recent incident, the impairment of corporate value suffered by a party whose operations were affected by a cleanup effort amounted to more than $10 million. Although this case was settled prior to trial, the evaluation of the company's consequential costs contributed significantly to the settlement. Therefore, an evaluation of the impairment of corporate value is of vital importance in order to fully determine the extent of an entity's economic loss arising out of environmental contamination.

§ 21.5   —Real Estate Owners

The consequential costs incurred by an individual or business entity that owns real estate fall into the same three primary categories identified for the owners of a manufacturing concern. However, although the categories remain the same, the conceptual analysis of the components that comprise each of these categories necessarily changes.

The consequential costs discussed in this section will primarily address the concerns of the owners of commercial real estate that is either already developed or is currently undergoing development. The consequential costs that would be incurred by the owners of undeveloped commercial real estate held for investment and/or residential property are principally limited to the diminution in the value of the land itself, and whatever health care issues that arise in the context of a personal injury action (as in the case of the toxic contamination of residential property).

Additional Expenses

The additional expenses incurred by the owners of commercial property to a large extent depend upon the status of the property's development at the time the environmental contamination is discovered. If the property is other than fully developed, the discovery of environmental contamination will no doubt result in considerable construction delays. It is possible that construction may be delayed for years while environmental assessments are performed and remedial efforts are determined and ultimately implemented. In this context one of the most obvious consequential costs is the increase in construction costs resulting from the delay itself.

Other additional expenses arising out of the environmental contamination are the carrying costs for the project during cleanup. Therefore, insurance, interest on financing provided to develop the property, fees, and interest to secure performance bonds, taxes, and all other carrying costs would fall into this category of consequential costs.

If a project is fully developed, as in the case of an older office building that must undergo asbestos abatement, the consequential costs are somewhat different and dependent upon the extent of the contamination. If it is necessary to remove all of the tenants from the building in order to remediate the contamination, then the analysis is similar to a delay in construction of a property under development, and all of the carrying costs would be additional expenses and therefore consequential damages. However, when only a portion of the property must be vacated, the carrying costs must be prorated for each portion of the property for the time it is vacant as a result of the environmental contamination.

An additional expense is the cost of tenant relocation to facilitate remediation. Tenants must have their office equipment moved; their phone, computer, and facsimile lines reconnected; and other concessions will have to be made in order to disrupt their business operations as little as possible. All of these relocation costs will necessarily be included as consequential costs, having been incurred but for the environmental contamination.

Also included as additional expenses are any contributions the owner is required to make under the tenant leases toward operating expenses, such as utilities, that will continue to be incurred as expenses during the remediation period. These operating expenses are considered separately from carrying costs and should be included as an element of consequential costs whether the entire property or only a portion of it is rendered vacant as the result of the environmental contamination.

Loss of Revenues

It is inevitable that certain portions of the property, if not the entire facility, will have to remain unoccupied in order to facilitate the cleanup of the environmental contamination. This in turn results in the obvious reduction of rental revenue from the property.[13] The calculation of the consequential cost from the nonreceipt of revenue is a fairly straightforward calculation. A more complex analysis is, however, required in order to

---

[13] The ability to require existing tenants who have been temporarily relocated to pay the full amount of their lease payments during that period of time is necessarily dependent upon: (1) applicable landlord/tenant laws; (2) the terms of the lease agreement; and (3) the quality of the temporary space provided relative to the tenants' existing arrangement. Such a determination is, therefore, highly fact-sensitive and dependent upon the jurisprudence of each applicable jurisdiction.

determine the full extent of the economic loss suffered as the result of these vacancies.

In order to fully consider the impact of forced vacancies on lost revenues, an analysis must be performed on the fluctuations in rental rates in the market in which the property is located. When the market becomes overbuilt, or is otherwise experiencing a downturn in rental rates for economic reasons (as is the situation in many markets today), the inability to obtain tenants due to forced vacancies can have a devastating effect on long-term revenue. This revenue loss may best be described by way of example. In order to facilitate environmental cleanup efforts, an owner is required to leave 200,000 square feet vacant at a time when market rent is $12 per square foot per month for similar space for a 10-year lease. After the cleanup effort is complete the market rate for similar space is only $8 per square foot per month for a 10-year lease because of a downturn in the economy. The yearly revenue loss due to the inability to lease the space during a time of higher rental rates is $800,000 every year for 10 years. Using a discount value of 10 percent, the present value of the revenue loss due to the environmental contamination is in excess of $4.9 million.

When the amount of square footage held unavailable for lease increases, as it would in the case of the delay of an entire project due to environmental contamination discovered during construction or renovation, the revenue loss increases rather dramatically. Therefore, as can readily be seen from this example, the full impact of the consequential cost to a property owner as the result of their inability to lease space in a timely fashion can be significant.

Impairment of Corporate Value

The impact of the consequential cost of the loss of corporate value is no less significant to the owner of commercial real estate than it is to the manufacturing concern discussed in **§ 21.4**. The consequential cost of the impairment of corporate value would again be represented by the difference between the fair market value of the entity owning the property in the present day and the fair market value of the company had the environmental contamination not occurred.

CHAPTER 22

ALLOCATION OF DAMAGES

Dale R. Jensen
Edward J. McGrath
Charlotte L. Neitzel*

Dale R. Jensen is a CPA and director of Litigation Services for the Denver, Colorado, office of Coopers & Lybrand. He has over twelve years experience in litigation services, auditing, and cost accounting, and specializes in environmental litigation and related financial consulting services. Mr. Jensen is a member of the American Institute of CPAs, the Colorado Society of CPAs, and the Colorado Bar Association's Legal Fee Arbitration Committee. He is an associate member of the ABA and its Natural Resources, Energy, and Environmental Law Section. He received his undergraduate degree in accounting from the University of Denver.

Edward J. McGrath is a partner with Holme Roberts & Owen in Denver, Colorado. He is a member of the bars of the District of Columbia, Maryland, and Colorado. Mr. McGrath heads the Environmental Section of the Litigation Department. Since joining the firm, he has concentrated on environmental litigation involving liability for toxic and hazardous wastes, liability for injuries related to hazardous and toxic wastes, compliance and enforcement of environmental laws, including civil and criminal penalty proceedings, and the representation of clients in licensing, permitting, and transactional matters pertaining to acquisition, development, and operation of industrial, commercial, mining, oil shale, geothermal, and petroleum facilities. He received an A.B. from Williams College and an LL.B. from Columbia University.

*The authors gratefully acknowledge the assistance of Richard Orman in the preparation of this chapter.

Charlotte L. Neitzel is a partner with Holme Roberts and Owen in Denver, Colorado, specializing in environmental law. Her practice emphasizes Superfund litigation, hazardous waste regulatory matters, environmental auditing, and environmental issues in real estate and lending. She graduated from the University of Texas Law School with honors. She has authored numerous articles on environmental law, and she is a frequent lecturer around the country on the Resource and Conservation and Recovery Act.

§ 22.1   Introduction

Allocation of damages resulting from environmental contamination can arise in several contexts. The primary federal statute under which damages are allocated is the Comprehensive Environmental Response, Compensation, and Liability Act (CERCLA).[1] This statute's liability net can ensnare hundreds of potentially responsible parties (PRPs) associated with landfills that fit within CERCLA's four categories of liable parties: present owners and operators, prior owners and operators, transporters, and persons who arranged for disposal or treatment at another facility. CERCLA's liability scheme has also spawned litigation involving myriad types of

---

[1] 42 U.S.C. §§ 9601–9675 (1988).

properties in which current owners or operators have sued prior owners or operators over costs to clean up contamination. Besides CERCLAs, litigation over asbestos has required allocation of damages among producers and sellers of asbestos and owners of buildings or other structures containing asbestos.

This chapter explains the liability scheme of CERCLA and identifies the factors and methods for apportionment that have been established by Congress, used by EPA, upheld by courts, and developed by PRPs and commentators. These factors and methods remain vague. Allocations are highly dependent on the facts associated with each site and on the methodology developed by EPA and PRPs after months and sometimes years of negotiations. The chapter therefore does not recommend a particular scheme. Rather, by summarizing apportionment schemes that have been used, it should enable the practitioner to develop his or her own scheme that will best suit the peculiar facts presented by the site at issue. The chapter concludes with the legal theories of apportionment that have developed in asbestos cases.

§ 22.2   CERCLA Joint and Several Liability

Early case law under CERCLA established that joint and several liability, even though not expressly authorized by the statute, could be imposed on the four types of PRPs. Under joint and several liability, each defendant is liable for the entire harm, not just the harm for which it is proximately responsible. The courts addressing joint and several liability also soon generally recognized a right of contribution against other PRPs by a PRP who paid more than its fair share. Congress recognized this right of contribution when it enacted the Superfund Amendments and Reauthorization Act (SARA) in 1986.[2] Although the right to contribution is clear, the case law reflects two different trends regarding when joint and several liability applies and when contribution and resulting apportionment occur.

§ 22.3   —Majority Rule

United States v. Chem-Dyne Corp.[3] represents the early expression of the majority trend[4] allowing the imposition of joint and several liability in

---

[2] *See id.* § 9613(f)(1).

[3] 572 F. Supp. 802 (S.D. Ohio 1983).

[4] *See, e.g.,* Dubuc & Evans, *Recent Developments under CERCLA: Toward a More Equitable Distribution of Liability,* 17 Envtl. L. Rep. (Envtl. L. Inst.) 10197, 10198 (1987); Allied Corp. v. Acme Solvents Reclaiming Inc., 691 F. Supp. 1100, 1116 (N.D. Ill. 1988); Note, *Misery Loves Company: Spreading the Costs of CERCLA Cleanup,* 42 Vand. L. Rev. 1469, 1478 (1989).

litigation filed by the United States. Following the *Restatement (Second) of Torts,* the court held that it must make a factual determination of whether the harm caused is divisible or indivisible. If the harm is divisible and reasonably subject to apportionment, the burden of proof as to apportionment is upon the defendants who are seeking it. If the harm is indivisible, each defendant is subject to joint and several liability. Under this approach, defendants seeking apportionment carry a heavy burden to prove that the harm is divisible. In *Chem-Dyne,* the defendants argued in a motion for summary judgment that the harm was divisible because they could establish the volume attributable to each generator. The court rejected the argument, stating that "the volume of waste of a particular generator is not an accurate predictor of the risk associated with the waste because the toxicity or migratory potential of a particular hazardous substance generally varies independently with the volume of the waste."[5]

After the *Chem-Dyne* decision, several courts focused on whether the burden as to indivisibility pertains to the particular remedial costs incurred or to the environmental harm caused at a site.[6] Most courts have held that environmental harm at the site, not the money that the government has spent on various activities, must be divisible. In the decision by the Fourth Circuit in *United States v. Monsanto Co.,*[7] for example, the court rejected the generator defendants' arguments that harm could be apportioned according to the volume deposited. According to the court, the generators presented no evidence showing a relationship between waste volume, the release of hazardous substances, and the harm at the site. In fact, substances "in every hazard class" were disposed at the site. Further, the court stated that, in light of the commingling of hazardous substances, the lower court could not have apportioned liability without some evidence of the individual and interactive qualities of the substances deposited at the site. Volume could be probative of contributory harm only if "independent factors had no substantial effect on the harm to the environment."[8] Courts have also pointed to the synergistic effects of the commingling of different wastes in holding that the harm at a landfill was indivisible.[9]

Under this reasoning, passive landowners who did not physically contribute to contamination have been found to be jointly and severally liable. *United States v. Monsanto, Co.*[10] held that these parties could be jointly

---

[5] United States v. Chem-Dyne Corp., 572 F. Supp. at 811. *See also* United States v. South Carolina Recycling & Disposal, Inc., 653 F. Supp. 984, 995 (D.S.C. 1986).

[6] *See, e.g.,* United States v. Western Processing Co., 734 F. Supp. 930, 937 (W.D. Wash. 1990).

[7] 858 F.2d 160, 172–73 (4th Cir. 1988), *cert. denied,* 109 S. Ct. 3156 (1989).

[8] *Id.* at 172 n.27.

[9] *E.g.,* United States v. Stringfellow, 661 F. Supp. 1053, 1060 (C.D. Cal. 1987).

[10] 858 F.2d at 171 n.22.

and severally liable because the harm to the environment was indivisible. In *United States v. Northernaire Plating Co.,*[11] the district court imposed joint and several liability on a landowner, simply stating that CERCLA imposes strict liability on landowners absent a third-party defense under § 107(b)(3).[12]

A few cases have suggested that the burden as to indivisibility can be directed at the governmental cleanup costs. *O'Neil v. Picillo,*[13] a 1989 First Circuit case, reflects this approach. The case involved a Rhode Island pig farm containing massive trenches and pits "filled with free-flowing, multi-colored, pungent liquid wastes" and thousands of "dented and corroded drums containing a veritable potpourri of toxic fluids."[14] The court stated that, although harm to groundwater would likely be indivisible, costs to remove barrels and soil might theoretically be apportioned if the costs were divisible. The court ultimately upheld the district court's finding of joint and several liability because the drums at the site could not be traced to individual generators. The court further questioned whether it could have apportioned costs to remove the barrels because it did not know the cost of removing the individual barrels. These costs would have been different because of the varying degrees of toxicity of the barrel contents. The court also stated that apportioning costs to remove the soil would have been arbitrary because wastes had commingled in the soil.[15]

Although it followed the *Chem-Dyne* approach, the court in *United States v. Miami Drum Services, Inc.*[16] acknowledged that waste volume might be used to establish divisibility if the information were available. The court described indivisible harm as a situation "where many parties have contributed to the contamination or other endangerment and there are no reliable records indicating who disposed of the hazardous waste and in what quantities."[17]

One court has, in fact, apportioned surface cleanup on the basis of volume. The court in *United States v. Ottati & Goss, Inc.*[18] used the drums sent by each generator to apportion liability. In that case, a total of 9,113 drums containing hazardous waste needed to be removed from a site. For

---

[11] 670 F. Supp. 742 (W.D. Mich. 1987).

[12] *See also* Kelley v. Thomas Solvent Co., 727 F. Supp. 1532, 1539–41 (W.D. Mich. 1989).

[13] 883 F.2d 176, 180 (1st Cir. 1989), *cert. denied sub nom.* American Cyanamid Co. v. O'Neil, 110 S. Ct. 1115 (1990).

[14] *Id.* at 177 (citing O'Neil v. Picillo, 682 F. Supp. 706, 709, 725 (D.R.I. 1988)).

[15] *Id.* at 183 n.11. *See also* Kelley v. Thomas Solvent Co., 727 F. Supp. at 1554 (court considered whether contaminants had commingled in the plume, as well as whether the response actions had been directed at the overall problem created by the contamination).

[16] 25 Env't Rep. Cas. (BNA) 1469, 1475 (S.D. Fla. Dec. 12, 1986).

[17] *Id.* at 1475 n.6.

[18] 24 Env't Rep. Cas. (BNA) 1152 (D.N.H. Mar. 3, 1986).

most of the generators, records reflected the exact number of drums contributed. For the others, the court estimated the number. By dividing each generator's total by the total of all drums found at the site, the court determined the percentage of liability for each generator.

§ 22.4   —Minority Rule

United States v. A&F Materials Co.,[19] a 1984 case from the Southern District of Illinois, established an alternative, more moderate approach to joint and several liability. Unlike the requirement in *Chem-Dyne* that defendants must prove both that the environmental injury is divisible and that there is a reasonable basis for apportionment, *A&F Materials* allowed courts to apportion liability even if the harm is indivisible. The court set forth the following "Gore factors"[20] to be used in such apportionment:

    (i)   the ability of the parties to demonstrate that their contribution to a discharge, release or disposal of a hazardous waste can be distinguished;

    (ii)   the amount of hazardous waste involved;

    (iii)   the degree of toxicity of the hazardous waste involved;

    (iv)   the degree of involvement by the parties in the generation, transportation, treatment, storage, or disposal of the hazardous waste;

    (v)   the degree of care exercised by the parties with respect to the hazardous waste concerned, taking into account the characteristics of such hazardous waste; and

    (vi)   the degree of cooperation by the parties with Federal, State or local officials to prevent any harm to the public health or the environment.[21]

The court noted that *Chem-Dyne's* approach would be "extremely harsh and unfair if it is imposed on a defendant who contributed only a small amount of waste to a site."[22]

The *A&F Materials* approach differs primarily from the *Chem-Dyne* approach in terms of when apportionment occurs. Under *A&F Materials,* apportionment occurs generally in § 106 and § 107 suits under CERCLA.[23] Under *Chem-Dyne,* apportionment occurs during contribution actions.

---

[19] 578 F. Supp. 1249 (S.D. Ill. 1984).

[20] The Gore Factors derive from an amendment to CERCLA introduced by Representative Gore which was passed by the House but not subsequently passed as part of CERCLA. *See* 126 Cong. Rec. H9461 (daily ed. Sept. 23, 1980).

[21] United States v. A&F Materials Co., 578 F. Supp. at 1256.

[22] *Id.*

[23] 42 U.S.C. §§ 9606, 9607.

Allied Corp. v. Acme Solvents Reclaiming[24] adopted the Gore factors approach in deciding that a claim by a PRP against other PRPs could result in joint and several liability. If joint and several liability could not be imposed in such suits, the court believed that a willing PRP would be discouraged from voluntarily cleaning up a site.[25] The court held that the Gore factors should govern whether joint and several liability applies.

§ 22.5   Contribution

As a result of the difficult burden required to establish divisibility and apportionment, virtually all allocations occur during the contribution phase of litigation. Section 113(f)(1) of CERCLA authorizes contribution actions against persons who are liable or potentially liable under § 107(a) "during or following" any civil action under § 106 or 107(a).[26] According to § 113(f)(1), "[i]n resolving contribution claims, the court may allocate response costs among liable parties using such equitable factors as the court determines are appropriate."[27]

Courts have developed no consistent apportionment methods for use in § 113(f)(1) contribution actions, but they have identified factors to be used in allocating liability. These factors have been described as the "relative culpability of each responsible party,"[28] the Gore factors,[29] or other factors.[30] The Gore factors have been used by many courts because they are based on comparative fault, which must be used in apportioning liability under CERCLA.[31]

Most of the contribution actions in which courts have allocated damages involve allocation among, and not within, the four categories of liable parties. As shown by the following cases, the factors used by the courts can vary, depending on which categories of PRPs are involved in allocation.

---

[24] 691 F. Supp. 1100, 1118 (N.D. Ill. 1988).

[25] *See also* Central Ill. Pub. Serv. Co. v. Industrial Oil Tank & Line Cleaning Serv., 730 F. Supp. 1498, 1505 (W.D. Mo. 1990) (defendant could be jointly and severally liable in action brought by PRP under §§ 107 and 113(f)(3)(B)).

[26] 42 U.S.C. § 9613 (f)(1).

[27] *Id.*

[28] United States v. Monsanto Co., 858 F.2d 160, 173 n.29 (4th Cir. 1988), *cert. denied,* 109 S. Ct. 3156 (1989).

[29] United States v. Western Processing Co., 734 F. Supp. 930, 938 (W.D. Wash. 1990); United States v. Stringfellow, 661 F. Supp. 1053, 1060 (C.D. Cal. 1987).

[30] *See e.g.,* South Fla. Water Management Dist. v. Montalvo, No. 88-8038-Civ-Davis, slip op. (S.D. Fla. Feb. 15, 1989), *reprinted in* Hazardous Waste Litig. Rep. (Andrews) 14,303 (Apr. 3, 1989).

[31] United States v. Conservation Chem. Co., 628 F. Supp. 391, 401–02 (W.D. Mo. 1985).

§ 22.6   —Owners versus Operators

South Florida Water Management District v. Montalvo[32] involved a private action for recovery of response costs brought by owners, including a company named New Farm, for cleanup of property used for a pesticide business. The suit was filed against a former operator of an aerial insecticide spraying company named Chemairspray and other former operators. The court found New Farm responsible for 25 percent of the costs incurred and the operator-defendants responsible for 75 percent. It expressly declined to use the Gore factors; rather, the court looked to whether the operators had generated sufficient spills and runoffs to create contaminated property, had profited from their business, and had engaged in a dangerous business. With respect to the owner, New Farm, the court considered that it had purchased the site with knowledge of Chemairspray's operations, that it was a major agricultural operator and should have understood the risks and regulations associated with the pesticide business, and that it had purchased the property without any survey or inspection, a practice "clearly discouraged by CERCLA." The court found these facts to constitute "acquiescence" in the operator's business. On the other hand, it found that New Farm did not have an interest in the operator's business and did not receive a discount on the purchase price as a result of the contamination. The court also examined whether the parties were cooperative with state and federal regulatory authorities and found that they had been.

United States v. Northernaire[33] involved a contribution suit in which the court imposed one-third of the liability on an owner of a property and two-thirds on an operator of an electroplating business located on the property. The court cited the Gore factors as the basis for its allocation. It considered that the owner had constructed and failed to maintain a defective sewer line, was aware of the manufacturing needs for a sewer line suitable for disposal, was instrumental in bringing the operator to the property, and had constructed the building that housed the facility. The owner also did not assist or cooperate with governmental officials. In evaluating the appropriate share of the operators, however, the court found that they primarily handled the effluent, abandoned the site after selling the property, and failed to cooperate with governmental officials.

---

[32] No. 88-8038-Civ-Davis, slip op. (S.D. Fla. Feb. 15, 1989), *reprinted in* Hazardous Waste Litig. Rep. (Andrews) 14,303 (Apr. 3, 1989).

[33] No. G84-1113-CA7, slip. op. at 5 (W.D. Mich. Sept. 18, 1989), *reprinted in* 18 Chem. Waste Litig. Rep. 1130 (Computer Law Nov. 1989).

§ 22.7   —Owners/Operators versus Generators

Amoco Oil Co. v. Dingwell[34] also used the Gore factors to allocate liability between the generators, who had conducted an investigation and signed a consent decree to undertake remediation, and a site operator. The court imposed 65 percent of the liability on the operator. It noted that the last three Gore factors were the most important in disputes between the generators and site operators. Applying these three factors, it found that the degree of involvement by all parties was "equally proportionate," because the generators were fully involved with generation and transportation and the site operator was fully involved with the treatment, storage, and disposal of waste. The degree of care involved weighed heavily in the court's analysis. Pursuant to their contractual relationship with the operator, the generators cleaned up tanks and disposed of waste. In contrast, the site operator had caused the environmental damages by failing to contain or dispose of waste properly. The court was also influenced by the third relevant factor. The generators had expended millions to finance the initial phase of remedial action and had negotiated the consent decree, whereas the operator had not cooperated actively in the cleanup.

United States v. Tyson[35] also relied on the Gore factors to impose 50 percent of the liability on an owner/operator of a disposal site in a suit for contribution by a generator. The court found that the owner/operator was an active participant in the operations that caused the environmental damage. The company knew or should have known at the time of purchase of the seller's unsound disposal practices, it benefitted financially from these practices, it initially hired an incompetent contractor after being notified by the government, and it thereafter refused to undertake response actions.

Advance Circuits, Inc. v. Carriere Properties[36] also dealt with allocation between operators and generators but used different factors in its analysis. Even though the case was decided under a state statute, commentators have suggested that the case could guide courts in determining what factors to consider in allocating damages in § 113(f)(1) actions.[37] In *Advance Circuits,* 13 generators had spent over $1 million cleaning up a site at an abandoned chemical recycling operation. In a suit against the former

---

[34] 690 F. Supp. 78, 86–87 (D. Me. 1988), *aff'd,* 884 F.2d 629 (1st Cir. 1989).

[35] No. 84-2663, slip op. (E.D. Pa. Dec. 29, 1989) (WESTLAW DCT) (1989 WESTLAW 159256).

[36] No. 84-3316, slip op. (D. Minn. Feb. 18, 1987), *aff'd,* No. C8-87-1436 (Minn. Ct. App. Feb. 16, 1988) (1988 WESTLAW 10,476).

[37] Dubuc & Evans, *Recent Developments Under CERCLA: Toward a More Equitable Distribution of Liability,* 17 Envtl. L. Rep. (Envtl. L. Inst.) 10,197, 10,201 (1987).

operators for contribution, the court found that the defendant operators were responsible for 70 percent of the response costs using the following eight factors:

(a) Defendants' actions and inactions were the substantial and material contributing cause of the release and threat of release of hazardous substances at the site.

(b) Defendants were principally responsible for all hazardous materials remaining at . . . facility at the time of cleanup; almost all of the materials were the byproducts of defendants' activities.

(c) There is no evidence that defendants' handling of the materials affected their toxicity.

(d) Defendants were completely and uniquely responsible for the care exercised in the treatment and storage of materials at the two sites in question.

(e) Defendants were generally uncooperative with the responsible authorities in addressing the problem created by defendants.

(f) [One] Defendant . . . represented himself as well-trained and expert in the area of recycling and metallurgy and implicitly aware of the hazardous nature of the substances which he was accepting and treating at the . . . facilities.[38]

The court imposed 30 percent of the liability on the generators, taking into account the following factors:

(a) The generators contributed to the release or threatened release only in the sense that they relied upon defendants' representations concerning proper handling of the materials that the generators delivered to the defendants for recycling.

(b) Collectively, the generators entrusted to the defendants the materials ultimately found at the . . . facilities.

(c) The generators have cooperated fully and completely with all government officials to prevent any harm to the public health and the environment.[39]

§ 22.8   —Current Owners/Operators versus Prior Owners/Operators

A few cases have also addressed allocation between current and prior owners of contaminated land. In *Smith Land & Improvement Corp. v. Celotex Corp.,*[40] the Third Circuit considered an action brought by a

---

[38] Advance Circuits, Inc. v. Carriere Properties, No. 84-3316, slip. op. at 4–5.

[39] *Id.* at 5.

[40] 851 F.2d 86, 90 (3d Cir. 1988), *cert. denied,* 109 S. Ct. 837 (1989).

purchaser seeking contribution to clean up an asbestos pile against the corporate successor to a company that had owned the land and produced the pile. The court held that defenses of caveat emptor and unclean hands had no place in CERCLA's liability scheme, which allowed actions for contribution. Although recognizing that a purchaser should not be entitled to double compensation, the court held that this fact should be taken into account in a contribution action. The amount of the discount, the cost of response, and any other considerations should be addressed in the allocation.

In *PVO International, Inc. v. Drew Chemical Corp.*,[41] the district court also considered whether the purchase price had taken into consideration the contaminated condition of the property. The court denied a motion for summary judgment to impose 100 percent of the cleanup costs on a prior owner in an action by the current owner under CERCLA. The court held that an equitable consideration in allocating liability between the parties was the increase in the value of the property if rid of hazardous waste. According to the court, the current owner could have paid a low purchase price to reflect the contamination.

In *BCW Associates, Ltd. v. Occidental Chemical Corp.*,[42] the court allocated liability between current and prior owners and operators of a warehouse that had become contaminated with lead dust. The court held that the equitable liability of one prior owner who owned the warehouse from 1980 to 1984 was "non-existent." That owner had used the warehouse to store raw materials and finished products and had used a color mixing process. The plaintiff, however, could not establish a link between this process and the lead contamination. This owner sold the property but continued to occupy the premises under a lease. The court characterized its activities as limited in scope, well-defined, and unrelated to disposal of hazardous substances. As between the prior owner who had owned the land from 1952 to 1980 and the current owner and lessee, the court imposed one-third of the liability on the prior owner and two-thirds on the present lessee and owner. The factors influencing the court were that the present owner purchased the property "as is" and received substantial collateral benefits from the cleanup. It also noted that the lessee was suspicious of the environmental condition of the warehouse and was responsible for the threatened release by allowing goods with lead dust to be shipped to customers and allowing shoes and clothing of workers to leave the warehouse.

---

[41] No. 87-3921, slip op. (D.N.J. June 27, 1988), *reprinted in* 16 Chemical Waste Litig. Rep. (Computer L. Rep., Inc.) 669 (Aug. & Sept. 1988).

[42] No. 86-5947, slip op. (E.D. Pa. Sept. 29, 1988) (WESTLAW DCT) (1988 WESTLAW 102641).

§ 22.9   Settlements as a Means of Allocation

Most of the allocations to date have been accomplished through settlements. As part of SARA, Congress included a provision, § 122, that encourages PRPs to settle with the government. These settlements can include covenants not to sue,[43] which generally have an exception for unknown conditions.[44] Under § 122, the government can negotiate with PRPs to apportion liability. The government also has the discretion to allow "mixed funding" settlements in which the government agrees to pay the so-called orphan share of liability attributable to unidentified or insolvent PRPs.[45]

Section 122 says little about how liability is to be allocated in settlements. Certain language indicates that EPA is to take into account both volume and toxicity. When sending special notice letters requesting PRPs to undertake response action, EPA is to provide PRPs with "[t]o the extent such information is available, the volume and nature of substances contributed by each potentially responsible party identified at the facility [and] . . . [a] ranking by volume of the substances at the facility, to the extent such information is available."[46] Section 122 also provides that EPA shall prepare guidelines for preparing nonbinding allocations of responsibility (NBARs). According to the statute:

> In developing these guidelines, the President may include such factors as the President considers relevant such as: volume, toxicity, mobility, strength of evidence, ability to pay, litigative risks, public interest considerations, precedential value, and inequities and aggravating factors. When it would expedite settlements under this section and remedial action, the President may, after completion of the remedial investigation and feasibility study, provide a non-binding preliminary allocation of responsibility which allocates percentages of the total cost of response among potentially responsible parties at the facility.[47]

To collect the necessary information, EPA can by subpoena require the attendance and testimony "of witnesses and production of reports, papers, documents, answers to questions, and other information that the President deems necessary."[48] The statute also says the NBARs cannot

---

[43] *See* 42 U.S.C. § 9622(f).

[44] *Id.* § 9622(f)(6).

[45] *Id.* § 9622(b). *See also* 54 Fed. Reg. 37,892 (Sept. 13, 1989) for EPA's proposal on how to implement mixed funding agreements.

[46] 42 U.S.C. §§ 9622(e)(1)(B), (C).

[47] *Id.* § 9622(e)(3)(A).

[48] *Id.* § 9622(e)(3)(B).

be admissible as evidence in any proceeding, cannot be reviewed by courts, and cannot constitute an apportionment or other statement on the divisibility of harm or causation.[49]

In 1987, EPA published interim guidelines for the preparation of NBARs.[50] These guidelines note that the preparation of NBARs is voluntary, and that a decision not to prepare NBARs is not appealable in a judicial proceeding. EPA also states that use of NBARs will not be routine, consistent with its policy that PRPs should work out allocation among themselves. Further, NBARs will typically be used only when the EPA invokes the special notice procedures.

If the EPA does prepare an NBAR, it will allocate 100 percent of responsibility, including that attributable to unknown parties.[51] Allocations among generators are decided primarily upon volume "for simplicity and other practical reasons," and upon settlement criteria, including the:

> strength of evidence tracing the wastes at a site to PRPs, ability of PRPs to pay, litigative risks in proceeding to trial, public interest considerations, precedential value, value of obtaining a present sum, certain inequities and aggravating factors, and the nature of the case that remains after settlement.[52]

EPA rejected models based on toxicity because they were too complex to apply and because the scientific community lacked agreement about degrees of toxicity of specific hazardous substances and synergistic effects. The EPA also noted that toxicity is usually causally related to the cost of cleanup for only a few substances, such as PCBs and dioxins.[53]

The liability of owners, operators, and transporters is also discussed in the NBAR guidelines. For owners and operators, culpability is the primary factor in allocation. An owner or operator who "managed waste badly" should, under the guidelines, receive a higher allocation than a passive or noncommercial landowner. If all other circumstances are equal, the relative allocation among successive owners and operators should be determined by the relative length of time each owned or operated the site.[54] Transporter liability may be based on volume, taking into account appropriate considerations such as packaging and placement of waste at a site.[55]

---

[49] *Id.* § 9622(e)(3)(C).

[50] 53 Fed. Reg. 19,919 (May 28, 1987) (request for public comment).

[51] *Id.* at 19,920.

[52] *Id.* at 19,919.

[53] *Id.* at 19,920.

[54] *Id.*

[55] *Id.* at 19,921–22.

In one of the uses of the NBAR procedure, EPA allocated liability on the basis of both volume and toxicity. The settlement, which involved the Re-Solve landfill site,[56] apportioned primarily on volume. Generators of toxic PCBs, however, were allocated a proportion greater than their volumetric contribution.

Section 122 of CERCLA also provides for de minimis settlements if the settlement involves only a minor portion of response costs at a facility and the conditions in the following subparagraph are met:

> (A)   Both of the following are minimal in comparison to other hazardous substances at the facility:
>
> (i)   The amount of the hazardous substances contributed by that party to the facility.
>
> (ii)   The toxic or other hazardous effects of the substances contributed by that party to the facility.[57]

As with NBARs, EPA has issued guidelines addressing de minimis settlements.[58] To be defined as a de minimis waste generator or transporter, the PRP must have contributed:

> an amount of hazardous substances which is minimal in comparison to the total amount at the facility. The PRP must also have contributed hazardous substances which are not significantly more toxic and not of significantly greater hazardous effect than other hazardous substances at the facility, as well as meeting the other conditions set forth in this guidance.[59]

A PRP would be disqualified if a minimal amount of its waste exhibited greater toxicity or more serious hazardous effects than other hazardous substances at a site, or required disproportionately high treatment and disposal costs.[60] As a result of its definition of de minimis parties, EPA must have adequate information about the identity, waste contributions, and viability of PRPs before a settlement can be reached. In determining the timing of such a settlement, EPA considers the amount of information available about the costs of remediating site contamination, the nature of reopeners included in the covenant not to sue, the amount of the premium to be paid by the settling parties, and the volume and toxicity criteria used

---

[56] *$40 Million Re-Solve Settlement Achieved,* Superfund (Pasha Publications Mar. 1, 1989).

[57] 42 U.S.C. § 9622(g)(1)(A).

[58] 52 Fed. Reg. 24,333 (June 30, 1987) (request for public comment); *see also* 52 Fed. Reg. 43,393 (Nov. 12, 1987) (interim model consent decree and administrative order on consent for de minimis settlements).

[59] 52 Fed. Reg. 24,335–36 (June 30, 1987).

[60] *Id.* at 24,336.

by EPA to distinguish between de minimis and other major parties at a site.[61] If such information is incomplete, any settlement should include expansive reopeners, substantial premiums, and low levels for volume and toxicity.[62] At a minimum, the EPA sets the amount of the cash offer at the de minimis party's volumetric share of the total past and projected response costs.[63] A premium is generally required in exchange for a covenant not to sue that does not include reopeners for costs overruns and future response actions.[64]

Section 122 also authorizes the following landowners to qualify for de minimis settlements:

(B)   the potentially responsible party—
    (i)   is the owner of the real property on or in which the facility is located;
    (ii)   did not conduct or permit the generation, transportation, storage, treatment, or disposal of any hazardous substance at the facility; and
    (iii)   did not contribute to the release or threat of release of a hazardous substance at the facility through any action or omission. This subparagraph (B) does not apply if the potentially responsible party purchased the real property with actual or constructive knowledge that the property was used for the generation, transportation, storage, treatment, or disposal of any hazardous substance.[65]

The EPA published its guidelines to implement this provision on August 18, 1989.[66] It interprets *any hazardous substance* to mean the hazardous substance that is the subject of the release or threatened release.[67] The guidelines also state that EPA will use the third-party defense in §§ 107(b)(3) and 101(35) of CERCLA[68] to determine whether landowners qualify.[69] It will question whether the landowner acquired the property without knowledge or reason to know of the disposal of hazardous substances.[70] To meet this test, the owner must have conducted all appropriate inquiry into the previous ownership and uses of the property consistent with good commercial or customary practice.[71] Unlike the information

---

[61] *Id.* at 24,335.

[62] *Id.*

[63] *Id.* at 24,338.

[64] *Id.*

[65] 42 U.S.C. § 9622(g)(1)(B).

[66] 54 Fed. Reg. 34,235 (Aug. 18, 1989).

[67] *Id.* at 34,237 n.6.

[68] 42 U.S.C. §§ 9607(b)(3), 9601(35).

[69] 54 Fed. Reg. 34,237 (Aug. 18, 1989).

[70] *Id.* at 34,238.

[71] *Id.*

compiled by EPA regarding a waste contributor's status as a de minimis party, the information regarding the landowner's status is to be provided by the landowner.[72] This information should include whether the landowner had actual or constructive knowledge of the previous ownership and uses of the property, exercised due care, and contributed to the release or threatened release through action or omission.[73]

§ 22.10   —Judicial Review of Consent Decrees Incorporating Settlements

Except for settlements accomplished through an administrative order on consent, EPA settlements with PRPs must be approved by a court in a consent decree.[74] In order to approve a consent decree, the court must determine that the settlement is "fair, reasonable, and consistent with the Constitution and the mandate of Congress."[75] In many cases, nonsettling PRPs oppose consent decrees on the basis of unfair allocations. Nonsettlors have a high stake in these settlements for two reasons. First, it leaves them open to contribution claims from settling defendants who have paid more than their proportionate share of liability.[76] Second, if the settling defendants have paid less than their proportionate share of liability, § 113(f)(2) apparently compels the nonsettlors to absorb the shortfall.[77] In considering challenges to consent decrees, courts consistently upheld the decrees, deferring to the terms of government-PRP settlements.

United States v. Cannons Engineering Corp.,[78] a 1990 First Circuit case, exhibits the extreme deference that courts have granted to EPA. In that case, EPA sent notices of liability to about 671 PRPs. De minimis administrative settlements were achieved with 300 generators who had sent less than 1 percent of the volume to the site. These generators paid 160 percent of their volumetric share and received a release from liability. The government filed suit against 84 PRPs who had rejected, or were ineligible for, the administrative settlement. It then filed two proposed consent decrees. The

---

[72] *Id.* at 34,239.

[73] *Id.*

[74] 42 U.S.C. §§ 9622(d)(1)(A), (g)(4).

[75] United States v. Cannons Eng'g Corp., 720 F. Supp. 1027, 1035–36 (D. Mass. 1989), *aff'd,* 899 F.2d 79 (1st Cir. 1990) (citing City of New York v. Exxon, 697 F. Supp. 677, 692 (S.D.N.Y. 1988)).

[76] 42 U.S.C. § 9613 (f)(3).

[77] United States v. Rohm & Haas Co., 721 F. Supp. 666, 676 n.10 (D.N.J. 1989) (citing City of New York v. Exxon Corp., 697 F. Supp. at 681 n.5).

[78] 899 F.2d 79 (1st Cir. 1990).

first embodied a settlement with the major PRPs and the second with 12 de minimis parties who had eschewed participation in the administrative settlement. These de minimis generators paid 260 percent of their volumetric share. The increased premium was in the nature of delay damages. When the government moved to enter the decrees, 7 nonsettling PRPs objected.

The court upheld the consent decrees under several factors, emphasizing that it was the policy of the law to encourage settlements.[79] Among the more significant factors, the court looked at whether the consent decree was fair from a procedural standpoint. It stated that Congress intended to give EPA broad discretion to structure classes of PRPs for settlement purposes, and that the 1 percent dividing line was well within the universe of plausibility.[80] The court also considered the substantive fairness of the settlements. Under this factor, the "settlement terms must be based upon, and roughly correlated with, some acceptable measure of comparative fault, apportioning liability among the settling parties according to rational (if necessarily imprecise) estimates of how much harm each PRP has done."[81] In discussing how comparative fault is to be measured, the court noted that there was no universally correct approach, and that:

> what constitutes the best measure of comparative fault at a particular Superfund site under particular factual circumstances should be left largely to the EPA's expertise. Whatever formula or scheme EPA advances for measuring comparative fault and allocating liability should be upheld so long as the agency supplies a plausible explanation for it, welding some reasonable linkage between the factors it includes in its formula or scheme and the proportionate shares of the settling PRPs.[82]

The EPA, according to the court, should also be allowed to diverge from a formula to address special factors, such as the uncertainty of future events and the timing of particular settlement decisions. A PRP's assumption of open-ended risks may merit a discount on comparative fault, while obtaining a complete release from uncertain events may call for a premium. The court was not disturbed by early settlements, even if precise information about the total extent of harm and the role of each PRP was unavailable. It stated that "[a]s long as the data that EPA uses to apportion liability for purposes of a consent decree falls along the broad spectrum of plausible approximations, judicial intrusion is unwarranted—regardless

---

[79] *Id.* at 84.

[80] *Id.* at 86.

[81] *Id.*

[82] *Id.*

of whether the court would have opted to employ the same data in the same way."[83] In response to the argument that EPA should have used relative toxicity to determine proportionate liability for response costs, instead of a strictly volumetric ranking, the court stated the the EPA need not show that the apportionment method was the best, or even the fairest, of all conceivable methods.

Courts have similarly rejected arguments that settlements were unfair because the nonsettlors would have had to pay more than their volumetric share. In *United States v. Acton,*[84] the court examined an allocation scheme developed by EPA in which the volume of the "primary settling defendants" was more than 1 percent and that of the "secondary settling defendants" was 0.1 to 1.0 percent of the total waste. These two groups had varying obligations to fund and perform cleanup, but were both jointly and severally liable, with each defendant's exact share of liability to be determined through an alternative dispute resolution process. One other group consisted of defendants whose waste volume did not exceed 0.1 percent. This group paid a fixed amount based on its volumetric share. The court rejected the nonsettlors' argument that settlement should be based solely on volume, stating that a PRP's liability in a settlement agreement may depend in part on the toxicity of wastes. The court refused to evaluate the toxicity of the nonsettlors' waste, despite the nonsettlors' argument that its toxicity was no greater than that of the settling defendants, because such an inquiry was well beyond its scope of review.

Courts have also approved consent decrees even though no allocation evidence had been developed. In *Kelley v. Thomas Solvent Co.,*[85] the court approved a consent decree for one defendant, called Grand Truck, in which it agreed to pay 75 percent of the total claim. The case involved three sites that had contaminated a public water supply. Grand Truck had been the owner of one site and the owner and operator of another site but had not been involved with the third site. Several PRPs challenged the consent decree. Using the deferential standard, the court held that, even though allocation evidence had not been developed, it was unlikely that Grand Truck's share would be greater than 75 percent.

In approving consent decrees, courts also rely on the threat posed by the site and the availability of funding to remedy the threat. In *United States v. Seymour Recycling Corp.,*[86] the court considered a consent decree in which 24 companies who shipped 50 percent of the wastes would

---

[83] *Id.* at 88.

[84] 733 F. Supp. 869, 873 (D.N.J. 1990).

[85] 717 F. Supp. 507, 517–18 (W.D. Mich. 1989).

[86] 554 F. Supp. 1334 (S.D. Ind. 1982).

pay $7.7 million for the surface cleanup. These PRPs had made their offer after the United States separated the remedy into two phases: a surface cleanup and a subsurface cleanup. The phased approach was intended to address as soon as possible the threat posed by 60,000 barrels of toxic chemicals. Several nonsettling PRPs challenged the consent decree, arguing that the remaining 300 companies who shipped the other 50 percent of the waste to the site were being asked to pay $15 million for groundwater cleanup, based on their volumetric share. The court approved the consent decree, relying on "the need to abate the hazardous conditions at the site as expeditiously as possible and the unavailability of any other prompt plan to undertake the cleanup."[87]

Nonsettling defendants also have unsuccessfully argued that the Uniform Comparative Fault Act (UCFA)[88] should preclude the government from pursuing nonsettlors for more than their fair share. Section 6 of the UCFA states that the claim by the releasing party, in this case the government, against other persons is reduced by "the amount of the released person's equitable share of the obligation," not by the amount of the settlement.[89] Most courts have ruled that § 113(f)(2) of CERCLA, which was added SARA, clarified that a settlement reduces the potential liability by the amount of the settlement.[90] Attempts by PRPs to circumvent this provision have been called "quixotic imprecations."[91] Only a few post-SARA opinions have indicated that the UCFA will govern a nonsettlor's contribution rights after a consent decree with the United States has been entered.[92]

Nonsettlors have been equally defeated in persuading courts to have a hearing to determine the effect of a settlement on nonsettling defendants or to decide issues of allocation and contribution prior to the entry of a consent decree.[93] Courts have reasoned that a hearing would subvert the very purpose of a settlement agreement, which is to avoid the costs of extended litigation.

---

[87] *Id.* at 1341.

[88] 12 U.L.A. 39 (1990 Cum. Supp.).

[89] *Id.* at § 6.

[90] United States v. Cannons Eng'g Corp., 899 F.2d at 92; United States v. Rohm & Haas Co., 721 F. Supp. at 677–78.

[91] United States v. Cannons Eng'g Corp., 899 F.2d at 92.

[92] United States v. Laskin, No. C84-2035Y, slip op. (N.D. Ohio Jan. 3, 1989) (1989 U.S. Dist LEXIS 4900); *United States v. Rohm & Haas Co.,* 721 F. Supp. at 677. *See* Lyncott Corp. v. Chemical Waste Management, Inc., 690 F. Supp. 1409, 1418 (E.D. Pa. 1988); Edward Hines Lumber Co. v. Vulcan Materials Co., No. 85 C 1142 (N.D. Del. Dec. 4, 1987) (WESTLAW, DCT) (1987 WESTLAW 27368) (cases applied the UCFA in settlements among private parties).

[93] United States v. Rohm & Haas Co., 721 F. Supp. at 686–87.

§ 22.11　—PRP Settlements

PRPs may want to settle among themselves without governmental involvement in order to conduct their own remedial activities and thus stave off governmental enforcement activities. In some government-PRP settlements, the terms of the agreement also merely state that settling PRPs are jointly and severally liable for a certain aggregate percentage of the liability, leaving allocation to the settlors.[94] Allocations among private parties are typically difficult and expensive. Large amounts of data must be collected, and determinations must be made on a variety of issues on which accurate data may not be available. Expertise in such determinations may come from private environmental consulting firms, who may have their own internal allocation methodologies, or who may create a methodology appropriate for each individual site. In addition, a number of lawyers and consultants have developed and published their own tests, criteria, and schemes for apportioning liability.

Coopers & Lybrand has developed a case study, set out in § 22.14, that demonstrates how liability can be apportioned at a landfill. The case study deals with generators, transporters, current and prior owners and operators, insolvent parties, and de minimis parties. It also addresses the difficult issues surrounding toxicity, mobility, and synergistic effects. The case study works through allocation mathematics on a step-by-step basis.

Another model for apportioning liability, called the DDA model, was developed by Robert Denbo and Dhamo Dhamotharan.[95] This model is based on the contribution of a waste to the cost of the remedy and not on other waste characteristics that have resulted in a hazardous classification. The authors believe that such characteristics as carcinogenicity, oral or dermal toxicity, and corrosivity relate to the urgency of closure but have little bearing on the cost of the remedy. Instead, the DDA model "assesses the contribution of each company's waste to the cost required to eliminate or minimize the combined threats of all waste present in the site."[96] The DDA model takes into account the unique geographical, geological, hydrological, and other factors of a particular site. According to the model, any given waste may necessitate three possible phases in a remediation:

---

[94] Consent decrees can be retrieved online by using the LEXIS legal information database. For examples of consent decrees in which liability was not apportioned among the individual PRPs, *see* United States v. Chevron Chem. Co., 1988 EPA Consent LEXIS 32; United States v. New Castle County, 1988 EPA Consent LEXIS 55.

[95] Denbo & Dhamotharan, *A Model for Apportioning the Cost of Closure of a Waste Site,* Proceedings of the Seventh Superfund Conference 56 (1986) (sponsored by the Hazardous Materials Control Inst.).

[96] *Id.* at 57.

surface closure, shallow subsurface closure, and groundwater remediation. The contribution of each waste to the overall total closure cost is the accumulation of the costs associated with each phase.[97] If the presence of one waste dictates a disposal technique, such as an incineration remedy for PCBs, the cost of the remedy without addressing PCBs can be deducted from the remedy that includes incineration. The added cost would be split in half, with one-half borne by the party who deposited the PCB waste and the other half apportioned among the remaining parties on the same basis as used in the DDA model approach. Although the model is interesting, the authors have failed to account for the situation in which information is lacking as to which PRPs contributed how much of each type of waste to the total at the site. The model also does not apportion costs among owners, operators, and transporters.

Kellogg Corporation has developed a similar cause/effect model.[98] Under this model, the volume of each type of waste disposed by each generator is determined. Each waste's contribution to specific site conditions, such as acidic soils or contaminated organics in an aquifer, is then determined. Each condition will necessitate one or more remedial actions. Each PRP's cost share is then determined by the PRP's percent contribution of each waste type that causes a particular remedial action to be undertaken. Under this approach, a generator of PCBs bears the entire burden of additional cleanup costs necessitated by the PCB contamination. Like all cost allocation models, the cause/effect model is dependent on the information gathered as to which PRPs contributed what waste.

Some commentators have questioned whether a pro rata division among PRPs should be used.[99] The pro rata approach would require each PRP to pay an even sum. Even though a pro rata apportionment may seem unjust to small volume/low toxicity PRPs, it has the distinct advantage of low cost. Protracted litigation, negotiation, scientific and engineering studies, and consulting firms to apportion costs can easily cost PRPs millions of dollars in large-scale CERCLA cases. Pro rata apportionment may be more appropriate when there are many PRPs and none with disproportional contributions to the contamination. This type of apportionment provides a simple means of dividing costs among generators, owners, operators, and transporters, as each group can be given an equal share of liability with apportionment of costs then prorated among its individual members.

---

[97] *Id.*

[98] Hengemihle, *A Cost/Effect Approach to Cost Allocation,* Environmental Perspectives 3 (Winter 1988) (a newsletter published by Kellogg Corporation, 26 West Dry Creek Circle, Littleton, CO).

[99] *Cf.* Miller, *Defending Superfund and RCRA Imminent Hazard Cases,* 15 Nat. Resources Law. 483, 490 (1983).

Because it may be difficult for PRPs to agree on any allocation, many commentators have suggested arbitration as a means of facilitating agreements.[100] Others have suggested management and psychologically based methods for dealing with large groups of PRPs.[101]

§ 22.12 Apportionment of Liability under State Laws

Many states have their own versions of CERCLA that apply coextensively with CERCLA or are broader.[102] Several of these laws contain detailed

---

[100] *E.g.,* Krickenberger & Berman, *Allocation of Superfund Site Costs Through Mediation by a Third Party Neutral,* 2 Toxics L. Rep. (BNA) 463 (Sept. 16, 1987); Couer, *Allocation of Superfund Cleanup Costs Among Potentially Responsible Parties: The Role of Binding Arbitration,* 18 Envtl. L. Rptr. (Envtl. L. Inst.) 10,158 (1988); United States v. Acton Corp., 733 F. Supp. 869, 871 (D.N.J. 1990).

[101] *E.g.,* Dore, *A Practical Guide to Negotiating Superfund Cost Allocation Agreements,* Def. Couns. J. 353 (July 1987); Garret, *Superfund: Apportionment of Liability,* 1 Nat. Res. & Env't 25 (Fall 1985); Graham & Stoll, *A Practical Guide to Negotiating Waste Site Cleanups,* 2 Toxics L. Rep. (BNA) 619 (Oct. 28, 1987); J. McKinney, A. Zetterberg, R. Tisch, & J. Zimmerman, PRP Organization Handbook (published by Information Network for Superfund Settlement) (1989).

[102] 38 states have laws that resemble CERCLA. Below is a list of all of them, along with the relevant statutory citations. States not listed have no equivalent to CERCLA, but they may have regulatory schemes controlling most facets of industrial use and disposal of hazardous substances and hazardous waste. Ala. Code §§ 22-30A-1 to -11. (Supp. 1989); Alaska Stat. §§ 46.03.010–.120 (1989); Ariz. Rev. Stat. Ann. §§ 49-901 to -944 (1988 & Supp. 1989); Ark. Stat. Ann. §§ 8-7-301 to -309 (Supp. 1989); Cal. Health & Safety Code §§ 25300–25395 (Deering 1988 & Supp. 1990); Colo. Rev. Stat. Ann. §§ 25-16-101 to -201 (1990); Conn. Gen. Stat. §§ 22a-133a to -133j (Supp. 1990); Del. Code Ann. tit. 7, §§ 6308–6309 (Supp. 1988); Fla. Stat. Ann. §§ 403.725–.726 (1989); Ga. Code Ann. § 12-8-75 (1988); Ill. Ann. Stat. ch. 111-1/2, paras. 1001-1003.67 (Smith-Hurd 1988 & Supp. 1990); Ind. Code Ann. §§ 13-6-1-1 to -6 (Burns 1987 & Supp. 1990); Iowa Code §§ 455B.381–.432 (1990); Kan. Stat. Ann. §§ 65-3452a to -3472 (1985 & Supp. 1989); Ky. Rev. Stat. Ann. § 224.877 (Baldwin Supp. 1988); La. Rev. Stat. Ann. §§ 30:2271–:2280 (West 1989); Me. Rev. Stat. Ann. tit. 38, § 1310E (1989); Mass. Gen. Laws Ann. ch 21E (West Supp. 1990); Minn. Stat. Ann. §§ 115B.01–.37 (West Supp. 1990); Mo. Ann. Stat. §§ 260.437–.470 (Vernon 1990); Mont. Code Ann. §§ 75-10-701 to -724 (1989); N.H. Rev. Stat. Ann. §§ 147-B:1 to -B:11 (Supp. 1989); N.J. Stat. Ann. §§ 58:10-23.1 to -23.24 (West Supp. 1990); N.M. Stat. Ann. §§ 74-4-1 to -11 (Supp. 1990); N.Y. Envtl. Conserv. Law §§ 27-1301 to -1327 (McKinney 1984 & Supp. 1990); N.C. Gen. Stat. §§ 130A-310 (1989); N.D. Cent. Code § 23-20.3-08 (Supp. 1989); Or. Rev. Stat. §§ 466.605–.680 (1989); Pa. Stat. Ann. tit. 35 §§ 6020.101 to -.1305 (Purdon 1990); S.C. Code Ann. § 44-56-200 (Law. Co-op. 1985); S.D. Codified Laws § 34A-10 (1986 & Supp. 1990); Tenn. Code Ann. §§ 68-46-201 to -222 (Supp. 1989); Tex. Health & Safety Code Ann. §§ 361.181-.345 (Vernon 1990); Utah Code Ann. §§ 26-14d-101 to -801 (Supp. 1990); Va. Code Ann. §§ 44-146.34 to -.40 (Supp. 1989); Wash. Rev. Code Ann.

apportionment schemes. For example, Utah's recently enacted Hazardous Substance Mitigation Act apportions liability on the basis of the volume, mobility, persistence, and toxicity of the hazardous wastes contributed by each PRP, and by the behavior of a responsible party compared to the behavior of other responsible parties in contributing to a release. If insufficient evidence is available for a PRP to meet the required burden of proof for apportioning its liability, the court will use what evidence it has to follow the above-mentioned factors. Joint and several liability is not allowed.[103] Most other states with such statutes instruct their courts to allocate liability on the basis of the Gore factors.[104]

§ 22.13   Asbestos Cases

The term *asbestos* refers to a group of fireproof minerals previously used in a large number of industrial applications, such as insulation, pipe and duct covering, and fabrics. Asbestos fibers can cause asbestosis, a lung disease, and mesothelioma, a form of cancer. Suits against the asbestos industry usually take the form of personal injury actions by those allegedly injured by asbestos, or actions to recover the cost of removing asbestos from buildings and other structures.

In many cases, plaintiffs are not able to identify the particular manufacturers responsible for their injury, and they have therefore attempted to sue a few large defendants based on a market share liability theory. Under this theory, the largest defendants would be held liable and have damages apportioned according to their percentage share of the asbestos market. Unfortunately for plaintiffs, the market share theory has been rejected in asbestos cases.[105] Courts have reasoned that asbestos cases are dissimilar to DES cases, which developed the market share theory. DES was a fungible product and produced pursuant to one formula. Pregnant women ingesting DES were therefore exposed to the same risk. In contrast, asbestos products vary as to the risk of harm they present, partially due to the six different

---

§§ 70-105D.010 to -.921 (Supp. 1990); W. Va. Code §§ 20-5G-1 to -6 (1989); Wis. Stat. Ann. § 144.442 (West 1989).

[103] Utah Code Ann. § 26-14d-402(2)(c) (Supp. 1990).

[104] *E.g.,* Ariz. Rev. Stat. Ann. § 49-285(E) (1989); Cal. Health and Safety Code § 25356.3(C) (Deering 1988); Minn. Stat. Ann. § 18D.115(b) (Supp. 1989); Mont. Code Ann. § 75-10-724(1) (1989); Pa. Stat. Ann. tit. 35, § 6020.705(b) (Purdon 1990).

[105] *See, e.g.,* Menne v. Celotex Corp., 861 F.2d 1453, 1468 n.24 (10th Cir. 1988); Vigiolto v. Johns-Manville Corp., 826 F.2d 1058 (3d Cir. 1987); Bateman v. Johns-Manville Sales Corp., 781 F.2d 1132, 1133 (5th Cir. 1986); Blackston v. Shook & Fletcher Insulation Co., 764 F.2d 1480 (11th Cir. 1985); Leng v. Celotex Corp., 196 Ill. App. 3d 647, 554 N.E.2d 468 (1990); Mullen v. Armstrong World Indus., Inc., 200 Cal. App. 3d 250, 246 Cal. Rptr. 32 (1988).

types of silicates, all of which have a different toxicity. In addition, other significant variables include the physical properties of the product itself, the percentage of asbestos used in the product, the form of the product, and the amount of dust it generates.[106]

Rather than the market share theory, courts have allocated liability on the basis of state statutes or common law that provide for allocation among tortfeasors. For example, Texas apportions damages in a products liability case among the defendants in accordance with their "relative roles in causing the injuries."[107] Under this system, the jury apportions responsibility among all—including nonsettling defendants, settling defendants, and the plaintiff—whose acts or products combined to produce the plaintiff's injuries. The nonsettling defendant's liability and the plaintiff's recovery are to be reduced by the total percentage share assigned to the settling defendants. The nonsettling defendant must establish the liability of the settling defendants in order to benefit from this system of comparative causation.[108] Using this system, the Fifth Circuit in *Moore v. Johns-Manville Sales Corp.*[109] rejected a pro rata allocation, stating that:

> [T]he jury . . . heard evidence that asbestosis is caused by the inhalation of asbestos fibers. It is a dose-related disease, in that the greater the quantity of asbestos fibers a person inhales and the longer the period of time during which he inhales the fibers, the more likely he is to contract the disease and the more severe it is likely to be. . . . [T]he evidence presented established that the products of the various defendants contained differing amounts of asbestos and that asbestos fibers were more readily released into the ambient air from some products than from others. . . . [S]ufficient evidence was presented to this jury to warrant its decision that exposure for different periods of time to products containing different amounts of asbestos fiber, emitted in different quantities, would play greater or lesser roles in causing the injury.[110]

Consistent with this approach, courts have also addressed allocation between a personal injury claimant and asbestos manufacturers under strict liability theories. Applying state law, certain cases allow a reduction of the manufacturer's share under comparative fault doctrines.[111] A defendant's liability share is reduced if the plaintiff voluntarily and unreasonably assumes a risk.

---

[106] Leng v. Celotex Corp., 554 N.E.2d at 470–71.

[107] Moore v. Johns-Manville Sales Corp., 781 F.2d 1061, 1062 (5th Cir. 1986).

[108] Whatley v. Armstrong World Indus., Inc., 861 F.2d 837, 839 (5th Cir. 1988).

[109] 781 F.2d 1061 (5th Cir. 1986).

[110] *Id.* at 1064–65.

[111] *See, e.g.,* Austin v. Raybestos-Manhattan, Inc., 471 A.2d 280 (Me. 1984).

Other courts have imposed prorated liability if a state law did not provide for comparative fault.[112] Under this theory, liability is prorated among all the defendants when the plaintiff has sued all or substantially all available, identifiable, or implicated manufacturers and the defendants are each found to have contributed some casually connected harm.

Owners of buildings that have products containing asbestos may face an easier burden in apportioning liability among manufacturers or suppliers. For instance, if a building has asbestos-containing insulation, pipe insulation, and soundproofing materials, each product may require a separate remedial action.[113] If the manufacturer and supplier of each product is known, each can be assigned the abatement costs associated with its product.

§ 22.14 Landfill Cost Allocation Case Study

To illustrate some of the issues relating to the allocation of remediation costs among potentially responsible parties (PRP), Coopers & Lybrand developed the following case study. The case study incorporates many of the current apportionment issues facing parties involved in the cleanup of a hazardous waste landfill.

In most instances in which apportionment is required, the methods used and factors considered will be unique. With this in mind, the case study was developed based on case history, logic, and the following underlying assumptions:

- All landfill operating activities have been discontinued.
- Allocation of costs is being negotiated between all solvent PRPs, except for de minimis settlors.
- All site investigation activities have been satisfactorily completed. All EPA and PRP response costs have been properly documented and are in accordance with all applicable requirements.
- All PRPs have been identified, as follows:
  - •• There are 25 generators (denoted by single letters), of which X and Y are insolvent, and G and J have negotiated de minimis settlements with the EPA.

---

[112] Menne v. Celotex Corp., 861 F.2d at 1469 (Nebraska law).

[113] Exactly what remedial action is necessary is likely to be a hotly contested subject. Three forms of remediation are possible: encapsulation, enclosure, and removal. Each method has different advantages and widely divergent costs. *See* Comment, *Asbestos Abatement: The Allocation of Liability,* 40 S.C.L. Rev. 1043, 1068 (1989).

•• There are four transporters (denoted by double letters).

With respect to the *transporters*, the following circumstances apply:

—AA   is the transporter for generators A through G. Each generator specifically instructed AA to deliver its hazardous wastes to this site.

—BB   is the transporter for generators H through L. Generators H, I, and J specifically instructed BB to deliver hazardous wastes to this site. Generators K and L left the determination of where to deliver wastes to the discretion of BB.

—CC   is the transporter for generators M through R. Each generator specifically instructed CC to deliver its hazardous wastes to this landfill.

—DD   is the transporter for generators S through Y. No specific instructions as to where to deliver wastes were given. DD made an independent decision to deliver wastes from these generators to this site.

•• There are three owners (denoted by triple letters)—one current and two past.

With respect to the *landowners*, the following circumstances apply:

—AAA   is the current owner. AAA purchased land from previous owner for considerably less than similarly situated, noncontaminated property. AAA carefully inspected the land and inquired into its past use prior to purchase. AAA has owned the land for five years. Landfill operations ceased after two years of AAA ownership.

—BBB   is the previous owner who purchased land from past owner for fair market value. BBB had owned the land for five years. Landfill operations occurred during BBB's entire ownership period.

—CCC   is the past owner. CCC sold the land for its fair market value. The land was undeveloped and unused prior to sale.

•• There are two operators (denoted by four letters)—one current and one past.

With respect to the *operators*, the following circumstances apply:

—AAAA is the current operator. AAAA took over as the landfill operator after the past operator and has acted in this capacity for the last four years. AAAA held itself out as an expert in the handling and storage of hazardous wastes. These representations were relied on by generators and transporters.

—BBBB is the past operator. BBBB was the initial operator of the landfill and acted in this capacity for three years. BBBB held itself out to be an expert in the handling and storage of hazardous wastes. These representations were relied on by generators and transporters.

- All volumes of contaminants are identifiable by generator.
- The degree of toxicity for each contaminant (ten contaminants) has been determined with I being the least toxic and X being the most toxic. Each contaminant has been weighted according to its degree of toxicity for purposes of allocating cleanup costs. The degree of toxicity is assumed to be directly proportional to the costs of the necessitated remedial actions.
- With the exception of contaminants I and IX, all contaminants have been determined to be nonmigratory.
- A synergistic effect has occurred with respect to contaminants I and IX. Contaminant IX is an extremely toxic substance with almost no mobility and, thus, no ability to contaminate groundwater. Contaminant I is virtually nontoxic but highly mobile. Contaminant I, however, has commingled with contaminant IX, forming a highly toxic, highly mobile substance that has contaminated the groundwater. The additional costs to cleanup contaminated groundwater due to the commingling and movement of contaminants I and IX is estimated to be $10,000,000. This cost is included in estimated future cleanup costs.
- Contaminant VIII, a relatively toxic substance, all of which was delivered while the site was being run by the original operator, was stored in drums. The drums leaked as a result of improper handling by the second operator (AAAA), causing a more costly cleanup than if the drums had not leaked. Furthermore, the original and current operators took no actions to reduce the level of toxicity of the substance contained in the drums. The additional costs relating to the leaking of these drums is estimated to be $2,800,000. This cost is included in estimated future cleanup costs.
- Remedial costs include:

$ 5	million of EPA investigation costs.
5	million of cleanup costs incurred by PRPs.
100	million of estimated future cleanup costs.
$110	million total costs.

- The following chart indicates the amounts of waste contributed by each generator and the amounts delivered by each transporter. These data provide the framework upon which the mathematics of the case study are built.

CONTAMINANT VOLUMES
by HAZARDOUS SUBSTANCE, by PRP

PRP	PRP Group	I	II	III	IV	V	VI	VII	VIII	IX	X	Total
A	(1)	2.0	1.0	3.0	0.0	0.0	4.0	0.0	6.0	2.0	1.0	19.0
B	(1)	60.0	0.0	20.0	7.0	1.0	2.0	0.0	7.0	2.5	0.0	99.5
C	(1)	6.0	0.0	0.0	0.0	1.0	1.0	1.5	6.0	2.0	6.0	23.5
D	(1)	2.5	0.0	7.0	1.0	1.0	1.5	2.5	4.0	0.0	0.0	19.5
E	(1)	0.0	1.0	1.0	1.0	0.0	7.0	1.0	0.0	0.0	6.0	17.0
F	(1)	1.0	7.0	2.0	3.0	0.0	0.0	0.0	0.0	0.0	0.0	13.0
G	(1)	0.0	1.0	1.0	1.0	.5	0.0	0.0	.5	1.0	1.5	6.5
H	(1)	8.0	0.0	1.0	7.0	0.0	1.0	3.0	0.0	0.0	0.0	20.0
I	(1)	35.0	4.0	6.0	0.0	8.0	0.0	4.0	0.0	1.0	0.0	58.0
J	(1)	0.0	0.0	0.0	3.0	0.0	0.0	0.0	1.0	0.0	0.0	4.0
K	(1)	6.5	0.0	.5	2.0	5.0	1.5	0.0	0.0	0.0	0.0	15.5
L	(1)	7.0	2.0	6.0	4.0	2.0	7.0	0.0	.5	2.5	0.0	31.0
M	(1)	7.0	2.5	0.0	0.0	0.0	0.0	9.0	0.0	0.0	0.0	18.5
N	(1)	4.0	1.0	.5	0.0	1.0	0.0	6.0	8.0	0.0	3.5	24.0
O	(1)	0.0	1.0	1.0	1.0	3.0	1.0	0.0	4.0	1.0	1.0	13.0
P	(1)	0.0	0.0	2.0	0.0	0.0	1.0	2.0	0.0	6.0	4.0	15.0
Q	(1)	7.0	0.0	0.0	0.0	0.0	1.0	3.0	4.0	2.0	4.0	21.0
R	(1)	0.0	1.5	6.0	1.0	2.0	0.0	3.5	0.0	4.5	1.0	19.5
S	(1)	2.0	0.0	2.0	0.0	3.0	5.0	7.0	4.0	0.0	0.0	23.0
T	(1)	1.0	7.0	0.0	0.0	0.0	0.0	0.0	3.0	6.0	9.0	26.0
U	(1)	0.0	4.0	2.0	0.0	0.0	0.0	3.0	5.5	7.0	0.0	21.5
V	(1)	1.0	0.0	0.0	0.0	0.0	1.0	0.0	0.0	3.0	10.0	15.0
W	(1)	10.0	1.0	89.0	9.0	7.0	4.0	0.0	0.0	0.0	0.0	120.0
X	(1)	0.0	2.0	1.0	0.0	0.0	6.0	6.5	2.0	1.0	1.0	19.5
Y	(1)	0.0	4.0	1.0	4.0	7.0	3.0	0.0	4.0	2.0	0.0	25.0
Total Tons		160.0	40.0	152.0	44.0	41.5	47.0	52.0	59.5	43.5	48.0	687.5
AA	(2)	71.5	10.0	34.0	13.0	3.5	15.5	5.0	23.5	7.5	14.5	198.0
BB	(2)	56.5	6.0	13.5	16.0	15.0	9.5	7.0	1.5	3.5	0.0	128.5
CC	(2)	28.0	6.0	89.5	2.0	6.0	3.0	23.5	16.0	13.5	13.5	201.0
DD	(2)	4.0	18.0	15.0	13.0	17.0	19.0	16.5	18.5	19.0	20.0	160.0
Total Tons		160.0	40.0	152.0	44.0	41.5	47.0	52.0	59.5	43.5	48.0	687.5

(1) Generator
(2) Transporter

Based on the underlying assumptions noted above, following is a description of the cost allocation model. The allocation model has been divided into distinct phases for ease of explanation. The first phase addresses the issues relating to de minimis settlements with two PRPs and how this affects the allocation of costs among other PRPs. Subsequent phases are based on calculations made in previous phases, thereby building a sequential allocation methodology. Note that rounding of amounts has occurred throughout the model.

PHASE I
De Minimis Settlements

As indicated in the underlying assumptions, two PRPs, G and J, reached de minimis settlements with the EPA, including a complete covenant not to sue, and are, therefore, not liable for cleanup costs in excess of their share of those costs currently incurred or estimated to be incurred at the time of settlement. De minimis settlements do not, however, come cheaply. For generators G and J, the cost to settle is assumed to be at a premium of 200 percent on their individual shares of the total response costs in proportion to their contributed volumetric shares.

At the time of EPA's settlement with the de minimis PRPs, estimated cleanup costs, including costs incurred at that time, were $80 million. Therefore, the costs to be paid under the de minimis settlements would be computed as follows:

PRP	Contributed Volume	Total Site Volume	% of Total	Estimated Site Cleanup Costs	Volumetric Share	Premium	De Minimis Settlement
G	6.5	687.5	.945%	$80,000,000	$756,000	200%	$1,512,000
J	4.0	687.5	.582%	80,000,000	465,600	200%	931,200
							$2,443,200

PHASE II
Allocation of remaining response costs to each PRP group

This case study will develop a model to allocate response costs among each PRP group and among individual PRPs based on the theory of relevant cases.

In the *United States v. Stringfellow*[114] case, the court found that the "the harm is theoretically and practically incapable of division among the defendants due to the synergistic effects of the commingling of different waste." Applying this theory to the case study, contaminants I and IX would have done little harm alone (I because of its low level of toxicity and IX because of its immobility); however, through commingling they do a greater amount of damage. Dividing harm and allocating costs becomes very difficult.

---

[114] 661 F. Supp. 1053 (C.D. Cal. 1987).

In the *United States v. A&F Materials Co.*[115] case, a line of reasoning for apportionment was developed utilizing the six so-called Gore Factors:

1. The ability of the parties to demonstrate that their contribution to a discharge, release or disposal of a hazardous waste can be distinguished
2. The amount of hazardous waste involved
3. The degree of toxicity of the hazardous waste(s) involved
4. The degree of involvement by the parties in the generation, transportation, treatment, storage, or disposal of the hazardous waste
5. The degree of care exercised by the parties with respect to the hazardous waste concerned, taking into account the characteristics of such hazardous waste
6. The degree of cooperation with federal, state, or local officials to prevent any harm to the public health or environment.

Although a degree of subjectivity does exist, the above theories will be considered in this case study in order to develop a framework from which to build an allocation model for PRPs, other than the de minimis settlors.
   PRPs to which costs are to be apportioned include:

Generators	21*
Operators	2
Transporters	4
Owners	2**
	29

*	Total Generators	25
	Less: Insolvent Generators	(2)
	Less: De Minimis Settlers	(2)
		21

**	Total Owners	3
	Less: Innocent Landowner	(1)
		(2)

Step 1:   Determination of cleanup cost factor for each contaminant.

• As indicated in the assumptions, contaminants are weighted according to their degree of toxicity. Higher degree contaminants are given a greater weight (as outlined below) which, in effect, allocates greater cleanup costs to more toxic substances.

---

[115] 578 F. Supp. 1249 (S.D. Ill. 1984).

- Weightings are assigned assuming an equal incremental cost for cleaning up each higher degree of contaminant.

(1) Contaminant	(2) Weighting Factor	(3) Unweighted Tonnage	(4) Weighted Tonnage	(5) Weighted Cleanup Cost Factor
I	1.00	160.0	160.00	.125
II	1.25	40.0	50.00	.039
III	1.50	152.0	228.00	.177
IV	1.75	44.0	77.00	.060
V	2.00	41.5	83.00	.065
VI	2.25	47.0	105.75	.082
VII	2.50	52.0	130.00	.101
VIII	2.75	59.5	163.63	.127
IX	3.00	43.5	130.50	.102
X	3.25	48.0	156.00	.122
		687.5	1,283.88	1.000

(1) and (3) – From assumptions.

(2) – Assigned assuming equal incremental cleanup costs for each higher level of contaminant.

(4) = (2) × (3)

(5) = Specific contaminant's weighted tonnage [column (4)] divided by 1,283.88.

Step 2: Determination of cleanup costs for each contaminant based on Weighted Cleanup Cost Factor.

Contaminant	Weighted Cleanup Cost Factor	Cleanup Costs	Additional Cleanup Costs	Total Cleanup Costs
I	.125	$ 11,844,600	$10,000,000 (1)	$ 21,844,600
II	.039	3,695,515		3,695,515
III	.177	16,771,952		16,771,952
IV	.060	5,685,408		5,685,408
V	.065	6,159,192		6,159,192
VI	.082	7,770,058		7,770,058
VII	.101	9,570,437		9,570,437
VIII	.127	12,034,114	2,800,000 (2)	14,834,114
IX	.102	9,665,194	(1)	9,665,194
X	.122	11,560,330		11,560,330
	1.000	$94,756,800	$12,800,000	$107,556,800

(1) With respect to commingled contaminants I and IX, it has been determined that cleanup costs for these two contaminants will be combined with the additional cost of cleaning up the associated contaminated groundwater, which is estimated to be $10,000,000. The total cleanup cost for these two contaminants is $31,509,794 ($21,844,600 + 9,665,194). This combined cost is to be allocated among all solvent PRPs as if it were a single contaminant.

(2) The additional cost to cleanup contaminant VIII due to leaking drums is estimated to be $2,800,000. Thus, total cleanup cost for contaminant VIII is $14,834,114. This will be described in more detail in later phases.

Step 3: Assumption of allocation percentages to each PRP group.

Generators: 40%— Overall responsibility for the generation of the waste lies with the generators themselves; liability has been determined.

Transporters: 5%— Transporters were involved in contributing to the problem at the site. Some transporters decided on their own where to deliver the contaminants.

Landowners: 5%— Although not directly involved in the contamination of the property, landowners AAA and BBB had full knowledge of what was occurring and made no attempt to discontinue the activities.

Operators: 50%— Both operators held themselves out to be experts in the handling and treatment of hazardous wastes. These representations were relied upon by generators, transporters, and owners. Further, as a result of improper handling by operator AAAA, contaminant VIII leaked from the drums in which it was stored. This leakage resulted in additional cleanup costs of $2,800,000. Because the additional costs were a direct result of operator AAAA's actions, it is assumed that AAAA will bear the entire burden of the $2,800,000 in addition to other allocated costs.

Step 4: Allocation of response costs by PRP group:

PRP Group	Allocation %	Allocated Costs (1)	Additional Costs (2)	Total Allocated Costs
Generators	40%	$ 41,902,720	0	$ 41,902,720
Transporters	5%	5,237,840	0	5,237,840
Landowners	5%	5,237,840	0	5,237,840
Operators	50%	52,378,400	$2,800,000	55,178,400
	100%	$104,756,800	$2,800,000	$107,556,800

(1) Costs remaining after de minimis settlements.

(2) Additional cleanup costs resulting from improper handling of drums by site operator AAAA.

Step 5:   Allocation of response costs by contaminant, by Generator PRP:

Contaminant	Total Response Costs	Generators' 40% Share
I, IX	$31,509,794	$12,603,918
II	3,695,515	1,478,205
III	16,771,952	6,708,780
IV	5,685,408	2,274,164
V	6,159,192	2,463,677
VI	7,770,058	3,108,023
VII	9,570,437	3,828,175
VIII	12,034,114	4,813,646
X	11,560,330	4,624,132
	$104,756,800	$41,902,720

PHASE III
Allocation of response costs to individual PRPs within each PRP group

Step 1:   Allocation of costs between generators.

- The amount of contaminants contributed to the site by the two de minimis generators (G and J) and by the two insolvent generators (X and Y) will be removed from the total, and a new pro-rata share for all other generators will be calculated.

CONTAMINANTS I, IX

Generator	Pro-rata Share of Total (1)	Costs Allocated to Generator for Contaminants I, IX
A	.020	$ 252,078
B	.313	3,945,027
C	.040	504,157
D	.013	163,851
E	.000	0
F	.005	63,020
H	.040	504,157
I	.180	2,268,706
K	.033	415,929
L	.048	604,988
M	.035	441,137
N	.020	252,078
O	.005	63,020
P	.030	378,118
Q	.045	567,176
R	.023	289,890
S	.010	126,039
T	.035	441,137
U	.035	441,137
V	.020	252,078
W	.050	630,195
	1.000	$12,603,918

(1) Based on PRP's tonnage contribution divided by base of 199.5 tons.

CONTAMINANT II

Generator	Pro-rata Share of Total (1)	Costs Allocated to Generator for Contaminant II
A	.030	$ 44,346
B	.000	0
C	.000	0
D	.000	0
E	.030	44,346
F	.213	314,857
H	.000	0
I	.121	178,863
K	.000	0
L	.061	90,171
M	.076	112,344
N	.030	44,346
O	.030	44,346
P	.000	0
Q	.000	0
R	.045	66,519
S	.000	0
T	.213	314,858
U	.121	178,863
V	.000	0
W	.030	44,346
	1.000	$1,478,205

(1) Based on PRP's tonnage contribution divided by base of 33 tons.

CONTAMINANT III

Generator	Pro-rata Share of Total (1)	Costs Allocated to Generator for Contaminant III
A	.020	$ 134,176
B	.135	905,685
C	.000	0
D	.048	322,021
E	.007	46,961
F	.013	87,215
H	.007	46,961
I	.040	268,351
K	.003	20,126
L	.040	268,351
M	.000	0
N	.003	20,126
O	.007	46,961
P	.013	87,215
Q	.000	0
R	.040	268,351
S	.013	87,215
T	.000	0
U	.013	87,215
V	.000	0
W	.598	4,011,850
	1.000	$6,708,780

(1) Based on PRP's tonnage contribution divided by base of 149 tons.

CONTAMINANT IV

Generator	Pro-rata Share of Total (1)	Costs Allocated to Generator for Contaminant IV
A	.000	$ 0
B	.194	441,187
C	.000	0
D	.028	63,677
E	.028	63,677
F	.083	188,756
H	.194	441,187
I	.000	0
K	.056	127,353
L	.111	252,432
M	.000	0
N	.000	0
O	.028	63,677
P	.000	0
Q	.000	0
R	.028	63,677
S	.000	0
T	.000	0
U	.000	0
V	.000	0
W	.250	568,541
	1.000	$2,274,164

(1) Based on PRP's tonnage contribution divided by base of 36 tons.

CONTAMINANT V

Generator	Pro-rata Share of Total (1)	Costs Allocated to Generator for Contaminant V
A	.000	$ 0
B	.029	71,447
C	.029	71,447
D	.029	71,447
E	.000	0
F	.000	0
H	.000	0
I	.235	578,963
K	.147	362,160
L	.059	145,357
M	.000	0
N	.029	71,447
O	.088	216,804
P	.000	0
Q	.000	0
R	.059	145,357
S	.088	216,804
T	.000	0
U	.000	0
V	.000	0
W	.208	512,444
	1.000	$2,463,677

(1) Based on PRP's tonnage contribution divided by base of 34 tons.

CONTAMINANT VI

Generator	Pro-rata Share of Total (1)	Costs Allocated to Generator for Contaminant VI
A	.105	$ 326,342
B	.053	164,725
C	.026	80,809
D	.039	121,213
E	.187	581,199
F	.000	0
H	.026	80,809
I	.000	0
K	.039	121,213
L	.184	571,876
M	.000	0
N	.000	0
O	.026	80,809
P	.026	80,809
Q	.026	80,809
R	.000	0
S	.132	410,259
T	.000	0
U	.000	0
V	.026	80,809
W	.105	326,342
	1.000	$3,108,023

(1) Based on PRP's tonnage contribution divided by base of 38 tons.

CONTAMINANT VII

Generator	Pro-rata Share of Total (1)	Costs Allocated to Generator for Contaminant VII
A	.000	$ 0
B	.000	0
C	.033	126,330
D	.055	210,550
E	.022	84,220
F	.000	0
H	.066	252,660
I	.088	336,879
K	.000	0
L	.000	0
M	.197	754,150
N	.132	505,319
O	.000	0
P	.044	168,440
Q	.066	252,660
R	.077	294,769
S	.154	589,538
T	.000	0
U	.066	252,660
V	.000	0
W	.000	0
	1.000	$3,828,175

(1) Based on PRP's tonnage contribution divided by base of 45.5 tons.

CONTAMINANT VIII

Generator	Pro-rata Share of Total (1)	Costs Allocated to Generator for Contaminant VIII
A	.115	$ 553,569
B	.135	649,842
C	.115	553,569
D	.077	370,651
E	.000	0
F	.000	0
H	.000	0
I	.000	0
K	.000	0
L	.010	48,136
M	.000	0
N	.153	736,489
O	.077	370,651
P	.000	0
Q	.077	370,651
R	.000	0
S	.077	370,651
T	.058	279,191
U	.106	510,246
V	.000	0
W	.000	0
	1.000	$4,813,646

(1) Based on PRP's tonnage contribution divided by base of 52 tons.

CONTAMINANT X

Generator	Pro-rata Share of Total (1)	Costs Allocated to Generator for Contaminant X
A	.022	$ 101,731
B	.000	0
C	.132	610,385
D	.000	0
E	.132	610,385
F	.000	0
H	.000	0
I	.000	0
K	.000	0
L	.000	0
M	.000	0
N	.077	356,058
O	.022	101,731
P	.088	406,924
Q	.088	406,924
R	.022	101,731
S	.000	0
T	.197	910,954
U	.000	0
V	.220	1,017,309
W	.000	0
	1.000	$4,624,132

(1) Based on PRP's tonnage contribution divided by base of 45.5 tons.

GENERATOR COST ALLOCATION SUMMARY
CONTAMINANTS

GENERATOR	I,IX	II	III	IV	V	VI	VII	VIII	X	TOTAL
A	$252,078	$44,346	$134,176	$0	$0	$326,342	$0	$553,569	$101,731	$1,412,242
B	3,945,027	0	905,685	441,187	71,447	164,725	0	649,842	0	6,177,913
C	504,157	0	0	0	71,447	80,809	126,330	553,569	610,385	1,946,697
D	163,851	0	322,021	63,677	71,447	121,213	210,550	370,651	0	1,323,410
E	0	44,346	46,961	63,677	0	581,199	84,220	0	610,385	1,430,788
F	63,020	314,857	87,215	188,756	0	0	0	0	0	653,848
H	504,157	0	46,961	441,187	0	80,809	252,660	0	0	1,325,774
I	2,268,706	178,863	268,351	0	578,963	0	336,879	0	0	3,631,762
K	415,929	0	20,126	127,353	362,160	121,213	0	0	0	1,046,781
L	604,988	90,171	268,351	252,432	145,357	571,876	0	48,136	0	1,981,311
M	441,137	112,344	0	0	0	0	754,150	0	0	1,307,631
N	252,078	44,346	20,126	0	71,447	0	505,319	736,489	356,058	1,985,863
O	63,020	44,346	46,961	63,677	216,804	80,809	0	370,651	101,731	987,999
P	378,118	0	87,215	0	0	80,809	168,440	0	406,924	1,121,506
Q	567,176	0	0	0	0	80,809	252,660	370,651	406,924	1,678,220
R	289,890	66,519	268,351	63,677	145,357	0	294,769	0	101,731	1,230,294
S	126,039	0	87,215	0	216,804	410,259	589,538	370,651	0	1,800,506
T	441,137	314,858	0	0	0	0	0	279,191	910,954	1,946,140
U	441,137	178,863	87,215	0	0	0	252,660	510,246	0	1,470,121
V	252,078	0	0	0	0	80,809	0	0	1,017,309	1,350,196
W	630,195	44,346	4,011,850	568,541	512,444	326,342	0	0	0	6,093,718
X	0	0	0	0	0	0	0	0	0	0
Y	0	0	0	0	0	0	0	0	0	0
	$12,603,918	$1,478,205	$6,708,780	$2,274,164	$2,463,677	$3,108,023	$3,828,175	$4,813,646	$4,624,132	$41,902,720

Step 2: Allocation of costs between transporters.

- The transporters have reached an allocation agreement that takes into consideration both the amount of contaminants transported and the degree of decision making exercised by each transporter, with respect to where hazardous wastes would be delivered. For example, transporter DD, who made the decision to deliver all wastes to this site autonomously, would be assessed a greater share of costs than transporter AA who was specifically instructed to deliver all wastes to this site.

- Percentage allocations based upon the degree of decision making exercised by each transporter are as follows:

  AA—20%

  BB —25%

  CC —20%

  DD—35%

- Allocations based on transported tonnage together with the above percentage allocations are reflected in the following table.

ALLOCATION OF RESPONSE COSTS
BETWEEN TRANSPORTERS

Transporter	Transported Volume	Decision Making Weighting Factor	Weighted Volume	Weighted Volume %	Cleanup Costs Allocated to Transporter
AA	198.0	20%	39.600	23.6%	$1,236,130
BB	128.5	25%	32.125	19.1%	1,000,427
CC	201.0	20%	40.200	24.0%	1,257,082
DD	160.0	35%	56.000	33.3%	1,744,201
	687.5	100%	167.925	100.0%	$5,237,840

Step 3: Allocation of costs between landowners.

- Landowner CCC, the original owner, will be assessed no response costs because CCC was assumed to be an "innocent landowner," since the land was undeveloped at the time it was sold.

- AAA and BBB will share costs allocated to landowner PRPs based initially on the percentage of time each owned the land while it was used as a landfill. Thus, AAA will be assessed 28.6% of the costs (2 years divided by 7 years) and BBB will be assessed 71.4% of the costs (5 years divided by 7 years).

- In addition, because AAA purchased the land from BBB at a considerable discount when compared to similarly situated, noncontaminated land, AAA and BBB have agreed to increase AAA's percentage of costs by 20%. Thus, final allocation percentages are AAA—48.6% and BBB—51.4%. This will prevent unjust enrichment to AAA who purchased the land at a discount and who will have land that could be sold for fair market value at the end of the cleanup.

ALLOCATION OF RESPONSE COSTS
BETWEEN LANDOWNERS

Landowner	Percentage Allocation	Allocated Costs
AAA	48.6%	$2,545,590
BBB	51.4%	2,692,250
		$5,237,840

Step 4:   Allocation of costs between operators.

- Response costs will be allocated between operators based on the length of time each acted as the operator. Thus, AAAA, who acted as the operator of the site for four years, will be assessed 57.1% of the response costs allocated to the operators (4 years divided by 7 years). Operator BBBB will be assessed 42.9% of response costs (3 years divided by 7 years). The additional cleanup costs of $2,800,000 for contaminant VIII will be allocated to operator AAAA.

ALLOCATION OF RESPONSE
COSTS BETWEEN OPERATORS

Operator	Percentage Allocation	Allocated Cleanup Costs	Additional Cleanup Costs	Total Cleanup Costs Allocated to Operators
AAAA	57.1%	$29,908,066	$2,800,000	$32,708,066
BBBB	42.9%	22,470,334	0	22,470,334
		$52,378,400	$2,800,000	$55,178,400

PHASE IV
Summary of response costs allocated to PRPs

RESPONSE COST ALLOCATION SUMMARY

PRP	PRP Group	Allocated Cleanup Costs
A	Generator	$1,412,242
B	Generator	6,177,913
C	Generator	1,946,697
D	Generator	1,323,410
E	Generator	1,430,788
F	Generator	653,848
G	Generator	1,512,000
H	Generator	1,325,774
I	Generator	3,631,762
J	Generator	931,200
K	Generator	1,046,781
L	Generator	1,981,311
M	Generator	1,307,631
N	Generator	1,985,863
O	Generator	987,999
P	Generator	1,121,506
Q	Generator	1,678,220
R	Generator	1,230,294
S	Generator	1,800,506
T	Generator	1,946,140
U	Generator	1,470,121
V	Generator	1,350,196
W	Generator	6,093,718
X	Generator	0
Y	Generator	0
AA	Transporter	1,236,130
BB	Transporter	1,000,427
CC	Transporter	1,257,082
DD	Transporter	1,744,201
AAA	Landowner	2,545,590
BBB	Landowner	2,692,250
CCC	Landowner	0
AAAA	Operator	32,708,066
BBBB	Operator	22,470,334
Total Costs		$110,000,000

CHAPTER 23

MANAGING THE REMEDIAL EFFORT

Evandro F. Braz
Kevin R. Bryson
Robert W. Myers
Alexandra Notaras

Evandro F. Braz is a partner in the international accounting and consulting firm of Coopers & Lybrand in New York, New York, and leads its national practice in project control services for owners of engineering and construction projects. He specializes in assisting project owners to manage the design and construction of their projects and to achieve on time, within budget, and quality performance. He is an experienced project manager and has directed a variety of major consulting assignments, including environmental dispute resolution. He is a certified management consultant, a professional engineer, and a commercial arbitrator. He received B.S. and M.S. degrees in engineering and an M.B.A. from Columbia University, and he has authored several technical and management publications.

Kevin R. Bryson is currently manager of Stone & Webster Environmental Services Division in Cherry Hill, New Jersey. Prior to that he was a project director with Hill International, Inc. As a registered professional engineer and lawyer, he has been involved with the regulatory and engineering aspects of environmental matters for over 20 years. Mr. Bryson is a graduate of the University of Lowell and Suffolk University Law School. He is a member of the New Jersey bar, its Environmental Law Committee, and the American Bar Association.

Robert W. Myers, group president of Hill International, Inc., in Willingboro, New Jersey, has extensive experience in engineering and construction, including construction problem solving, claims evaluation, presentations, and resolution. Some of these assignments on behalf of owners and contractors involved investigating and evaluating claims and damages based on arguments of differing site conditions, defective specifications or construction, construction methods, extra work, inefficiency, and delay. He has authored several papers on improving technical specifications, soils, impacts of differing site conditions, minimizing claims, underground construction and hazardous waste disposal contracting, and soil influence on landfill leachates. He is a member of numerous industry and professional organizations and has spoken before professional societies.

Alexandra Notaras is a senior associate in the international accounting and consulting firm of Coopers & Lybrand in the Project Control Services Group in New York, New York. Prior to joining the firm, she practiced architecture for ten years and has gained extensive experience in management and control of the construction process. She received a B.S. in architecture from the University of Illinois, an M.A. in architecture from the University of Washington, and an M.B.A. from Harvard University.

§ 23.1   Introduction

This chapter discusses how an owner of property with known hazardous waste problems should utilize its internal operations, select its outside consultants and contractors, and manage and control the remedial process. Business variables that must be considered and decisions that an owner must make in order to effectively complete the remedial effort on its property are explored. The approach and procedures herein defined are applicable whether the problem is discovered prior to or during the construction of a project. As discussed in previous chapters, responsible parties are those parties who currently own the property or have contributed to the problem in some way or manner in the past. For this reason, the term *owner* as used in this chapter will refer to any and all responsible parties.

Failure to properly plan, manage, and control the remedial process can be disastrous. Moreover, under certain circumstances the consultants advising the owner may end up sharing the responsibility and liability. Therefore, a thorough understanding of the extensive liability and other legal implications, as well as proper management and execution of the remedial process, are critical.

Statutes and more stringent monitoring enforcement by environmental agencies have resulted in an atmosphere in which every owner of property must seriously address the environmental aspects as part of the planning process of a project. Planning for the remedial process is not inexpensive but may prove far more costly. Legal liabilities, delays in design, approvals, and construction, and extreme financial penalties are among the potential consequences of failing to plan.

In addition, the current public awareness of the hazards associated with environmental remediation sites can result in short- and long-term impacts on the acceptability and feasibility of a project. The public will focus on any written accounts or rumors of potential hazards and will closely scrutinize the environmental management efforts. Therefore, it is critical for an owner to state its intentions up front and assign a point person to keep interested parties aware of the remediation process.

§ 23.2   Assembling the Team

The approach recommended in this chapter is applicable for cleanups at Superfund sites initiated by potentially responsible parties (PRP's); remediation efforts at nonSuperfund sites where construction for a new project has begun; and in situations in which the site does not meet the criteria for being included on the National Priorities List. However, it does not apply to those cleanup efforts undertaken by the federal government or by state agencies under the appropriate legislation. In these latter matters, responsible parties have little involvement in the direction or control of the cleanup efforts; their involvement is generally limited to their share of the payment obligation for the cleanup effort.

Following the initial discovery and definition of the specific environmental issues affecting the project and establishment of the source of funding to carry out the remediation, the scope of work must be established and the team to accomplish this effort must be assembled. In most situations the owners do not have the in-house expertise to drive the effort associated with remediation. If they do have such expertise, it may be focused elsewhere and unavailable to dedicate sufficient time to the remediation effort.

In most instances, the owner must work very closely with appropriate federal and/or state environmental regulatory agencies in preparing and obtaining approval for the final remediation program to be implemented at the site. Therefore, it is essential that the owner select and engage a competent environmental attorney. The environmental attorney can assist the owner in dealing with regulatory agencies, protecting against future liabilities, selecting the other important members of the team, and providing overall direction and guidance in selecting the remedial approach. The following is a description of the overall program to carry out these efforts.

§ 23.3   Establishing Program Description, Budget, Scope, and Objectives

The initial investigation process typically consists of two phases. The first phase is what is generally known as a *remedial investigation feasibility study (RI/FS)*. During this process an examination of the conditions at the site is conducted to identify the nature and extent of the problem. Once the problem has been characterized, various remedial action alternatives for the cleanup are investigated to determine the most appropriate method. Following the selection of the method, the detailed design of the appropriate and cost-effective method is completed, and actual construction follows.

These preliminary investigations and the resulting feasibility study assist the owner in establishing the requirements and approach to correct the environmental problems affecting the property. After gathering the initial information concerning available techniques, reliability, cost, and time to implement, the owner is then in a position to chose a method and present and defend its selection before the various regulatory agencies. Prior to presenting a remediation program to the regulatory agencies, the owner should seek assurance from its investigative team that variables have been explored, and that the preliminary environmental studies have adequately considered all reasonable alternatives.

§ 23.4   Establishing the Selection Committee

The best means of providing the owner with assurances that the preliminary findings of the site investigation are representative of the actual situation is for the owner to establish its own team of experts. This team should be comprised of individuals with diverse expertise. As with any action group, this committee should have a defined, written purpose to guide its activities. To be effective, it must be empowered to act as the owners' representative throughout the life of the program. The consistent continuity of such a task force is critical to its success, and achieving this continuity should be a factor considered when selecting committee members.

In addition, the committee should be of manageable size. The size of the team will depend upon the extent of the scope and complexity of the project and the number of individual owners associated with the cleanup effort. The team leader should be a person who has the time to investigate alternatives, has access to upper management, and is able to make timely decisions. This leader should also be able to guide the committee to a consensus or unified decision and ideally have the authority to demand action from all parties involved. Finally, this leader should be charged with and have authority to formulate the project's objectives, commit resources, and apportion the work between the members of the project. The committee will administer the activities of the owners' on-site project management team and will act as liaison between these on-site personnel and upper management.

§ 23.5   Project Management Team

Establishing the owner's project management team is another important aspect. Most owners do not have a project management team in place and may have to rely on their engineering or facilities group to perform this function. Larger firms generally have appropriate individuals on their staffs, but smaller firms may have to recruit from the outside or elect to delegate the owner's representative responsibilities to an outside consultant.

Because the owner assumes the highest level of risk in this process and usually bears the majority of the costs, it is imperative that the individual selected to represent the owner's perspective and interests be able to:

Plan
Organize
Coordinate
Implement controls
Operate under sometimes conflicting authorities
Adjust to the situation.

§ 23.6   Selecting the Environmental Consultant

In most cases the owner will not have sufficient experience with hazardous waste cleanup, so it should not attempt to act as its own environmental consultant. An environmental consulting firm can provide not only the specific knowledge it has but also its experience on similar work and specialized judgment. One can almost suggest that the fact-gathering process is the simple part. The expert becomes valuable in the interpretation of these facts and the extrapolation of the best course of action evaluated against the associated potential consequences to the owner.

Owners should be familiar with the various types of environmental firms that exist in today's market and the services offered by these firms, which include:

Geotechnical
Hydrogeology
Air/Water/Groundwater
   Quality Monitoring
Air/Water/Groundwater
   Modelling
Regulatory Assistance
Environmental Sciences

Remediation Technologies
Design, Engineering, and Construction
   Services
Quality Assurance
Risk Assessment
Health and Safety
Sampling/Laboratory Services

Some firms supply all of these services and have the capability to provide comprehensive services on a turnkey basis. Others provide specialty services in one or more of these areas and are generally utilized to assist the owner in understanding the scope of the problem and arranging for services as required. Selection of the type of firm and its particular qualifications is, of course, dictated by the in-house capability of the owner and the anticipated extensiveness of the remediation effort.

Environmental consultants and specialists who perform remediation work are in high demand. As a result of this demand, there are many new entrants to the market. Some of the firms that have already performed several assignments may have been successful because of the favorable supply/demand situation, not because of experience of their staff or the quality of their performance. Therefore, the owner of the remediation project, especially if it is a one-time buyer of the environmental consultant's services, should exercise extreme caution when selecting the consultant.

§ 23.7 —Method of Selection

A number of methods for choosing a consultant are available to the owner.

Direct selection based on referrals or on client's prior experience. This method of selection presumes an owner who is a knowledgeable buyer of environmental services and who is relatively comfortable with the consultants it has worked with in the past, or who trusts the opinion of the entity making the referral. The advantage of this method of selection is that the time frame for solicitation of services is shortened and the consultant and the owner are knowledgeable of each other's culture, structure, and capabilities. The disadvantage may result from the fact that the owner did not explore all the alternatives available or that the price of the services is not competitive. This method of selection typically favors the more established environmental consulting firms, because it presupposes a proven client base that results in client referrals or repeat clients. When selecting on this basis, it is important to verify the firm's prior experience in handling very similar situations and the specific people within the firm who were responsible for the project services.

Comparative selection based on proposals and qualifications. With this method, the owner makes a selection based on more objective criteria. It allows the owner to explore the different options available to it. It is considered the fairest method of selection because the owner is making a selection based on the specific qualifications of each proposing firm.

Competitive selection based on price. This method of selection is the most controversial because it may lead to price cutting and unfair competition among bidders. Remedial work involves so many unknowns that initial price estimates rarely reflect the actual cost of the work. As a result, selecting one's consultant based solely on price may not be a valid alternative, especially if qualifications and prior experience are not closely investigated. Proponents of this method of selection state that the exposure of environmental consultants to risk and liability guarantees a level of performance and, therefore, price is a valid criterion for selection. However, it should be noted that in most hazardous waste situations liability remains with the owner. Even if the owner receives indemnification from the consultant, this indemnification is limited to the consultant's ability to pay, and this should be considered when evaluating alternatives.

§ 23.8   —Criteria for Selection

Regardless of the method of selection, the owner must choose consultants. To facilitate the evaluation and selection process, it is advisable that the owner establish an evaluation matrix that assigns value to each criterion according to its needs, goals, and program objectives. Depending upon the owner's experience in these matters, help in establishing an evaluation system may be required.

A sample list of criteria that an owner may use to qualify and select its consultants follows. Individual needs of each project and the scope of the work should govern the assignment of weights accordingly.

Objective or Factual

Following is a list of objective criteria that an owner should easily obtain for each bidder under consideration, to assist in the selection process:

1. Size of firm. The firm's size is a very good indicator of the breadth and depth of the services it provides. Typically, larger firms have a more varied staff and larger resources to draw upon.

2. Qualifications of staff. An owner should solicit a list of qualifications of each staff member to be assigned to the project. In addition, it would be advantageous for an owner to be aware of the mix of qualifications and specialization of the firm as a whole.

3. Experience. A successful record of previous similar work is the best indicator of the consultant's ability to perform the type of services that the owner requires. A listing of work that is similar in scope completed for other clients will demonstrate the consultant's ability to perform satisfactory services for an owner.

4. Structure of firm. A description of the structure of the firm will allow the client to inquire about project management issues that may affect its project. Ramifications on overall control, quality,

efficiency, and accountability can be easily assessed if the buyer of services understands the principles of internal organization the consultant follows.

5. Availability. Knowing that a proposed team is immediately available to pursue the owner's objectives is of significant importance whenever selecting a firm. In addition, it is recommended that the assigned team be committed to the project for the duration of the work.

Subjective Criteria

An owner should interview consultants under consideration to assess the following:

1. Compatibility of firm's objectives and interests with those of the owner. Learning about the "personality" of the firm prior to contractual commitment will assist the owner in avoiding conflicts later in the process. Understanding up front how a consultant will react and communicate as well as having an insight on the principles that guide its decision-making process will assist the owner in determining if there is a fit between it and the consultant.

2. Level of commitment. The interview process will reveal the consultant's enthusiasm and level of commitment to the project. The level of energy a consultant devotes to getting the work usually correlates with the execution effort later on.

Fee Structure

Although the price for services should not be the sole basis for selection, it is an important consideration. Many consultants will consider performing services under alternate compensation arrangements. As a result, it is up to the owner to arrive at the arrangement most appropriate for his project.

Following is a list of the most typical types of fee structures:

Multiplier. This method of compensation is most appropriate when the scope of services is difficult to define. The consultant keeps track of all its direct salary cost, then applies an agreed-upon multiple.

The percent fee. Percentage fee based on the final cost of the project is the most traditional method of compensating design professionals. However, this type of compensation may not reflect the actual effort put into the project and generally creates a conflict of interest. There is no incentive to the consultant to keep costs down. In addition, in the case of environmental remediation, where the exact scope of the work is the hardest to define at the onset, this method gives very few guidelines to an owner whenever it is trying to establish the budget for consultants' fees. When an owner specifies this type of compensation, it should track costs of materials and labor supplied by its forces in order to eliminate the possibility that the consultant will claim that those costs should be included in the final cost when calculating his fee. In addition, prior to the execution of an agreement, the owner should establish a fee schedule based on percentage of work completed, in order to avoid paying a disproportionate amount up front.

Lump sum. The lump sum requires, more than other methods, a detailed scope of the work, to provide a good basis for estimating the amount of effort required of the consultant. Furthermore, this method of compensation requires the owner to exercise the greatest amount of control in order to regulate extent of services performed in each phase and to avoid the situations in which the consultant has used up its fee prior to the completion of the work. In addition, under this method of compensation, the consultant may be tempted not to devote the time and attention that is required on certain aspects of the job to compensate for miscalculations on its part regarding the actual amount of effort required to complete a task. On long-term engagements, the owner should specify escalation costs to be applied on the direct salaries over the duration of the project. The owner should also require the consultant to preestablish the mix of the professionals to be involved in the effort.

With this method the owner is paying the consultant for the exact amount of time it takes to perform the service. Upon occasion, a guarantee for a maximum cost of the service (GMP), or a not-to-exceed figure, may be attached to this method.

Hourly or daily charge. Under this method of compensation, the owner compensates the consultant on the basis of an agreed-upon schedule of hourly or daily professional service fees. This arrangement is most appropriate for services performed by primarily professional level staff when the scope is well defined. It has the advantage over the multiple method in that the owner pays a prescribed rate on the basis of the staff qualifications, and not payroll. Thus, there is no incentive to load the project with high salary staff or give excessive raises that will return more overhead allowance or profit.

§ 23.9   Implementation Contract

The next step in effective planning is the selection of the agreements to carry out the construction and disposal aspects of the program.

General Contractor

Depending on the environmental issues facing an owner, utilizing a general contractor may be the most appropriate selection. Opponents to this form of contracting point out that a general contractor is not acting as an owner's agent and thus its principle duty is to protect its own interests at a time of conflict. Several conditions should exist before the services of a General Contractor should be contemplated:

In house expertise. Experienced personnel representing the owner's interests should be available to control the general contractor. Failure to monitor and control cost and schedule as the work progresses, the inability to control change orders due to unforeseen field conditions and resulting scope changes, as well as the possible lack of control over quality and safety issues, can have very adverse financial and legal consequences.

Sufficient time. Sufficient time should be available to develop a thorough set of specifications that meet the owner's needs. Traditionally, general contractors do not get involved in the planning of the remediation work but rather in just the execution.

Budgeting experience. Having a quantity take-off and estimate prepared in advance of soliciting quotes or bids for the implementation phase will avoid a situation in which the bids exceed the available funding.

Construction Manager

The owner in this approach retains a Construction Manager (CM) after engaging the environmental consultant. The CM's role is to provide, early on in the process, support concerning such issues as budgeting, cost estimating, scheduling, and evaluation of appropriate construction methods. He acts as the owner's agent and is likely to assume coordination of project meetings, review of budget and schedule, select contractors, perform contract administration, and review progress payments, claims, change orders, and project close-out procedures. An owner should consider engaging a Construction Manager when the following conditions exist:

The work is of increased scope and complexity. As projects become larger and more complex, every step of the planning and the execution become more complex. As a result, more hands-on expertise is required earlier on in the process. Increased risks to the owner may require the integration of expert services regarding the execution of the remedial effort into the planning stages.

Lack of in-house expertise. Engaging a CM as the owner's agent safeguards against potential lack of control and typically results in savings of cost and time. In addition, it reduces an owner's staff requirements because the owner's team under this system is involved in the review of the CM's recommendations and the overall management and decision making, rather than the day-to-day monitoring of the project's execution.

Insufficient time. The CM system is suited well for the owner who is interested in reducing overall project duration. By developing comprehensive schedules, activities can be shortened or overlapped, and by dividing a project into separate and distinct subprojects, remediation can start before planning is complete.

Need for early budget planning. When overall cost of the project is of concern, a CM's experience in cost estimating techniques may prove invaluable.

Other Approaches

Design/Build.   Under this type of agreement the owner holds one contract under which the consultant provides both the planning input as well as the execution for one stated price. An owner should consider this approach whenever its needs require a simplified reporting relationship.

Turnkey.   The turnkey system is a variation of the design/build concept in which the contracted entity provides the financing in addition to the planning and execution.

§ 23.10   Selecting the Contractors

The most important step in the process of selecting a contractor is the *prequalification.* The objective of prequalification is to limit the providers of remedial services to contractors with satisfactory resources and experience to provide the work, a demonstrated record of performance, and adequate financial backing.

Contacting firms directly or advertising to interested parties through specialized periodicals, journals, and associations will give an owner a pool of potentially interested bidders from which to select. Each firm should then be evaluated by the owner (team) with the assistance of its environmental consultant under the objective criteria stated in **§ 23.9.**

The list of providers of remedial work should be restricted to approximately ten. Meetings with these prequalified firms and further evaluation under the subjective criteria stated in **§ 23.9** should reduce the number of possible firms to five or six. This number is generally considered to be the optimum number of firms with which an owner can successfully enter into negotiations.

To avoid confusion at the time of selection, it is advisable for an owner to establish the format in which proposals are to be received. In this way, it will be simpler when comparing fees, schedule durations, and the exact scope services between bidders.

The process of prequalification has acquainted the owner with each firm's capabilities and strengths. As a result, a short interviewing process and the use of a weighted evaluation matrix should provide the owner with an objective selection.

§ 23.11   Considerations when Preparing and Evaluating Bids

Hazardous wastes remediation projects are unique situations, not only for the owner, but also for the contractor engaged to do the cleanup. These projects may involve problems related to varying site conditions; environmental protection requirements; and health and safety requirements. Therefore, due consideration must be given by the contractor when preparing the bid and the owner when evaluating bids.

§ 23.12   —Variable Site Conditions

Although the environmental consultant has a duty to use due care in defining the nature and extent of the hazardous waste, it is not unusual that situations will change once the contractor begins the remediation project. This is particularly true when the hazardous waste exists on previous industrial or commercial sites. On such sites, it is unlikely that all underground utilities will be identified. Also, experience has shown that the amount of excavated contaminated material that is actually encountered may differ substantially from that estimated. Given that the cost of disposal for this material can be $300–$400 per ton, a small variation can amount to a significant increase in cost. An appropriate method of evaluating these variables should be developed for use in the bid evaluation process, and an explanation should accompany all estimated and nominal quantities to be bid.

§ 23.13   —Environmental Protection Requirements

Special provisions for environmental protection are required in the bidding process. The invitation to bid and the bidder's response should set out these requirements and should also indicate who has responsibility for each. Such items may include:

1. Air monitoring
2. Dust and odor control
3. Solid and liquid waste handling and disposal
4. Spill prevention and control program
5. Soil erosion and sediment control
6. Weighing systems (waste disposal monitoring)
7. Documentation programs
8. Public relations.

Each of these items is important, but the disposal of waste frequently presents the most significant problem. Typically, a waste disposal program requires that the waste be sampled and classified, and the transportation and disposal of those which are hazardous must comply with specific legal requirements under various state and federal laws. Included in these requirements is the need to manifest each shipment of waste to provide assurances that each shipment is transported and disposed of in a proper manner. See **Chapter 8**. In addition, the generator (usually the owner) of the waste is required to maintain records of the disposition of the wastes for a period of years after the disposal occurs. This is a specific legal requirement but it is also a practical one. At some point in time the owner may be engaged in litigation to recover costs from parties who contributed to the hazardous waste situation at the site, and the manifests will provide one of the material facts in proving these costs. In addition, if the disposal of waste removed from the site should be improper, the owner may become party to an entirely new remediation project, and the manifests then can be used to allocate the owner's portion of these cleanup costs.

§ 23.14 —Health and Safety Concerns

A health and safety plan should be developed as an integral part of the project work plan. This plan should, among other things, specify how workers will be protected from exposure to any harmful conditions that may exist at the site. In addition, this plan should identify other areas of concern and specify how they will be monitored and controlled if required. Areas of concern include public protection at site boundaries, dust suppression, vapor control, poisonous chemical monitoring, and explosive and ignitable hazardous situations.

Regardless of the hazardous situation anticipated or actually encountered during a remediation project, certain requirements must be met to protect workers on the site. Included in these are training, personnel protective equipment (PPE), medical examinations, emergency procedures, and decontamination. The Occupational Safety and Health Administration (OSHA) has provided regulations governing these and other criteria for workers involved at remediation projects at 29 C.F.R. 1900.120. A summary of these regulations is presented in § **23.23**. The reader is also referred to a publication entitled *Occupational Safety and Health Guidance Manual for Hazardous Waste Site Activities.*[1]

In planning activities associated with hazardous material cleanup, consideration should be made for the loss of time and efficiency that accompanies the use of personnel protection equipment (PPE). Various studies have indicated that worker efficiencies can be significantly affected by the use of PPE.[2] Efficiencies can vary from 10 to 90 percent of that experienced without PPE. This range of efficiencies is affected by the level of protection required and the ambient conditions, as heat stress has also been shown to be a factor in loss of efficiency.

The health and safety program developed as part of the project work plan would generally be under the control of the owner's Health and Safety Officer (HSO). Among other things, the HSO is responsible for ensuring that the workers on the site are not exposed to any hazardous situations and to specify when and what types of safety measures should be implemented. Therefore, the HSO exercises a great deal of control over areas of the project that, under different circumstances, would lie with the contractor. Because of this, the contractor and the owner should realize that there may be delays which are neither expected or avoidable and for which the contractor may have to be compensated.

§ 23.15 Awarding the Contracts

Awarding the contract is the last step in the process of assembling the remediation team. Several forms of agreement are available to the owner. It is recommended that whatever form of agreement used, it should be carefully reviewed by the owner's legal counsel to ensure that the owner's interests are protected both in legal terms as well as from a business point of view.

---

[1] U.S. Dep't Health and Human Servs., Occupational Safety and Health Guidance Manual for Hazardous Waste Site Activities (Oct. 1985).

[2] R. Stillman, *Estimating the Remediation of Hazardous Waste Sites,* AACE Transactions (1990); J. D'Annunzio & M. Renda, *Bidding a Hazardous Waste Project* in Hazardous Waste Disposal and Underground Construction Law (R. Cushman & B. Ficken, eds., John Wiley & Sons 1987).

§ 23.16   Determining Responsibility

As noted in § **23.1**, the term *owner* in this chapter refers to a singular entity or several parties identified as liable for the cleanup, typically referred to as potentially responsible parties (PRPs). Liability for these PRPs will be both strict and joint and several for all costs incurred in remediating a project. These parties frequently include present and former owners and operators of the site, transporters who brought waste to the site, off-site entities that generated or arranged for disposal or treatment of wastes ultimately disposed of at the site, and, more recently, lenders.

Each PRP, as well as the other project participants involved in the planning/design and cleanup operations, should be identified as early as possible in the process. A detailed description of each party's duties and responsibilities should be established, and each party should be held contractually responsible to the commitments.

PRPs share the common goals that remediation satisfy all legal obligations and avoid unnecessary expenditures. As the work progresses, the PRPs share the mutual objective of identifying and minimizing potential risks and addressing unforeseen developments promptly. An additional objective is that all relevant information be readily available and accessible to all project participants in a timely manner.

To accomplish this, methods of communication as well as channels to effectively handle decisions affecting the process must be established as soon as practical. Furthermore, distribution of pertinent information and methods for resolution of conflict among participants must be planned in the early stages of the remediation effort.[3]

In order to expedite and effectively carry out a remediation project, it is essential also to develop and implement reporting relationships that assign responsibility and define program management plans.

§ 23.17   The Program Management Plan

A program management plan or project execution plan is the primary tool that will disseminate program planning and management/control information from all program participants to an owner as well as communicate owner requirements to the team. A successful plan ensures that all stages and phases of work are identified and managed, that a program management system is established and its component elements, cost, schedule, and technical baselines defined, and that interfaces between all program participants are delineated and controlled.

---

[3] *See* Morgan, Lewis & Bockius, *Information Network for Superfund Settlements* in PRP Organization Handbook (June 1989).

Specifically, the plan should state the measurable objectives of the project, the management organization structure and the detailed responsibilities of each team, the work plan to be followed, and the recommended milestones for the project. It should also identify the subplans necessary to effectively manage the remedial effort. It should be developed, maintained, controlled, and enforced on a continual basis throughout the project's duration.

A program management plan provides the owner with:

1. Integration of all program participants' data. By delineating the exact scope of services of each project participant and by having one set format for the presentation of every participant's inputs, the integration of the various teams' efforts can easily be assembled into one comprehensive progress report.
2. Management of uncertainty, prevention of surprises. Identification of deficiencies or failures to conform to a base plan allow for early corrective actions that will have a lesser impact on cost, schedule, quality, and safety.
3. Confidence. A single document of complete management planning that delineates scope, schedule, budget, and responsibility provides an owner with the assurance that the design, implementation, and technical, operational, schedule, and budgetary considerations are planned, implemented, and evaluated appropriately.

§ 23.18   Establishing the Management Control Systems

After the appropriate teams have been selected and their duties, responsibilities, and reporting relationships have been defined, an owner must establish a wide variety of controls to monitor and control performance and progress. These control systems, or at least an understanding of the exact controls that will be required, should be in place prior to the start of the remediation effort.

Controls are necessary because not only do they measure and report progress but they also provide a framework for taking timely and corrective action to meet project objectives. Through effective controls, a project can be monitored to see that it is proceeding according to plan, and variances can be reported. Deviations from plan can then alert management and project team members in time, and appropriate corrective measures can be established before the situation gets out of hand. (It should also be noted that controls can provide strong evidence of prudent action in support of any subsequent cost recovery litigation that may result.)

Adequate controls should be viewed as a management tool and not as additional paperwork. Of course, a certain amount of report preparation is required to effectively portray actual progress, but the essence of control is the analysis of the situation that ensues and the timely corrective actions that will bring the project back to plan.

An owner should keep in mind that not all projects require the same level of control. As a result, the first step for an owner is to establish an understanding of the risks associated with each project and then protect its interests against each one of these risks accordingly.

The belief in the need for control must be shared by all the people involved in the project. The team should believe in submitting reports at fixed periodic intervals with the associated backup documentation. Management, in turn, should demonstrate that it can utilize these reports to implement corrective actions and to improve the progress and quality of the project.

Effective control is both informative and motivating, and should be regarded as such. However, the areas to be covered by the reports and the format of the report must be decided prior to the start of the work. Each report should focus on predefined criteria, should strike a balance between necessary information and desirable information, and most of all should be kept simple.

Project organization is the key to achieving the goals and objectives of the remedial effort. Furthermore, the team that is challenged by the work and is inspired by strong leadership is far more likely to follow the recommended project execution strategy and achieve cost, schedule, and quality goals. Thus, the key to effective leadership and project success is a clearly defined, efficient, and responsible project organization.

The duties and responsibilities of key positions must be clearly defined and understood thoroughly by the individual assigned to carry them out. Furthermore, because the remediation process typically involves many teams, each of which is responding to different project requirements, lines of authority should be clear without gaps or overlaps.

The owner should keep in mind that project organization needs change as the project progresses through its various stages. Accordingly, the project organization should be reviewed periodically and changes should be implemented as appropriate. It is in the owner's best interest to establish feedback mechanisms to allow for information to filter up as well as down through the project teams. Thus, by being kept current, an owner can improve upon the existing structure, can monitor the internal flow of information, and can maintain the necessary flexibility that the remediation effort requires.

It is in the owner's best interest to continuously monitor performance of each team relative to the tasks assigned to it. Members of the project should be held accountable for their performance and deviations from an owner-developed, objective, project-specific measurement system should require an explanation.

§ 23.19   Cost Control Systems

Actual costs may vary substantially depending on the remedial alternative selected; remedial work is very expensive. Owners are very susceptible to cost overruns. Frequently, remedies prove insufficient, and further work is required. Given the inherent complexities presented by the number of uncertainties involved, the potential financial liabilities confronting an owner can rise to staggering levels. As a result owners are concerned about controlling costs and seek manageable financial controls.

A framework to allocate costs to the different aspects of the work is essential, because many PRPs are involved but each may be responsible for only certain aspects of the remediation program. Also, there may be a government reimbursement program involved. Even if only a single party is responsible for the cost, its insurance may cover certain areas but not others. A basis for cost allocation is a must. Secondly, because cleanup work involves uncertainties regarding the work scope, careful documentation of actual funds expended are necessary to avoid potential penalties that may be imposed by regulatory agencies for failure to meet predetermined obligations.

For internal monitoring purposes, the owner's project manager is typically responsible for monitoring and tracking the overall project costs expended against the original budget estimate. All project participants should be expected to provide input to the project manager for the work assigned to them and should alert the owner whenever deviations from the original budget are encountered.

A project cost control system should provide an owner with the controls required to account for and manage the project expenditures. The controls should include procedures for reviewing and approving transactions and invoices of consultants and contractors, procedures for approval of the authorization of funds, and procedures for achieving documentation for all project-related transactions.

In addition to properly authorized and well documented transactions, a cost control system provides the following advantages:

1. Potential problems are identified in time for corrective or cost minimizing actions to be taken
2. Project team members are informed of the costs allocated to their own area of responsibility and are aware of how their portion of their work fits into the total project budget

3. A cost-conscious environment is created in which all team members are aware of the impact of their decisions on project costs
4. Forecasting of remaining costs is possible from comparison of costs expended to date versus control estimates.

Changes to the original plan are very likely to occur during the remedial process, and typically the owner is responsible for that cost. Therefore, an owner should set aside a reasonable contingency to pay for these legitimate changes that arise either from further exploration of alternatives or from unanticipated field conditions. The contingency is again a best gross estimate, but it should consider the complexity of the site, the thoroughness of the investigation, and the ability and timing of obtaining substantial additional remedies and funding, if necessary.

§ 23.20   Operational Control Systems

A formal and structured project management process and a defined control environment is required to successfully conduct the remedial effort. The control objectives should be as follows:

Contractual Provisions

The project control starting point for owners is the contract and all related documents incorporated into it by reference, that is, design and specification documents, whole statutes, labor contract provisions, affirmative action plans, and the like. An owner should make a checklist of all the financial, management, and operational controls it wants to exercise on the project, identify how they will be enforced, and specify the levels of authority for making changes. Then the owner must make sure that all the desired controls are spelled out in the contract prior to its signing.

In the environmental remediation arena especially, carefully drawn documents may allow owners to minimize certain financial and legal risks. Furthermore, because each consultant will attempt to offer its own form of contract with provisions that best protect its interests, it is advisable for an owner to include a draft copy of the agreement in its request for proposal for consultant's services.

Scope Control

The most important aspect in controlling costs is that of controlling the scope of the work. Most remedial projects have two distinct phases: the feasibility/investigative study, during which the team explores the alternatives available to it and decides on the most advantageous course of action; and the implementation or remediation phase, during which the team executes the requirements of the feasibility study. Both of these phases require explicit scope control. During the investigative phase the team experiences the highest level of ambiguity in its tasks or in its appropriate course of action. As a result, the job cannot be easily scoped at the beginning of the engagement. Depending upon the facts discovered, the scope may increase or decrease and the investigation may proceed in varying directions.

The best method of control under such circumstances is achieved when the owner requires the consultant to submit progress reports and look-ahead work plans. These reports should be submitted on a predetermined regular interval, typically on a monthly basis, and the owner should approve the proposed plan and its associated budget prior to proceeding to the next phase of the work.

In addition, for a multi-phased project, it may be prudent to hire a different consultant to perform the investigatory work and another to carry out the remediation process in order to avoid conflict of interest. At a minimum, the owner should contractually commit to one phase of the project at a time in order to maintain the consultant's integrity.

During the implementation phase, changes caused by safety concerns, unanticipated field conditions, environmental or regulatory requirements, or changes with a significant economic benefit to the owner should be permitted. Thus, the concept of *design freeze* should be considered and a scope change control system should be developed.

Schedule Control

A milestone schedule should be prepared at the beginning of the project, and it should include target dates, durations sequences, and dependencies of critical activities for feasibility analysis, bidding, contract awards, remediation, and close-out. Whenever appropriate, the duration of the project can be reduced by releasing portions of the work for remediation while other portions of design continue (that is, fast-tracking).

Throughout the project's duration, the project milestone schedule should be updated at predetermined intervals. If events are not keeping pace with the schedule, the first priority should be to correct those events, not the schedule. All team members should be required to complete activities within the project milestone schedule and establish due dates for submissions and deliverables accordingly.

Team members should provide the owner with monthly schedule reports. These subtier schedules provide a detailed breakdown of each activity and will be compiled into the milestone schedule. In general, subtier schedules allow the team to prepare for upcoming events, whereas the milestone schedule gives an overall picture of the project.

Projects with multiple phases or long durations should be scheduled using critical path methodology (CPM). In addition, a project schedule tracking system should be implemented on the project to help ensure the following:

1. The milestone and completion dates can be met
2. Delays and their causes are identified and necessary actions can be taken to put the project back on track
3. Changes to the original project are properly reflected and the target schedule is adjusted accordingly
4. Consultant's and contractor's monthly progress payments are being made according to actual progress reported.

Document Control

The presence of good records and a reliable, workable system to process, record, and retrieve project information should be devised.

Effective and expeditious exchange of information, especially on critical issues, can be achieved through the use of a *document distribution chart*. All incoming and outgoing project information and correspondence should be labeled by project number, date, and appropriate file number and should be stored in a central accessible area. In addition, a project document control report will assist an owner in tracking the documents received against the documents normally expected per the contract.

Change Order/Claims System

The biggest contributor to cost and schedule overruns is the lack of control over changes that occur over the normal course of a project. Therefore, a change order status file and a change order tracking system, kept with the project tracking system or separately, are necessary to allow the owner to track currently cumulative expenditures on the project as well as to allow forecasting of final costs and completion dates.

The contract should set procedures for the issuance and control of change orders, including their initiation, approval, and processing. Change orders should show estimated completion dates, total cost, and impact on the overall project schedule and should be approved by the owner in writing.

One control that is often needed to protect the owner's financial interests is a procedure for going ahead with change in the scope of the contract before the price is negotiated. This is usually accomplished by issuing a written notice to the contractor to proceed with the change pending negotiation of price, with the stipulation that the calculation of price follow as soon as possible. In addition, because it takes time to prepare a complete estimate for a change and the project must proceed, owners should consider issuing pending change orders to the contractor. This allows the contractor to be notified of an expected change so it can proceed with other work until the price can be agreed upon and the change order can be issued.

Finally, the change order tracking system should reflect all current and future/pending change orders. If the cumulative cost of all change orders and pending changes exceeds the contingency amounts (or other available funds), an owner will have to seek additional financing for the project. Thus, the ability to know current costs as well as the ability to forecast total project costs may save the owner the embarrassment of depleting available funds prior to the completion of work.

§ 23.21   Project Management Oversight/Audit Program

In addition to the active owner involvement in all phases of the remedial effort, an owner should consider engaging a specialized project management oversight (PMO) consultant. This will assist an owner to exercise the maximum level of control, to forestall or at least lessen the impact of cost and schedule overruns, and to better achieve the desired quality level.

A PMO consultant helps verify the existence or nonexistence of project problems and facilitates the identification and implementation of timely and prudent management decisions. The function is usually performed by an independent party who is not involved in the remedial process and is charged by the owner to give an objective assessment on how well the project is proceeding. Although the amount and type of necessary oversight will vary with the circumstances of the project, for any combination of circumstances there is an appropriate level of oversight.

The PMO approach should be flexible and allow selection of specific tasks to be performed in a particular project. It should use interdisciplinary skills to anticipate and monitor the many variables that can lead to cost overruns and schedule delays. The PMO team, for example, could include professionals with expertise in engineering, construction, accounting, tax, information systems, contracts, and risk management.

PMO techniques should be participative, should reinforce the capabilities of the owner's management organization, and should follow the life cycle of the project. During the early stages, the emphasis should be on verifying the existence of appropriate procedures and guidelines and in setting up any missing control mechanisms. During the later compliance phase, PMO entails verifying compliance with controls and project procedures established earlier, identifying signs of impending problems, and formulating corrective measures.

The most important difference between the services offered by the PMO consultant and the services offered by the owner's project management organization lies in the PMO's independence and objectivity. The PMO consultant reports directly to the owner's senior management, and, as a result, the project status information and required corrective actions have not been filtered or biased by the influence of project team members. At the owner's request, the PMO consultant can also evaluate the performance of the project implementation organization, including the owner's project management staff. In addition to the objectivity feature, owners may want to use PMO services as a supplement to their own project management resources, especially when the project is a one-time endeavor for which the owner does not need to build permanent staff.

§ 23.22   Cost Recovery Aspects

To the person or persons who have to pay for them, cleanup projects are unwanted and expensive. It certainly would lessen the burden if the costs were borne or shared by someone else. Therefore, in most instances in which owners are required to clean up hazardous wastes, they seek compensation for the cleanup from all parties who may have contributed to the problem. As discussed in previous chapters, various legal theories are available for owners to assess liability on other parties. However, in nearly all hazardous wastes cleanup activities, it is the extent of the liability, that is, a party's share of the costs, and not the liability itself that becomes the focus of attention. Therefore, to successfully pursue recovery of these costs, the party seeking reimbursement must be prepared to demonstrate that the approaches taken were necessary and reasonable and that the consequential costs were directly related to these decisions. The most effective proof is documentation that supports these claims.

Documentation should begin when the decision to enter into the remediation is made. Preliminary decisions discussed earlier in the chapter (such as selecting the team and the environmental consultant) should be sufficiently annotated with correspondence and meeting notes.

In most cases decisions relative to the selection of a remedial program are accomplished with significant involvement of the appropriate regulatory agencies, and approval of the program by the regulatory agencies may be sufficient to satisfy the claimant's burden of proof. However, if this is not the case, the owner should perform an evaluation similar to that conducted under the EPA's superfund program (see **Chapter 2**) and document each step of the process.

As discussed in **§ 23.12**, site characterizations frequently do not identify all obstacles to construction. Therefore, disruptions in the work may occur. As with any construction project on which the work is disrupted, the owner should to the extent practical collect, carefully document, and categorize all of the necessitated changes and their associated costs. It is not sufficient to merely report the costs associated with the changes; the change orders or other documents requesting additional funding should identify the reason for the change, the difference between proposed work and the planned work, and provide a sufficient breakout of costs so that their reasonableness can be demonstrated to an independent party. Time lost for such unusual activities as employee physicals may be easily documented. However, time loss and production inefficiencies that may occur as a consequence of distractions or concerns of workers for their health and safety may be real and significant but much more difficult to measure and prove. Disruptions may also be caused by external factors such as added regulatory requirements or reaction by local community groups. Should this occur, it is likely that the administrative record and also local newspapers will report on the matter. These accounts will help to substantiate the significance of the events and bolster the credibility of claims made for delays in accomplishing the effort.

Selection of contractors should also be documented. If the contract for services is competitively bid, bid comparisons should be conducted and maintained as part of the project record. If sole-source contracts are let, the necessity for this should be justified.

In some circumstances the remediation project may be conducted as a separate and distinct part of a development project. Whether the remediation project is being conducted in parallel or the original project is stopped during remediation, it is imperative that the procedures discussed above be employed and maintained as a function separate from the development project. Furthermore, delays and other impacts on the development project that are attributable to the remediation effort should also be carefully documented. This may include, among other things, increases in labor and material costs as a result of escalation, overtime to meet the original schedule, and impacts on the original project design as a result of interferences caused by the remedial design project. It should be noted that a differentiation should be made between necessary design changes and those that result in improvements to the original project, which would most likely not be recoverable.

Adequate record-keeping procedures will usually facilitate any subsequent cost recovery process, but they may impose a significant burden on an owner's staff. For this reason, consideration should be given to employing an independent third party to provide for project management oversight services. See § **23.21.**

§ 23.23   Summary of OSHA Regulations for Cleanup Sites

OSHA has promulgated regulations under 29 C.F.R. § 1910.120 governing working conditions for persons involved in a hazardous waste site cleanup. These regulations are summarized here.

The regulations apply to employers, employees, contractors, and subcontractors engaged in:

1. Hazardous substance response under CERCLA
2. Major corrective actions under RCRA
3. Operations involving hazardous waste storage, disposal, and treatment facilities
4. Hazardous waste operations sites designated for cleanup by state or local governmental authorities
5. Emergency response operations and post-emergency response operations.

General requirements—safety and health program.   Employers shall develop and implement a written safety and health program for their employees, contractors, and subcontractors involved in hazardous waste operations. The program shall be designed to identify, evaluate, and control safety and health hazards and provide for emergency response for hazardous waste operations.

Site characterization and analysis.   Hazardous waste sites shall be evaluated to identify specific site hazards and to determine the appropriate safety and health control procedures needed to protect employees from the identified hazards.

Site control.   Appropriate site control procedures shall be implemented before cleanup work begins in order to control employee exposure to hazardous substances. This program is to be part of the employer's health and safety program.

Training.   Initial or review training shall be provided to employees before they are permitted to engage in hazardous waste operations that could expose them to hazardous substances, safety, or health hazards. All employees (such as, but not limited to, equipment operators and general laborers) exposed to hazardous substances, health hazards, or safety hazards shall be thoroughly trained in the use of protective equipment, work practices, engineering controls, and other pertinent information.

Medical surveillance.   Medical surveillance shall be provided to employees exposed or potentially exposed to hazardous substances or health hazards or who wear respirators.

Engineering controls, work practices, and personal protective equipment for employee protection.   Engineering controls, work practices, personal protective equipment, or a combination of these shall be implemented to protect employees from exposure to hazardous substances and health hazards, to the extent they are feasible. Engineering controls that may be feasible include, but are not limited to, the use of pressurized cabs or control booths on equipment and/or the use of remotely operated material-handling equipment. Other work practices that may be feasible are removing all nonessential employees from potential exposure during opening of drums, wetting down dusty operations, and locating employees downwind of possible hazards.

Monitoring.   Monitoring shall be performed to assure proper selection of engineering controls, work practices, and personal protective equipment so that employees are not exposed to levels that exceed established permissible exposure limits for hazardous substances.

Informational programs.   Employers shall develop and implement a program, which is part of the employer's safety and health program, to inform employees, contractors, and subcontractors (or their representatives) actually engaged in hazardous waste operations of the nature, level, and degree of exposure likely as a result of participation in such hazardous waste operations. Employees, contractors, and subcontractors working outside of the operations part of a site are not covered by this standard.

Handling drums and containers.   Hazardous substances and contaminated soils, liquids, and other residues and their associated drums and containers shall be handled, transported, labeled, and disposed of so as to meet the appropriate DOT, OSHA, and EPA regulations for the wastes that they contain.

Decontamination.   Procedures for all phases of decontamination shall be developed and communicated to employees. Standard operating procedures shall be developed to minimize employee contact with hazardous substances or with equipment that has contacted hazardous substances.

Emergency response plan.   An emergency response plan shall be developed and implemented by affected employers to handle anticipated emergencies prior to the commencement of hazardous waste operations. The plan shall be in writing and available for inspection and copying by employees, their representatives, and OSHA personnel. Employers who will evacuate their employees from the workplace when an emergency occurs and who do not permit any of their employees to respond to assist in handling the emergency are exempt from these requirements. They provide an emergency action plan complying with 29 C.F.R. § 1910.38(a).

Illumination.   Areas accessible to employees shall be lighted to appropriate illumination as specified.

Sanitation in temporary workplaces.   Facilities for employees must be provided. These facilities are to include: potable and nonpotable water supplies, each clearly identified; toilet facilities, the number to be determined by the number of employees; requirement for food handling; sleeping quarters; washing, showering, and change facilities.

PART V

PROCEDURAL CONSIDERATIONS

CHAPTER 24

DISPOSITION OF ENVIRONMENTAL DISPUTES WITHOUT LITIGATION

Maureen A. Brennan*
John E. Frazier

Maureen A. Brennan, a member of the firm of Baker & Hostetler in Cleveland, Ohio, specializes in environmental law with particular emphasis on Superfund, RCRA, wetlands, and the impact of environmental law on business transactions. Her previous experience included service as an attorney for the United States Environmental Protection Agency (USEPA) and as an environmental attorney for TRW. Ms. Brennan received a B.A., magna cum laude, from Bryn Mawr College and a J.D., cum laude, from Boston College. She is a member of the Ohio and Pennsylvania Bar Associations. She has helped organize and has lectured in workshops about changing environmental laws, and she is also the recipient of the USEPA's bronze medal for achievement for her work on a municipal sewage treatment plant case.

*The author thanks Michael R. Hope, Esquire of the Denver Baker & Hostetler office for his assistance in preparing this chapter.

John E. Frazier is partner-in-charge of the Real Estate, Environmental, and Construction Group within the Business Investigation Services (BIS) practice of Coopers & Lybrand's Philadelphia office. He is responsible for delivering a wide range of financial, business, and litigation advisory services involving real estate, environmental, and construction matters to troubled or reorganizing businesses. Mr. Frazier received a B.A. degree in English and economics from the University of Alabama, an M.A. degree in international relations from the University of Arkansas (European campus), and a Ph.D. in political science from Pennsylvania State University. A member of the Urban Land Institute, he has over 15 years of experience in real estate-related banking, investment, and corporate finance.

§ 24.1   Introduction

Environmental disputes involving hazardous wastes and hazardous substances usually involve complex legal, factual, and engineering issues. Solutions to CERCLA and RCRA problems require detailed cleanup or remedial plans that are usually the source of bitter controversy between agency and private industry experts. Sometimes a citizen group interested in the issue will have a technical expert as well. Such controversies rely on the application of scientific and engineering principles for their resolution are frequently resolved more expeditiously by negotiation rather than by trial. In fact, most CERCLA and RCRA disputes are not litigated through trial. As the frequent notices from the Department of Justice in the *Federal Register* attest, most cases are settled by agreement among the parties.

In Superfund situations in which many cleanup solutions can actually solve the problem, it is more efficient to have engineers reach agreement on the remedy. If this cannot be done, considerable time is consumed in litigation arguing over the scope of the EPA's administrative record, and/or disputing the EPA's choice of remedy on the basis that the selection was arbitrary or capricious or not supported by the record.

Negotiated solutions conserve the resources of all parties, and money can be spent on cleanup rather than on transaction costs.

There are several non-trial mechanisms used to settle environmental disputes. If the agency involved has chosen a civil lawsuit as its enforcement mechanism, consent decrees are the settlement tools. If the agency has chosen an administrative enforcement mechanism, consent orders (also called administrative orders on consent) embody a negotiated solution.

In certain circumstances environmental disputes have been submitted to arbitration. Various alternative dispute resolution mechanisms have also been used to resolve portions of environmental disputes, such as controversies over the allocation formulas in Superfund sites.

SETTLEMENTS UNDER FEDERAL LAWS

§ 24.2   Federal Hazardous Substance Settlements

Environmental disputes under the Comprehensive Environmental Response, Compensation and Liability Act (CERCLA)[1] may be resolved both

---

[1] 42 U.S.C. §§ 9601–9675 (1983 & Supp. 1990).

administratively and judicially. The EPA can issue administrative orders or sue for injunctive relief under CERCLA § 106[2] to force potentially responsible parties (PRPs) to engage in remedial or response action or undertake a remedial investigation and feasibility study (RI/FS), and it also can sue to recover its cleanup costs under CERCLA § 107.[3] The EPA may also issue an order or sue to compel compliance with an EPA request for information from a PRP under CERCLA § 104(e).[4]

However, most environmental disputes under CERCLA are settled. PRPs have become increasingly desirous to settle CERCLA claims with the EPA because of the agency's record of judicial success in prior litigation. Rather than engage in costly litigation or contest § 106 administrative orders, which could result in treble damages, most PRPs have chosen to work with the EPA to structure administrative or judicial settlements of CERCLA claims.

The Superfund Amendments and Reauthorization Act (SARA),[5] Congress's 1986 amendments to CERCLA, codified EPA settlement procedures in order to "expedite effective remedial actions and minimize litigation."[6] These provisions were meant to foster settlement by engaging PRPs early in the investigatory process, granting qualified protection to settling PRPs from future liability and/or contribution claims, and penalizing nonsettling PRPs.[7] Settlements typically take the form of either judicially entered consent decrees or EPA-authorized administrative orders on consent, also called consent orders. In practice, however, the EPA has never given full effect to these provisions.

§ 24.3 Consent Decrees

Consent decrees are agreements negotiated between PRPs and the EPA and entered in federal district court as a resolution to a lawsuit filed previously or concomitantly by the Department of Justice. Federal district courts have limited judicial review over consent decrees. A court may only approve or reject a consent decree; it may not modify its terms.[8] To approve a consent decree, a court must deem it "fair, reasonable, and

---

[2] 42 U.S.C. § 9606(a) (1983).

[3] 42 U.S.C. § 9607(a) (Supp. 1990).

[4] *Id.* § 9604(e).

[5] Pub. L. No. 99-499, 100 Stat. 153 (1986) (codified as amended at 42 U.S.C. §§ 9601–9675 (1983 & Supp. 1990)).

[6] 42 U.S.C. § 9622(a) (Supp. 1990).

[7] *Id.* § 9622.

[8] United States v. Jones & Laughlin Steel Corp., 804 F.2d 348 (6th Cir. 1986).

consistent with the Constitution and the mandate of Congress."[9] Factors involved in the court's decision on the fairness of the decree might include "the strength of the Government's case, the good faith efforts of the negotiators, the possible risks of any transaction costs involved in litigation under CERCLA, and the effect of the proposed settlement on non-settling parties."[10] The court's primary concern is that the consent decree protect the public interest as expressed in CERCLA.[11] Although approval is at the court's discretion, courts strongly favor voluntary settlement and defer to the technical decisions of the parties and the authority of the EPA. Therefore, the presumption of validity of consent decrees is strong.[12]

Under CERCLA § 122,[13] consent decrees may involve cost recovery claims under CERCLA § 107,[14] remedial or recovery action under CERCLA §§ 104(a) or 106(a),[15] or an RI/FS litigation under CERCLA §§ 104(b) and 106(a).[16] CERCLA § 122(d)(1)(a) provides that all agreements with respect to remedial action must be entered as consent decrees.[17] Examples of a pure cost recovery consent decree as well as a combined cost recovery and prospective relief consent decree are found in §§ 24.6 and 24.7. PRPs and the EPA may also settle a claim under CERCLA § 104(e)[18] regarding a PRP's failure to respond to information requests made by the EPA.

Consent decrees typically include sections on determinations and findings, parties bound, description and schedule of work to be performed and/or costs to be repaid, penalties for noncompliance, force majeure, and covenant not to sue. Given the broad statutory authority of the EPA and the climate of judicial deference to EPA decision making, PRPs typically do not possess much leverage in negotiating the terms of such settlements. The EPA is drafting a *model consent decree*. The EPA claims that many of the provisions of this model will be non-negotiable. This will further reduce the ability of private parties to negotiate with the EPA. As of this

---

[9] United States v. Cannons Eng'g Corp., 720 F. Supp. 1027, 1035–6 (D. Mass. 1989). *See also, e.g.,* United States v. Seymour Recycling Corp., 554 F. Supp. 1334, 1337–38 (S.D. Ind. 1982).

[10] United States v. Rohm & Haas Co., 721 F. Supp. 666, 680 (D.N.J. 1989).

[11] *Id.*

[12] United States v. Hooker Chem. & Plastics Corp., 776 F.2d 410, 411 (2d Cir. 1985).

[13] 42 U.S.C. § 9622 (Supp. 1990).

[14] *Id.* § 9607.

[15] 42 U.S.C. §§ 9604(a), 9606(a) (1983 & Supp. 1990).

[16] *Id.* §§ 9604(b), 9606(a).

[17] 42 U.S.C. § 9622(d)(1)(A) (Supp. 1990). Remedial action settlements with de minimis PRPs, ordinarily identified by the EPA as those PRPs who have contributed a 1% or less volumetric share of hazardous substances to a site, may also be settled by consent order.

[18] 42 U.S.C. § 9604(e) (Supp. 1990).

writing, the EPA had not released its model consent decree for remedial cleanups.

Pursuant to CERCLA §§ 122(d)(2)(B) and 122(i)[19] and Department of Justice policy,[20] notice of proposed consent decrees is published in the *Federal Register* in order to invite written comments. The comments are solicited over a 30-day period. The Department of Justice must respond to the comments submitted and may refuse final agreement with PRPs on the basis of such comments.[21] If the comments do not upset the agreement among the parties and the court deems the agreement fair, the court signs and enters the consent decree.

CERCLA provides that violation of the dictates of a consent decree can bring penalties of up to $25,000 per day. Subsequent violations can bring penalties of up to $75,000 per day.[22]

§ 24.4   Consent Orders

The EPA has authority under CERCLA § 106 to issue administrative orders "as may be necessary to protect public health and welfare and the environment."[23] Administrative orders have become an increasingly popular tool of the EPA because they are easier to administer than consent decrees and the terms of the orders are not immediately judicially contestable.

The EPA negotiates consent orders with PRPs in order to facilitate timely settlement as well as to encourage PRP input into RI/FS and remedial and removal action decisions. Typically, the EPA lets parties know that they are being investigated as PRPs and that they should consider settlement, or it issues an administrative order but delays the effective date, providing a window for negotiation.

Under CERCLA §§ 122(d)(3), 122(g)(4) and 122(h)(1),[24] all de minimis settlements as well as other RI/FS and cost recovery settlements may be embodied in consent orders. CERCLA § 122(d)(1)[25] provides that all agreements with PRPs[26] with respect to remedial action must be entered as consent decrees, although in practice the EPA often mandates what is

---

[19] *Id.* § 9622(i).

[20] 28 C.F.R. § 50.7 (1990).

[21] *See, e.g.,* United States v. Cannons Eng'g Corp., 720 F. Supp. at 1035.

[22] 42 U.S.C. §§ 9622(l), 9609(c)(4), 9609(c)(5) (Supp. 1990).

[23] 42 U.S.C. § 9606(a) (1983).

[24] 42 U.S.C. §§ 9622(d)(3), 9622(g)(4), 9622(h)(1) (Supp. 1990).

[25] *Id.* § 9622(d)(1).

[26] Settlements with de minimis PRPs may be by consent decree or consent order. *Id.* § 9622(g)(4).

really remedial action in consent orders that are never entered in court.[27] Consent orders have provisions similar to consent decrees, but they generally also include an admission by PRPs of imminent and substantial endangerment. Model language for administrative orders on consent has been promulgated by the EPA.[28]

In accordance with CERCLA § 122(i) and standard Department of Justice procedure, notice of proposed consent orders typically appears in the *Federal Register* with a 30-day opportunity for public comment, similar to consent decrees.

Violations of consent orders, like consent decrees, may carry penalties of up to $25,000 per day.[29] Furthermore, failure of a PRP to carry out the removal required under an administrative order may subject the PRP to treble damages.[30] A court can require the respondents to the order to pay three times the cost incurred by the EPA to carry out the work.

§ 24.5   Settlement Policies

The EPA has developed numerous policy memoranda over the years to guide its staff in carrying out the Superfund program. EPA headquarters in Washington, D.C., issues written policies. Occasionally, the regional offices of EPA have written policies that guide negotiations. Given the volume of policies,[31] very few EPA staff are aware of all policies applicable to any one situation. There are policies on settlements with small contributors (de minimis parties) to CERCLA sites, on the structure of settlement documents, and on technical cleanup issues.

Sometimes these policies are published in the *Federal Register* and therefore can be discovered through computer-assisted legal research. More frequently, however, they are disseminated only to EPA personnel. Only through articles in environmental journals, responses to Freedom of Information Act requests, and word of mouth do these policies surface. The policies change over time. Therefore, the journals need to be reviewed periodically for changes in major policies.

---

[27] This is possible becuase the EPA has successfully blocked PRP attempts to litigate the validity of consent orders in federal court, and because the EPA usually makes PRPs waive their ability to contest EPA jurisdiction when consenting to such orders.

[28] EPA Office of Solid Waste and Emergency Response (OSWER) Directive No. 9835.3-1A, Model Administrative Order on Consent for CERCLA Remedial Investigation/Feasibility Study (Jan. 30, 1990).

[29] 42 U.S.C. §§ 9622(l), 9609(c)(4), 9609(c)(5) (Supp. 1990).

[30] CERCLA § 107(c)(3), 42 U.S.C. § 9607(c)(3) (1983).

[31] III Inside EPA's Superfund Report, No. 5 (Mar. 1, 1989).

§ 24.6 Sample: Pure Cost Recovery Consent Decree

Lexis now has a data base in the ENVIRN library called CONDEC. This contains the full text of CERCLA consent decrees. Copies of consent decrees may also be obtained through a Freedom of Information Act request to the EPA. This section contains an example of a pure cost recovery consent decree, and § 24.7 sets forth a combined cost recovery and prospective relief consent decree.

UNITED STATES OF AMERICA,
   Plaintiff

          vs.

A CORPORATION, B COMPANY,
C INC., D PRODUCTS,
   Defendants

No. 86 C 9107

---

*   *   *   *   *   *

CONSENT DECREE

WHEREAS, on November 24, 1986, plaintiff United States of America filed a complaint in the United States District Court for the Northern District of Illinois asserting claims under section 107 of the Comprehensive Environmental Response, Compensation, and Liability Act of 1980 (CERCLA), 42 U.S.C. § 9607, for the recovery of costs incurred in responding to releases and threatened releases of hazardous substances and hazardous wastes at the Disposal Site (complaint);

WHEREAS, each of the Settling Defendants denies that it is liable in any way to the United States or to any other person with respect to the Disposal Site;

WHEREAS, the parties to this decree desire to settle this matter in good faith without adjudication of any alleged liability or any issues of law or fact in an attempt to avoid further litigation with respect to said response costs, but not to discharge any nonsettlers from liability with respect to such response costs;

WHEREAS, this decree shall not release, relieve, or absolve any nonsettling defendant from liability to the settling Defendants arising from said response costs or future costs; and

WHEREAS, this decree shall not create any presumption that any Settling Defendant is a responsible person or is liable in any way for any future damages or response costs that the United States or any other person may incur or seek to recover with respect to the Disposal Site or any other site;

NOW THEREFORE, it is hereby ordered, adjudged and decreed as follows:

I. JURISDICTION

This Court has jurisdiction of the subject matter herein and of the parties consenting hereto for purposes of this Consent Decree.

II. PARTIES

This consent decree shall apply to and be binding upon the parties to this decree and upon their officers, directors, agents, employees, contractors, successors, and assigns, and upon all firms or persons acting under or for them. The undersigned representative of each party certifies that he or she is authorized by the party or parties whom he or she represents to enter into this Consent Decree.

III. DEFINITIONS

A. *Disposal site* mans ABC Incineration site as defined in plaintiff's Complaint.

B. *Response costs* means all past costs incurred with respect to the Disposal Site that may allegedly be recoverable by the United States or by any other person under CERCLA and/or RCRA, including, without limitation, administrative, overhead, interest, litigation, enforcement, investigatory, and remedial and removal costs.

C. *Covered matters* means liability for all response costs incurred by the United States prior to and including the date of entry of this Consent Decree, and any costs incurred by the United States in connection with the administration of this consent decree.

D. *Responsible person* shall mean the classes of persons defined in Section 107(a) of CERCLA, 42 U.S.C. § 9607(a).

E. *Settling Defendants* means B Company and D Products. Defendants A Corporation and C Inc. are not Settling Defendants as that term is defined for purposes of this Consent Decree and are not parties to this Consent Decree.

IV. PAYMENT

A. Within 30 days after the entry of this decree, the Settling Defendants shall pay to the United States the sum of One Hundred Fifty-five Thousand, One Hundred Fifty-seven Dollars and 99/100 ($155,157.99). The payment made by Settling Defendants is not to be construed to allocate in any way any alleged liability among the Settling Defendants or to release in any way any nonsettling defendants from any liability to the Settling Defendants for part or all of that sum, nor shall such payment or anything in this Consent Decree be construed in any way as an admission of alleged liability to plaintiff or to any other person.

B.   The Settling Defendants shall make such payment in the form of a certified check payable to EPA Hazardous Substance Superfund (Fund), identifying payment as for the Disposal site, and transmitted to the U.S. Environmental Protection Agency, Superfund Accounting, P.O. Box 371003M, Pittsburgh, Pennsylvania 15251. Copies of the check and any associated transmittal letter shall be provided to each of the following:

1.   CERCLA Enforcement Section (5HE-12);
2.   Financial Accounting Section (5MF-14);
3.   Office of Regional Counsel (5CS-16) Attention: SWERB Branch Secretary; at U.S. Environmental Protection Agency, Region V, 230 South Dearborn Street, Chicago, Illinois 60604.

C.   Each Settling Defendant shall pay the sum that is shown for the settling Defendant in the attachment to this Consent Decree. The monies paid by each settling Defendant pursuant to this Consent Decree are not penalties. The monies paid by Settling Defendants shall reimburse the above-referenced Fund for the monies expended by the United States for covered matters.

D.   Each of the Settling Defendants represents that it is paying in good faith a percentage of the $155,157.99 settlement amount as negotiated among the settling Defendants. Nothing herein shall be construed as any admission or presumption (a) that any Settling Defendant is liable in any way for matters not included in covered matters, including but not limited to any future costs that may be incurred with respect to the Disposal site, (b) that any settling Defendant is liable or responsible for any alleged percentage or share of any such costs, or (c) that any nonsettling defendant is not liable or is released from liability for part or all of such costs.

E.   Failure of any Settling Defendant to pay its share of the total amount as set forth in the attachment shall not relieve the remaining Settling Defendants of their obligation to pay the Plaintiff the total amount of $155,157.99 stated in the attachment. In the event that any Settling Defendant fails to pay its share as set forth in the attachment and the remaining settling Defendants accordingly pay that share to the Plaintiff, nothing in this Consent Decree shall be construed to limit the rights of those remaining Settling Defendants to take any necessary action to collect from any Settling Defendant the share that it failed to pay.

V.   PLAINTIFF'S COVENANT NOT TO SUE

A.   In consideration of the payments made by the Settling Defendants required by the terms of this decree, plaintiff covenants not to initiate or maintain any civil suit, administrative action or proceeding, including but not limited to any complaint, third-party complaint, cross-claim or counterclaim, against any Settling Defendant for any claim or cause of action asserted, or which could have been asserted, for covered matters. The parties to this decree intend that this covenant shall not be construed as a covenant not to sue any person, firm, or corporation not a party to this decree for any claim plaintiff may have with respect to covered matters.

B.   This covenant not to sue shall not become effective as to the Settling Defendants, or any of them, until timely payment is made by the Settling Defendants of the full amount specified in Section IV herein.

C.   This covenant not to sue shall not preclude the United States from taking any action or from initiating or maintaining any proceeding against any Settling Defendant for matters other than covered matters, including any proceeding for injunctive relief to abate any release, threat of release or conditions at the Disposal Site.

D.   The Settling Defendants have resolved their liability to the United States in this judicially approved and good faith settlement and therefore shall not be liable for claims for contribution regarding matters addressed in the settlement.

VI.   SETTLING DEFENDANTS' COVENANT NOT TO SUE

A.   For and in consideration of the covenants and promises made herein by the United States, the Settling Defendants covenant not to sue or to bring any claims, demands, or causes of action, including any claims for reimbursement from the Hazardous Substances Responses Trust Fund, against the United States, its subdivisions, departments, agencies, or entities acting on its behalf, for any of its actions related to covered matters at the Disposal Site. This covenant not to sue shall not waive any other cause of action any Settling Defendant may have against Plaintiff and/or any other Settling Defendant for matters other than covered matters.

B.   The Settling Defendants covenant not to maintain or initiate suit, including but not limited to any complaint, third-party complaint, cross-claim, or counterclaim, against each other for covered matters.

C.   The Settling Defendants do not admit any legal right of Plaintiff to seek or recover relief from the settling Defendants for any costs incurred by the United States with reference to the Disposal Site subsequent to the date of entry of this Consent Decree for natural resource damage claims or for past and future costs incurred by the United States at any other site for materials removed from the Disposal Site during plaintiff's response action or for injunctive or other relief at law or equity arising out of any occurrence resulting from the presence of those materials at any other such site.

D.   The Settling Defendants reserve all rights that each may have to assert claims against nonsettling defendants or parties arising out of the Disposal Site or its operation and ownership, including without limitation claims for breach of contract, tortious conduct, indemnity, contribution, nuisance, and claims under applicable federal, state, and local laws.

VII.   ATTORNEYS' FEES

The Plaintiff and the Settling Defendants shall bear their respective costs and attorneys' fees.

VIII. DISMISSAL OF ACTION

The plaintiff's complaint is hereby dismissed as to the Settling Defendants without prejudice but subject to the terms hereof.

* * * * *

JUDGE MARVIN E. ASPEN, UNITED STATES DISTRICT JUDGE, NORTHERN DISTRICT OF ILLINOIS

ATTACHMENT

This schedule is attached to

and made a part of:

CONSENT DECREE

between

THE UNITED STATES OF AMERICA

AND

B COMPANY

§ 24.7   Sample: Cost Recovery-Prospective Relief Consent Decree

IN THE UNITED STATES DISTRICT COURT
FOR THE NORTHERN DISTRICT OF OHIO
EASTERN DIVISION

UNITED STATES OF AMERICA
  Plaintiff,
              v.
ALVIN, et al.,
  Defendants.
	CIVIL ACTION NO.

CONSENT DECREE
I. BACKGROUND

The United States Environmental Protection Agency (U.S. EPA), pursuant to § 105 of the Comprehensive Environmental Response, Compensation, and Liability Act of 1980 (CERCLA), 42 U.S.C. § 9605, placed the Oil Site (the Site as specifically defined in Paragraph V.4.U of this Consent Decree) on the National Priorities List, which is set forth at 40 C.F.R. Part 300, Appendix B, by publication in the *Federal Register* on September 1982, 47 Fed. Reg. 30000.

In 1982, in response to a release or a substantial threat of a release of a hazardous substance at or from the Site, the U.S. EPA commenced a Remedial Investigation and Feasibility Study (RI/FS) pursuant to 40 C.F.R. § 300.68 to determine the need for and type of remedial action necessary to mitigate potential or actual harm to human health and the environment posed by such releases or threats of releases at or from the Site. The RI was completed on December 23, 1988, and the Feasibility Study was completed on April 7, 1989.

On or about April 12, 1989, U.S. EPA, pursuant to § 117 of CERCLA, 42 U.S.C. § 9617, published notice of the completion and availability of the RI/FS, and of the proposed plan for remedial action developed pursuant to § 117(a) of CERCLA, 42 U.S.C. § 9617(a), and provided opportunity for public comment, including comments by the state of Ohio, to be submitted in writing to U.S. EPA by May 12, 1989, or orally at a public meeting held on April 26, 1989.

U.S. EPA, pursuant to § 117 of CERCLA, 2 U.S.C. § 9617, has kept a transcript of the public meeting and has made this transcript available to the public as part of the administrative record located at U.S. EPA, Region V, 230 South Dearborn Street, Chicago, Illinois, the Ashtabula County Public Library, located in Ashtabula, Ohio, and at the Ashtabula County Disasters Services offices.

On April 19, 1989, U.S. EPA, pursuant to § 122 of CERCLA, 42 U.S.C. § 9622, notified certain parties that the U.S. EPA determined each party to be a potentially responsible party (PRP) regarding the proposed remedial action.

In accordance with § 121(f)(1)(F) of CERCLA, 42 U.S.C. § 9621(f)(1)(F), U.S. EPA notified the state of Ohio on April 4, 1989, of negotiations with PRPs regarding the scope of the remedial design and remedial action for the Site, and U.S. EPA has provided the State with an opportunity to participate in such negotiations and be a party to any settlement.

Certain persons, including several PRPs and the state of Ohio, have provided comments on U.S. EPA's proposed plan for remedial action, and to such comments U.S. EPA provided a summary of responses, all of which have been included in the administrative record referred to above.

Considering the proposed plan for remedial action and the public comments received, U.S. EPA has reached a decision on a remedial action plan, which is embodied in a document called a Record of Decision (ROD) signed by the Regional Administrator of Region V of U.S. EPA on June 29, 1989, which includes a discussion of U.S. EPA's reasons for the remedial action to be undertaken at the Site and for any significant changes from the proposed remedial action plan published with the RI/FS.

The defendant signatories to this Consent Decree (Settling Defendants, as defined in Paragraph 4.S of this Consent Decree) are in agreement with U.S. EPA's proposed remedial action and the RODs.

U.S. EPA, pursuant to § 117(b) of CERCLA, 42 U.S.C. § 9617(b), has provided public notice of adoption of the remedial action plan embodied in the form of the ROD, including notice of the ROD's availability to the public for review in the same locations as the administrative record referred to above.

Pursuant to § 117(d) of CERCLA, 42 U.S.C. § 9617(d), that notice has been published in a major local newspaper of general circulation and the notice includes an explanation of any significant changes and the reasons for such changes from the proposed remedial action contained in the proposed plan.

Pursuant to § 121(d)(1) of CERCLA, 42 U.S.C. § 9621(d)(1), U.S. EPA and Settling Defendants (the Parties) believe that the remedial action plan adopted by U.S. EPA will attain a degree of cleanup of hazardous substances, pollutants, and contaminants released into the environment and of control of further release which will at a minimum assure the protection of human health and the environment at the Site.

The parties believe the remedial action adopted by U.S. EPA will provide a level or standard of control for such hazardous substances, pollutants, or contaminants which at least attains legally applicable or relevant and appropriate standards, requirements, criteria, or limitations under federal or state environmental law or facility siting law, in accordance with § 121(d)(2) of CERCLA, 42 U.S.C. § 9621(d)(2), and that the remedial action plan is in accordance with § 121 of CERCLA and is consistent with the National Contingency Plan (NCP), 40 CFR Part 300.

Settling Defendants agree to implement the remedial action adopted by U.S. EPA in the RODs, as set forth in Appendices A and B to this Consent Decree and incorporated by reference herein, and U.S. EPA has determined that the Work required under the Consent Decree will be done properly by Settling Defendants, and that Settling Defendants are qualified to implement the remedial action contained in the ROD.

It is the policy of U.S. EPA to identify potentially responsible parties not signatories to this Consent Decree, and, subject to its nonreviewable prosecutorial discretion, to seek reimbursement of past response costs, and/or to take appropriate action against such nonsignatories pursuant to the provisions of CERCLA. Such nonsignatories remain potentially jointly and severally liable to U.S. EPA for all response costs incurred before entry of this Consent Decree, for any remedial action necessary at the Site, and for any response costs incurred at the Site.

The Parties recognize and intend to further the public interest in expediting the cleanup of the Site by entering into this Consent Decree and to avoid prolonged and complicated litigation between the Parties which might delay the cleanup.

NOW, THEREFORE, it is hereby Ordered, Adjudged and Decreed:

II. JURISDICTION

1. This Court has jurisdiction over the subject matter herein, and over the parties consenting hereto, pursuant to 28 U.S.C. §§ 1332 and 1345, and 42 U.S.C. §§ 9601 *et seq.* Settling Defendants shall not challenge this Court's jurisdiction to enter, modify, and enforce this Consent Decree.

III.   PARTIES BOUND

2.   This Consent Decree applies to and is binding upon the undersigned parties and their successors and assigns. The undersigned representative of each party to this Consent Decree certifies that he or she is fully authorized by the party or parties whom she or he represents to enter into the terms and conditions of the Consent Decree and to execute and legally bind that party to it. Settling Defendants shall provide a copy of this Consent Decree to the contractor hired to perform the work required by this Consent Decree and shall require the contractor to provide a copy thereof to any subcontractor retained to perform any part of the work required by this Consent Decree.

IV.   GOOD FAITH SETTLEMENT AND ADMISSIBILITY

3.   This Consent Decree was negotiated and executed by the parties in good faith to avoid expensive and protracted litigation and is a settlement of claims that were vigorously contested, denied, and disputed as to validity and amount. The execution of this Decree is not an admission of any fact or liability on any issue dealt with in this Decree, except in an action to enforce this Decree brought by the Plaintiff, wherein Settling Defendants and Settling *De Minimis* Defendants agree not to contest either the entry of the Decree, their liability with respect to the matters covered in the Decree or, except as provided in Section XV regarding dispute resolution, any factual matter or finding or any conclusion of law set forth in this Decree. Accordingly, with the exception of this proceeding and any other proceeding to enforce this Decree, the Settling Defendants and Settling *De Minimis* Defendants do not consent to the admissibility of this Consent Decree in any judicial or administrative proceeding, except that it may be admissible in a judicial or administrative proceeding between the Settling Defendants and Settling *De Minimis* Defendants and their respective insurers, or any other person or entity other than Plaintiff in an action for private cost recovery, contribution, or indemnification.

V.   DEFINITIONS

4.   Whenever the following terms are used in this Consent Decree and the Exhibits and Appendices attached hereto, the following definitions specified in this Paragraph shall apply:

A.   *Architect* or *Engineer* means the company or companies retained by the Settling Defendants to prepare the construction plans and specifications necessary to accomplish the remedial action described in the ROD, and in the Statement of Work (SOW) which is attached to this Consent Decree as Appendix C.

B.   *Contractor* means the company or companies retained by or on behalf of Settling Defendants to undertake and complete the work required by this Consent Decree. Each contractor and subcontractor shall be deemed to be related by contract to each Settling Defendant within the meaning of 42 U.S.C. § 9607(a).

C.   *Consent Decree* means this Decree and all appendices hereto.

D.   *Future liability* refers to liability arising after U.S. EPA's Certification of Completion is issued pursuant to Paragraph XXVI of this Consent Decree.

E.   *Hazardous substance* shall have the meaning provided in § 101(14) of CERCLA, 42 U.S.C. § 9601(14).

F.   *National Contingency Plan* (NCP) shall be used as that term is used in § 105 of CERCLA, 42 U.S.C. § 9605.

G.   *Non-Settling PRP* means any potentially responsible party (PRP), as that term is used in § 107(a) of CERCLA, 42 U.S.C. § 9607(a), which is potentially liable to the United States with respect to this Site and which does not enter into this Consent Decree.

H.   *OEPA* means the Ohio Environmental Protection Agency.

I.   *Operable Unit* means the Source Removal Operable Unit remedial action that is required to be performed by certain potentially responsible parties (PRPs) under an administrative order issued by U.S. EPA on February 26, 1988, consistent with the Source Removal Operable Unit Record of Decision signed by the Regional Administrator of Region V of the U.S. EPA on September 30, 1987. Performance of the remedial action required under the Source Removal Operable Unit has been incorporated into the obligations of all Settling Defendants under the SOW and this Consent Decree.

J.   *Operation and Maintenance* (O&M) means operation and maintenance of the remedial construction Work performed or installed at the Site, including operation and maintenance of the dioxin vault. O&M shall commence for each portion of the Work at the time that construction of such portion is complete.

K.   *Oversight costs* means all costs incurred by the Plaintiff, not inconsistent with the NCP, in reviewing, overseeing, or directing performance of all or any part of the Work required under this Consent Decree, including O&M and any Additional Work required under Section IX of this Decree, but not including costs of obtaining access under Section XI.

L.   *Owner Settling Defendants* refers to Alvin, et al.

M.   *RD/RA Work Plan* means the Work Plan for Source Removal Operable Unit and the Work Plan for Final Remediation which the Settling Defendants are required to submit under the SOW.

N.   *Parties* means the United States of America, the Settling Defendants, and the Settling *De Minimis* Defendants.

O.   *Performance standards* and *cleanup standards* mean standards that are required to be achieved by the remedial measures to be performed pursuant to this Consent Decree, and the standards for performance of the Work required under Section VII of this Consent Decree, as set forth in the RODs and the SOW.

P.   *Plaintiff* means the United States of America.

Q.   *Response costs* means any costs incurred by Plaintiff pursuant to 42 U.S.C. § 9601 *et seq.* in connection with the Site, other than those costs incurred by the United States which were reimbursed under the terms of the Consent Decree entered in *United States of America v. Alvin, et al.,* Civil Action No. C-84, on March 3, 1989.

R.   *Records of Decision* (RODs) means: (1) the Source Removal Operable Unit Record of Decision, signed by the Regional Administrator of Region V, U.S. EPA on September 30, 1987 and attached hereto and incorporated herein as Appendix A; and (2) the Final RD/RA Record of Decision, signed by the Regional Administrator of Region V, U.S. EPA on June 29, 1989, and attached hereto and incorporated herein as Appendix B.

S.   *Settling Defendants* means those entities other than the Plaintiff and Settling *De Minimis* Defendants who have signed this Consent Decree and who are listed on Appendix D to this Consent Decree.

T.   *Settling De Minimis Defendants* means those potentially responsible parties listed on Appendix E to this Consent Decree who have contributed quantities of materials to the site that are less than seven thousand (7,000) gallons of hazardous substances or waste materials, as reflected on Appendix F to this Consent Decree, and whose contributions are minimal in both quantity and toxicity relative to the total volume of materials contributed to the Site by all PRPs.

U.   *Site* means the Oil site, located in Ashtabula County, Ohio. This area is a *facility* within the meaning of § 101(9) of CERCLA, 42 U.S.C. § 9601(9), and is the area delineated on the map attached hereto as Appendix G.

V.   *Statement of Work* (SOW) means the plan for implementation of the remedial design, remedial action, and operation and maintenance of the remedial action for the Site, as set forth in Appendix C, including work to be performed consistent with the requirements of the Source Removal Operable Unit ROD.

W.   *United States* means the United States of America.

X.   *U.S. EPA* means the United States Environmental Protection Agency.

Y.   *U.S. DOJ* means the United States Department of Justice.

Z.   *Waste Material* means any hazardous substances, as defined in § 101(14) of CERCLA, 42 U.S.C. § 9601(14), and any associated contaminated material, pollutant or contaminant as defined by § 101(33) of CERCLA, 42 U.S.C. § 9601(33).

AA. *Work* means the design, construction, implementation, operation, and maintenance, in accordance with this Consent Decree, of the tasks described in (1) the ROD; (2) this Consent Decree; and (3) the Statement of Work attached hereto; and any schedules, plans, or other documents required to be submitted by the Settling Defendants pursuant thereto. The Work shall include the obligations set forth in the unilateral administrative order issued under § 106 of CERCLA, 42 U.S.C. § 9601, to 45 PRPs on February 26, 1988, which shall be incorporated into the SOW and the obligations of Settling Defendants under this Decree.

VI. GENERAL PROVISIONS

5. Commitment of Plaintiff and Settling Defendants:

A. Settling Defendants agree jointly and severally to finance and perform the Work as defined in Section V, Paragraph AA hereof.

B. The Work shall be completed in accordance with all requirements of this Decree, the RODs and the SOW, including the standards, specifications, and the time periods set forth in Section VII hereof and in the SOW.

6. Permits and Approvals:

A. All activities undertaken by the Settling Defendants pursuant to this Consent Decree shall be undertaken in accordance with the requirements of all applicable local, state, and federal laws, regulations, and permits. The United States has determined that the obligations and procedures authorized under this Consent Decree are consistent with the authority of the United States under applicable law to establish appropriate remedial measures for the Site.

B. The United States has determined, pursuant to § 121(e)(1) of CERCLA, 42 U.S.C. § 9621(e)(1), that no federal, state, or local permits are required for Work conducted entirely on-site, within the meaning of § 121(e)(1), as described in the SOW. Settling Defendants shall obtain all permits or approvals necessary for off-site work under federal, state, or local laws and shall submit timely applications and requests for any such permits and approvals.

C. The standards and provisions of Section XIV hereof describing Force Majeure shall govern delays in obtaining permits required for the Work and also the denial of any such permits.

D. Settling Defendants shall include in all contracts or subcontracts entered into for work required under this Consent Decree, provisions stating that such contractors or subcontractors, including their agents and employees, shall perform all activities required by such contracts or subcontracts in compliance with all applicable laws and regulations. This Consent Decree is not, nor shall it act as, nor is it intended by the Parties to be, a permit issued pursuant to any federal or state statute or regulations.

7. Conveyance of the Site

A. Within 30 days of approval by the court of this Decree, the Owner Settling Defendants shall record a copy of this Decree with the Recorder's Office, Ashtabula County, State of Ohio.

B. The Site as described herein may be freely alienated provided that at least 60 days prior to the date of such alienation, the Owner Settling Defendants notify Plaintiff of such proposed alienation, the name of the grantee, and a description of the Owner Settling Defendants' remaining obligations under this Decree, if any, to be performed by such grantee. In the event of such alienation, all of Settling Defendants' obligations pursuant to this Decree shall continue to be met by all Settling Defendants and the grantee.

C.   (1)   Owner Settling Defendants agree that any deed, title, or other instrument of conveyance that transfers any right, title, or interest or that permits any use of the property of Owner Settling Defendants, shall contain a notice that the Site is the subject of this Decree, setting forth the style of the case, case number, and court having jurisdiction herein. Owner Settling Defendants further agrees that they will impose restrictions on use of their property by recording with the Ashtabula County Recorder's Office, within 30 days of entry of this Consent Decree, a document incorporating such restrictions, in a form acceptable to the United States. Owner Settling Defendants agree that such restrictions shall bar any future use of the Site that U.S. EPA determines is inconsistent with the remedial action Work to be performed under this Consent Decree, including a bar on any excavation, grading, filling, drilling, mining, or other construction or development, or farming or parking, on the property, or, any other activity which U.S. EPA determines would present conditions that would not be protective of human health or the environment. Owner Settling Defendants shall not use or permit the use of groundwater or surface water on their property except with the advance written approval of U.S. EPA. Such restrictions shall expressly bar removal of the cap, or any excavation or closure or modification of the diversion trench, except with the express written approval of U.S. EPA, and only if such activity is in furtherance of the Performance Standards and purposes of the remedial action set forth in the RODs and the SOW.

(2)   U.S. EPA's determination of which restrictions shall be required and the form of such restrictions shall not be subject to the Dispute Resolution provisions of Section XV.

(3)   In exchange for resolution of the claims against them and other good and valuable consideration, Owner Settling Defendants agree not to assert any claims against the United States related to any loss of use or value of their property, including but not limited to claims under the Tucker Act, 28 U.S.C. § 507, or CERCLA, 42 U.S.C. §§ 9601 *et seq.*

8.   Trust Agreement

A.   Performance of the requirements of this Consent Decree will be funded by a trust fund to be governed by a Trust Agreement among the Settling Defendants. The Trust Agreement shall confer upon the Trustee all powers and authority necessary to fund the obligations of the Settling Defendants under this Consent Decree. The Trust Shall be established, and the Trustee appointed, within five days of the date of entry of this Consent Decree. Creation of a Trust Fund, selection and appointment of a Trustee, and payment of any funds into the Trust by Settling Defendants shall in no way relieve Settling Defendants of their obligations and responsibilities under this Consent Decree. After entry of this Consent Decree, the Trustee shall be deemed the agent of the Settling Defendants for purposes of compliance with this Consent Decree.

B.   The Trust Agreement shall instruct the Trustee to pay the expenses that are required to be paid by the Settling Defendants pursuant to this Consent Decree. Funding and/or the payment of money by the Settling

Defendants to the Trust Fund is not a fact admissible in evidence for any reason except to the extent expressly provided by the Federal Rules of Evidence.

C.   The Settling Defendants represent that they are capable of funding the Trust to cover all anticipated expenditures that may be required of the Settling Defendants under this Consent Decree, including but not limited to the Work, oversight costs and O&M, and shall make available, upon the request of the United States, indicia of their financial ability to provide for such expenditures. In the event that one or more Settling Defendants fails to meet its obligations to pay into the Trust Fund, the other Settling Defendants agree, and the Trust Agreement shall so provide, that the remaining Settling Defendants are jointly and severally liable for and shall make up any shortfall.

D.   The Trust Agreement shall provide that, within 30 days of appointment of a Trustee, and on a quarterly basis thereafter, said Trustee shall submit to the Settling Defendants, and to the U.S. EPA, financial reports that include a balance sheet for the period ended and a projected expense statement for all Consent Decree-related obligations of Settling Defendants, including but not limited to the expenses for the next quarter. The Trust Agreement shall provide that at all times sufficient funds shall be maintained in the Trust Fund to cover the expenses projected to be incurred in connection with the implementation of this Consent Decree for the next year of activities to be performed pursuant to this Consent Decree. The initial and subsequent payments by Settling Defendants into the Trust Fund shall at least equal the anticipated annual expenses and obligations of Settling Defendants under this Consent Decree during the first and each subsequent year of performance hereunder, respectively. No later than 45 days after the entry of the Consent Decree, Settling Defendants shall deposit funds into the Trust Fund sufficient to fund the Settling Defendants' obligations under the Consent Decree for the first year. If the funds in the Trust Fund are insufficient to meet the projected expenses for the upcoming year with regard to the implementation of this Consent Decree, the Settling Defendants shall promptly deposit funds into the Trust Fund to cover the projected costs of performance for the next year.

E.   If Settling Defendants fail to maintain sufficient funds in the Trust Fund by this Section, Plaintiff may require that Settling Defendants provide additional financial assurances as permitted by 40 CFR 264.145 in order to insure that their obligations under the Consent Decree will be fully funded.

VII.   PERFORMANCE OF THE WORK BY SETTLING DEFENDANTS

9.   All remedial design work to be performed by Settling Defendants pursuant to this Consent Decree shall be under the direction and supervision of a qualified professional architect or engineer. To the extent that they have not already done so, prior to the initiation of remedial design work for the Site, the Settling Defendants shall notify U.S. EPA, in writing, of the name, title, and qualifications of any engineer or architect proposed to be used in carrying out the remedial design work to be performed pursuant to this Consent

Decree. Selection of any such architect or engineer shall be subject to approval by U.S. EPA in consultation with the OEPA. Such approval shall not be unreasonably withheld.

10.   All remedial action Work to be performed by the Settling Defendants pursuant to this Consent Decree shall be under the direction and supervision of a qualified professional engineer. To the extent that they have not already done so, prior to the initiation of remedial action work at the Site, the Settling Defendants shall notify U.S. EPA, in writing, of the name, title, and qualifications of the proposed engineer, and the names of principal contractors and/or subcontractors proposed to be used in carrying out the Work to be performed pursuant to this Consent Decree. Selection of any such engineer or contractor and/or subcontractor shall be subject to approval by the U.S. EPA in consultation with the OEPA. Such approval shall not be unreasonably withheld.

11.   Appendix C to this Consent Decree provides a Statement of Work (SOW) for the completion of remedial design and remedial action at the Site. This SOW is incorporated into and made an enforceable part of this Consent Decree.

12.   The following work shall be performed:

A.   Within 60 calendar days of the effective date of this Consent Decree, the Settling Defendants shall submit a work plan to the U.S. EPA for the remedial design and remedial action activities to be conducted in accordance with the RODs at the Site. The RD/RA Work Plan shall be developed in conformity with the SOW, U.S. EPA Superfund Remedial Design and Remedial Action Guidance (OSWER Directive 9355.0-4A, dated June 1986), and any additional guidance documents provided to Settling Defendants by U.S. EPA in accordance with the notice provisions of Section XXII of this Consent Decree.

B.   The RD/RA Work Plan submitted shall include, but not be limited to, a schedule for submittal of the following project plans: (1) a site safety plan; (2) a health and safety plan; (3) a sampling and monitoring plan; (4) an air monitoring plan; (5) an incinerator generic operation and maintenance plan; (7) a contingency plan; (8) a preliminary inspection, maintenance, and monitoring plan; and (9) a regulatory compliance plan. The RD/RA Work Plan shall also include a schedule for implementation of the RD/RA tasks and submittal of RD/RA reports.

C.   The RD/RA Work Plan and other required documents and reports (hereinafter referred to as documents) shall be subject to review, modification, and approval by U.S. EPA in consultation with the OEPA.

D.   Within 45 calendar days of receipt of any document, the U.S. EPA Remedial Project Manager will notify Settling Defendants, in writing, of approval or disapproval of the document, or any part thereof. In the event that a longer review period is required, the U.S. EPA Remedial Project Manager shall notify Settling Defendants of that fact within 30 calendar days of receipt of the documents. In the event of any disapproval, U.S. EPA shall specify, in writing, any deficiencies and the reasons for the determination of any deficiency, any required modifications, and the reason for such modifications, to the document. Nothing herein shall negate U.S. EPA's right to approve or disapprove a submittal by Settling Defendants should the time stated in this Paragraph be exceeded by U.S. EPA.

E.   Within 30 calendar days of receipt by the Settling Defendants from U.S. EPA of any written notice of document disapproval of a document, the Settling Defendants shall submit a revised document to U.S. EPA that incorporates the U.S. EPA modifications, or shall provide a notice of dispute pursuant to Section XV below.

F.   Settling Defendants shall proceed to implement the work detailed in the RD/RA Work Plan when the Work Plan is fully approved by U.S. EPA. Unless otherwise directed by U.S. EPA, the Settling Defendants shall not commence field activities until approval by U.S. EPA of the RD/RA Work Plan. The fully approved RD/RA Work Plan shall be deemed incorporated into and made an enforceable part of this Consent Decree as Appendix H. All Work shall be conducted in accordance with the National Contingency Plan, the U.S. EPA Superfund Remedial Design and Remedial Action Guidance (OSWER Directive 9355.0-4A, dated June 1986), any additional guidance provided by U.S. EPA to Settling Defendants by U.S. EPA in accordance with the notice provisions of Section XXII of this Consent Decree, and the other requirements of this Consent Decree, including the standards, specifications, and schedules contained in the RODs, the SOW and the RD/RA Work Plan.

13.   The Remedial Action required under this Decree shall include activities set forth in the RODs and as more fully described in the Statement of Work. The Settling Defendants shall, at the Site, perform each of the described actions in accordance with the Performance Standards and the schedules set forth in the RODs, the SOW, and the RD/RA Work Plan. Settling Defendants shall meet the performance and cleanup standards and specifications in the conduct of the Work at the Site, with respect to soils, sediments, groundwater, surface water, and air. The construction, operation, and maintenance of containment, collection, diversion, and treatment devices and techniques shall also be in conformity with the performance goals and standards set forth in the RODs, the SOW, and the RD/RA Work Plan.

14.   The parties acknowledge and agree that approval of the SOW and/or the RD/RA Work Plan does not constitute a warranty or representation of any kind by Plaintiff that the performance of the Work under the SOW or RD/RA Work Plan will achieve the performance goals and standards set forth in the ROD and the SOW, and nothing herein shall foreclose Plaintiff from seeking performance of all terms and conditions of this Consent Decree, including applicable performance or cleanup standards specified in the SOW or as required by § 121 of CERCLA, 42 U.S.C. § 9621.

VIII.   U.S. EPA PERIODIC REVIEW TO ASSURE PROTECTION OF HUMAN HEALTH AND ENVIRONMENT

15.   To the extent required by § 121(c) of CERCLA, 42 U.S.C. § 9621(c), and any applicable regulations, U.S. EPA shall review the remedial action at the Site at least every five years from initiation of the Work or after the entry of the Consent Decree, whichever is sooner, to assure that human health and the

environment are being protected by the remedial action being implemented. If upon such review, U.S. EPA determines that further response action in accordance with §§ 104 or 106 of CERCLA, 42 U.S.C. §§ 9604 or 9606, is appropriate at the Site, then, consistent with the covenant not to sue provisions of Section XIX of this Consent Decree, the U.S. EPA may take or require such action. The U.S. EPA shall notify the Settling Defendants in accordance with the notice provisions of Section XXII of this Decree of the initiation of the periodic review process. Failure of U.S. EPA to so notify the Settling Defendants shall not present or provide a defense to Settling Defendants' obligations under this Section.

16. Settling Defendants shall be provided with an opportunity to confer with U.S. EPA on any response action proposed as a result of the periodic review provided for under Paragraph 15 above, and to submit written comments for the record. After the period for submission of written comments is closed, the Regional Administrator of U.S. EPA, Region V, shall in writing either affirm, modify, or rescind the order for further response action. The final decision of U.S. EPA shall be subject to judicial review pursuant to the dispute resolution provisions in Section XV to the extent permitted by § 113 of CERCLA, 42 U.S.C. § 9613.

IX. ADDITIONAL WORK

17. In the event that U.S. EPA in consultation with OEPA, or the Settling Defendants, determines that additional work, including additional remedial design or remedial action, is necessary to meet the performance standards specified in the RODs and the SOW, written notification of such additional work will be provided to the other parties as provided in Section XXII below.

18. Any additional work determined to be necessary by Settling Defendants is subject to approval by U.S. EPA in consultation with OEPA.

19. Any additional work determined to be necessary by Settling Defendants and approved by U.S. EPA in consultation with OEPA, or determined to be necessary by U.S. EPA in consultation with OEPA in order to meet the performance or cleanup standards described in the RODs and the SOW, shall be completed by Settling Defendants in accordance with the levels, specifications, and schedules approved by U.S. EPA in consultation with OEPA. Notwithstanding the above, any dispute among the parties relating to any additional work shall be resolved in accordance with the dispute resolution provisions of Section XV of this Consent Decree.

X. QUALITY ASSURANCE

20. Settling Defendants shall use quality assurance, quality control, and chain of custody procedures in accordance with U.S. EPA's *Interim Guidelines and Specifications for Preparing Quality Assurance Project Plans* (QAM-005/80) and shall use any subsequent amendments to such guidelines upon notice from U.S. EPA in accordance with the notice provisions of Section XXII of this Decree for subsequent sampling and analytical events after such notice. Prior

to the commencement of any monitoring project under this Consent Decree, Settling Defendants shall submit a Quality Assurance Project Plan (QAPP) to U.S. EPA that is consistent with the SOW and applicable guidelines. U.S. EPA, after review of Settling Defendants' QAPP and the OEPA's comments thereon, will notify Settling Defendants of any required modifications, conditional approval, disapproval, or approval of the QAPP. Upon notification of disapproval or any need for modifications, Settling Defendants shall make all required modifications in the QAPP, subject to the dispute resolution provisions of Section XV. Sampling data generated consistent with the QAPP shall be admissible as evidence in any proceeding under Section XV (Dispute Resolution) of this Decree or otherwise to enforce the terms of this Decree. Settling Defendants shall assure that U.S. EPA personnel or authorized representatives are allowed access during normal business hours to any laboratory utilized by Settling Defendants in implementing this Consent Decree. In addition, Settling Defendants shall have any laboratory employed by Settling Defendants for analysis of samples subject to the QAPP analyze samples, subject to the QA/QC provisions of the QAPP, submitted by U.S. EPA for quality assurance monitoring.

XI. ACCESS, SAMPLING, DOCUMENT AVAILABILITY

21.   Owner Settling Defendants shall allow and provide access to their property that is part of the Site by any officer, employee, or representative of the U.S. EPA or the OEPA, or any employee, agent, or representative of any Settling Defendant or any contractor or subcontractor retained by Settling Defendants in connection with the performance of the Work required under this Consent Decree. Such access shall include permission to perform any and all activities listed in the SOW or required under this Consent Decree to effectuate the RODs and the SOW.

22.   To the extent that the Site or other areas where Work is to be performed hereunder are presently owned by persons other than Owner Settling Defendants, except as otherwise provided above, Settling Defendants shall use best efforts to secure from such persons access for Settling Defendants' contractors, the United States, and its authorized representatives, as necessary to effectuate this Consent Decree. If access is not obtained within 60 days of the date of entry of this Decree, Settling Defendants shall promptly notify the United States. If the U.S. EPA determines that the Settling Defendants have used their best efforts to obtain access, the United States thereafter shall assist Settling Defendants in obtaining access, to the extent necessary to effectuate the remedial action for the Site. The United States' costs in this effort shall be reimbursed by Settling Defendants. Payment shall be made in accordance with the reimbursement provisions of Paragraph 48 of this Consent Decree.

23.   Settling Defendants shall submit to U.S. EPA the results of all sampling and test, and other data generated by Settling Defendants with respect to the implementation of this Consent Decree, and shall submit the results of all sampling and tests, and other data that are subject to QA/QC procedures, in

monthly progress reports as described in Section XII of this Consent Decree. Any results that are not subject to QA/QC procedures shall be submitted to U.S. EPA in the next monthly report after they are obtained.

24.   At the request of Settling Defendants and at Settling Defendants' cost, U.S. EPA shall make available to Settling Defendants the results of all sampling and/or tests and other data that are subject to the QA/QC standards set by U.S. EPA for such information, with respect to the implementation of this Consent Decree, within a reasonable period after such data become available and a request therefor is received from Settling Defendants. Such request shall be made in accordance with the notice provisions of Section XXII of this Decree. The obligations of this Paragraph shall not apply to samples being collected by U.S. EPA that are not within the scope of QA/QC monitoring and oversight or are being collected for enforcement purposes that are not directly related to ensuring satisfactory performance of the Work required under this Consent Decree or that may be related to investigation of civil or criminal claims or causes of action.

25.   At the request of U.S. EPA, Settling Defendants shall allow split or duplicate samples to be taken by U.S. EPA and/or its authorized representatives, of any samples collected by Settling Defendants pursuant to the implementation of this Consent Decree. Settling Defendants shall notify U.S. EPA not less than 14 days in advance of any sample collection activity, except in the event of an emergency or with prior approval of the RPM. In the case of an emergency, notice shall be given as early as practicable. In addition, U.S. EPA shall have the right to take any additional samples that U.S. EPA deems necessary.

26.   At the request of Settling Defendants and at Settling Defendants' cost, U.S. EPA shall allow split or duplicate samples to be taken by Settling Defendants and/or their authorized representatives, of any samples collected by U.S. EPA at the Site. Such request shall be made in accordance with the notice provisions of Section XXII of this Decree. To the extent practicable, U.S. EPA shall notify the Settling Defendants at least seven days in advance of any such sample collection activity. The obligations of this Paragraph shall not apply to samples being collected by U.S. EPA that are not within the scope of QA/QC monitoring and oversight or samples that may be collected for enforcement purposes that are not directly related to ensuring satisfactory performance of the Work required under this Consent Decree or that may be related to prosecution of civil or criminal claims or causes of action.

XII.   REPORTING REQUIREMENTS

27.   Settling Defendants shall require the contractor to prepare and provide to U.S. EPA written monthly progress reports which: (1) describe the actions which have been taken toward achieving compliance with this Consent Decree during the previous month; (2) include all results of sampling and tests and all other data that have been subjected to QA/QC procedures and have been received by Settling Defendants during the course of the Work; (3) include all plans and procedures completed under the RD/RA Work Plan during the previous month; (4) describe all actions, data collection activities,

and plans that are scheduled for the next month, and provide other information relating to the progress of construction as is customary in the industry; (5) include information regarding percentage of completion, unresolved delays encountered or anticipated that may affect the future schedule for implementation of the Statement of Work or the RD/RA Work Plan, and a description of efforts made to mitigate those delays or anticipated delays. These progress reports are to be submitted to U.S. EPA by the tenth day of every month following the effective date of this Consent Decree.

28.   If the date for submission of any item or notification required by this Consent Decree falls upon a weekend or state or federal holiday, the time period for submission of that item or notification is extended to the next working day following the weekend or holiday.

29.   Upon the occurrence of any event during performance of the Work which, pursuant to § 103 of CERCLA, 42 U.S.C. § 9603, requires reporting to the National Response Center, Settling Defendants shall promptly orally notify the U.S. EPA Remedial Project Manager (RPM) and OEPA Project Coordinator, or in the event of the unavailability of the U.S. EPA RPM, the Emergency Response Section, Region V, United States Environmental Protection Agency, in addition to the reporting required by § 103 of CERCLA, 42 U.S.C. § 9603. Within 20 days of the onset of such an event, Settling Defendants shall furnish to Plaintiff a written report setting forth the events that occurred and the measures taken and to be taken in response thereto. Within 30 days of the conclusion of such an event, Settling Defendants shall submit a report setting forth all actions taken to respond thereto.

XIII.   REMEDIAL PROJECT MANAGER/PROJECT COORDINATORS

30.   U.S. EPA shall designate a Remedial Project Manager (RPM) and/or On Scene Coordinator (OSC) and the OEPA may designate a Project Coordinator for the Site, and the U.S. EPA may designate other representatives, including U.S. EPA employees and federal contractors and consultants, to observe and monitor the progress of any activity undertaken pursuant to this Consent Decree. The RPM and/or OSC shall have the authority lawfully vested in a Remedial Project Manager and/or On-Scene Coordinator by the National Contingency Plan, 40 CFR Part 300. In addition, when conditions at the Site, or at off-Site locations where Work required under this Consent Decree is being performed, may present an imminent and substantial endangerment to public health or welfare or the environment, the RPM and/or OSC shall have authority to halt, conduct, or direct any work required by this Consent Decree and to take or direct any necessary response action. Settling Defendants shall also designate a Project Coordinator who shall have primary responsibility for implementation of the Work at the Site.

31.   To the maximum extent possible, except as specifically provided in the Consent Decree, communications between Settling Defendants, OEPA, and U.S. EPA concerning implementation of the Work under this Consent Decree shall be made between the Project Coordinators and the RPM and/or OSC.

32.   Within 20 calendar days of the effective date of this Consent Decree, Settling Defendants and U.S. EPA shall notify each other, in writing, of the name, address, and telephone number of the designated Project Coordinators and Alternate Project Coordinators, and RPM and/or OSC and Alternate RPM and/or OSC.

XIV.   FORCE MAJEURE

33.   *Force majeure,* for purposes of this Consent Decree, is defined as any event arising from causes beyond the control of Settling Defendants which delays or prevents the performance of any obligation under this Consent Decree. Force majeure shall not include increased costs or expenses or nonattainment of the performance or cleanup standards set forth in the RODs and the Statement of Work.

34.   When circumstances occur that may delay the completion of any phase of the Work, or delay access to the Site or to any property on which any part of the Work is to be performed, whether or not caused by a force majeure event, Settling Defendants shall promptly notify the RPM orally, or in the event of their unavailability, the Director of the Waste Management Division of U.S. EPA and the OEPA Office of Corrective Action. Within five days of the event which Settling Defendants contend is responsible for the delay, Settling Defendants shall supply to Plaintiff a written statement of the reason(s) for and anticipated duration of such delay, the measures taken and to be taken by Settling Defendants to prevent or minimize the delay, and the timetable for implementation of such measures. Failure to give oral notice to the RPM and to give written explanation to Plaintiff in a timely manner shall constitute a waiver of any claim of force majeure.

35.   If U.S. EPA agrees that a delay is or was attributable to a force majeure event, the Parties shall modify the RD/RA Work Plan to provide such additional time as may be necessary to allow the completion of the specific phase of Work and/or any succeeding phase of the Work affected by such delay, with such additional time not to exceed the actual duration of the delay.

36.   If U.S. EPA and Settling Defendants cannot agree on whether the reason for the delay was a force majeure event, or on whether the duration of the delay is or was warranted under the circumstances, the parties shall resolve the dispute according to Section XV hereof. Settling Defendants have the burden of proving force majeure as a defense to compliance with this Consent Decree.

XV.   DISPUTE RESOLUTION

37.   As required by § 121(e)(2) of CERCLA, 42 U.S.C. § 9621(e)(2), the Parties to this Consent Decree shall attempt to resolve expeditiously and informally any disagreements concerning implementation of this Consent Decree or any Work required hereunder.

38.   In the event that any dispute arising under this Consent Decree is not resolved expeditiously through informal means, any party desiring dispute

resolution under this Paragraph shall give prompt written notice to the other parties to the Decree.

39.   Within ten days of the service of notice of dispute pursuant to Paragraph 38 above, the party who gave the notice shall serve on the other parties to this Decree a written statement of the issues in dispute, the relevant facts upon which the dispute is based, and factual data, analysis, or opinion supporting its position, and all supporting documentation on which such party relies (hereinafter the Statement of Position). Opposing parties shall serve their Statements of Position, including supporting documentation, no later than ten days after receipt of the complaining party's Statement of Position. In the event that these 10-day time periods for exchange of Statements of Position may cause a delay in the Work, they may be shortened upon and in accordance with notice by U.S. EPA.

40.   An administrative record of a dispute under this Section may be maintained by U.S. EPA. The U.S. EPA shall maintain an administrative record with respect to any dispute involving adequacy and selection of remedial action for the Site, including the Work to be performed by the Settling Defendants that was required under the Source Removal Operable Unit ROD and which has been incorporated into this Decree. In all other disputes, the U.S. EPA shall give written notice to the other parties of its intention to maintain an administrative record. The record shall include the written notification of such dispute, the Statement of Position served pursuant to the preceding subparagraphs, and any other information deemed relevant by the U.S. EPA. The record shall be available for review and copying by all parties.

41.   Upon review of the administrative record, the Director of the Waste Management Division, U.S. EPA, Region V, shall issue a final decision and order resolving the dispute. This order shall be enforceable administratively pursuant to § 121(e)(2) of CERCLA, 42 U.S.C. § 9621(e)(2), subject to the rights of judicial review set forth in Paragraph 42.

42.   Any decision and order of U.S. EPA pursuant to the preceding Paragraph 38 shall be reviewable by this court, provided that a motion for review of the dispute is filed with the Clerk's office within ten days of receipt of U.S. EPA's decision and order. In any event, judicial review of decisions involving the adequacy and selection of the remedy for the Site shall be limited in scope to the administrative record, and the standard of review shall be whether the determination of the U.S. EPA is arbitrary and capricious or otherwise not in accordance with law.

43.   The invocation of the procedures stated in this Paragraph shall not extend or postpone Settling Defendants' obligations under this Consent Decree with respect to the disputed issue unless such delay is attributable to a force majeure event or and until U.S. EPA finds, or the court orders, otherwise.

44.   The provisions of this Section XV shall not be applicable to the determination of U.S. EPA concerning acceptability of an alternative cap proposed by the Settling Defendants under the provisions of Paragraph 2.2 of the SOW, nor shall they be applicable to determinations of the U.S. EPA regarding forgiveness of stipulated penalties under Paragraph 68 below, nor shall they be applicable to the provisions of Paragraph 21 above regarding restrictions to be placed upon use of Owner Settling Defendants' property.

XVI.   RETENTION AND AVAILABILITY OF INFORMATION

45.   Settling Defendants shall make available to U.S. EPA and shall retain, during the pendency of this Consent Decree or for a period of six years after the initiation of construction as defined in the SOW, whichever period is longer, one complete set of all records and documents in their possession custody, or control relating to the performance of this Consent Decree, including, but not limited to, documents reflecting the results of any sampling, tests, or other data or information generated or acquired by any of them, or on their behalf, with respect to the Site, and all documents pertaining to their own or any other person's liability for response action or costs under CERCLA. After the later of either (1) termination of this Decree, or (2) six years after initiation of construction, Settling Defendants shall notify U.S. DOJ and U.S. EPA at least 90 calendar days prior to the destruction of any such documents, and upon request by U.S. EPA, Settling Defendants shall relinquish custody of the documents to U.S. EPA. Settling Defendants may not withhold any documents that are subject to the public disclosure provisions of § 104(e)(7)(F) of CERCLA, 42 U.S.C. § 9604(e)(7)(F).

46.   Settling Defendants may assert business confidentiality claims covering part or all of the information provided in connection with this Consent Decree in accordance with § 104(e)(7) of CERCLA, 42 U.S.C. § 9604(e)(7), and pursuant to 40 C.F.R. § 2.203(b). Information acquired or generated by Settling Defendants in performance of the Work that is subject to the provisions of § 104(e)(7)(f) of CERCLA, 42 U.S.C. § 9604(e)(7)(f), shall not be claimed as confidential by Settling Defendants.

47.   Information determined to be confidential by U.S. EPA will be afforded the protection specified in 40 C.F.R. Part 2, Subpart B. If no such claim accompanies the information when it is submitted to the U.S. EPA, the public may be given access to such information without further notice to Settling Defendants.

XVII.   REIMBURSEMENT

48.   Settling Defendants and Settling *De Minimis* Defendants acknowledge that the United States claims that the unreimbursed past response costs incurred by it prior to September 30, 1989 in connection with the Site total $5,578,674.48.

49.   Settling Defendants and Settling *De Minimis* Defendants shall pay, within 30 days of the entry of this Consent Decree, to the U.S. EPA Hazardous Substances Superfund, and delivered to:

> U.S. Environmental Protection Agency
> Region V
> Attn: Superfund Accounting
> P.O. Box 70753
> Chicago, Illinois 60673

by a certified or cashier's check payable to "EPA Hazardous Substances Superfund," and referencing CERCLA Number 5TJB05B403 and DOJ Case Number

90-11-3-38B, in an amount to be determined in accordance with the provisions of Paragraph 50 below. A copy of such check shall be sent to the Director, Waste Management Division, U.S. EPA, Region V. A copy of the check shall also be sent to the Chief, Environmental Enforcement Section, Land and Natural Resources Division, U.S. Department of Justice, 10th and Pennsylvania, Washington, D.C. 20530. The payments made under this Paragraph are reimbursement of past response costs claimed by the United States in this action. Upon receipt of the payment required above, the United States covenants not to sue Settling Defendants and Settling *De Minimis* Defendants for any costs incurred prior to the date of lodging of this Consent Decree (past response costs) pursuant to CERCLA, 42 U.S.C. § 9601 *et seq.*, as set forth in Paragraphs 71 and 80.

50.   The payment of past response costs required of Settling Defendants and Settling *De Minimis* Defendants under Paragraph 49 above shall be calculated according to the following procedure. Settling Defendants and Settling *De Minimis* Defendants jointly and severally agree to pay the following sums in reimbursement of past response costs, according to the degree of volumetric participation of the Settling Defendants and Settling *De Minimis* Defendants, based upon the aggregate shares of such parties as reflected in column 2 of Appendix F:

A.   If the aggregate level of participation is 65 percent or less, Settling Defendants and Settling *De Minimis* Defendants shall pay no past response costs. If the aggregate level of participation is greater than 65 percent but less than 70 percent, the Settling Defendants shall pay Past Response Costs according to the following formula: Amount owed in millions of dollars = −16.25 + (0.25 × percentage of participation). For example, if the aggregate participation is 68.5 percent, the amount to be paid is −16.25 + (0.25 × 68.5) = \$0.875 million.

B.   If the aggregate level of participation equals 70 percent but less than 75 percent, Settling Defendants and Settling *De Minimis* Defendants shall pay \$1.25 million of past response costs, plus an incremental amount for any degree of participation over 70 percent but less than 75 percent to be calculated according to the following formula: Amount owed in millions of dollars = −19.75 + (0.30 × percentage of participation). For example, if the aggregate participation is 74.2 percent, the amount to be paid is −19.75 + (0.30 × 74.2) = \$2.51 million.

C.   If the aggregate level of participation equals 75 percent but less than 80 percent, Settling Defendants and Settling *De Minimis* Defendants shall pay \$2.75 million of past response costs, plus an amount for any degree of participation over 75 percent but less than 80 percent to be calculated according to the following formula: Amount owed in millions of dollars = −8.5 + (0.15 × percentage of participation). For example, if the aggregate participation is 79 percent, the amount to be paid is −8.5 + (0.15 × 79) = \$3.35 million.

D.   If the aggregate level of participation equals 80 percent but less than 85 percent, Settling Defendants and Settling *De Minimis* Defendants shall pay \$3.5 million of Past Response Costs, plus an amount for any degree of participation over 80 percent but less than 85 percent to be calculated according to the following formula: Amount owed in millions of dollars = −9.3 + (0.16 × percentage of participation). For example, if the aggregate participation is 83.8 percent, the amount to be paid is −9.3 + (0.16 × 83.8) = $4.108 million.

   E.   If the aggregate level of participation equals 85 percent or greater, Settling Defendants and Settling *De Minimis* Defendants shall pay all past response costs set forth in Paragraph 48 above.

   51.   Neither the Settling Defendants nor the Settling *De Minimis* Defendants shall challenge the volumetric ranking in Appendix F for purposes of this Consent Decree. The volumetric ranking in Appendix F is not and shall not be considered a nonbinding preliminary allocation of responsibility pursuant to § 122 of CERCLA, 42 U.S.C. § 9622. Appendix F is not to be used for any purpose other than to calculate the percentage participation of Settling Defendants and Settling *De Minimis* Defendants in this Consent Decree to determine the amount of past response costs to be paid to the United States under this Section. Appendix F does not determine the liability of any person and shall not be construed as evidence of the liability of any person.

   52.   Settling Defendants shall pay the first $350,000 of the U.S. EPA's oversight costs incurred in connection with the review or development of plans, reports, and other items or with the oversight or verification of Work to be performed under this Consent Decree. Settling Defendants shall be relieved of responsibility for reimbursement of any oversight costs of the United States in connection with the Site which exceed $350,000, up to $1,750,000, except that if the aggregate volumetric participation of Settling Defendants and Settling *De Minimis* Defendants exceeds 90 percent of the volumetric total reflected in Appendix F, Settling Defendants shall pay all oversight costs of the United States. Settling Defendants shall, unless obliged under the preceding sentence to pay all oversight costs, reimburse the United States for all oversight costs that exceed $1,750,000. Payment of the first $350,000 shall be made within ten days of the date of entry of this Consent Decree. Payment of U.S. EPA's oversight costs in excess of $1,750,000 shall be made on an annual basis and within 30 days after U.S. EPA makes a demand for payment of such costs. The United States shall submit its demand for oversight costs as soon as practicable after each anniversary date of this Consent Decree. Payment shall be made in the manner specified in Paragraph 49 above. In consideration of and upon payment of all oversight costs as required by this Paragraph, the United States covenants not to sue Settling Defendants for any oversight costs incurred in overseeing the Work.

   53.   If oversight costs related to the work which Settling Defendants are required to pay are outstanding at the time the United States plans to terminate this Consent Decree, Settling Defendants shall, within 30 days of receipt of U.S. EPA's oversight cost demands and before termination of this Consent Decree, pay such oversight costs.

   54.   The response costs, including oversight costs, to be paid by Settling Defendants as set forth in this Section of this Consent Decree shall not be inconsistent with the National Contingency Plan.

55.   Nothing in this Decree shall constitute a preauthorization of any claim against the Hazardous Substance Superfund under the Comprehensive Environmental Response, Compensation, and Liability Act (CERCLA), 42 U.S.C. §§ 9601 et seq.

56.   On or before August 24, 1989, Settling Defendants shall provide executed original signature pages for each Settling Defendant. If the aggregate volumetric share of contributions of waste materials of all signatory Settling Defendants as of that date does not equal or exceed 50 percent of the volumetric total of all contributions of waste materials to the Site reflected in Appendix F, this Consent Decree shall be null and void and of no force and effect. On or before September 24, 1989, Settling Defendants shall provide to the United States a final update of the list of Settling Defendants, and signed signature pages from each additional defendant party entering into this Decree. Said final list shall determine the percentage share of contributions of waste materials to be used in calculating the reimbursements due to the United States and required under this Section XVII.

XVIII.   STIPULATED PENALTIES

57.   Settling Defendants shall pay stipulated penalties in the amount set forth in Paragraph 58 below to the United States for each violation of the requirements of the schedule under Paragraph VIII for delivery of reports or documents required to be delivered under Paragraph VII of the SOW and/or each violation of the construction schedule set forth under Paragraph 6.1 of the SOW, unless such failure is excused under Section XIV (Force Majeure) or forgiven by U.S. EPA pursuant to Paragraph 69. Violation by Settling Defendants shall include any failure to complete an activity under this Consent Decree or plan approved under this Consent Decree or any matter under this Consent Decree in an acceptable manner and within the specified time schedules in and approved under this Consent Decree. Any modifications of the time for performance shall be in writing and approved by U.S. EPA.

58.   The following stipulated penalties shall be payable per violation per day to the United States for any noncompliance with the schedule of deliverables set forth in Paragraphs 3.1 through 3.9, and Paragraph 4.1., of the SOW for plans or reports:

Amount Per Day	Period of Noncompliance
$100	1st through 14th day
$250	15th through 30th day
$1000	31st day and beyond

59.   The following stipulated penalties shall be payable per violation per day to the United States for any noncompliance with the construction schedule set forth in Paragraph 6.1 of the SOW for Work at the Site, or for late payment of the amounts owed to the United States as reimbursement of past response costs under Paragraph 49 above:

Amount Per Day	Period of Noncompliance
$ 1,000	1st through 14th day
$ 2,500	15th through 30th day
$ 5,000	31st day through 60th day
$10,000	61st day and beyond

60. All penalties begin to accrue on the day after the day on which complete performance is due or a violation occurs, and continue to accrue through the final day of correction of the noncompliance. Nothing herein shall prevent the simultaneous accrual of separate penalties for separate violations of this Consent Decree.

61. Following U.S. EPA's determination that Settling Defendants have failed to comply with the requirements of this Consent Decree, U.S. EPA shall give Settling Defendants written notification of the same and describe the noncompliance. This notice shall also indicate the amount of penalties due.

62. All penalties owed to the United States under this Section shall be payable within 30 days of receipt of the notification of noncompliance, unless Settling Defendants invoke the dispute resolution procedures under Section XV. Penalties shall accrue from the date of violation regardless of whether U.S. EPA has notified Settling Defendants of a violation. Interest shall begin to accrue on the unpaid balance at the end of the 30-day period pursuant to Paragraph 67 of this Section. Such penalties shall be paid by certified check to the Hazardous Substance Superfund and shall contain Settling Defendants' complete and correct address, the site name, and the civil action number. All checks shall be mailed to:

U.S. Environmental Protection Agency
Region V
Attn: Superfund Accounting
P.O. Box 70753
Chicago, Illinois 60673

A copy of each such check shall be mailed to:

Assistant Attorney General
Land & Natural Resources Division
U.S. Department of Justice
10th & Pennsylvania Avenue, N.W.
Washington, D.C. 20530

63. Neither the filing of a petition to resolve a dispute nor the payment of penalties shall alter in any way Settling Defendants' obligation to complete the performance required hereunder.

64. Settling Defendants may dispute the United States' right to the stated amount of penalties by invoking the dispute resolution procedures under Section XV. Penalties shall accrue but need not be paid during the dispute resolution period. If the District Court becomes involved in the resolution of the dispute, the period of dispute shall end upon the rendering of a decision by

the District Court regardless of whether any party appeals such decision. If Settling Defendants do not prevail upon resolution, the United States has the right to collect all penalties that accrue prior to and during the period of dispute. In the event of an appeal, such penalties shall be placed into an escrow account until a decision has been rendered by the final court of appeal. If Settling Defendants prevail upon resolution, no penalties shall be payable.

65.   No penalties shall accrue for violations of this Consent Decree caused by events determined by U.S. EPA to be beyond the control of Settling Defendants as identified in Section XIV (Force Majeure). Settling Defendants have the burden of proving force majeure or compliance with this Consent Decree.

66.   This Section shall remain in full force and effect for the term of this Consent Decree.

67.   Pursuant to 31 U.S.C. § 3717, interest shall accrue on any amounts overdue at a rate established by the Department of Treasury of any period after the date of billing. A handling charge will be assessed at the end of each 30-day late period, and a 6 percent per annum penalty charge will be assessed if the penalty is not paid within 90 days of the due date.

68.   If Settling Defendants fail to pay stipulated penalties, Plaintiff may institute proceedings to collect the penalties. Notwithstanding the stipulated penalties provisions of this Paragraph, U.S. EPA may elect to assess civil penalties and/or to bring an action in U.S. District Court pursuant to § 109 of CERCLA, 42 U.S.C. § 9609, as amended by SARA, to enforce the provisions of this Consent Decree. Payment of stipulated penalties shall not preclude U.S. EPA from electing to pursue any other remedy or sanction to enforce this Consent Decree, and nothing shall preclude U.S. EPA from seeking statutory penalties against Settling Defendants for violations of statutory or regulatory requirements.

69.   A.   U.S. EPA may forgive stipulated penalties for the untimely submission of plans for the design, construction, and operation of the remedial action required under this Consent Decree if the Settling Defendants complete all required remedial construction activities required under the SOW within 795 days after the date of entry of this Consent Decree.

B.   U.S. EPA may forgive stipulated penalties for failure to meet an interim construction deadline set forth in Paragraph VII of the SOW for a major element of construction, including construction related to the Source Removal Operable Unit, if Settling Defendants complete construction of that major element on or before the date scheduled under Paragraph 6.1 of the SOW.

C.   Any penalties for the untimely submission of any plan or document required under Paragraphs 3.1 through 3.9 or 4.1 of the SOW, or the completion of any element of construction scheduled under Paragraph 6.1 of the SOW, shall be collected as specified in Paragraph 62 above, but shall be paid into an interest-bearing escrow account to be established by the Settling Defendants, subject to the approval of the United States, and shall remain there until four months after the completion of construction at the Site, as defined in Paragraph 7.0 of the SOW. If the Settling Defendants do not satisfy the criterion for forgiveness of any stipulated penalty paid into the escrow account pursuant to this Paragraph 69, the United States may instruct the escrow agent to pay to United States the amount of each penalty not forgiven, together with interest accumulated thereon, within 30 days. Amounts due to the United States shall be paid to the Hazardous Substance Superfund, as provided in Paragraph 62 of this Section. Copies of the check shall also be sent to the Department of Justice, at the address specified in Paragraph 62. This provision shall not be subject to the dispute resolution provisions set forth in Section XV above.

XIX.   COVENANT NOT TO SUE

70.   In consideration of actions that will be performed and payments that will be made by the Settling Defendants under the terms of the Consent Decree, and except as otherwise specifically provided in this Decree, the United States covenants not to sue Settling Defendants for covered matters. *Covered matters* shall include any and all claims available to Plaintiff under §§ 106 and 107 of CERCLA, 42 U.S.C. §§ 9606 and 9607, and § 7003 of RCRA, 42 U.S.C. § 6973, relating to the Site, on the facts surrounding the transactions or occurrences as described in Plaintiff's complaint against the Settling Defendants. With respect to future liability, this covenant not to sue shall take effect upon certification by U.S. EPA of the completion of the remedial action concerning the Site. With respect to oversight costs, this covenant not to sue shall take effect upon payment of the last of such costs demanded by the U.S. EPA. The covenant not to sue under this Paragraph shall not apply to Owner Settling Defendants until they have executed and recorded documents as required under Paragraph 7.C above.

71.   *Covered Matters* does not include:

(a)   Liability arising from hazardous substances removed from the Site;

(b)   Natural resources damages;

(c)   Criminal liability;

(d)   Claims based on a failure by the Settling Defendants to meet the requirements of this Consent Decree;

(e)   Any matters for which the United States is owed indemnification under Section XX hereof;

(f)   Liability for violations of federal law that occur during implementation of the remedial action;

(g)   Unreimbursed portions of the claims of the United States that were the subject of the action in *United States v. Alvin, et al.,* 84C, Northern District of Ohio, unless a Settling Defendant has previously resolved such claim as a Settling Defendant in the Consent Decree entered in that action on March 3, 1989; and

(h)   Any and all claims relating to final disposal of materials to be placed in the dioxin vault to be constructed on the Site in accordance with the SOW.

72.   Notwithstanding any other provision in this Consent Decree, (1) the United States reserves the right to institute proceedings in this action or in a new action or to issue an Order seeking to compel the Settling Defendants to perform any additional response work at the Site, and (2) the United States reserves the right to institute proceedings in this action or in a new action seeking to reimburse the United States for its response costs for any response action undertaken by U.S. EPA under CERCLA, relating to the Site, if:

a.   for proceedings prior to U.S. EPA certification of completion of the remedial action concerning the Site,

(i)   conditions at the Site, previously unknown to the United States, are discovered after the entry of this Consent Decree, or

(ii)   information is received, in whole or in part, after the entry of this Consent Decree,

and these previously unknown conditions or this information indicates that the remedial action is not protective of human health and the environment; and

b.   for proceedings subsequent to U.S. EPA certification of completion of the remedial action concerning the Site,

(i)   conditions at the Site, previously unknown to the United States, are discovered after the certification of completion by U.S. EPA, or

(ii)   information is received, in whole or in part, after the certification of completion by U.S. EPA,

and these previously unknown conditions or this information indicates that the remedial action is not protective of human health and the environment.

73.   Notwithstanding any other provisions in this Consent Decree, the covenant not to sue in this Section shall not relieve the Settling Defendants of their obligation to meet and maintain compliance with the requirements set forth in this Consent Decree, including the conditions in the RODs and the SOW, which are incorporated herein, and the United States reserves its rights to take response actions at the Site in the event of a breach of the terms of this Consent Decree and to seek recovery of costs incurred after entry of this Consent Decree: 1) resulting from such a breach; 2) relating to any portion of the Work funded or performed by the United States; or 3) incurred by the United States as a result of having to seek judicial assistance to remedy conditions at or adjacent to the Site.

74.   Nothing in this Consent Decree shall constitute or be construed as a release or a covenant not to sue regarding any claim or cause of action against any person, firm, trust, joint venture, partnership, corporation, or other entity not a signatory to this Consent Decree for any liability it may have arising out of or relating to the Site. Plaintiff expressly reserves the right to continue to sue any person other than the Settling Defendants, in connection with the Site.

75.   The United States acknowledges that information currently known to the United States indicates that all persons listed in Appendix E to this Consent

Decree (the Settling *De Minimis* Defendants) contributed to the Site quantities of Waste Materials not greater than the amounts attributed to each such person in column 2 of Appendix F, that the Settling *De Minimis* Defendants have made or have agreed to make payments to the Settling Defendants in the amounts listed in column 6 of Appendix F, and that the Settling *De Minimis* Defendants are eligible for a *de minimis* settlement under the provisions of § 122(g) of CERCLA, 42 U.S.C. § 9622.

76.   The Parties acknowledge and agree that Settling Defendants and Settling *De Minimis* Defendants who have resolved their liability to Plaintiff shall not be liable for claims for contribution regarding matters addressed in this settlement, in accordance with and under the provisions of § 113 of CERCLA, 42 U.S.C. § 9613. Settling Defendants and Settling *De Minimis* Defendants acknowledge and agree that resolution of the matters addressed in this Consent Decree resolves all claims and controversies relating to the Site existing between all Defendants that are signatories to this action, and all Parties covenant not to pursue any claim for contribution or other cause of action against any party to this Consent Decree regarding the matters addressed in this Consent Decree. Nothing in the Consent Decree shall preclude any of the Parties from asserting such claims as they may have against nonsettling PRPs.

77.   Nothing in this Consent Decree constitutes a covenant not to sue or take action or otherwise limits the ability of the United States or the U.S. EPA to seek or obtain further relief from any of the Settling *De Minimis* Defendants, and the covenant not to sue in Paragraph 80 of this Consent Decree is null and void if information not currently known to the United States is discovered which indicates that any Settling *De Minimis* Defendant contributed hazardous substances or waste materials to the Laskin Site in such greater amount or of such greater toxic or other hazardous effect that the Settling *De Minimis* Defendant no longer qualifies as a *de minimis* party because such party contributed greater than 7,000 gallons of hazardous substances or waste materials, or contributed disproportionately to the cumulative toxic or other hazardous effects of the hazardous substances or waste materials at the Site.

78.   Certification by Settling De Minimis Defendants. By signing this Consent Decree, each Settling *De Minimis* Defendant certifies, to the best of its knowledge and belief, the following:

A.   The Settling *De Minimis* Defendant has made reasonable inquiry to gather all information that relates in any way to its ownership, operation, generation, treatment, transportation, storage, or disposal of hazardous substances or waste materials at or in connection with the Site, and has provided to the United States all such information; and

B.   The information provided under Paragraph 78.A above is materially true and correct with respect to the amount of waste materials that the Settling *De Minimis* Defendant may have shipped to the Site, and to the best of the Settling *De Minimis* Defendant's knowledge and belief, the volume and toxicity of hazardous substances or waste materials delivered by the Settling *De Minimis* Defendant to the Site is minimal in relation to the total volume and general nature of the hazardous substances or waste materials delivered to the Site.

79.   Nothing in this Consent Decree constitutes a covenant not to sue or to take action or otherwise limits the ability of the United States to seek or obtain any and all available relief against any Settling *De Minimis* Defendant, and the covenant not to sue in Paragraph 80 of this Consent Decree is null and void if information not currently known to the United States is discovered that indicates that such Settling *De Minimis* Defendant contributed hazardous substances or waste materials to the Site in such greater amount or of such greater toxic or other hazardous effect that such Settling *De Minimis* Defendant no longer qualifies as a Settling *De Minimis* Defendant at the Site because that party's contribution materially exceeds the amount attributed to it in Appendix F or contributed materially and disproportionately to the cumulative toxic or other hazardous effects of waste materials at the Site.

80.   Subject to the reservation of rights in Paragraph 83 (regarding the dioxin vault) below, upon payment of the amount specified in Appendix F to this Consent Decree, the United States covenants not to sue or to take any other civil or administrative action against any Settling *De Minimis* Defendant for *de minimis* covered matters. *De minimis covered matters* shall include any and all civil liability to the United States relating to the Site for (1) reimbursement of response costs of the United States pursuant to § 107(a) of CERCLA, 42 U.S.C. § 9607(a), or (2) for injunctive relief pursuant to § 106 of CERCLA, 42 U.S.C. § 9606, or (3) claims for injunctive relief pursuant to § 7003 of RCRA, 42 U.S.C. § 6973, on the facts surrounding the transactions or occurrences as described in Plaintiff's Complaint in this action.

De minimis covered matters does not include:

(a)   Natural resources damages;
(b)   Criminal liability; and
(c)   Any and all claims relating to final disposal of materials to be placed in the dioxin vault to be constructed on the Site in accordance with the SOW.

81.   In consideration of the United States' covenants not to sue in Paragraphs 70 and 80 of this Section, Settling Defendants and Settling *De Minimis* Defendants agree not to assert any claims or causes of action against the United States or the Hazardous Substance Superfund, or to seek any other costs, damages, or attorneys' fees from the United States, arising out of covered matters.

82.   For and in consideration of the mutual benefits and considerations set forth above, the U.S. EPA agrees that, upon entry of this Decree by the Court and in the absence of an appeal or other judicial action that suspends or terminates this Decree, and subject to the provisions of Paragraph 74 herein, the obligations imposed by the unilateral administrative order, attached hereto as Appendix I, issued to 45 PRPs with respect to the Site under § 106 of CERCLA, 42 U.S.C. § 9606, on February 26, 1988, shall be deemed to become a part of this Consent Decree and shall be enforceable in the same manner against all Settling Defendants as all other obligations under this Decree, and the order

shall continue to have full force and effect against the Respondents thereto except as it has been incorporated into this Decree and performed by the Settling Defendants. Notwithstanding any other provision of this Consent Decree, the U.S. EPA expressly reserves all rights, causes, or claims of action that it may have against any potentially responsible party other than a Settling Defendant or a Settling *De Minimis* Defendant for the Source Removal Operable Unit pursuant to the February 26, 1988 administrative order for the Site, including, but not limited to, costs, injunctive relief, or penalties related to noncompliance with the terms of said administrative order.

83.   The Parties expressly recognize and agree that at the time of the entry of this Consent Decree, no approved final disposal option exists for the dioxin-contaminated materials that are addressed in the SOW, and that enclosure of these materials in the vault required under the SOW is intended to be an interim resolution of the potential for release or threat of release of these materials that provides interim protection of human health and the environment. Notwithstanding any other provision of this Consent Decree, the United States reserves, and this Consent Decree is without prejudice to, the right to seek from Settling Defendants or Settling *De Minimis* Defendants, or any other person, in this action or in a new action, any and all response costs that are associated with final removal, treatment, and disposal of dioxin-contaminated material to be placed in a vault on the Site during performance of the Work required under this Consent Decree. The United States also reserves the right to issue administrative orders, perform the necessary removal, treatment, and disposal, and recover its costs associated therewith, or seek injunctive relief against Settling Defendants or Settling *De Minimis* Defendants, or any other person, in this action or in a new action requiring the removal, treatment, and final disposal of these dioxin-contaminated materials or reimbursement of such costs.

XX.   INDEMNIFICATION; OTHER CLAIMS

84.   Settling Defendants agree to indemnify, save, and hold harmless U.S. EPA and/or its representatives from any and all claims or causes of action arising from acts or omissions of Settling Defendants and/or their representatives in carrying out the activities pursuant to this Consent Decree. U.S. EPA shall notify Settling Defendants of any such claim or actions promptly after receipt of notice that such a claim or action is anticipated or has been filed. The indemnification and hold harmless agreement between the Settling Defendants and the U.S. EPA shall not apply to claims or causes of action for any injuries or damages to persons or property arising out of actions that the Settling Defendants are directed to take or refrain from taking by the RPM or the OSC, to the extent that the actions directed by the RPM or the OSC are not contemplated in or are materially different from the Work required in the SOW, and prior to performing the actions directed by the RPM or the OSC, the Settling Defendants advise the RPM or the OSC that such actions present an unreasonable risk or injury to persons or property.

85.   U.S. EPA is not to be construed as a party to, and does not assume any liability for, any contract entered into by Settling Defendants in carrying

out the activities pursuant to this Consent Decree. The proper completion of the Work under this Consent Decree is solely the responsibility of Settling Defendants.

86.   Settling Defendants waive their rights to assert any claims against the Hazardous Substances Trust Fund under CERCLA that are related to any past costs incurred in the Work performed pursuant to this Consent Decree, and nothing in this Consent Decree shall be construed as U.S. EPA's preauthorization of a claim against the Hazardous Substance Superfund.

XXI.   INSURANCE/FINANCIAL RESPONSIBILITY

87.   Prior to commencing any on-site work, Settling Defendants, or their Contractors and Subcontractors, together shall secure, and shall maintain for the duration of this Consent Decree, automobile liability insurance, including bodily injury liability and property damage liability with a minimum of $1 million for each person and each occurrence; and comprehensive general liability insurance, which includes, but is not limited to, coverage for contractual liability, property damage, and bodily injury with coverage of $5 million combined single limit. The United States and the U.S. EPA shall be named as additional insureds. Prior to commencement of the Work at the Site, Settling Defendants shall provide U.S. EPA with a certificate of insurance and a copy of the insurance policy for U.S. EPA's approval.

88.   In the event that Settling Defendants or their Contractors or Subcontractors are unable through their best efforts to obtain some or all of the comprehensive general liability insurance specified in Paragraph 87 of this Section, or can only obtain such insurance at unreasonable costs, they shall send U.S. EPA written notice of their inability to obtain such insurance. The notice shall identify which kinds of insurance are unavailable, describe Settling Defendants' efforts to obtain such insurance, and summarize the key terms, including the cost, of any insurance that the Settling Defendants claim to be available only at unreasonable rates. If U.S. EPA determines that Settling Defendants did exercise their best efforts to obtain the required coverage and that such coverage was not obtainable or was only available at unreasonable rates, U.S. EPA and the Settling Defendants may mutually agree on reasonable alternative coverage, including self-insurance.

XXII.   NOTICES

89.   Whenever, under the terms of this Consent Decree, notice is required to be given, a report or other document is required to be forwarded by one party to another, or service of any papers or process is necessitated by the dispute resolution provisions of Section XV hereof, such correspondence shall be directed to the following offices or individuals at the addresses specified below: [Addresses omitted].

*   *   *   *   *

XXIII.   CONSISTENCY WITH NATIONAL CONTINGENCY PLAN

90.   The United States agrees that the Work, if properly performed as set forth in Sections VI and VII hereof, is consistent with the provisions of the National Contingency Plan promulgated at 40 C.F.R. Pat 300, pursuant to 42 U.S.C. § 9605.

XXIV.   RESPONSE AUTHORITY

91.   Nothing in this Consent Decree shall be deemed to limit the response authority of the United States under §§ 104 and 106 of CERCLA, 42 U.S.C. §§ 9604 and 9606.

XXV.   COMMUNITY RELATIONS

92.   Settling Defendants shall cooperate with U.S. EPA in providing information to the public, regarding the progress of remedial design and remedial action at the Site. As requested by U.S. EPA, Settling Defendants shall participate in the preparation of all appropriate information disseminated to the public and in any public meeting which may be held or sponsored by U.S. EPA to explain activities at or concerning the Work to be performed or under way at the Site.

XXVI.   EFFECTIVE AND TERMINATION DATES

93.   This Consent Decree shall be effective upon the date of its entry by the Court.

94.   Certification of Completion of Remedial Action

a.   Application. When the Settling Defendants believe that the demonstration of compliance with cleanup and performance standards has been made and that the operation of remedial Work required under Section VII above has been completed in accordance with this Consent Decree, they shall submit to the United States a Notification of Completion of Remedial Action and a final report that summarizes the work done, and modification made to the SOW or Work Plan(s) thereunder relating to the cleanup standards, and data demonstrating that the cleanup standards have been achieved. The report shall include or reference any supporting documentation.

b.   Certification. Upon receipt of the Notice of Completion of Remedial Action, U.S. EPA shall review the final report and any other supporting documentation and the remedial actions taken. U.S. EPA shall issue a Certification of Completion of Remedial Action upon a determination that Settling Defendants have demonstrated compliance with cleanup and performance standards as required by the RODs and the SOW, that operation of the remedial Work in accordance with the terms of this Consent Decree has been completed, and that no further corrective action is required. Any negative determination on the part of U.S. EPA shall set forth the manner in which the work has not been satisfactorily completed. Settling Defendants shall thereafter have a reasonable opportunity to respond and correct any deficiencies in performance. Upon such a demonstration by the Settling Defendants, the Certificate of Completion shall not be unreasonably withheld or delayed.

95.   Termination. Upon the filing of U.S. EPA's Certification of Completion pursuant to the preceding Paragraph, and a showing that the other terms of this Consent Decree, including payment of all costs and stipulated penalties due hereunder, have been complied with, this Consent Decree shall be terminated upon motion of either party. However, in consideration of the mutual promises, covenants, and undertakings set forth in this Decree, the Settling Defendants agree that as between the parties, the obligations, rights, and authorities under, and the provisions of, the terms of this Decree shall survive the termination of the Consent Decree and shall be enforceable by the United States, by re-institution of this action or by institution of a new action.

ENTERED this _____ day of _____, 19_____.

_____

U.S. District Judge

[Signatures omitted.]

LIST OF APPENDICES

APPENDIX A.   Record of Decision for Source Removal Operable Unit
APPENDIX B.   Record of Decision for Final Remedial Design and Remedial Action
APPENDIX C.   Statement of Work
APPENDIX D.   List of Settling Defendants
APPENDIX E.   List of Settling *De Minimis* Defendants
APPENDIX F.   List of Volumetric PRP Contributions and Amounts to Be Paid by Settling *De Minimis* Defendants
APPENDIX G.   Map of Site
APPENDIX H.   RD/RA Work Plan
APPENDIX I.   Unilateral Section 106 Source Removal Operable Unit Administrative Order

SETTLEMENTS UNDER STATE LAWS

§ 24.8   Ohio's Statutory Scheme

State mechanisms for settlement of hazardous substance disputes are similar to those used by the federal government. **Sections 24.8** through **24.12** describe representative state schemes.

The Ohio Environmental Protection Agency (Ohio EPA) is required by statute to take "appropriate" action to clean up a hazardous waste site whenever the agency determines that the site constitutes a substantial threat to public safety or is contributing or threatening to contribute to air, water, or soil contamination.[32] This action must be taken not only regarding present hazardous waste facilities, but also regarding any location where hazardous waste was treated, stored, or disposed. The specific actions that the agency is authorized to take include issuing administrative orders, requesting the attorney general to bring actions for injunctive relief and civil penalties, and requesting the attorney general to bring criminal charges against a violator. Once the agency initiates or proposes action, it commonly negotiates with the party against whom the action is directed. The results of this negotiation are consent decrees, consent orders, or plea agreements.

Administrative Orders

The Ohio EPA has the power to issue administrative enforcement orders to force cleanup of a hazardous waste site. Specifically, the statute authorizes the agency to issue orders "directing [any person] to abate violation or to prevent any threatened violation" of the hazardous waste laws.[33] The Ohio EPA is required to specify a reasonable time for compliance with such orders, but it can also issue emergency orders, without prior notice, that require immediate compliance.[34] No emergency order may remain in effect for more than 120 days, however, and the violator must be given a hearing "as soon as possible" upon application to the agency, but not later than 30 days after such application.[35]

The procedural rules promulgated by Ohio EPA with regard to enforcement orders require the agency to issue a proposed order before issuing a final order.[36] There is an exception to this requirement if the statutes specifically give a violator the right to appeal to the Ohio Environmental Board of Review and the right to a hearing on such appeal.[37] The rules also require the agency to give public notice of all actions.[38] The foregoing rules are not applicable to emergency orders, however, to the extent they conflict with the procedures applicable to such orders.[39]

---

[32] Ohio Rev. Code Ann. § 3734.20(B) (Baldwin 1989).

[33] Id. § 3734.13(A).

[34] Id. § 3734.13(B).

[35] Id.

[36] Ohio Admin. Code § 3745-47-05(A) (1988).

[37] Id. § 3745-47-05(E).

[38] Id. § 3745-47-07.

[39] Id. § 3745-47-29(A).

If an administrative order of the agency is not complied with, the agency can request that the attorney general bring civil or criminal actions to enforce the order.[40] The Ohio EPA rules require that this request be made when there is "cause to believe" that administrative remedies have been or appear likely to be ineffective.[41] In the alternative, the agency can clean up a site itself.[42] Before the agency undertakes cleanup, it is required to attempt to reach an agreement with the site owner, specifying the measures to be performed and providing for reimbursement of any cleanup costs incurred by the agency.[43] These costs become a lien against the cleaned property and the agency can direct that the attorney general institute an action to recover them.[44]

Injunctive Relief and Civil and Criminal Penalties

The Ohio EPA is authorized to bring actions for both injunctive relief and civil penalties against violators of the hazardous waste laws, and the Ohio statutes give precedence to these actions over all other cases.[45] In the case of injunctive relief, the agency can require that the attorney general bring an action against any person who "has violated, is violating or is threatening to violate" the hazardous waste laws.[46] In the case of civil penalties, the agency can "request" that the attorney general bring an action.[47] In either case, the attorney general has no independent power to bring the action without an EPA request.[48]

The Ohio Courts of Common Pleas are required to grant injunctive relief upon a showing of a violation or threatened violation, but they are not required to impose civil penalties.[49] If imposed for hazardous waste violations, these penalties, which can be as much as $25,000 per day of violation, are paid into the hazardous waste cleanup fund.[50]

The Ohio EPA can also require that the attorney general criminally "prosecute to termination" any person violating the Ohio hazardous waste

---

[40] Ohio Rev. Code Ann. §§ 3734.10, 3734.13(C) (Baldwin 1989).

[41] Ohio Admin. Code § 3745-49-04 (1988).

[42] Ohio Rev. Code Ann. § 3734.20(B) (Baldwin 1989).

[43] *Id.* § 3734.22.

[44] *Id.* § 3734.20(B).

[45] *Id.* §§ 3734.10, 3734.13(C).

[46] *Id.* § 3734.10.

[47] *Id.* § 3734.13(C).

[48] Holcomb v. Schlicter, 34 Ohio App. 3d 161, 517 N.E.2d 1001 (1986); Ohio *ex rel.* Brown v. Rockside Reclamation, 47 Ohio St. 2d 76, 351 N.E.2d 448 (1976).

[49] Ohio Rev. Code Ann. §§ 3734.10, 3734.13(C) (Baldwin 1989).

[50] *Id.* §§ 3734.13(C), 3734.13(E).

laws.[51] Penalties of up to four years' imprisonment and $25,000 per day of violation are provided.[52]

Findings and Orders on Consent

The Ohio EPA commonly negotiates agreements for hazardous waste cleanups. One negotiated agreement used by Ohio EPA is the *administrative consent order*. This document, called Findings and Orders, is similar to the consent decree, discussed below, except that it is an administrative order and not a judicial judgment. It is therefore treated and enforced as an administrative order.

One Ohio court has expressly approved the use of administrative consent orders in the environmental context.[53] The court concluded that the absence of the word "consent" in the section of Ohio's air pollution statutes that authorized the agency to issue enforcement orders was "not of such legal gravity that an entry of consent is forbidden."[54] The court stated that it would be "too confining" to prohibit consent orders[55] and noted that by issuing a consent order the agency could accomplish within a reasonable time what the violator would have eventually been required to do after much litigation.[56]

The Ohio EPA has reported that between January 1988 and August 1990, it issued 55 consent Findings and Orders for violations of Ohio's hazardous waste laws, as compared with 23 unilateral Findings and Orders. An example of a recent consent Findings and Orders is found in § 24.9.

The Consent Decree

Another type of agreement, the *consent decree,* sometimes referred to as a consent order, is used when a court action has been filed by the agency against a violator. This decree is essentially a contract between the parties but is entered and enforced as a judgment by the court.[57] The parties agree

---

[51] *Id.* § 3734.10.

[52] *Id.* § 3734.99.

[53] Broadway Christian Church v. Williams, 59 Ohio App. 2d 243, 394 N.E.2d 330 (1978).

[54] *Id.* at 246.

[55] *Id.* at 247.

[56] *Id.* at 249.

[57] Ohio State Medical Bd. v. Zwick, 59 Ohio App. 2d 133, 139, 392 N.E.2d 1276 (1978) (citing 49 C.J.S. *Judgments* §§ 173, 178 (1947); *see also* Gilbraith v. Hixson, 32 Ohio St. 3d 127, 129, 512 N.E.2d 956, 959 (1987).

on the terms of the decree, and the court has no power to supply terms not previously agreed to by the parties.[58]

In general, a court has a duty to enter a consent decree as a judgment unless it determines that one or both of the parties are not capable of binding themselves by consent or have not consented to the decree, that the court lacks jurisdiction, or that the decree is illegal.[59] In addition, some courts have held that a court must inquire whether the terms of the decree are fair and adequate, whether the decree is reasonable, and whether the public interest is adequately protected.[60]

According to the Ohio EPA, 32 actions brought by the Ohio Attorney General between January 1988 and August 1990 were settled by consent decrees. An example of a recent Ohio state court consent decree is found in § 24.10.

The Plea Agreement

The third negotiated agreement the Ohio EPA can use is the plea agreement. Once criminal charges have been brought by the attorney general, the plea agreement often can be used as leverage to negotiate the cleanup of hazardous waste sites.

§ 24.9   —Sample: Ohio Findings and Order

Issue Date   January 23, 1990
Effective Date   January 23, 1990

BEFORE THE
OHIO ENVIRONMENTAL PROTECTION AGENCY

In the Matter of:

C CORPORATION
A Avenue
Cleveland, Ohio 44105
       Respondent

*Director's Final
Findings and Orders*

---

[58] 49 C.J.S. *Judgments* § 173 (1947).

[59] *Id.* § 174; *see generally* Note, *The Consent Judgment as an Instrument of Compromise,* 72 Harv. L. Rev. 1314, 1316 (1959).

[60] *See, e.g.,* United States v. Rohm & Haas Co., 721 F. Supp. 666, 680 (D.N.J. 1989), United States v. Seymour Recycling Corp., 554 F. Supp. 1334, 1337 (S.D. Ind. 1982); United States v. Katchikan Pulp Co., 430 F. Supp. 83, 86 (D. Alaska 1977).

PREAMBLE

It is hereby agreed by and among the parties hereto as follows:

I. JURISDICTION

These Director's Final Findings and Orders (Orders) are issued to the C Corporation (Respondent) pursuant to the authority vested in the Director of the Ohio Environmental Protection Agency (Ohio EPA) under §§ 3734.13 and 3745.01 of the Ohio Revised Code (ORC).

II. PARTIES

These Orders shall apply to and be binding upon the Respondent and successors in interest.

III. DEFINITIONS

Unless otherwise stated, all terms used in these Orders shall have the same meaning as used in Chapter 3734. of the Ohio Revised Code and the regulations promulgated thereunder.

IV. FINDINGS OF FACT

The Director of the Ohio EPA has determined the following findings of fact:

1. The Respondent owns and operates a manufacturing facility located at A Avenue, Cuyahoga County, Cleveland, Ohio (Facility) and was licensed to do business in the state in 1972.
2. The Respondent is a *person* as defined in §§ 1.59 and 3734.01 of the ORC and rule 3745-50-10 of the Ohio Administrative Code (OAC).
3. Rule 3745-51-06 of the OAC provides that facilities that store recyclable materials before they are recycled are regulated under all applicable provisions of Chapters 3745-54, 3745-55, 3745-65 and 3745-66, and rules 3745-50-44, 3745-56-20 to 3745-56-59 and 3745-67-20 to 3745-67-57 of the OAC. The recycling process itself is exempt from regulation.
4. The Respondent stored *recyclable materials* from off-site facilities, as that term is defined in rule 3745-51-06(A)(1) of the OAC, at the Facility before they were recycled.
5. By letters dated September 18 and November 12, 1986, Ohio EPA informed the Respondent that it was required to submit a Part A of the hazardous waste facility installation and operation permit application by June 30, 1986; for the storage of spent chromic acid from off-site facilities prior to reclamation of the spent chromic acid. In addition, Ohio EPA informed the Respondent that it was subject to all applicable requirements contained in Chapters 3745-65 and 3745-66, and rules 3745-67-20 to 3745-67-57 of the OAC at the Facility.

6. On November 10, 1986, the Respondent submitted Part A of the hazardous waste facility installation and operation permit (permit) application for the Facility to Ohio EPA. The application listed the storage and treatment of hazardous wastes in tanks and storage of hazardous wastes in containers, as hazardous waste management activities conducted at the Facility.

7. The Respondent generates *hazardous waste* identified and listed under Chapter 3734. of the ORC and the regulations adopted thereunder at the Facility as that term is defined by section 3734.01 of the ORC and rule 3745-51-03 of the OAC.

8. Rule 3734-52-34 of the OAC provides that a hazardous waste generator may accumulate hazardous waste on-site without a hazardous waste installation and operation permit, provided that: the waste is placed in containers and the generator complies with the container use and management requirements of rules 3745-66-70 through 3745-66-77 of the OAC; the date upon which each period of accumulation begins is clearly marked on each container and each container is labelled or marked clearly with the words "Hazardous Waste" as required by rule 3745-52-34 of the OAC; and the generator complies with the requirements concerning Preparedness and Prevention and Contingency Plan and Emergency Procedures in Chapter 3745-65 of the OAC and with the personnel training requirements set forth in rule 3745-65-16 of the OAC.

9. On January 27, 1989, Ohio EPA inspected the Facility and determined that the Respondent:

    (a) failed to ensure that Facility personnel successfully completed a program of classroom instruction, or on-the-job training, that teaches them to perform their duties in a way that ensures the Facility's compliance with the hazardous waste regulations, in violation of rule 3745-65-16 of the OAC;

    (b) failed to maintain documents and records at the Facility which include the job titles and written job descriptions for each position at the Facility related to hazardous waste management, written descriptions of the type and amount of training that will be given to each person filling a position related to the hazardous waste management, and records that document that the required training has been given, in violation of rule 3745-65-16 of the OAC;

    (c) failed to maintain aisle space at the Facility adequate to allow the unobstructed movement of personnel, fire protection equipment, spill control equipment, and decontamination equipment, in violation of rule 3745-65-35 of the OAC;

    (d) failed to keep a written waste analysis plan at the Facility which describes the procedures to be implemented in order to obtain detailed chemical and physical analyses of a representative samples of the wastes, in violation of rule 3745-65-13 of the OAC;

    (e) failed to immediately amend the contingency plan for the Facility when the list of emergency coordinators changed, in violation of rule 3745-65-54 of the OAC;

    (f)   failed to keep a written operating record at the Facility, in violation of rule 3745-65-73 of the OAC;

    (g)   failed to prepare and submit a facility annual hazardous waste report to the Director of Ohio EPA by March 1, 1988, in violation of rule 3745-65-75 of the OAC;

    (h)   failed to maintain a written closure plan at the Facility, in violation of rule 3745-66-12 of the OAC; and

    (i)   failed to keep a container holding hazardous waste at the Facility closed during storage, in violation of rule 3745-66-73 of the OAC.

10.   By a letter dated February 7, 1989, Ohio EPA notified the Respondent of the violations discovered during the January 27, 1989, inspection and directed the Respondent to demonstrate that the violations occurring at the Facility had been abated.

11.   By letter dated April 19, 1989, Ohio EPA informed the Respondent that Ohio EPA had not received the documentation that violations cited in the February 7, 1989, Ohio EPA letter had been abated.

12.   In a letter received by Ohio EPA on April 24, 1989, the Respondent acknowledged the receipt of Ohio EPA's April 19, 1989, letter; however, the Respondent did not demonstrate that the violations found at the Facility had been abated.

13.   By letter dated April 27, 1989, the Respondent responded to the February 7, 1989, Ohio EPA notice of violation letter by stating that:

    (a)   a formal training program would begin the week of May 15, 1989, at which time training documentation would be updated, as required by rule 3745-65-16(A)(B) and (C) of the OAC;

    (b)   analyses were being maintained for all incoming chromic acid solutions received for recycling and returned to the customer and that because all materials received are similar in nature the Respondent understood that a written waste analysis plan is not required by rule 3745-65-13 of the OAC;

    (c)   adequate aisle space would be maintained around drums containing hazardous wastes at the Facility, as required by rule 3745-65-35 of the OAC;

    (d)   the contingency plan for the Facility had been amended to reflect the change in the emergency coordinators, as required by rule 3745-65-54(D) of the OAC;

    (e)   a description of the quantity and treatment date of recyclable materials and documentation concerning the return of recyclable material to the generator was being maintained at the Facility, as required by rule 3745-65-73 of the OAC;

    (f)   the annual treatment, storage, and disposal operating report for 1987 for the Facility was submitted on April 27, 1989, as required by rule 3745-65-75 of the OAC;

    (g)   all hazardous wastes would be stored in closed containers at the Facility, as required by rule 3745-66-73 of the OAC; and

    (h)   because their reclamation process uses the same equipment as their usual operations, a closure plan would only include changing the Respondent's status from a hazardous waste storage facility to a hazardous waste generator.

14. By letter dated May 9, 1989 Ohio EPA requested that the Respondent document the abatement of the following violations found during the January 7, 1989 inspection:

   (a) documentation of personnel training, as required by rule 3745-65-16 of the OAC;

   (b) a written waste analysis plan, as required by rule 3745-65-13 of the OAC;

   (c) a written operating record for 1989, as required by rule 3745-65-73 of the OAC; and

   (d) a written closure plan for the hazardous waste storage units at the Facility, as required by rule 3745-66-12 of the OAC.

15. By letter dated May 11, 1989, the Respondent submitted facility annual hazardous waste reports for the years ending on December 31, 1987, and December 31, 1988, and a generator annual hazardous waste report for the year ending on December 31, 1988, in accordance with rules 3745-65-75 and 3745-52-41 of the OAC.

16. By letter dated May 31, 1989, the Respondent submitted a waste analysis plan for the Facility. The Respondent stated that personnel training for Facility personnel had been postponed until mid-June and that the Respondent did not believe that a closure plan for the Facility was required. In addition, the Respondent stated that no off-site hazardous waste was received for storage at the Facility during the 1989 calendar year.

17. Rule 3745-66-12(D) of the OAC provides that the owner or operator of a hazardous waste facility shall submit a written closure plan for the facility to the Director of Ohio EPA at least 45 days prior to the date on which the owner or operator expects to begin final closure of a facility with tanks or container storage. The date when the owner or operator expects to begin closure must be either within 30 days after the date on which any hazardous waste management unit receives the known final volume of hazardous wastes, or if there is a reasonable possibility that the hazardous waste management unit will receive additional hazardous wastes, no later than one year after the date on which the unit received the most recent volume of hazardous waste.

18. The Respondent is not in compliance with the financial requirements for owners or operators of hazardous waste facilities. Specifically, the Respondent: does not have a detailed written estimate of the cost of closing the Facility in accordance with the applicable closure requirements in rules 3745-66-10 through 3745-66-20 of the OAC as required by rules 3745-66-42 and 3745-66-43 of the OAC; has not established financial assurance for closure of the Facility as required by rules 3745-66-43 and 3745-66-45 of the OAC; and has not demonstrated financial responsibility for bodily injury and property damage to third parties caused by sudden and non-sudden accidental occurrences

arising from the operations of the Facility as required by rule 3745-66-47 of the OAC.

19. By a letter dated June 1, 1989, Ohio EPA directed the Respondent to comply with the financial assurance requirements in rules 3745-66-42 through 3745-66-48 of the OAC.

20. By letter dated August 11, 1989, Ohio EPA informed the Respondent of the following violations of the state's hazardous waste laws that remained unabated:

    (a) Ohio EPA had not received documentation demonstrating that the Respondent had provided personnel training at the Facility, as required by rule 375-65-16 of the OAC;

    (b) the written waste analysis plan for the Facility submitted by the Respondent did not meet the requirements of rule 3745-65-13 of the OAC;

    (c) the Respondent did not have a closure plan for the Facility, as required by rule 3745-66-12 of the OAC, and

    (d) the Respondent had not submitted documentation that demonstrated that adequate aisle space was being maintained and that containers were maintained in a closed condition at the Facility, as required by rules 3745-65-35 and 3745-66-73 of the OAC.

21. During an October 10, 1989 meeting with Ohio EPA, the Respondent submitted documentation sufficient to demonstrate compliance with rules 3745-65-13, 3745-65-35, 3745-65-73 and 3745-66-73 of the OAC.

22. Ohio EPA finds that the Respondent has not submitted documentation sufficient to demonstrate compliance with the following requirements:

    (a) personnel training at the Facility, as required by rule 3745-65-16 of the OAC;

    (b) maintenance of documents and records at the Facility concerning personnel training, as required by rule 3745-65-16 of the OAC;

    (c) maintenance of a written closure plan for the Facility, as required by rule 3745-66-12 of the OAC; and

V. ORDERS

Respondent shall achieve compliance with Chapter 3734. of the ORC and the regulations promulgated thereunder according to the following compliance schedule:

1. Within 45 days from the effective date of these Orders, the Respondent shall submit for approval a closure plan for the Facility that conforms to the requirements of rules 3745-66-10 through 3745-66-20 of the OAC. The closure plan shall be submitted to the Director of Ohio EPA and the Ohio EPA, Northeast District Office.

2. Within 60 days from the effective date of these Orders, the Respondent shall submit to the Director of the Ohio EPA a closure cost estimate, documentation of financial assurance for closure, and liability

coverage for the Facility in accordance with rules 3745-66-42, 3745-66-43 and 3745-66-47 of the OAC.

3. Within 45 days from the effective date of these Orders, the Respondent shall submit to Ohio EPA Northeast District Office documentation sufficient to demonstrate compliance with rule 3745-65-16 of the OAC, concerning personnel training and documentation of personnel training.

4. Respondent shall give notice of these Orders to any successor in interest prior to transfer of interest and shall verify to the Director of Ohio EPA that such notice has been given. The Respondent shall be subject to this Order until released of the same by the Director of EPA, in writing, which shall be forwarded upon determination that the Respondent has otherwise fully complied with these Orders.

5. Within 30 days from the effective date of these Orders, the Respondent shall pay to Ohio EPA the amount of $28,380 in settlement of Ohio EPA's claims for civil penalties that may be assessed pursuant to Chapter 3734. of the ORC. Payment shall be made by tendering a certified check in the stated amount to counsel for the Director of Ohio EPA made payable to Treasurer, State of Ohio.

6. The Respondent shall comply with all the applicable requirements under Chapter 3734. of the ORC and the rules promulgated thereunder to the Ohio EPA.

VI. OTHER CLAIMS

Nothing in these Orders shall constitute or be construed as a release from any claim, cause of action, or demand in law or equity against any person, firm, partnership, or corporation not a signatory to these Orders for any liability arising out of or relating to the operation of Respondent's hazardous waste facility.

VII. OTHER APPLICABLE LAWS

All actions required to be taken pursuant to these Orders shall be undertaken in accordance with the requirements of all applicable local, state, and federal laws and regulations. Nothing in these Orders shall be construed as waiving or compromising in any way the applicability and enforcement of any other statutes or regulations applicable to Respondent's operation of its hazardous waste facility. The Ohio EPA reserves all rights and privileges except as specified herein.

VIII. NOTICE

All documents demonstrating compliance with these Orders, and other documents required under these Orders to be submitted to the Ohio EPA, shall be addressed to: [Addresses omitted] as specified in these Orders or to such persons and addresses as may be otherwise specified in writing by the Ohio EPA.

IX. RESERVATION OF RIGHTS

Nothing contained herein shall be construed to prevent Ohio EPA from seeking legal or equitable relief to enforce the terms of these Orders or from taking other administrative, legal, or equitable action as deemed appropriate and necessary, including penalties against the Respondent for noncompliance with these Orders. Nothing contained herein shall be construed to prevent the Ohio EPA from exercising its lawful authority to require the Respondent to perform additional activities pursuant to Chapter 3734. of the Ohio Revised Code or any other applicable law in the future. Nothing herein shall restrict the right of the Respondent to raise any administrative, legal, or equitable claim of defense with respect to such further actions that the Ohio EPA may seek to require of the Respondent. Nothing in these Orders shall be construed to limit the authority of the Ohio EPA to seek relief for violations not addressed in these Orders.

X. SIGNATORIES

Each undersigned representative of a signatory to these Orders certifies that he or she is fully authorized to enter into these Orders and to legally bind such signatory to this document.

IT IS SO ORDERED:

_____   January 23, 1990
Richard L. Shank Ph.D.   Date
Director

XI. WAIVER

Without admission of fact, violation, or liability, and in lieu of further enforcement action by Ohio EPA for only the matters addressed in these Findings and Orders, the Respondent agrees that these Findings and Orders are lawful and reasonable, that the times provided for compliance herein are reasonable and that it agrees to comply with these Orders. Compliance with these Orders shall be a full accord and satisfaction for the Respondent's liability for the violations cited herein.

The Respondent hereby waives the right to appeal the issuance, terms, and service of these Orders, and it hereby waives any and all rights it might have to seek judicial review of said Findings and Orders either in law or equity.

In the event that these Findings and Orders are appealed by any other party to the Environmental Board of Review or any court, nothing in these Findings and Orders shall preclude the Respondent from seeking to intervene in such appeal.

IT IS SO AGREED:

[Signatures omitted.]

§ 24.10 —Sample: Ohio State Court
Consent Decree

IN THE COURT OF COMMON PLEAS
CUYAHOGA COUNTY, OHIO

STATE OF OHIO, ex rel. ATTORNEY GENERAL OF OHIO Plaintiff, vs. B, INC., Defendants	CASE NO. 126971 JUDGE JAMES J. McMONAGLE *CONSENT ORDER BETWEEN THE STATE OF OHIO AND T., R., J., AND B.A.*

The Plaintiff, State of Ohio, ex rel. Attorney General of Ohio (State or Plaintiff), filed the amended Complaint in this action on March 3, 1989 against Defendants B, Inc., T., R., J., and B.A. to enforce the State of Ohio's hazardous waste laws and water pollution laws and the rules promulgated thereunder concerning the Defendants' waste handling and disposal practices at the B, Inc. facility located in Cleveland, Cuyahoga County, Ohio (hereinafter the facility). The case against B, Inc., was resolved through a default judgment. Plaintiff and Defendants T., R., J., and B.A. consent to entry of this Order:

THEREFORE, without trial or admission of any issue of law or of fact, and upon the consent of the Plaintiff and Defendants T., R., J., and B.A. hereto, it is hereby ORDERED, ADJUDGED and DECREED as follows:

I. PERSONS BOUND

The provisions of this Consent Order shall apply to and be binding upon Defendants T., R., J., and B.A. (hereinafter defendants). These defendants shall provide a copy of this Consent Order to each consultant or contractor they employ to perform the work referenced herein.

II. SATISFACTION OF LAWSUIT

Compliance with the terms of this Consent Order shall constitute full satisfaction of any civil liability by Defendants for all claims against said Defendants alleged in the Complaint. Nothing in this Consent Order shall be construed so as to limit the authority of the State of Ohio to seek relief for claims or conditions not alleged in the Complaint, including violations or conditions that occur after the filing of the Complaint. Nothing in this Consent Order shall be construed so as to limit the authority of the State of Ohio to undertake any action against any person, including Defendants to eliminate or mitigate conditions arising after the date hereof that may present a threat to the public health, welfare, or the environment.

III. JURISDICTION AND VENUE

The Court has both personal and subject matter jurisdiction over Defendants. The Complaint states a claim upon which relief can be granted against Defendants under Chapters 3734 and 6111 of the Ohio Revised Code and the rules promulgated thereunder. Venue is proper in this court.

IV. CLOSURE PLAN

Defendants shall fully implement the closure plan attached hereto as Attachment 1, which is incorporated herein as if fully restated. Said Defendants are enjoined and ordered to fully implement the closure plan as approved by the Ohio EPA and comply with the rules contained in O.A.C. 3745-65-14, 3745-66-10, 3745-66-11, 3745-66-12, 3745-66-14, 3745-66-15, 3745-66-16 and (without admission by any Defendant of legal status as a "generator") the generator requirements of R.C. Chapter 3734 and O.A.C. 3745-52 et seq.

In addition, Defendant T. shall determine the whereabouts of the fiberglass tank referenced in Item 2 of the closure plan that has been removed from the facility, and Defendants T., R., and J. shall demonstrate decontamination of such tank by the methods provided in the approved closure plan. As part of the closure, Defendants shall specifically provide for closure of the additional sump unit as provided by Condition 4 of the approved closure plan.

Defendants shall complete waste removal from the facility as soon as possible but no later than 90 days after entry of this consent order. Defendants shall complete closure of the facility within 150 days after entry of this order and certify closure pursuant to O.A.C. 3745-66-15 no later than 180 days after the entry of this consent order.

Should implementation of the closure plan after the entry of this order reveal that amendments to the closure plan are required because of subsequent discoveries of contamination at the facility, Defendants shall amend the closure plan within the time frames set forth in O.A.C. 3745-66-12(C)(2). Defendants shall comply with the amended closure plan as approved by Ohio EPA. Such amended closure plan shall be attached to this consent order as attachment 2 and incorporated herein as if fully restated. Defendants shall comply with the amended closure plan.

V. PERMANENT INJUNCTION

Except as provided in Section 4 above, Defendants are permanently enjoined to comply with O.R.C. Chapter 6111 and the rules adopted thereunder and O.R.C. Chapter 3734 and the rules adopted thereunder.

VI. CIVIL PENALTY

It is hereby ordered that Defendants shall each pay a civil penalty of $10,000 each. This civil penalty shall be paid by checks made payable to

Treasurer, State of Ohio, which checks shall be delivered by mail, or otherwise, to Treasurer or his successor in office at his office at the Ohio Attorney General's Office, Environmental Enforcement Section, 30 East Broad Street, 25th Floor, Columbus, Ohio 43266-0410, within 30 days of the Court's entry of this order. This penalty shall be paid into the hazardous waste clean-up fund created by R.C. 3734.28.

Failure to pay the penalty in a timely fashion will result in the imposition of statutory interest that begins to accrue at the time the payment becomes delinquent. Defendants shall pay the statutory interest accrued by the next scheduled payment date for civil penalty.

VIII.   RETENTION OF JURISDICTION

The Court will retain jurisdiction of this action for the purpose of overseeing that Defendants, subject to further order of the court, carry out the terms and conditions of this Consent Order and comply with O.R.C. Chapter 3734, and the rules adopted thereunder.

IX.   INSPECTIONS

Pursuant to O.R.C. 3734.07, Defendants are ordered to allow employees, representatives, and agents of the Ohio EPA, upon proper identification, to enter upon the facility at reasonable times, to inspect, investigate, take samples and pictures, and examine or copy records in order to determine compliance with the terms of this Consent Order and O.R.C. Chapter 3734. and the rules promulgated thereunder. Nothing in this Consent Order shall limit the rights of the Ohio EPA or U.S. EPA to conduct regular and routine inspections pursuant to statute or regulation at the B, Inc. facility.

X.   NOTICE

Any submission to the Ohio EPA as required by this Consent Order, unless otherwise indicated, shall be delivered to:

[Addresses omitted.]

XI.   COURT COSTS

Defendants shall pay the court costs of this action incurred to date.

XII.

For the purposes of effectuating the cleanup of the facility, the Defendants are jointly and severally liable. The remaining issues joined in this lawsuit shall be set for trial on February 6, 1990. Nothing herein shall be construed as a waiver of rights or defenses of parties involved in the remaining issues of this case.

[Signatures omitted.]

§ 24.11   Colorado's Statutory Scheme

The state of Colorado has been active in regulating both hazardous waste management and the cleanup of abandoned sites. The state does not have statutes and regulations dealing with both areas and specifically has no statutory counterpart to the federal CERCLA program. Colorado has been aggressively litigating seven CERCLA cases in federal court since 1983, but the state relies entirely on federal law for its authority to do so. A state fund does exist that is used to pay the state's 10 percent match on Superfund-financed cleanups,[61] but there are no state hazardous substance liability provisions similar to the federal liability provisions in CERCLA.

The Colorado General Assembly has established a state counterpart to the federal RCRA program.[62] Under the Colorado Hazardous Waste Act, the Colorado Department of Health is charged with "regulation of hazardous waste management."[63] The state regulations under the Act are virtually identical to the federal RCRA regulations, and the state program operates in lieu of the federal hazardous waste program.

The one area in which the state regulations go beyond the federal regulations concerns the siting of treatment, storage, or disposal facilities for hazardous waste.[64] For example, § 2.5.3 of the siting regulations provides:

> The geological and hydrological conditions of a site in which hazardous wastes are to be disposed shall be such that reasonable assurance is provided that such wastes are isolated within the designated disposal area of the site and away from natural environmental pathways that could expose the public for 1,000 years.[65]

Consent Decrees

Consent decrees have been used by Colorado to require hazardous waste cleanups primarily in the state CERCLA cases rather than the state RCRA

---

[61] Colo. Rev. Stat. § 25-16-104.6 (1988).

[62] Colorado Hazardous Waste Act, Colo. Rev. Stat. § 25-15-191 *et seq.* (1990).

[63] *Id.* § 25-15-301 (1).

[64] 6 Colo. Code Regs. § 1007-2 pt. 2 (1984).

[65] *Id.*

cases because the state has the authority to issue administrative orders in RCRA matters. Without such authority in its CERCLA cases, the state must rely on judicially enforceable consent decrees to resolve those cases.

In the past, the Colorado CERCLA consent decrees were patterned loosely on federal EPA models because the state was acting more or less independently of the EPA. The United States District Court for the District of Colorado has approved three state consent decrees under CERCLA.[66]

All of these consent decrees share certain features. For example, each incorporates a remedial action plan that describes the cleanup to be performed in great detail. In addition, each consent decree has provisions for: oversight of the cleanup by the state; modifying the consent decree should it ever become necessary; establishing a formal dispute resolution process before a special master; special state authority to respond to emergency situations; stipulated penalties for certain violations; payment of the state's past and future response costs and natural resource damages; and eventual termination of the consent decree following completion of the cleanup.

Administrative Consent Orders

The Colorado Department of Health has the power to issue administrative enforcement orders to require the cleanup of a hazardous waste site under the Colorado Hazardous Waste Act. Specifically, the statute provides:

> Whenever the department finds that any person is in violation of any permit, rule, regulation, or requirement of [the state hazardous waste management program], the department may issue an order requiring such person to comply with any such permit, rule, regulation, or requirement and may request the attorney general or bring suit for injunctive relief or for penalties.[67]

Thus, both injunctive relief and penalties can be requested by the state in appropriate cases.

In recent years, Colorado has issued administrative consent orders in three cases.[68] These consent orders all include findings of fact, conclusions of law, and orders on consent issued by the Department of Health and agreed to by the responsible party. With regard to specific provisions, the consent orders include detailed statements of the cleanup activity to

---

[66] Colorado v. Union Carbide Corp., No. 83-C-2384 (signed Feb. 23, 1987); Colorado v. Cotter Corp., No. 83-C-2389 (signed Apr. 4, 1988); and Colorado v. Gulf & W. Indus., Inc., No. 83-C-2387 (signed June 24, 1988).

[67] Colo. Rev. Stat. § 25-15-308(2)(1990).

[68] Colorado Dep't of Health v. Martin Marietta Corp., No. 86-CV-2034, (signed May 7, 1986); In re United States Dep't of Energy, Rocky Flats (Colorado) Site, CERCLA/RCRA-VIII-89- (filed Dec. 1989); and In re Syntex Chems., Inc., No. 88-08-12-01 (filed Aug. 12, 1988). A copy of the In re Syntex consent order is included in § **24.12**.

be performed by the responsible party, payments to the state, releases from liability, force majeure provisions, and many other provisions commonly found in federal consent orders. One interesting aspect to several of the state consent orders is that the state has allowed responsible parties to dispute some of its findings of fact or conclusions of law, so long as the responsible party agrees to perform the work specified in the order. Typically, these provisions are the result of very intense negotiations between the state and the responsible party, but they do allow the discussions to focus on remedial issues rather than liability issues. A sample Colorado administrative consent order appears in § **24.12**.

§ **24.12** —Sample: Administrative Consent Order

BEFORE THE HAZARDOUS MATERIALS AND
  WASTE MANAGEMENT DIVISION
DEPARTMENT OF HEALTH
STATE OF COLORADO
COMPLIANCE ORDER ON CONSENT NO. 88

IN THE MATTER OF S, INC. AND S CORPORATION

This Compliance Order on Consent (Consent Order) is being entered into by the Colorado Department of Health through the Hazardous Materials and Waste Management Division (the Department), S, Inc. and S Corporation (collectively, S) pursuant to the Department's authority under Colo. Rev. Stat. § 25-15-308 (1982 and 1987 Supp.). The Department and S may be referred to collectively as the Parties.

FINDINGS OF FACT

The Department makes the following findings of fact:

1. S, Inc. is a Delaware corporation authorized to do business in Colorado, with its principal place of business in Colorado located at Boulder, Colorado 80301.
2. S Corporation is incorporated in the Republic of Panama.
3. S, Inc. owns a chemical waste landfill located in Boulder (the Landfill). The Landfill was owned by S Corporation from 1965 to 1971. The Landfill is situated in a rural, agricultural area. The general location of the Landfill is depicted on Exhibit 1, attached hereto.
4. Between 1965 and 1971, S Corporation, and between 1971 and 1976 S, Inc. or S, Inc.'s predecessor, disposed of chemical manufacturing wastes and other debris in the Landfill in the area designated as the lower disposal area (LDA) and in the area designated as the upper disposal area

(UDA) on Exhibit 2, attached hereto. No materials have been placed in the Landfill since 1976.

5. At an unknown time or times, certain chemicals began leaching into the groundwater beneath and adjoining the Landfill trenches. The chemicals continue to leach from the trenches but remain on S, Inc.'s property.

6. Between 1980 and 1987, S conducted a voluntary remedial program, including installation of trenches, drains, and a sump from which collected leachate was removed. However, these remedial actions did not prevent wastes in the trenches from migrating in the groundwater inside S's property boundary.

7. Between 1980 and 1987, S also conducted an investigation of the Landfill, including the installation, sampling, and analysis of numerous monitoring wells and the performance of other geological and geophysical investigations. The Department and the Colorado Geological Survey have informally reviewed and commented on the investigation and the investigation reports. The results of the investigation as of July, 1987, are summarized in a report, incorporated herein by reference as Exhibit 4, prepared by IT Corporation and entitled "Phase II Remedial Investigation, S Landfill Site, Boulder (Phase II Report).

8. In December 1987, the Department and S, Inc. executed an interim Compliance Order on Consent No. 87-12-08-01 (the 1987 Order) to facilitate negotiation of a final remediation plan for the Landfill. The 1987 Order is attached hereto for convenience, as Exhibit 3.

9. Pursuant to paragraph 11 of the 1987 Order, S has implemented, as approved by the Department, a Waste Characterization Plan designed to determine the necessity for and feasibility of treatment and removal strategies for contaminated soils in and near the disposal trenches. The study results are reported in "Landfill Characterization Investigation Data Report" (July 1988), prepared by IT Corporation for S, Inc. (Landfill Characterization Report, incorporated herein by reference as Exhibit 5).

10. Pursuant to paragraph 10 of the 1987 Order, S implemented a Groundwater Control Program to halt the flow through groundwater of contaminant plumes associated with both the Upper and Lower Disposal Areas. According to data submitted through July, 1988, the Groundwater Control Program has succeeded in halting the spread of the contaminant plume associated with the Lower Disposal Area through the Shallow Benton and Lower Greenhorn Units, and has contained the contaminant plume associated with the Upper Disposal Area. The Groundwater Control Program has also reduced contaminant concentrations in these plumes.

11. Contaminants which have leaked and continue to leak from the trenches to surrounding soils and groundwater include chlorobenzene and toluene. S has used these compounds in its manufacturing processes for their solvent properties.

12. The Phase II Report states that spent solvents have been disposed at the Landfill.

13. S does not have a permit to interim status to dispose of hazardous wastes at the Landfill.

CONCLUSIONS OF LAW

The Department makes the following conclusions of law:

14. 6 CCR 1007-3, Section 261.31 includes the following spent solvents in its listing of hazardous wastes: chlorobenzene (F002) and toluene (F005).

15. 6 CCR 1007-3, Section 261.33 lists the following discarded commercial chemical products as hazardous wastes: chlorobenzene (U037) and toluene (U220).

16. Section 25-15-101(3.5), C.R.S. (1987 Supp.) defines *disposal* to include the "discharge . . . leaking, or placing of any hazardous waste into or on any land or water so that such hazardous waste or any constituent thereof may enter the environment or be emitted into the air or discharged into any waters, including groundwaters."

17. Section 25-15-308(1)(b), C.R.S. (1987 Supp), prohibits the on-site disposal of any hazardous waste without a permit or interim status.

18. The leaking from the Landfill of chlorobenzene, toluene and other substances identified in the Phase II Report since November 2, 1984, constitutes the disposal of hazardous waste without a permit or interim status, in violation of Section 25-15-308(1)(b), C.R.S. (1987 Supp.)

S's DENIAL OF CONCLUSIONS OF LAW

19. S and its affiliates deny the conclusions of law set forth in paragraphs 14 through 18. S and its affiliates deny that they individually or collectively are in violation of Section 25-15-308(1)(b) or any other state or federal laws or regulations with respect to the Landfill. S and its affiliates specifically deny that hazardous wastes listed in sections 261.31 or 261.33 have moved from the original disposal areas and affirmatively assert that any movement of materials from the original disposal areas does not require interim status or a permit and is not subject to any other requirements or authorities. S and its affiliates do not admit, accept, or acknowledge any liability or fault by virtue or S's entry into this Consent Order or performance of its terms.

S's CONSENT TO ORDER

20. Notwithstanding paragraph 19, S consents to the issuance of this Consent Order and agrees to abide by its terms and conditions. S also agrees not to challenge the Department's authority to bring, or the court's jurisdiction to hear, any civil action to enforce the terms of this Consent Order.

ORDER ON CONSENT

21. The remedial action at the Landfill shall be conducted in accordance with this paragraph 21., and all submittals required under this paragraph

shall likewise be consistent with this paragraph. The remedial action shall consist of two components: Landfill Excavation and Groundwater/ Non-Aqueous Phase Liquid (NAPL)/vadose zone Remediation System (Groundwater Remediation System or GRS). The Department or its designee shall oversee all remedial actions, and shall retain authority to enforce compliance with the requirements of this Consent Order and submittals required hereunder, subject to paragraph 41. The Department will utilize an On-Scene Coordinator to oversee Landfill Excavation activities.

Landfill Excavation

a. S shall excavate to their original dimensions the 16 original pits and trenches of the Upper and Lower Disposal Areas, as shown in Exhibit 1. S shall also excavate the disposed materials present above the original ground surface, but not in distinct pits or trenches, in Subareas B, E and H. Except for soil backfill material, all excavated material shall be manifested as hazardous waste and shall be transported to a permitted hazardous waste treatment or disposal facility for incineration or landfill disposal. *Soil backfill material* is defined to be material above the depth of first occurrence of contamination by disposed chemical materials, as determined by visual inspection. Soil backfill material may be set aside on site for replacement in the excavated areas. Such replacement may occur only as authorized by the Department's On-Scene Coordinator (OSC).

b. S shall also excavate for disposal or incineration at a permitted hazardous waste treatment or disposal facility materials in the bottom or sides of an excavation that are outside the boundaries of the original trench or pit when those materials are visually significantly contaminated with disposed chemical materials over a significant area. Material is "visually significantly contaminated with disposed chemical materials over a significant area" when it contains more contamination than a superficial layer, such as that which would occur solely within narrow bedding planes or joints. In determining whether material is visually significantly contaminated with disposed chemical materials over a significant area, the OSC shall consider that the purpose of this requirement is to remove any material that is so contaminated that it cannot be timely and effectively removed by the GRS.

c. Excavation of the Landfill shall proceed in accordance with the requirements and schedules contained in the Landfill Excavation Plan, attached hereto as Exhibit 6 and incorporated by reference. S desires to complete Landfill excavation by November 7, 1988. S's failure to excavate all materials described in subparagraphs 21.a. and 21.b. by November 7, 1988, shall not relieve it of its obligation to excavate such material for incineration or disposal at a permitted hazardous waste treatment or disposal facility. By October 12, 1988, S shall submit to the Department for its approval a contingency plan addressing alternative treatment/disposal options in the event Landfill excavation is not complete by November 7, 1988. The plan shall include:

(i)   an estimate of the amount of material, if any, that will remain to be excavated after November 7, 1988;

(ii)   a minimum of three alternative treatment/disposal options for the material identified in (i); and

(iii) a schedule for implementing each of the options described in (ii) that will ensure S will be able to implement one of the options by November 7, 1988, or as soon thereafter as practicable.

S shall follow each of the schedules established in the contingency plan until it has made final arrangements to implement the selected alternative, at which point it will follow the schedule for that alternative; provided that no alternative need be selected if excavation is completed prior to November 7, 1988.

Groundwater Remediation System

d.   S shall continue to operate the Groundwater Remediation System approved under the 1987 Order until Plume Remediation Levels established pursuant to subparagraph 21.j. are achieved. S shall submit any proposed modifications to the Groundwater Remediation System to the Department for its approval, except that normal maintenance, repair and replacement of equipment shall not require Departmental approval.

e.   S shall install and operate a compliance monitoring well network (Compliance Boundary) within its property. The Compliance Boundary shall consist of monitoring wells completed in the Shallow Benton, Lower Greenhorn Limestone, and Muddy Sandstone hydrogeologic units. The Shallow Benton and Muddy units monitoring wells will be located approximately as shown in Exhibit 7. The Lower Greenhorn monitoring well or wells will be installed and operated following an exploration program to the Lower Greenhorn Limestone. The objective of said exploration program is to optimize the location of the monitoring wells with respect to areas of increased permeability downgradient and in the direct path of the known contaminant plume. If there is hydrogeologic evidence that a separate pathway exists in the area, the number of monitoring wells will be increased appropriately. All complaince monitoring wells shall be completed and operable by December 30, 1988.

f.   The Groundwater Compliance Standards set forth below shall not be verifiably exceeded at the Compliance Boundary.

Compliance Standard Contaminant	mg/1
benzene	0.005
chlorobenzene	0.10
1,2-dichloroethane	0.005
toluene	2.0

The Groundwater Compliance Standards listed above are based on promulgated or proposed Maximum Contaminant Levels (MCLs) established by the U.S. EPA under the Safe Drinking Water Act. MCLs are the health protective standards that specify the allowable concentrations of contaminants in public drinking water supplies. Within 45 days of the effective date of this Order, S shall submit to the Department for its approval proposed Groundwater Compliance Standards for diethyl ether and tetrahydrofuran. The scientific data and techniques used to develop these standards will be similar to the methods used to develop MCLs. Within 150 days of the effective date of this Consent Order, S shall submit to the Department for its approval a contingency plan that shall be implemented if any Groundwater Compliance Standard is verifiably exceeded at a Compliance Boundary. If any Groundwater Compliance Standard is continuously verifiably exceeded for more than 60 days, S shall reassess the contingency plan and propose any necessary modifications for Departmental approval.

g. Monitoring of the Compliance Boundary wells will consist initially of one year of background monitoring on a quarterly basis for each of the 6 Compliance Standard Contaminants (THF, benzene, 1,2 dichloroethane, toluene, chlorobenzene, diethyl ether), general chemistry parameters specified in Exhibit 8, and U.S. EPA Hazardous Substance List for volatile organic compounds specified in Exhibit 9. In addition, water level and water temperature shall be recorded on a quarterly basis the first year. After the first year's background data have been obtained, the Compliance Boundary wells will be sampled and analyzed for these same parameters on a semi-annual basis during the spring runoff and the low groundwater level periods. If the Activation Levels at an Action Line are exceeded, quarterly monitoring of the Compliance Boundary wells will be instituted. Quarterly monitoring will continue until concentrations of contaminants at the Action Line are reduced to Action Line Deactivation Levels, as specified in the Action Line Plan. At that point, the Groundwater Remediation System may be turned off, and semi-annual monitoring of the Compliance Boundary wells will resume as described above.

h. Within 45 days of the effective date of this Consent Order, S shall submit to the Department for its approval an Action Line Plan for establishing Action Lines of monitoring wells for the Shallow Benton, Lower Greenhorn Limestone and Muddy Sandstone hydrogeologic units. Action Line wells for each hydrogeologic unit shall be located within the hydraulic capture zone of the associated Groundwater Remediation System. The Action Lines provide for the management of the groundwater plumes emanating from the LDA and UDA such that the Groundwater Compliance Standards will not be exceeded at the compliance boundary. The Action Line Plan shall provide for:

   (i)   number and location of the Action Line wells for each hydrogeologic unit;

   (ii)   the depths of completion and length of screen intervals on the Action Line wells;

   (iii)   quarterly monitoring of Action Line wells for the Compliance Standard Contaminants, general chemistry parameters (table 1), and water levels and water temperature;

   (iv)   Activation and Deactivation Levels for each Compliance Standard Contaminant which will ensure that the Groundwater Compliance Standards are not exceeded. The Activation and Deactivation Levels will be established using the RANDOM WALK SOLUTE TRANSPORT model, or other computer programs approved by the Department, in conjunction with an appropriate safety factor, to predict the concentrations in the Action Line wells which would not cause the Groundwater Compliance Standards to be exceeded at the compliance boundary;

   (v)   documentation of the methodology used to derive the Activation and Deactivation Levels;

   (vi)   a schedule for activating the Groundwater Remediation System when the Activation Levels have been verifiably exceeded;

   (vii) procedures for deactivating the Groundwater Remediation System when the Deactivation Levels have been achieved; and

   (viii) provisions for re-evaluation of Plume Remediation Levels in the event the Activation Levels are verifiably exceeded.

i.   S shall implement the approved schedule for activating the Groundwater Remediation System within two working days of receipt of the first validated analytical results indicating that the Activation Levels have been exceeded.

j.   Within 90 days of the effective date of this Consent Order, S shall submit to the Department for its approval a Plume Remediation plan for determining when the Groundwater Remediation Systems for the Shallow Benton, Lower Greenhorn, and Muddy Sandstone hydrogeologic units can be deactivated. The Plume Remediation plan shall provide:

   (i)   the number and location of Plume Remediation Level monitoring wells for each hydrogeologic unit;

   (ii)   the depths of completion and length of screen intervals on the Plume Remediation Level monitoring wells;

(iii) monitoring of Plume Remediation Level monitoring wells for the complaince standard contaminants, general chemistry parameters (Exhibit 8), water levels and water temperature;

(iv) procedures for addressing dry monitoring wells;

(v) Plume Remediation Levels to assure that the Groundwater Remediation System can be shut down without causing the Activation Levels to be exceeded. The Plume Remediation Levels will be established using the RANDOM WALK SOLUTE TRANSPORT model or other computer programs approved by the Department, in conjunction with an appropriate safety factor;

(vi) documentation of the methodology used to derive the Plume Remediation Levels;

(vii) a schedule for deactivating the Groundwater Remediation System after the Plume Remediation Levels have been reached in all Plume Remediation Level monitoring wells; and

(viii) provisions for long-term monitoring of the Action Line and Compliance Boundary wells for thirty years from completion of Landfill excavation, unless the Parties agree to another time period.

The Groundwater Remediation System may not be deactivated until the Plume Remediation Levels have not been exceeded at any Plume Remediation Level monitoring well for at least six months, or two consecutive sampling events, whichever is longer.

k. Within 120 days of the effective date of this Consent Order, S shall submit to the Department for its approval a plan for studying the impacts of the NAPL and vadose zone contaminants on the length of operation of the Groundwater Remediation System. The study will be conducted pursuant to the schedule included in the approved plan. If the results of the study indicate that the remaining NAPL or vadose zone contaminants would significantly extend the length of operation of the Groundwater Remediation System, S shall submit a plan for accelerated in situ remediation of the NAPL and/or vadose zone contaminants.

l. For purposes of this Order, a verified exceedance of an Action Line Activation Level or Groundwater Compliance Standard (applicable standard) at a monitoring well shall be defined as follows:

(i) The original sample results will be validated using laboratory analytical data validation procedures defined by the U.S. Environmental Protection Agency Technical Directive Document No. HQ-8410-01. Validated analytical results shall be provided to the Department within six weeks of collection.

(ii) If, after validation, the analytical results exceed the applicable standard, S shall immediately collect another sample from the well. Validated analytic results of the second sample shall be provided to the Department within three weeks of collection.

> (iii)   If the validated results of this second sample exceed the applicable standard, then the applicable standard will be considered to be verifiably exceeded.
>
> (iv)   If a compliance standard contaminant is not detected in a sample and the limit of detection is higher than the applicable standard, then the applicable standard shall not be considered to have been exceeded.

m.   All wells shall be constructed and monitored pursuant to procedures approved by the Department.

n.   Whenever the Department's approval is required pursuant to any paragraph of this Consent Order, the Parties shall attempt to resolve any differences informally. If they are unable to agree, either Party may submit the matter for dispute resolution pursuant to paragraph 41.

SCOPE AND EFFECT OF AGREEMENT

22.   The intent of the Parties in entering into this Consent Order is to protect public health and the environment by establishing procedures and standards for the final remediation of the Landfill, including the disposal trenches and contaminated groundwater and surrounding soils. Remedial actions taken pursuant to this Consent Order shall also be timely and cost-effective, to the extent such considerations are consistent with the preceding sentence.

23.   Upon the effective date of this Consent Order, the 1987 Order is terminated, and any requirements of the 1987 Order that have not yet been fulfilled are excused.

24.   The Parties' obligations under this Consent Order are limited to matters expressly stated in the Consent Order or in submissions required hereunder.

25.   a.   This Consent Order shall not constitute evidence in any proceeding (other than any dispute resolution proceeding pursuant to paragraph 41 or any proceeding to enforce this Consent Order), and shall in no event constitute an admission or adjudication with respect to any facts or conclusions set forth herein. Nor shall S's complaince with the requirements of this Consent Order, and specifically its compliance with the manifesting and financial assurance requirements, constitute such an admission or adjudication.

b.   The Department's approval of any submission, standard, or action under this Consent Order shall not constitute a defense to, nor excuse, any subsequent violation of any requirement of this Consent Order.

c.   Except as otherwise provided in this Consent Order, the Parties do not waive any claims, defenses or other rights either Party may have.

26.   Except as specifically provided in the following paragraph, upon the effective date of this Consent Order, the State of Colorado hereby releases

and covenants not to sue S regarding all matters arising out of con-tamination of the Landfill under any common law theory or state or federal statutory provision, including, but not limited to, the Resource Conservation and Recovery Act, P.L. No. 94-580, as from time to time amended; the Comprehensive Environmental Response, Compensation and Liability Act, P.L. No. 96-510, as from time to time amended in-cluding any claims by the State of Colorado for damages to natural re-sources; the Colorado Hazardous Waste Act, Section 25-15-101 to 313, C.R.S. (1982 and 1987 Supp.), as from time to time amended, and the Colorado Water Quality Act, Section 25-8-101 to 703, C.R.S. (1982 & 1987 Supp.).

27. The release and convenant not to sue described in the preceding para-graph shall not apply:

   a. to any liability S may have arising from conditions at the Landfill that are unknown to the Department as of the effective date of this Consent Order, if such conditions may pose an imminent and sub-stantial endangerment to human health or the environment;

   b. if the Department receives any new information, in whole or in part after the effective date of this Consent Order, which indicates that the remedial action required under this Consent Order is not pro-tective of human health and the environment;

   c. if S fails to conduct the remedial action required under this Consent Order;

   d. to any liability that may arise from S's negligence in performing the remedial action required under this Consent Order; or

   e. to any liability arising out of the transportation, handling, treatment, storage or disposal of materials removed from the Landfill and re-quired to be manifested as hazardous waste, including contami-nated groundwater, once those materials have been excavated, pumped, or otherwise removed from the Landfill.

28. Nothing in this Consent Order resolves any claims against S which may be asserted for damages to natural resources by or on behalf of the Depart-ment of Interior or other federal trustees. Nothing in this Consent Order resolves any claims, counter-claims or cross-claims against S which may be brought by any person other than the State of Colorado.

29. Upon the effective date of this Consent Order, S hereby releases and covenants not to sue the State of Colorado as to all common law or statutory claims or counter-claims arising out of the Landfill.

30. a. S shall obtain any permits or approvals necessary to conduct the remedial activities required by this Consent Order. S shall use its best efforts to obtain those permits or approvals in a timely manner. The Department shall use its best efforts, consistent with its legal authority, to assist S in obtaining such permits and approvals. If S is unable to obtain on a timely basis a necessary permit or other ap-proval, except on terms that would prevent or materially alter the performance of any activity required by this Consent Order, S shall verbally notify the Department the same day it receives actual

notice. If S receives actual notice on a non-working day, it shall attempt to notify the Department that day and shall verbally notify the Department the next working day. S shall also provide the Department written notice within 5 working days.

b. S shall propose to the Department, as soon as practicable following notification pursuant to paragraph 30(a), an alternative action that will assure an equivalent or greater degree of protection of human health and the environment. If the Department approves the proposed alternative, the Parties shall modify this Consent Order accordingly. If the Department and S cannot agree on the proposed alternative, the matter shall be resolved pursuant to the dispute resolution procedures set forth in paragraph 41. If S complies with the requirements of sub-paragraph 30(a), delays in, or changes to, the performance of activities required under this Consent Order due to S's inability to obtain a required approval as described above shall not be considered violations of the Consent Order.

c. The Department has determined that treatment of contaminated groundwater from the Landfill at S's wastewater treatment unit at its Boulder facility does not require a hazardous waste treatment permit because it meets the requirements of 6 CCR 1007-3, Sections 260.10, 264.1(g)(6), and 100.10(a)(6).

LIMITATION OF LIABILITY

31. The Department shall not be liable for any injuries or damages to persons or property resulting from acts or omissions of S, its employees, agents or contractors in carrying out the activities pursuant to this Consent Order. S agrees to indemnify the Department for all claims by any party which arise from such acts or omissions of S, its employees, agents or contractors, including the Department's costs and attorneys' fees expended in responding to any such claim. In no event shall S contend that the Department is, or should be treated as, a party to any contract entered into by S, its employees, agents or contractors in carrying out activities pursuant to this Consent Order, or an owner or operator of the Landfill.

FORCE MAJEURE

32. If S learns or has reason to learn of the occurrence of any event that it reasonably believes may delay or prevent the timely performance of any activities required under this Consent Order, it shall verbally notify the Department the same day it learns of such an occurrence. If S learns of the occurrence on a non-working day, it shall attempt to notify the Department that day and shall verbally notify the Department the next working day. Within 5 working days after such oral notification, S shall submit to the Department a written description of the event which may

delay or prevent performance, the expected duration of the delay or nature of the prevented performance, and actions which will be taken to mitigate any delay or failure to perform.

33. Any unforeseeable event beyond the reasonable control of S that delays or prevents performance of any of S's obligations under this Consent Order constitutes a Force Majeure. Delays or failure to perform obligations caused by a Force Majeure shall not constitute violations of this Consent Order. If the parties cannot agree that a particular event constitutes a Force Majeure, they may submit the dispute to resolution as provided in paragraph 41. S shall have the burden of establishing the existence of a Force Majeure. S's failure to obtain any required permit or other authorization shall not constitute a Force Majeure, but shall be handled under paragraphs 30 or 31.

STIPULATED PENALTIES

34. S shall pay stipulated penalties as set forth below for the following violations of this Consent Order. Penalties shall be paid within 30 days of demand therefor by the Department. Disputes concerning stipulated penalties shall be resolved in the district court for Boulder County. In a proceeding to resolve such a dispute, the only issue before the court shall be occurrence of the violation.

   a.   (i)   S shall pay $60,000 as a stipulated penalty in the event any Groundwater Compliance Standard is verifiably exceeded at the Compliance Boundary for either the Upper or Lower Disposal Area. The Compliance Boundary for the Upper Disposal Area consists of all Compliance Boundary monitoring wells completed in the Muddy Sandstone hydrogeologic unit. The Complaince Boundary for the Lower Disposal Area consists of all Compliance Boundary monitoring wells completed in the Shallow Benton and Lower Greenhorn hydrogeologic units. Verified exceedances of any Compliance Boundary Standard at both the UDA and LDA Compliance Boundaries shall constitute separate violations of this Consent Order. After a Groundwater Compliance Standard is verifiably exceeded, S shall immediately implement the contingency plan required under paragraph 21. f., and an additional $60,000 stipulated penalty shall be assessed only if any of the Groundwater Compliance Standards are verifiably exceeded during every sampling event during the 120-day period following the initial verified exceedance.

   a.   (ii)   S shall pay stipulated penalties according to the following schedule for delays in implementing the approved contingency plan required under paragraph 21.f. following a verified exceedance of any Compliance Boundary Standard:

            days 1–10 of failure to
            implement the contingency plan $6,000/day

days 11–20 of failure to
implement the contingency plan $7,000/day

every day thereafter of
failure to implement the
contingency plan $9,000/day

b. For each day that Landfill excavation continues beyond October 3, 1989, S shall pay stipulated penalties according to the following schedule:

days 1–10	$4,000/day
days 11–20	$5,000/day
each day thereafter	$6,000/day

c. For each day of delay in implementing the schedule for activating the Groundwater Remediation System following a verified exceedance of an Action Line Activation Level, S shall pay stipulated penalties according to the following schedule:

days 1–10	$4,000/day
days 11–20	$5,000/day
each day thereafter	$6,000/day

d. S shall pay $5,000 for the first truck containing materials removed from the Landfill or adjoining soils, or contaminated ground water, that is not manifested as hazardous waste in accordance with 6 CCR 1007-3, part 262. For subsequent violations of the manifesting requirement, the stipulated amount shall be $10,000 per unmanifested truck. The stipulated penalty for trucks which have improperly completed manifests shall be $500.00 for the first truck and $1,000.00 for every truck thereafter.

e. Except as provided in subparagraphs 34. a., b., and c., S shall pay $500 per day for each day it is overdue in meeting any deadline set forth in paragraph 21 or any schedule established thereunder.

REIMBURSEMENT OF OVERSIGHT AND REVIEW COSTS

35. S shall reimburse the Department or its designee for the actual cost of the following oversight activities:

a. The services of an on-scene coordinator to perform the duties specified in paragraph 21.

b. Reasonable review and oversight by Department and Colorado Geological Survey personnel of activities and submittals required under this Consent Order in accordance with the procedures established in Department's Document Review fees, 6 CCR 1007-3, Subpart 100.3 (1-88).

S shall also reimburse the Department $30,000 for its past costs in reviewing documents submitted under the 1987 Order. The reimbursement shall be in the form of a check, made payable to The Hazardous Waste Service Fund. S shall make this payment within 21 days of the effective date of this Consent Order. The Department shall provide S with documentation of its costs.

FINANCIAL ASSURANCE

36. S shall comply with the financial assurance requirements of 6 CCR 1007-3, part 266, provided that the financial instruments set forth in part 266 shall be modified as necessary to reflect the nature of this Consent Order.

NOTICE REGARDING USE AND TRANSFER OF LAND

37. Within fifteen (15) days after the effective date of this Consent Order, S, Inc. shall file with the County Clerk and Recorder in Boulder, Colorado a "Notice Regarding the Use and Transfer of Land" regarding the property. The Notice shall state:

> "There is a Consent Order requiring remediation, long-term care, maintenance and monitoring which affects the following described land: [legal description omitted].

> The Consent Order was executed in August, 1988, by the Colorado Department of Health, S, Inc., and S Corporation. Copies of the Order are on file with the Colorado Department of Health, Hazardous Materials and Waste Management Division and the Boulder County Land Use Department.

The Notice shall be filed and recorded as instruments affecting title to property which are normally examined during a title search.

38. Complaince with any of the requirements of this Consent Order by S Corporation or by S, Inc., shall constitute complaince for S.

PUBLIC AVAILABILITY OF DOCUMENTS

39. All documents submitted pursuant to this Consent Order are public records within the intendment of section 24-72-202, C.R.S. (1982), and shall be available for inspection by any person in accordance with the Department's regulations. S shall not make any claim of confidentiality regarding any documents, or portions thereof, submitted pursuant to this Consent Order.

NOTICES

40. Unless otherwise specified, any reports, notices or other communications required under this Consent Order shall be in writing and shall be sent to: [addresses omitted].

DISPUTE RESOLUTION

41. If the parties are unable to resolve any dispute arising under this Consent Order, either party may file a complaint in the district court for Boulder County seeking a declaration of rights of the Parties under this Consent Order. The Parties hereby agree and stipulate to the appointment of Judicial Arbiters Group, Inc., as a special master to resolve the dispute. If unavailable, another person approved by both Parties may be appointed special master. If the dispute concerns the technical adequacy of any of S's submissions required by this Consent Order, the special master may refer the issue to a qualified technical consultant approved by the Parties for a recommendation. The special master's proceedings shall be conducted pursuant to Rule 53 of the Colorado Rules of Civil Procedure. Findings of fact by the special master shall be binding on the Parties unless the findings are contrary to the weight of the evidence.

MODIFICATIONS

42. The Parties may, by mutual agreement, modify this Consent Order.

TERMINATION

43. S's obligations under this Consent Order, except those under paragraphs 29 and 31, shall terminate at the end of the long-term monitoring program required by sub-subparagraph 21. j. (viii).

APPLICABILITY AND AUTHORIZATION TO SIGN

44. This Consent Order shall be binding upon the State of Colorado and S and S's successors in interest and assigns. The undersigned warrant that they are authorized to legally bind their respective principals to this Consent Order. This Consent Order shall become effective when all required signatures have been obtained. This Consent Order may be executed in multiple counterparts, each of which shall be deemed an original, but all of which shall constitute one and the same agreement.

Approved as to form:

S, INC. COLORADO ATTORNEY GENERAL'S OFFICE

[Signatures omitted.]

DATE: _____

MECHANISMS FOR ACHIEVING NEGOTIATED SETTLEMENTS

§ 24.13   Alternative Dispute Resolution

The EPA encourages alternative methods of dispute resolution (ADR) for cost recovery actions under Superfund.[69] EPA generally favors nonbinding ADR methods, though it has provided for binding arbitration for small claims.[70] However, although it supports ADR, EPA has resolved few cost recovery actions through these methods. Private parties may also resolve disputes under Superfund through ADR.

EPA's support for ADR in selected cost recovery contexts reflects general federal policy to encourage ADR for administrative disputes.[71] In a 1987 guidance memorandum, EPA outlined its policy to promote ADR in enforcement situations[72] and reaffirmed its support in a 1989 memorandum. EPA stated that its goal was to provide "explicit opportunities for using non-binding [sic] alternative dispute resolution (ADR) where it would expedite settlement . . . [and to] consider innovative use of ADR as well as traditional forms of ADR such as non-binding [sic] arbitration and mediation."[73]

The 1987 guidance memorandum for ADR in enforcement cases is the most extensive EPA statement regarding ADR. It outlines appropriate ADR methods, case selection, and third-party neutral selection. It also provides for confidentiality of revealed information.

§ 24.14   —ADR Methods

EPA specifically recommends mediation, arbitration, fact-finding, and mini-trials[74] as methods of alternate dispute resolution.

---

[69] 42 U.S.C. § 9622.

[70] *See* 40 C.F.R. § 304 (1989). See § **24.8**.

[71] The Administrative Conference recommends that federal agencies use ADR to resolve disputes. *Agencies' Use of Alternative Means of Dispute Resolution,* 1 C.F.R. § 305.86-3 (1986). A bill that further encourages federal agencies to use ADR was signed into law on Nov. 15, 1990. Administrative Dispute Resolution Act, Pub. L. No. 101-522 (H.R. 2497, 101st Cong., 1st Sess., 135 Cong. Rec. S5166 (1989)).

[72] EPA, Guidance on Alternative Dispute Resolution Techniques in Enforcement Actions (1987) [hereinafter EPA 1987 Guidance].

[73] EPA, Superfund Enforcement Strategy and Implementation Plan (1989).

[74] EPA 1987 Guidance § II.

Mediation.   In mediation, a third-party neutral facilitates discussions.[75] The mediator generally will not take a position but will help the parties clarify their positions.[76] Parties may withdraw from mediation prior to settlement if the mediation has been long and unsuccessful, chances for settlement appear remote, or the mediator's conduct has been inappropriate.[77] Mediation may be conducted as an adjunct to ongoing litigation.[78]

Arbitration.   An arbitrator is a third-party neutral who decides issues through party-determined procedures.[79] Arbitration under Superfund is generally nonbinding, though it may be binding in certain small claim situations.[80] Arbitration is particularly appropriate in cases that do not justify expenditures for a formal administrative proceeding or court trial.[81]

Fact-finding.   In fact-finding, a third-party expert independently investigates particular issues specified by the parties.[82] The neutral may hold party meetings to gather information.[83] The fact-finder produces a report of findings and recommendations, which may then be used in settlement negotiations.[84] If the parties have agreed to make the neutral's report binding, the report may be admissible as fact in a subsequent formal proceeding.[85] The fact-finder's report is only advisory if the parties have not agreed to make it binding.[86]

---

[75] *Id.* § II(A). The guidance outlines protocols for EPA mediation cases. *Id.* Attachment D to guidance. The protocols include provisions about mediation participants, decision making, safeguards, schedule, press, mediator, approval of proposals, and effective date of decisions. *Id.*

[76] *Id.* § VIII(B)(1).

[77] *Id.* § VIII(B)(3).

[78] *Id.* § VIII(B)(4).

[79] EPA 1987 Guidance § II(B). EPA included suggested arbitration procedures in the guidance. *Id.* Attachment C to guidance. These procedures are largely reflected and refined by the regulatory scheme outlined in 40 C.F.R. § 304 (1989).

[80] EPA 1987 Guidance § II(B). EPA is "conducting further research regarding [arbitration] . . . to decide factual issues."

[81] *Id.* § VIII(A)(2). An arbitrator may handle technical disputes requiring expertise better than would an administrative or district court judge.

[82] *Id.* §§ II(C), VIII(D)(1). EPA attached a form, Agreement to Institute Fact-Finding Procedures, to the 1987 Guidance.

[83] *Id.* § VIII(D)(1).

[84] *Id.*

[85] *Id.* §§ II(C), VIII(D)(1).

[86] EPA 1987 Guidance § II(C).

Mini-trials. A mini-trial is a forum in which the parties present their cases to principals with authority to settle.[87] A third-party neutral may also be present.[88] The parties determine the procedure of the mini-trial, and they usually provide an opportunity for each of the principals to directly examine the opposing side.[89] The parties negotiate after the mini-trial.[90] If a third-party neutral is present, he or she acts as a mediator or advisor during the negotiations.[91] Mini-trial results are not binding but should narrow issues and give principals a "realistic view" of their cases.[92] The evidence presented at the mini-trial is not admissible in formal litigation unless the parties so agree.[93] Mini-trials are most useful when a small number of parties are involved, a party has overestimated its bargaining position, difficult policy issues surface, or the expert neutral's assistance would help resolve the case.[94]

§ 24.15   —Case Selection

ADR may be appropriate if ongoing litigation is slow, negotiations have stalled, or ADR would efficiently help resolve the dispute.[95] ADR may be especially useful in technical disputes because an expert third-party neutral's assistance may eliminate the need for a master.[96] ADR may also be appropriate when outside persons or organizations are affected.[97] ADR allows these parties to become involved in the dispute resolution.[98]

Any involved person at EPA or any PRP may suggest that a case or issue use ADR.[99] After the party communicates the suggestion to the appropriate

---

[87] *Id.* § II(D). EPA attached a form, Agreement to Institute Mini-Trial Proceedings, to the 1987 Guidance.

[88] *Id.* § II(D).

[89] *Id.* § VIII(C)(1).

[90] *Id.* § II(D).

[91] *Id.* §§ II(D), VIII(C)(2).

[92] EPA 1987 Guidance § II(D).

[93] *Id.* § VIII(C)(2).

[94] *Id.* § VIII(C)(3).

[95] *Id.* § III. Although the parties may introduce ADR at any point in a case, they should suggest it before EPA refers the case to the Department of Justice (DOJ). *Id.* ADR may be particularly efficient if (1) EPA has considerable experience and the case law and remedies are well defined; or (2) many parties or issues are involved and ADR can help manage the case. *Id.* § III(B).

[96] *Id.* § III.

[97] *Id.* § III(C). For instance, the case may affect a state or local government, a citizens group, or the site's surrounding community.

[98] EPA 1987 Guidance § III(C).

[99] *Id.* § IV(B).

EPA regional office, the EPA-designated decision maker will determine whether to nominate the case for ADR.[100] The office will refer nominations to EPA headquarters and the Department of Justice.[101] If EPA suggests ADR, it should approach PRPs with its suggestion and reasoning, though it retains the option to proceed with "vigorous" litigation.[102]

§ 24.16   —Third-Party Neutral Selection

Parties participating in ADR preferably should determine the method of ADR before selecting a neutral.[103] EPA suggests various measures for choosing a third-party neutral, such as proposing names of neutrals until the parties agree or choosing names from a list.[104] The parties may consult with the Chief, Legal Enforcement Policy Branch, for guidance in selecting a neutral.[105]

EPA suggests certain qualifications for third-party neutrals, though every qualification need not be met.[106] Specified qualifications for individual neutrals include demonstrated experience, independence, subject matter expertise, and *single role,* which means that the neutral should not be serving in another capacity that might create bias in the case.[107] A corporation that wishes to serve as the neutral must meet the same qualifications as an individual and must submit a list to the parties of everyone who might be significantly involved in ADR.[108] EPA and involved PRPs share the cost of retaining the neutral.[109]

§ 24.17   —Confidentiality

Many parties considering ADR may be concerned about the confidentiality of information they reveal. Records and communications revealed during ADR will not be admissible in formal proceedings if not otherwise

---

[100] *Id.* EPA provided a form nomination statement for both binding and nonbinding ADR (Attachments A and B to 1987 Guidance).

[101] *Id.* § IV(B).

[102] *Id.*

[103] EPA 1987 Guidance § V(A).

[104] *Id.*

[105] *Id.*

[106] *Id.* § V(B).

[107] *Id.* § V(B)(1)(d).

[108] *Id.* § V(B)(2). These indivdiuals must also meet the individual qualifications. *Id.*

[109] EPA 1987 Guidance § VII(B).

discoverable.[110] ADR agreements should include clauses imposing sanctions for revealing confidential information.[111] If a court supervises the case, a court order may protect confidentiality.[112]

§ 24.18   Binding Arbitration for Small Superfund Cost Recovery Claims

The United States may settle its cost recovery claims under Superfund through binding or nonbinding arbitration.[113] Under Superfund, EPA may promulgate regulations governing arbitration when its response costs are $500,000 or less.[114] EPA outlined a procedural framework for arbitration in a 1989 regulation.[115]

Arbitration may be binding only when response costs are $500,000 or less, excluding interest.[116] If a claim exceeds $500,000, the parties may agree to nonbinding arbitration under the same procedural guidelines outlined in the regulation.[117] These parties may agree to accept the arbitrator's decision as an administrative settlement pursuant to 42 U.S.C. § 9622(h)(1), subject to the attorney general's approval and public comment.[118]

EPA or a PRP may initiate arbitration. If EPA determines a claim is "appropriate" for arbitration, it must notify all identified PRPs for the subject facility so that they may discuss potential arbitration.[119] A PRP may propose arbitration to EPA only after EPA has demanded payment and before any civil litigation regarding the claim has commenced.[120] If practicable, the PRP or EPA must notify other PRPs at the facility of potential arbitration.[121]

---

[110] Id. § VII(C).

[111] Id.

[112] Id. Confidentiality is also protected by professional ethics codes. EPA is considering promulgating more regulations to "further ensure the confidentiality of ADR proceedings."

[113] 42 U.S.C. § 9622(h)(2) (1990).

[114] Id.

[115] 40 C.F.R. § 304 (1989).

[116] Id. § 304.20(a)(1).

[117] Id. § 304.20(b)(1).

[118] Id. § 304.20(b)(2).

[119] Id. § 304.21(a).

[120] Id.

[121] 40 C.F.R. § 304.21(a).

The Joint Request

EPA and the PRPs that wish to arbitrate must submit a joint request for arbitration to the National Arbitration Association.[122] The request should include a description of the situation and a statement of the issues as well as statements ensuring a binding decision.[123] Any party may later modify the request and add issues if the other parties agree.[124] The arbitrator's decision is binding only regarding the issues described in the request.[125]

In the joint request, parties may seek allocation of costs and specify factors the arbitrator should consider.[126] An arbitrator will allocate 100 percent of the response costs among liable participating PRPs unless the joint request specifies that a lower percentage is acceptable.[127] The participating PRPs have the burden of establishing appropriate allocation,[128] which means that EPA has no obligation to participate in allocation discussions before the arbitrator.[129] Participating PRPs may request an allocation even if they have not submitted the issue of liability to the arbitrator.[130]

The Arbitral Proceeding

In the arbitral proceeding, parties select an arbitrator, submit pleadings, and participate in a pre-hearing conference. All parties participate in selection of the arbitrator, who should be chosen from the National Panel of Environmental Arbitrators.[131] EPA has not yet selected a group to serve on the National Arbitration Association, which would list a National Panel of Environmental Arbitrators.[132] However, EPA and participating PRPs may now choose an arbitrator on a case-by-case basis.[133]

---

[122] *Id.* § 304.21(b)(1).

[123] *Id.*

[124] *Id.* § 304.21(c).

[125] *Id.* § 304.20(c).

[126] *Id.* § 304.20(d)(4). The parties may seek allocation even if the harm is indivisible.

[127] *Id.* § 304.20(d)(4)(ii).

[128] *Id.* § 304.20(d)(4)(iii).

[129] Telephone interview with Richard Robinson, Senior Attorney, Office of Waste Programs Enforcement, EPA Headquarters (June 15, 1990).

[130] 40 C.F.R. § 304.20(d)(5)(1989).

[131] *Id.* § 304.22(b).

[132] Telephone interview with Richard Robinson, Senior Attorney, Office of Waste Programs Enforcement, EPA Headquarters (June 15, 1990).

[133] 40 C.F.R. § 304.22(e)(1989).

Participating PRPs may withdraw from the arbitral proceeding within 30 days after they receive notice of the arbitrator's appointment.[134] After the parties select the arbitrator, EPA must submit a pleading statement that describes the facts, evidence, issues, and costs of its response to the problem situation.[135] Participating PRPs must then answer, challenging any disputed EPA statements, actions, or documentation.[136] EPA may file a response, and any participating PRP may reply.[137] The arbitrator conducts a pre-hearing conference and possibly a hearing on disputed issues.[138]

A PRP may challenge EPA's response action in the arbitral proceeding but must prove that EPA's selection was inconsistent with the National Contingency Plan.[139] A PRP must show that EPA costs either were not in curred through its response or were clearly excessive.[140]

Nonparticipating PRPs may move to intervene in the arbitral proceeding and, if approved by all participating parties, will be included through modification of the joint request.[141]

The arbitrator proposes a decision after the hearing or the pre-hearing conference if no hearing is held.[142] The *Federal Register* publishes the proposed decision, and nonparties may file comments.[143]

After the proposed decision is published, EPA must enter a statement. EPA may seek modification of the proposed decision or withdrawal from the arbitral proceeding based on concerns raised by public comments.[144] Otherwise, the arbitrator's proposed decision becomes final 30 days after EPA has issued its statement.[145] If EPA requests modification or withdrawal, the parties may settle by modifying the proposed decision.[146] If they do not settle, the decision is null.[147]

---

[134] *Id.* § 304.24(b).

[135] *Id.* § 304.30(b).

[136] *Id.* § 304.30(c).

[137] *Id.* § 304.30(d), (e).

[138] *Id.* §§ 304.31, 304.32.

[139] 40 C.F.R. § 304.20(e)(1).

[140] *Id.* § 304.20(e)(3), (4). The PRP must prove the costs were "arbitrary and capricious or otherwise not in accordance with law." *Id.* § 304.20(e)(4).

[141] *Id.* § 304.24(a).

[142] *Id.* § 304.33(a), (b).

[143] *Id.* § 304.33(e).

[144] 40 C.F.R. § 304.33(e).

[145] *Id.* § 304.33(e)(2).

[146] *Id.*

[147] *Id.*

The arbitration does not affect participating PRPs' contribution rights against nonparticipating PRPs.[148] The effectiveness of arbitration is limited because participating PRPs may still need to litigate against nonparticipating PRPs to establish allocation and enforce contribution rights.

EPA has utilized ADR in Superfund cost recovery actions on only a few occasions. EPA promulgated the binding arbitration regulation in August 1989, but it had not used the provisions as of July 1990.[149]

The only type of ADR that EPA has used in the Superfund cost recovery context is mediation,[150] which it used in four situations. Each of the cost recovery mediations has occurred in Region V, the only regional office that has actively promoted and proposed mediation projects.[151] EPA used mediation for Spechtrochem in Oregon, Wisconsin;[152] the City of Youngstown, Ohio;[153] Greiner's Lagoon in Fremont, Ohio;[154] and Revere Cooper and Brass in Detroit, Michigan.[155] Region V has also instigated mediation at two remedial design/remedial action sites involving E.H. Schilling in Lawrence County, Ohio,[156] and Onalaska Landfill in Onalaska, Wisconsin.[157] Various regions have used facilitation, a form of mediation, in noncost recovery Superfund contexts.[158]

---

[148] Telephone interview with Richard Robinson, Senior Attorney, Office of Waste Programs Enforcement, EPA Headquarters (June 15, 1990).

[149] *Id.*

[150] Second telephone interview with Richard Robinson, Senior Attorney, Office of Waste Programs Enforcement, EPA Headquarters (June 20, 1990).

[151] Telephone interview with Suzanne Orenstein, Senior Associate, Program on Environmental Dispute Resolution, Conservation Foundation (July 10, 1990). EPA has contracted with the Conservation Foundation to employ approved mediators. The Conservation Foundation has handled each of the cost recovery mediation situations.

[152] For more information, contact T. Krueger, Assistant Regional Counsel, Office of Regional Counsel, EPA Region V.

[153] For more information, contact P. Andrews, Assistant Regional Counsel, Office of Regional Counsel, EPA Region V.

[154] For more information, contact R. Nagle, Assistant Regional Counsel, Office of Regional Counsel, EPA Region V.

[155] For more information, contact T. Kenney, Assistant Regional Counsel, Office of Regional Counsel, EPA Region V.

[156] This mediation was not completed in July 1990. For more information, contact Carolyn Lane-Wenner, Attorney Advisor, Office of Enforcement, EPA Headquarters.

[157] This mediation case was in its early stages in July 1990. For more information, contact P. Andrews, Assistant Regional Counsel, Office of Regional Counsel, EPA Region V.

[158] EPA and PRPs have used facilitation specifically for community relations purposes. *See* Cassel, *Negotiating Better Superfund Settlements: Prospects and Protocols,* 16 Pepperdine L. Rev. S117 (1989) [hereinafter Cassel, *Better Settlements*].

§ 24.19   ADR among Private Parties

PRPs often negotiate among themselves to formulate a plan for a site cleanup to avoid a more expensive EPA-run cleanup or a cost recovery action.[159] PRPs may seek the help of outside neutrals on various issues involved in the cleanup, including their organization or representation and allocation of their cleanup costs.[160] If private parties choose to involve an outside neutral, they often enlist the assistance of an organization. Clean Sites, Inc., ICF, Inc., and the Center for Public Resources (Center) are the three primary organizations that assist in Superfund disputes. Private parties may also work with neutrals who are not affiliated with an organization.

The PRPs, not the EPA, bring in facilitating organizations.[161] From 1984 to 1989, PRPs at approximately 70 sites invoked the assistance of mediators.[162] Clean Sites, ICF, and the Center are all heavily involved in Superfund disputes.

Clean Sites is a nonprofit organization[163] that assists the multiple PRPs involved at targeted sites to resolve disputes.[164] Clean Sites may help parties resolve disputes regarding their organization or representation before the government, their allocation responsibilities, or their legal liability.[165] Clean Sites conducts the research necessary to resolve these issues as equitably and efficiently as possible.[166] It recently agreed to work with

---

[159] Cohen, *Allocation of Superfund Cleanup Costs Among Potentially Responsible Parties: The Role of Binding Arbitration,* 18 Envtl. L. Rep. (Envtl. L. Inst.) 10158 (May 1988) [hereinafter Cohen, *Role of Arbitration*].

[160] Rennie, *Private Facilitating and Adjudicative Functions: A. Superfund Disputes and the Role of Clean Sites, Inc.,* 17 Envtl. L. Rep. (Envtl. L. Inst.) 10263 (July 1987) [hereinafter Rennie, *Role of Clean Sites*]. Sandra Rennie was Coalescing Executive, Clean Sites, Inc., in 1987. She now manages the Toxic and Hazardous Waste Mediation practice at ICF, Inc.

[161] Rennie, *Kindling the Environmental ADR Flame: Use of Mediation and Arbitration in Federal Planning, Permitting, and Enforcement,* 19 Envtl. L. Rep. (Envtl. L. Inst.) 10479 (Nov. 1989) [hereinafter Rennie, *Kindling the ADR Flame*].

[162] *Id.* at 10480.

[163] Rennie, *Role of Clean Sites* at 10264. Clean Sites was founded in 1984. Krickenberger & Rekar, *Superfund Settlements: Breaking the Logjam,* 19 Envtl. Rep. (BNA) 2384 (March 1989). [hereinafter Krickenberger & Rekar]. It is based in Alexandria, Virginia. *Legal Times,* July 22, 1985, at 6.

[164] Rennie, *Role of Clean Sites* at 10264. Clean Sites has been asked to assist in disputes involving from three parties to 4,000 parties. The typical case has about one hundred PRPs.

[165] *Id.* at 10264, 10265.

[166] *Id.* at 10266.

the American Arbitration Association to promote ADR and choose potential arbitrators.[167]

EPA and Clean Sites have had a mixed history. EPA financially supports Clean Sites,[168] but it generally perceives Clean Sites as having a bias in favor of PRPs.[169] EPA has not allowed Clean Sites to mediate disputes between itself and PRPs.[170]

ICF, Inc. is a broader organization than Clean Sites but still does much Superfund work.[171] When involved at a site, ICF generally performs the same functions as Clean Sites.[172]

Parties may also involve the Center, which is based in New York City.[173] The Center has on its board of directors general counsels of many Fortune 500 companies and partners from large law firms.[174] The Center focuses primarily on cost allocation issues.[175]

§ 24.20   —Use of Nonaffiliated Neutrals

Parties may choose to hire a nonaffiliated neutral to implement certain ADR methods. The only mini-trial case conducted under Superfund as of July 1990 involved a nonaffiliated neutral.[176] In this case, Goodyear Tire and Rubber Company and the Department of Defense were named PRPs by EPA, and they used a mini-trial to allocate responsibility for the cleanup

---

[167] Cohen, *Role of Arbitration* at 10162. The American Arbitration Association has a panel of neutrals from which PRPs may select an arbitrator.

[168] Krickenberger & Rekar at 2387. Clean Sites is primarily funded by the industry and has received grants from private foundations. *Id.* at 2387, 2388. *See also* Memorandum from J. Winston Porter, Assistant Administrator, EPA Office of Solid Waste and Emergency Response and Thomas L. Adams, Assistant Administrator, EPA Office of Enforcement and Compliance Monitoring, *Role of Clean Sites, Inc. at Superfund Sites,* dated Apr. 24, 1987. [hereinafter Porter & Adams, *Role of Clean Sites*].

[169] Krickenberger & Rekar at 2388. This belief is based on industry funding of Clean Sites.

[170] Porter & Adams, *Role of Clean Sites* at 4. EPA delayed deciding on its policy toward using Clean Sites in mediation until EPA guidelines and procedures for instituting mediation are in place. EPA may use Clean Sites in pilot cases, though Clean Sites would be evaluated equally with other potential third-party neutrals.

[171] Cassel, *Better Settlements* at S159. ICF specializes in energy, health, and safety issues as well as environmental issues.

[172] Telephone interview with Kathy Holtgrieve, Senior Associate, Alternative Dispute Resolution Division, ICF, Inc. (July 18, 1990).

[173] *Alternative Dispute Resolution Gaining Prominence as Way of Solving Environmental Issues, Avoiding Rising Litigation Costs,* [May-Dec.] Env't Rep. (BNA) No. 21, at 908 (Sept. 20, 1985).

[174] *Id.* at 912.

[175] *Id.*

[176] Rennie, *Kindling the ADR Flame* at 10480.

costs.[177] The Army Corps' Omaha District Engineer and the Goodyear Vice President for Government Environmental Safety and Health Assurance Programs attended the 1988 mini-trail.[178] A neutral advisor assisted them.[179] The mini-trial was successful, and the parties reached an agreement after three days of negotiations.[180]

PRPs have also involved arbitrators that were not affiliated with a particular organization. PRPs from at least four sites have involved a non-affiliated arbitrator.[181] PRPs used binding arbitration at the Wauconda Sand and Gravel Landfill in Lake County, Illinois, and the Hardage/Criner site in McClain County, Oklahoma.[182] PRPs have used nonbinding arbitration at various sites including the Bayou Sorrel site in Iberville Parish, Louisiana, and the MOTCO site near LaMarque, Texas.[183]

DISPOSITION OF PROPERTY IN BANKRUPTCY PROCEEDINGS

§ 24.21   Bankruptcy Issues

The intersection of environmental law and bankruptcy law has engendered a large number of difficult legal and policy dilemmas. The Bankruptcy Code (the Code) is designed to give businesses a fresh start and to distribute the debtor's assets equitably among its creditors. The Code's design allows for preservation of the estate's assets for the corporation's successful reorganization or, in the case of dissolution, allows a corporation's creditors to collect what is owed to them based on the security that they bargained for in contracts with the debtor.

The goals of environmental law in general and CERCLA in particular conflict notably with those of the bankruptcy scheme. The Superfund is

---

[177] U.S. Army Corps of Engineers, Case Study #5—Goodyear Tire & Rubber Co. 1 (1989).

[178] *Id.* at 6.

[179] *Id.* The advisor was Professor Richard C. Collins, Director, Institute for Environmental Negotiation, University of Virginia.

[180] *Id.* at 8.

[181] Rennie, *Role of Clean Sites* at 10480.

[182] Cohen, *Role of Arbitration* at 10158. *See also* 16 Envtl. L. Rep. Admin. Materials (Envtl. L. Inst.) 30043 (Mar. 1986); 18 Envtl. L. Rep. Admin. Materials (Envtl. L. Inst.) 30132 (Sept. 1988).

[183] Cohen, *Role of Arbitration* at 10158. *See also* 18 Envtl. L. Rep. Admin. Materials (Envtl. L. Inst.) 30131 (Sept. 1988); 15 Envtl. L. Rep. Admin. Materials (Envtl. L. Inst.) 30020 (Nov. 1985). Parties at the Bayou Sorrel site also employed Clean Sites to assist them in allocating costs. *Alternative Dispute Resolution,* Gaining Prominence as Way of Solving Environmental Issues, [May–Dec.] Env't Rep. (BNA) No. 21, at 908 (Sept. 1985).

designed to protect public health and safety by ensuring that contamination is contained or cleaned up so that it will not pose an ongoing threat to the environment and public welfare. Whereas bankruptcy law seeks to protect the debtor and as many of the creditors as possible, Superfund seeks to protect the public fisc (without regard to other creditors) by requiring responsible parties to pay for environmental cleanups. Given the large expense of environmental cleanups, Superfund judgments often have the potential to deplete the debtor's assets so thoroughly that nothing remains for the other creditors.

The tensions between the two legal schemes have played themselves out in the courts in a variety of areas. Among the most litigated questions are whether a debtor can abandon a piece of property that has an environmental hazard associated with it under 11 U.S.C. § 554(a) and whether the automatic stay under 11 U.S.C. § 362 applies to government efforts to enforce judgments against debtors responsible for environmental hazards. A survey of the case law in these areas lends some insight into the kinds of settlements that the government and debtors have reached.

§ 24.22   Abandonment of Affected Property

Section 554(a) of the Code provides that "After notice and a hearing, the trustee may abandon any property of the estate that is burdensome to the estate or that is of inconsequential value and benefit to the estate."[184] Such property may be abandoned to anyone with a possessory interest in it. This provision appears to authorize a trustee to abandon *any* property of the estate that the bankruptcy court finds to be burdensome to the estate or of inconsequential benefit. In *Midlantic National Bank v. New Jersey Department of Environmental Protection,*[185] however, the Supreme Court ruled that a bankruptcy court

> does not have the power to authorize an abandonment without formulating conditions that will adequately protect the public's health and safety . . . a trustee may not abandon property in contravention of a state statute or regulation that is reasonably designed to protect public health or safety from identified hazards.[186]

The Court stressed that Congress did not intend for trustees to have an absolute right to ignore nonbankruptcy law: "Where the Bankruptcy Code has conferred special powers on the trustee and where there was no common law limitation on that power, Congress has expressly provided that

---

[184] 11 U.S.C. § 554(a).

[185] 474 U.S. 494, *reh'g denied,* 106 S. Ct. 1482 (1986).

[186] *Id.* at 507.

the efforts of the trustees to marshal and distribute the assets of the estate must yield to the governmental interest in public health and safety."[187] The *Midlantic* Court qualified this exception to the trustee's abandonment power:

> This exception to the abandonment power vested in the trustee . . . is a narrow one. It does not encompass a speculative or indeterminate future violation of such laws that may stem from abandonment. The abandonment power is not to be fettered by laws and regulations not reasonably calculated to protect the public health or safety from imminent or identifiable harm.[188]

Litigation on abandonment after *Midlantic* has focused on how narrowly the exception to abandonment must be interpreted. Bankruptcy courts have continued to allow trustees to abandon contaminated property but only under controlled circumstances. The bulk of the cases allowing abandonment distinguish *Midlantic* on the facts.

Thus, in *In re Franklin Signal Corp.,*[189] the bankruptcy court found that 14 drums of chemicals (at least one of which was identified as hazardous) did not present any threat of imminent harm to the public and it authorized the trustee to abandon them. The court in *Franklin Signal* fashioned a five-factor test to determine whether abandonment is proper on a case-by-case basis. The factors it had to consider include:

1. The imminence of danger to public health and safety
2. The extent of probable harm
3. The amount and type of hazardous waste
4. The cost of bringing the property into compliance with environmental laws
5. The amount and type of funds available for cleanup.

Although the abandonment was permitted in *Franklin Signal,* it was not unconditional. The trustee was required to take intermediate steps to protect public health and safety, including hiring an environmental specialist to assess the gravity of the situation; fencing off contaminated areas to prevent public access and sealing storage tanks to prevent discharge; conducting an investigation to determine which hazardous substances burden the property; and advising state and federal agencies of its intent to abandon.

In *In re Purco,*[190] the bankruptcy court applied the five-factor *Franklin Signal* test and took a similarly narrow view of the *Midlantic* exception. It

---

[187] *Id.*

[188] *Id.* at 507 n.9.

[189] 65 Bankr. 268 (Bankr. D. Minn. 1986).

[190] 76 Bankr. 523 (Bankr. W.D. Pa. 1987).

ruled that the trustee could abandon approximately 200 drums containing asphalt and other substances because the Pennsylvania Department of Environmental Resources was not involved (which led the court to conclude the drums posed no immediate threat) and because there was no showing of clear and immediate danger. The court noted that abandonment is permitted when conditions are such that abandonment will not render public health and safety inadequately protected.

The Fourth Circuit further stressed the narrowness of the *Midlantic* exception in the case of *In re Smith Douglas, Inc.*[191] The Fourth Circuit concluded:

> [I]n describing the contours of the exception [to 11 U.S.C. § 554(a)], the Court appears to have intended to fashion a narrow exception to the trustee's abandonment power in order to protect public safety rather than a broad exception to shield the state treasury.[192]

The court looked, once again, to the presence or absence of enforcement by a state or federal agency to decide whether a threat was present, and noted:

> The Bankruptcy Court does not have the power to substitute its judgment for that of the state as to what constitutes a serious health or safety risk. The bankruptcy court must therefore determine whether the risk of imminent harm exists in reference to the design of the state law or regulation alleged to have been violated.[193]

Even though the court chose to allow the abandonment in the case before it, it noted in dicta that when an estate has unencumbered assets, the bankruptcy court should require strict compliance with state environmental law before it permits the trustee to abandon property.

In the case of *In re Peerless Plating Co.,*[194] the bankruptcy court interpreted *Midlantic* to say that abandonment is improper unless one of three conditions could be met: (1) the environmental law is so onerous as to interfere with bankruptcy adjudication; (2) the environmental law is not designed to protect public health and safety from identifiable hazards; or (3) a violation caused by abandonment would be merely speculative or indeterminate.[195] The court said that in the absence of one of the three factors, a trustee must comply with state and federal environmental law and was not authorized to abandon the property. The court noted that the Supreme Court in *Midlantic* failed to give an example of what would be so

---

[191] 856 F.2d 12 (4th Cir. 1988).

[192] *Id.* at 16.

[193] *Id.*

[194] 70 Bankr. 943 (Bankr. W.D. Mich. 1987).

[195] *Id.* at 947.

onerous as to interfere with the bankruptcy adjudication itself. It concluded, however, that depletion of resources does not qualify as such an example. The bankruptcy court reasoned that "The normal course of affairs . . . is to deplete the estate by liquidating it and distributing it to creditors as required by law. The fact that one claimant or creditor receives the lion's share does not render that claim onerous."[196] Because the court concluded that the Peerless plant also passed the second and third tests, it refused to permit abandonment.

Overall, a survey of the case law reveals that the abandonment issue still tends to be decided on a case-by-case basis. The *Midlantic* exception survives but its impact has been limited by the decisions that succeeded it.

§ 24.23   Automatic Stay

A second issue subject to considerable litigation is whether the automatic stay of judicial, administrative, or other actions or proceedings against the debtor under § 362 applies to government attempts to enforce environmental regulations. The automatic stay is not universal. Sections 362(b)(4) and (5) contain some important exceptions to the application of the automatic stay. Section 362(b)(4) exempts from the stay "commencement or continuation of an action or proceeding by a governmental unit to enforce such governmental unit's police or regulatory power." Section 362(b)(5) similarly exempts from the automatic stay the "enforcement of a judgment, other than a money judgment, obtained in an action or a proceeding by a governmental unit to enforce such governmental unit's police or regulatory power." Together these provisions distinguish between the government's right to collect money judgments from the debtor and the government's right to pursue actions to enforce its regulatory and police powers. Because most police and regulatory actions can be reduced to money judgments, there has been considerable debate in the courts over how to apply this distinction.

In *Penn Terra Ltd. v. Department of Environmental Resources,*[197] the Third Circuit Court of Appeals concluded that the automatic stay provision of 11 U.S.C. § 362 did not apply to the state's seeking of an injunction against a debtor to require the debtor to comply with environmental laws. The court held that the suit aimed to enforce the police powers of the state, not to enforce a monetary judgment. The court thus narrowed the scope of the automatic stay by limiting the definition of a money judgment that an automatic stay protects to judgments rendered by a court or jury requiring debtors to pay a fixed sum.

---

[196] *Id.*

[197] 733 F.2d 267 (3d Cir. 1984).

In *Thomas Solvent Co. v. Kelley,*[198] the bankruptcy court noted that although the § 362(b)(5) exception to the automatic stay allows the state to enjoin a debtor from continuing its operation, without taking immediate steps to comply with a state court judgment, and permits the entry of a money judgment, it does not extend to permitting enforcement of a money judgment.[199] The court characterized a state court order to clean up contaminated ground water as an order to enforce a money judgment. It allowed the preliminary injunction to stand and permitted the automatic stay to remain in effect for 90 days. At the end of the 90 days, the stay would be lifted unless the debtor devised a plan that included compliance with environmental regulation or unless the case was converted to a Chapter 7 liquidation case. The court explained its reasoning:

> In the case of a Chapter 11 debtor engaged in an ongoing business, 28 U.S.C. § 959(b) would expressly apply so as to require an operating trustee or debtor in possession to operate its business according to local law. The State would have the power to enjoin such a debtor from continuing its operations without taking immediate steps to comply with a state court judgment. A debtor in possession may not preserve its viability as a business entity, yet avoid its responsibility to society simply by filing a Chapter 11 petition.[200]

In *United States v. Nicolet,*[201] by contrast, the Third Circuit ruled that a Chapter 11 bankruptcy filing did not stay the federal government's Superfund action against a company to recover cleanup costs of an asbestos-contaminated site. The court ruled that the Superfund action fell under the police and regulatory exceptions to the automatic stay set out in 11 U.S.C. § 361(b)(4) and (5). The court noted that CERCLA's purpose, which authorizes the government to protect public welfare and safety, supersedes the automatic stay provisions of the Bankruptcy Act.

Because regulatory proceedings almost always have financial components, the cases cannot be reconciled. In each decision about whether to allow a regulatory proceeding to be stayed, courts make a difficult policy choice.

§ 24.24   Settlements

Given the complexity and ambiguity created when bankruptcy and environmental law intersect, it is not surprising that settlements between the government and debtors have taken many forms.

---

[198] 44 Bankr. 83 (Bankr. W.D. Mich. 1984).

[199] *Id.* at 86,065.

[200] *Id.* at 86,067.

[201] 857 F.2d 202 (3d Cir. 1988).

For example, *Thomas Solvent Co. v. Kelley*[202] involved a stipulation between the state of Michigan, EPA, several citizens' groups, and the debtor, Thomas Solvent Company. The EPA had filed a proof of claim which it amended several times. The claim arose from costs it incurred in responding under CERCLA to releases or threats of releases from the Thomas Solvent facility. EPA sought to have these costs treated as administrative expenses. The debtor objected. Michigan also filed a proof of claim, and citizens claiming harm from pollution also filed claims.

The parties signed a stipulation in 1986 recognizing the claims of the EPA, Michigan, and the citizens' groups as general unsecured claims so that the remaining assets of the debtor could be distributed in a Chapter 11 liquidation.

In re Hartman Material Handling Systems, Inc.[203] also involved a stipulation agreement whereby EPA obtained money for CERCLA cleanups. In that 1988 stipulation, issues involving numerous Superfund sites were consolidated. The stipulation concerning what reimbursement EPA would receive had to be approved by the bankruptcy court and the district court.

The mechanism of a consent order was used in *United States v. Continental Steel Corp.*[204] to set up a fund using money from the bankrupt's estate to close a hazardous waste facility. The bankruptcy trustee paid money into a trust account established for the benefit of the Indiana Department of Environmental Management to take care of cleanup at the site.

---

[202] No. NK 84-00843 (Bankr. W.D. Mich. 19___).

[203] Nos. 87 B 11,225–87 B 11,242 (Bankr. S.D.N.Y. 1988) (cases not settled as of Dec. 1990).

[204] No. IP86-849C (S.D. Ind. July 12, 1989).

CHAPTER 25

CHALLENGING THE EPA'S CLEANUP DECISIONS

Mitchell E. Burack*
Craig M. Jacobsen
David Richman

Mitchell E. Burack is a partner in the Philadelphia, Pennsylvania, office of Pepper, Hamilton & Scheetz, concentrating in environmental regulatory, counseling, and litigation practice. His experience includes representation of clients in state and federal enforcement actions related to hazardous waste, water and air pollution, as well as environmental compliance and liability from ongoing operations, or the acquisition of new facilities. Prior to joining the firm, Mr. Burack was an enforcement attorney with United States EPA in Washington, D.C. Mr. Burack is a graduate of Washington University School of Law and is a member of the bars of Pennsylvania, District of Columbia, Illinois, and Oklahoma. He was the 1990 chairman of the Philadelphia Bar Association's Environmental Law Committee.

Craig M. Jacobsen is partner in charge of Coopers & Lybrand's litigation/bankruptcy practice in the southwestern states. He has extensive experience evaluating contractors' costs and related performance. As part of these assignments, he regularly assesses overhead and indirect cost charges. Mr. Jacobsen has testified in numerous forums regarding these issues.

*The authors wish to acknowledge the substantial assistance rendered by Ms. L.B. Kregenow, an associate at Pepper, Hamilton & Scheetz, in preparing this chapter.

David Richman is a partner in the Philadelphia, Pennsylvania, office of the law firm of Pepper, Hamilton & Scheetz and co-chairs the firm's Environmental Practice Group. His practice is concentrated in environmental and toxic tort litigation and includes counseling and representation on related insurance and criminal matters. Mr. Richman graduated *cum laude* from the University of Pennsylvania Law School and served as an assistant district attorney for the City of Philadelphia for five years. Mr. Richman has chaired an ABA Litigation Section Subcommittee on Environmental Trials, lectures frequently on hazardous waste litigation, has served as a regional instructor for the National Institute of Trial Advocacy, and has represented clients in a number of government and private Superfund enforcement actions.

§ 25.1   Introduction

Suits under the Comprehensive Environmental Response, Compensation, and Liability Act (CERCLA)[1] typically involve three overriding substantive issues: who is liable for the release or threatened release of a hazardous substance under the expansive liability standard fixed in § 107(a); how shall the cost of investigation and cleanup be allocated among the liable parties; and what remedy should be adopted to prevent or abate environmental harm.

This chapter is concerned with the third issue of remedy selection. CERCLA empowers the United States Environmental Protection Agency to investigate a hazardous waste site, develop a cleanup plan, and either order the responsible parties to carry out the plan, seek injunctive relief requiring responsible parties to carry out the plan, or implement the plan unilaterally using money from the Superfund. If the Superfund is used, the EPA may bring a cost recovery suit against a potentially responsible party (PRP) for reimbursement of its "response" costs, including, notably, the cost of implementing the cleanup plan. The Superfund Amendments and Reauthorization Act of 1986 (SARA) limits the ability of PRPs to obtain judicial review of the EPA's choice of remedy. No challenge may be brought until the EPA brings an enforcement or cost recovery suit, and when such a challenge is finally allowed, the scope and standard of judicial review are quite narrow, even in comparison to judicial review of other administrative agency decisions.

The object of this chapter is to provide an overview of the process of administrative record making and judicial review under CERCLA as amended by SARA. Recent court decisions illustrating the limited scope of judicial review are analyzed, and the constitutionality of the scheme is considered under the due process clause. Finally, we discuss how PRPs can best challenge the EPA's choice of a remedy, the administrative record-making process, and the defense of injunctive or cost recovery actions.

CHOOSING REMOVAL AND
REMEDIAL PLANS

§ 25.2   NCP Requirements in General

When the EPA decides that a site requires response action, it has three potential options under CERCLA § 106: it may (1) seek injunctive relief in federal district court, (2) issue an administrative order, or (3) implement

---

[1] 42 U.S.C. §§ 9601–9675 (1988).

the response action unilaterally and seek reimbursement under § 107. Should the EPA choose the third option and implement its own investigation and cleanup, the PRP will be liable only for those costs that were not inconsistent with the National Contingency Plan (NCP).[2]

The NCP sets forth "methods and criteria for determining the appropriate extent of response authorized by CERCLA."[3] Response actions fall into two categories: removal and remedial actions. *Removal actions* are intended to "prevent, minimize, or mitigate" any immediate dangers caused by the release or threatened release of hazardous substances through analysis, removal, and/or containment of the substances;[4] *remedial activities* are designed to prevent further damage to the environment or public health through long-term, permanent remedies.[5] In practice, removal actions are not necessarily limited to emergency situations and will be undertaken whenever EPA sees fit to initiate interim cleanup or containment activities. Moreover, CERCLA defines *removal* broadly to include investigatory activities.[6]

The NCP requires that the EPA first conduct a site evaluation to determine such things as the source of the release or threatened release and the magnitude of the danger to public health and welfare that might be involved.[7] Using the findings of that preliminary study and taking a number of enumerated factors into consideration, the EPA must determine whether removal actions are required.[8] The NCP offers a list of "appropriate" removal actions for particular situations, such as fencing, controlling drainage, stabilizing structures, capping, removing highly contaminated soils, removing drums and other bulk containers, or providing alternate water supplies.[9]

---

[2] 42 U.S.C. § 9607(a)(4)(A) (1980 & Supp. 1990). CERCLA also allows private parties who have incurred response costs to bring a cost recovery suit against other liable parties. *Id.* § 9607(a)(4)(B). The provision is used, for example, when one or more PRPs perform response actions at a site and then seek reimbursement from other, nonparticipating PRPs. § 9607(a)(4)(B) makes a defendant liable for costs that were incurred "consistent with the national contingency plan." Therefore, the following discussion of NCP requirements applies equally to cost recovery suits brought by private parties or by the EPA.

[3] 40 C.F.R. § 300.400(a) (1989).

[4] 42 U.S.C. § 9601(23) (Supp. 1990).

[5] *Id.* §§ 9601(24), 9604(a)(2). *See also* United States v. Hardage (*Hardage II*), 733 F. Supp. 1424, 1431–32 (W.D. Okla. 1989).

[6] 42 U.S.C. § 9601(23).

[7] 40 C.F.R. § 300.410.

[8] *Id.* § 300.415(b).

[9] *Id.* § 300.415(d).

The NCP also delineates the steps to be taken before a remedial plan may be implemented at a hazardous release site. The EPA must conduct a preliminary assessment[10] followed by a Remedial Investigation/Feasibility Study (RI/FS).[11] As part of the feasibility study, the EPA must develop remedial alternatives, "taking into account the scope, characteristics, and complexity of the site problem that is being addressed."[12] All remedial options must be developed and screened using effectiveness, implementability, and cost as criteria.[13] After this initial screening, a more detailed analysis of each remaining remedial alternative must be conducted.[14] Each proposal must be evaluated according to nine factors:

1. Overall protection of human health and the environment
2. Compliance with applicable or relevant and appropriate requirements of federal and state environmental laws (ARARs)
3. Long-term effectiveness and permanence
4. Reduction of toxicity, mobility, or volume through treatment
5. Short-term effectiveness
6. Implementability
7. Cost
8. State acceptance
9. Community acceptance.[15]

The EPA must then select a remedial alternative for presentation to the public. The overall protection of human health and the environment and compliance with applicable ARARs are threshold requirements that an alternative must meet before it can be chosen as the final remedy.[16] The Agency is also required to choose a "cost-effective" remedy, although the

---

[10] *Id.* § 300.420(b), (c).

[11] *Id.* § 300.430(d), (e).

[12] *Id.* § 300.430(e)(2). The 1988 version of the NCP required the EPA to develop at least one remedial alternative in five specified categories. The EPA had to propose a remedy that would require off-site treatment or disposal, one that would attain all federal health and environmental requirements, one alternative that would exceed such federal requirements, one that would not attain the federal requirements but would nevertheless be a significant improvement over the present situation, and one that would require no remedial action at all. Hazardous Substances Response, 40 C.F.R. § 300.68(f)(1) (1988). The 1990 regulations provide the EPA with more flexibility in deciding what kind of remedial options to propose.

[13] 40 C.F.R. § 300.430(e)(7).

[14] *Id.* § 300.430(e)(9).

[15] *Id.* § 300.430(e)(9)(iii).

[16] *Id.* § 300.430(f)(1)(i)(A).

determination of whether a remedial alternative is cost-effective, pursuant to the NCP, includes several factors, of which only one is cost.[17] After the public has had an opportunity to comment on the proposed plan, the Agency must review and respond to any significant comments and new data before making its final choice.[18] The remedial action that is ultimately selected must be set forth in a Record of Decision (ROD).[19] The EPA may then implement its chosen remedial plan at the particular site.

There has been a substantial amount of CERCLA litigation concerning a PRP's ability to challenge the EPA's choice of remedy. Because CERCLA allows the EPA to use Superfund monies to respond to a hazardous waste site and then bring a cost recovery suit against any of the liable parties, remedy selection is of vital importance to the parties who will eventually be found liable to pay the costs. As discussed in § 25.3, CERCLA § 113 places sharp and controversial limits on the avenues through which PRPs may challenge in court the EPA's remedial decisions.[20]

§ 25.3   Judicial Review of Response Actions

In CERCLA § 113, which is one of the provisions SARA added to Superfund, Congress granted the EPA broad discretion to devise cleanup plans and limited judicial review of the selection and implementation of remedies.[21]

SARA allows judicial review of challenges to EPA response action in certain specified judicial proceedings only:

1. A cost recovery action brought pursuant to § 107
2. An enforcement action brought pursuant to § 106(a)
3. An action for reimbursement under § 106(b)(2)

---

[17] *Id.* § 300.430(f)(1)(ii)(D):

> Cost-effectiveness is determined by evaluating the following three of the five balancing criteria . . . to determine overall effectiveness: long-term effectiveness and permanence, reduction of toxicity, mobility, or volume through treatment, and short-term effectiveness. Overall effectiveness is then compared to cost to ensure that the remedy is cost-effective. A remedy shall be cost-effective if its costs are proportional to its overall effectiveness.

[18] 40 C.F.R. § 300.430(f)(3)(i).

[19] *Id.* § 300.430(4)(i).

[20] 42 U.S.C. § 9613 (1986 & Supp. 1990).

[21] *See, e.g.,* United States v. Northeastern Pharmaceutical, 810 F.2d 726, 748 (8th Cir. 1986) ("Because determining the appropriate removal and remedial action involves specialized knowledge and expertise, the choice of a particular cleanup method is a matter within the discretion of the EPA.").

4. A citizens' suit alleging that a removal or remedial action was in violation of some provision of CERCLA

5. An action under § 106 in which the United States has moved to compel a remedial action.[22]

The legislative intent behind limiting judicial review was, presumably, to expedite response action by avoiding delays associated with litigation.[23] As a result of this limited jurisdiction, a PRP cannot challenge EPA's choice of remedial action until the EPA goes to court.[24] By that time, of course, the EPA typically has expended vast sums of money.[25]

In an effort to obtain judicial consideration of EPA's remedial plan before its implementation and without awaiting EPA's institution of suit, several PRP groups have attempted to enjoin implementation of a remedy pursuant to § 113(h)(4), which grants federal court jurisdiction over citizens' suits. For example, in *Cabot Corp. v. EPA,*[26] the PRPs claimed that EPA failed to take certain steps, which were required under CERCLA, to limit the cost of implementing the chosen remedial plan. The court noted that although the statutory language would seem to allow such a suit,

---

[22] 42 U.S.C. § 9613(h).

[23] *See, e.g.,* Jefferson County v. United States, 644 F. Supp. 178, 182 (E.D. Mo. 1986) ("[J]udicial review of agency clean-up activities would hinder and delay the hazardous waste disposal. This delay would be inconsistent with the intent of Congress to allow swift clean-up actions.") *But see* Voluntary Purchasing Groups, Inc. v. Reilly, 889 F.2d 1380, 1388–89 (5th Cir. 1989) (holding that a PRP could not bring a post-cleanup declaratory judgment action because § 113(h) forbade such actions regardless of whether it would interfere with the cleanup process).

[24] *See* Voluntary Purchasing Groups, Inc. v. Reilly, 889 F.2d at 1386–87. Many courts held that the federal courts did not have jurisdiction to hear pre-enforcement challenges to the EPA's remedial actions even before SARA became effective in 1986. *See* Aminoil, Inc. v. EPA, 599 F. Supp. 69, 71 (C.D. Cal. 1984) (CERCLA's statutory language, the legislative history, and interpretive case law all indicate that Congress did not intend to allow pre-enforcement review, although the statute itself did not expressly prohibit such review).

[25] The costs incurred in government cleanups of hazardous waste sites vary widely, but all are sizable. As of June 1989, the average cost of Superfund cleanups was over $30 million. EPA Report, Management Review of the Superfund Program (June 1989).

Because 42 U.S.C. § 9607(a)(4)(A) makes liable parties responsible for "all costs of removal or remedial actions incurred by the United States Government . . . not inconsistent with the national contingency plan," and because such response costs are broadly defined in CERCLA § 101(25), defendants have been held liable for millions of additional dollars in EPA payroll and travel costs as well as Department of Justice enforcement costs. *See* United States v. Hardage, 733 F. Supp. 1424, 1437 (W.D. Okla. 1989) (granted government's motion for summary judgment, thereby holding a PRP group liable for $5,441,201.25 in administrative costs).

[26] 677 F. Supp. 823 (E.D. Pa. 1988).

§ 113(h)(1) explicitly requires PRPs to wait until after EPA initiates a cost recovery suit before challenging remedial plans and their implementation.

> If the PRPs here, in the guise of citizens, were permitted to raise the same challenges in a citizen suit timed in accordance with § 9613(h)(4) that they, as PRPs, would have to wait to raise under § 9613(h)(1), subsection (4) would eviscerate subsection (1). In order to avoid reading §§ 9659 [defining citizen's suits] and 9613(h)(4) as permitting an "end-run" around the ban on pre-enforcement review that would otherwise apply here, § 9613(h)(4) must be read as applying only to those claims that would not otherwise be deferred under § 9613(h)(1), (2), (3) or (5).[27]

In determining whether a claimant is acting as a PRP or as a citizen, the court, says *Cabot,* should look at the kind of harm alleged by the complaining party. If the PRP alleges that the EPA's response action will cause irreparable harm to human health or the environment, a citizen's suit under § 113(h)(4) is appropriate. If, on the other hand, the claimant is alleging merely financial injury, the action should be deferred pursuant to § 113(h)(1).[28]

The *Cabot* case initially generated optimism that courts would be receptive to pre-enforcement citizens' suits alleging that EPA's remedy would likely be harmful to health or the environment. However, subsequent decisions have all but closed the door on even this limited opportunity. For example, in *Schalk v. Reilly,*[29] the court held that a removal action could not be challenged while implementation of a final remedy was pending. A similar result was reached in *Alabama v. EPA.*[30] In a somewhat less restrictive opinion, the court in *Neighborhood Toxic Cleanup Emergency v. Reilly,*[31] held that a citizen's group could not challenge the health aspects of a remedial plan until at least a discrete portion of the plan had been implemented. This opinion at least left open the possibility of challenging remedy selection before implementation of the entire remedy.

The legislative history supports the position that challenges under § 113(h)(4) need not be deferred until the entire response action is completed, but only until the separate and distinct phase that is at issue has been implemented.[32]

---

[27] *Id.* at 828.

[28] *See id.* at 829.

[29] 900 F.2d 1091, 1095 (7th Cir. 1990).

[30] 871 F.2d 1548, 1557 (11th Cir.), *cert. denied,* 110 S. Ct. 538 (1989). ("The plain language of the statute indicates that section 113(h)(4) applies only after a remedial action is actually completed.").

[31] 716 F. Supp. 828 (D.N.J. 1989).

[32] H.R. Conf. Rep. No. 962, 99th Cong., 2d Sess. 224, *reprinted in* 1986 U.S. Code Cong. & Admin. News 3276, 3317.

§ 25.4 —Scope of Judicial Review

In any challenge to a response action taken or ordered by the EPA, the general view is that a reviewing court may only consider the administrative record upon which the EPA has based its decision.[33] This limited scope of review precludes, in most instances, introduction of non-record documentary evidence, the introduction of favorable fact or expert testimony, or the cross-examination of government employees or consultants.[34] In addition, pretrial discovery, although not specifically addressed in § 113 or elsewhere in SARA, has been held to be inconsistent with administrative record review because discovery, in most instances, seeks information that is not part of the administrative record.[35]

Congress chose to circumscribe judicial review in the belief that "limiting judicial review of response actions to the administrative record expedites the process of review, avoids the need for time-consuming and burdensome discovery, reduces litigation costs, and ensures that the reviewing court's attention is focused on the criteria used in selecting the response."[36] Although efficiency and expedition are appropriate goals of public policy, SARA arguably departs from our constitutional tradition

---

[33] 42 U.S.C. § 9613(j)(1). *See* United States v. Mexico Feed & Seed Co., 729 F. Supp. 1250, 1256 (E.D. Mo. 1990); *In re* Acushnet River & New Bedford Harbor, re: Alleged PCB Pollution, 722 F. Supp. 888, 890–91 (D. Mass. 1989). This limitation applies only to those claims that relate to the selection of a remedy. The court is not limited to the administrative record when determining liability or whether the EPA actually incurred certain costs. Such issues must be determined at a de novo proceeding. However, de novo review is not applicable when a party is merely challenging the reasonableness of costs incurred (which is seen as an attempt to challenge the reasonableness of the remedy itself). United States v. Bell Petroleum Servs. Inc., 734 F. Supp. 771, 780 (W.D. Tex. 1990) (*Bell Petroleum II*).

[34] The rule precluding non-record evidence may be relaxed in instances in which the administrative record produced before the court is incomplete or too complicated to be properly reviewed by a non-technical judge. *See* §§ **25.17** and **25.18**.

[35] *See* United States v. Wastecontrol of Fla., Inc., 730 F. Supp. 401, 404 (M.D. Fla. 1989) ("there will generally be no need for discovery" because the review process set forth in § 113(j) limits the reviewing court to the administrative record to determine whether EPA's actions were arbitrary and capricious). *See generally,* Camp v. Pitts, 411 U.S. 138, 142 (1973) ("the focal point for judicial review should be the administrative record already in existence, not some new record made initially in the reviewing court"); Citizens to Preserve Overton Park, Inc. v. Volpe, 401 U.S. 402, 407–09 (1971); United States v. Morgan, 313 U.S. 409, 422 (1941). *But see* United States v. Bell Petroleum Servs., Inc., 718 F. Supp. 588, 591 (W.D. Tex.), *reconsideration denied,* 31 Env't Rep. Cas. (BNA) 1365 (W.D. Tex. 1989) (*Bell Petroleum I*) (administrative record review is required by the statute but some discovery may be necessary).

[36] H.R. Rep. No. 99-253, 99th Cong., 2d Sess. 81, *reprinted in* 1986 U.S. Code Cong. & Admin. News 2835, 2863.

insofar as it makes these values paramount to the fundamental political values fostered by the process of judicial review.

The Administrative Procedure Act,[37] which generally governs judicial review of agency actions in the absence of provisions addressing the subject in the regulatory statute on which the administrative decision is based, clearly contemplates a limited scope of judicial review of the actions of administrative agencies. In most instances, however, there has already been an evidentiary hearing conducted at the agency level, so that the record presented to the court for review includes the evidence and testimony offered at this hearing. SARA, on the other hand, expressly forbids the EPA from holding an adjudicatory hearing in order to develop the administrative record.[38] Thus, SARA designs an administrative review process that not only limits the scope of review to the administrative record, but also limits the means for developing that record to written submissions. Judicial review of an administrative record developed without opportunity for an adjudicatory hearing before the agency has been upheld by the Supreme Court so long as no hearing is required by the statute authorizing the agency action nor mandated by the constitution.[39] Thus, subject to possible due process requirements, a court reviewing EPA's chosen remedy is limited to the record compiled and produced by the agency, regardless of the fact that the defendant has had no opportunity for an adjudicatory hearing through which to shape the record.

§ 25.5   —Standard of Review

If a party seeks to challenge the EPA's choice of remedial action during a cost recovery proceeding, the PRP faces a very strict standard of review. The objecting party must demonstrate that the EPA's choice is "arbitrary and capricious or otherwise not in accordance with law."[40] The Supreme Court in *Motor Vehicles Manufacturers Association v. State Farm Mutual Automobile Insurance Co.,*[41] articulated the standard as follows:

> The scope of review under the "arbitrary and capricious" standard is narrow and a court is not to substitute its judgment for that of the agency.

---

[37] 5 U.S.C. § 706 (1977).

[38] 42 U.S.C. § 9613(k)(2)(C).

[39] *Cf.* Wong Yang Sung v. McGrath, 339 U.S. 33 (1950) (deportation order invalid because proceedings underlying the order did not satisfy APA procedural requirements for adjudicatory hearings).

[40] 42 U.S.C. § 9613(j)(2). *See* United States v. Mexico Feed & Seed Co., 729 F. Supp. 1250, 1256 (E.D. Mo. 1990); *In re* Acushnet River & New Bedford Harbor, 722 F. Supp. 888, 890–91 (D. Mass. 1989); United States v. Akzo Coatings of Am., Inc., 719 F. Supp. 571, 586 (E.D. Mich. 1989).

[41] 463 U.S. 29 (1983).

Nevertheless, the agency must examine the relevant data and articulate a satisfactory explanation for its action including a "rational connection between the facts found and the choice made." In reviewing that explanation, we must "consider whether the decision was based on a consideration of the relevant factors and whether there has been a clear error of judgment." Normally, an agency rule would be arbitrary and capricious if the agency has relied on factors which Congress has not intended it to consider, entirely failed to consider an important aspect of the problem, offered an explanation for its decision that runs counter to the evidence before the agency, or is so implausible that it could not be ascribed to a difference in view or the product of agency expertise. The reviewing court should not attempt itself to make up for such deficiencies; we may not supply a reasoned basis for the agency's action that the agency itself has not given. We will, however, "uphold a decision of less than ideal clarity if the agency's path may reasonably be discerned."[42]

The courts must conduct a thorough review of the administrative record in order to ensure that the EPA followed the prescribed procedures and considered all of the factors that Congress (in CERCLA as amended by SARA) and the EPA (in the NCP) have deemed relevant. Such a thorough review may lead the court to find that an EPA determination was arbitrary and capricious even though it was based on substantial evidence.[43] If, for example, there is substantial evidence supporting an agency's conclusion, but the court finds that the agency failed to consider certain relevant factors or drew irrational conclusions from the facts before it, the court may set aside the agency's decision as arbitrary and capricious.[44]

In order to show that the EPA's choice of remedial action is arbitrary and capricious, a party may attempt to prove that key factual premises on which the EPA relied in making its decision are contradicted by evidence within the administrative record.[45] However, even though the scientific data in the record may be incomplete or conflicting, the EPA's decision is not automatically invalid. In such cases, policy considerations

---

[42] *Id.* at 43 (citations omitted). *See also* Natural Resources Defense Council v. EPA, 790 F.2d 289, 297–98 (3d Cir.), *cert. denied,* 479 U.S. 1084 (1986).

[43] *See* Bowman Transp. Inc. v. Arkansas-Best Freight Sys., Inc., 419 U.S. 281, 284, *reh'g denied,* 420 U.S. 956 (1974) ("though an agency's findings may be supported by substantial evidence . . . it may nonetheless reflect arbitrary and capricious action."); Erco Indus., Ltd. v. Seaboard Coast Line R.R., 644 F.2d 424, 432 n.5 (5th Cir. 1981).

[44] *See* Motor Vehicles Mfrs. Assn. v. State Farm Mut. Auto. Ins. Co., 463 U.S. at 43.

[45] *See generally* Mizerak v. Adams, 682 F.2d 374, 376 (2d Cir. 1982) (stating that "an agency decision is arbitrary and must be set aside when it rests on a crucial factual premise shown by the agency's records to be indisputably incorrect," the court determined that an air traffic controller's discharge was arbitrary and capricious because the agency mistakenly thought a directive had been issued to him). *See also* American Iron & Steel Inst. v. EPA, 568 F.2d 284, 309–10 (3d Cir. 1977) (water pollution regulations remanded because EPA may have proceeded on a mistaken assumption of fact).

may be taken into account. However, decisions based on environmental policy choices are judged under an even more deferential standard because the EPA's expertise is assumed to be greater in the area of environmental policy.[46]

A PRP may also challenge the EPA's choice of response action by showing that it rests upon assumptions or conclusions that are not supported by the facts in the administrative record. Courts reviewing EPA actions under other programs have been willing to review critical agency decisions when the company being regulated has offered its own pollution reduction plan that the EPA has ignored or summarily dismissed. Conclusory statements that the EPA's chosen plan of action is preferable have not been considered sufficient explanation for the EPA's actions.[47]

EPA's response choice must be defended on the record that served as the basis for the decision. Any data acquired after that time, even if it supports the EPA's choice of remedy, can be challenged as a post-hoc rationalization that is irrelevant to the administrative record review. The court may therefore find that a decision was arbitrary and capricious if it was unsupported at the time it was made, even though the same decision would have been a valid choice if made at a later date.[48]

§ 25.6 Judicial Review of Enforcement Actions

Judicial review of EPA's selected remedy is relevant not only to cost recovery actions under CERCLA § 107(a) but also to injunctive or enforcement actions brought by the EPA pursuant to CERCLA § 106(a). The form of the suit may also affect the scope and standard of review available to the PRPs.

CERCLA § 106(a) confers on the district courts jurisdiction to hear injunctive actions brought by the United States and the power to "grant such

---

[46] *See* Environmental Defense Fund v. EPA, 636 F.2d 1267, 1277–78 (D.C. Cir. 1980).

[47] *See* Bethlehem Steel Corp. v. EPA, 651 F.2d 877, 875–77 (3d Cir. 1981), *cert. denied,* 457 U.S. 1105 (1982) (EPA's choice of costly emission control system over the company's less expensive proposal was arbitrary and capricious when the EPA's explanation for its action was so inadequate that meaningful judicial review was frustrated); Asarco, Inc. v. EPA, 616 F.2d 1153, 1161–63 (9th Cir. 1980) (EPA's insistence on its own remedial plan was arbitrary and capricious; court found no reasoned scientific basis for the EPA's decision that the company's proposed emission control system was impractical).

[48] *See* Tanners' Council of Am. v. Train, 540 F.2d 1188, 1192–93 n.13 (4th Cir. 1976) (court set aside regulations on effluent limitations, in part because EPA's finding that certain effluent levels were achievable was not supported by record evidence, and EPA's attempt to rely on data accumulated after the decision was made was rejected as a post-hoc rationalization).

relief as the public interest and the equities of the case may require."[49]
This language, which was not amended by SARA, has been interpreted as
giving courts a much broader range of discretion when trying injunctive
actions than when hearing EPA's cost-recovery claims.[50] In *United States
v. Ottati & Goss, Inc.,* the court ruled that when the EPA seeks injunctive
relief against a PRP, as opposed to seeking to enforce an order or recover
costs, the court need not adopt the remedial alternative recommended by
the EPA.[51] In *Ottati & Goss,* the EPA sought a mandatory injunction requiring defendants to implement a response plan selected by the EPA. The
court refused, noting that the first sentence of § 106(a) pertaining to injunctive relief implies court-selected, not government-selected remedies.
In addition, if the EPA wished to have control over the formulation of the
response action, "it can compile an administrative record, reach a decision, and issue an order."[52] *Ottati* supports the position that at least when
the EPA seeks injunctive relief, the court is not limited to the administrative record and is not required to find that agency action was arbitrary
and capricious in order to overrule the EPA's selected remedy.[53]

On the other hand, the court in *United States v. Seymour Recycling
Corp.*[54] refused to hold a de novo hearing when reviewing the remedy selected by the EPA in a § 106(a) injunctive action. Although the language
in SARA § 113(j)(1) limits the courts' jurisdiction only when reviewing
actions "taken or ordered [by the EPA]," the court held that the arbitrary
and capricious standard discussed in § 113(j)(2) should apply to "any judicial action under this Act."[55]

There is substantial case law that suggests that in CERCLA actions for
injunctive relief, the court may hold a de novo hearing on the remedy issue
and make its own judgment as to the appropriate remedy to be implemented. However, no similar latitude has been recognized in cases in
which the EPA has issued an administrative order pursuant to § 106(a).

---

[49] 42 U.S.C. § 9606(a).

[50] *See* United States v. Ottati & Goss, Inc., 900 F.2d 429, 434 (1st Cir. 1990) (asserting
that the grant of jurisdiction implies that the court has "discretionary legal power").

[51] *Id.* at 434.

[52] *Id.* (emphasis omitted).

[53] *See also* United States v. Conservation Chem. Co., 661 F. Supp. 1416, 1417 (W.D. Mo.
1987) (EPA invoked the court's full equitable powers, including the power to determine
the appropriate remedy, when it filed a § 106(a) action for injunctive relief); United
States v. Hardage, 663 F. Supp. 1280, 1285 (W.D. Okla. 1987) (*Hardage I*) (CERCLA
and SARA afford "greater deference to remedies which the government chooses to implement and finance itself, by restricting review thereof to the administrative record,
and favors defendants when the government seeks to force its own remedy upon
them . . . by allowing *de novo* review in such cases.").

[54] 679 F. Supp. 859, 862–63 (S.D. Ind. 1987).

[55] 42 U.S.C. § 9613(j).

When the government invokes the jurisdiction of the court to compel compliance with a § 106(a) order, a challenge to the response action so "ordered" will be subject to administrative record review under the arbitrary and capricious standard. Both the *Ottati & Goss* and *Hardage I* opinions note that the scope and standard of review are more stringent when the government has actually ordered a response action than when it is merely seeking injunctive relief to implement a proposed plan.

As a practical matter, EPA is unlikely to initiate or prosecute a significant number of § 106(a) injunctive relief actions in the future. Section 106 orders are currently favored by EPA in the belief that the threat of treble damages for noncompliance will induce swift PRP compliance with the Agency's cleanup demands.

§ 25.7 —Retroactivity of SARA

SARA became effective on October 17, 1986. Whether these amendments, and in particular § 113(j), apply to cost recovery cases filed before SARA's effective date is of vital importance to PRPs involved in long-term cases with the EPA. If SARA does not apply retroactively, de novo review of EPA's response action selection is more likely to be granted.[56]

As a general rule, courts will apply the law in effect at the time the decision was rendered.[57] There are two primary exceptions to this rule. The first is when there is a legislative expression of intent not to have a statute applied retroactively. SARA's provisions and legislative history, however, seem to indicate that Congress intended that it apply to pending cases.[58]

The second exception is that a law will not be applied retroactively if doing so would cause a "manifest injustice."[59] In cases instituted before

---

[56] Before SARA's enactment, the standard and scope of judicial review of the EPA's remedy selection were uncertain. Although statements in the legislative history of SARA evidence Congressional belief that § 113 simply "clarifies and confirms" the role of judicial review in the selection of a remedy, S. Rep. No. 11, 99th Cong., 1st Sess. 57 (1985), that Congress saw fit to legislate on the subject suggests that the application of the arbitrary and capricious standard to the administrative record was not universal. *See* United States v. Allied Signal Corp., 30 Env't Rep. Cas. (BNA) 2129 (N.D. Cal. 1990) ("Some courts applied a deferential standard to record review; others undertook *de novo* review. Congress apparently passed § 113(j) for just that reason.").

[57] *See generally* Bradley v. School Bd., 416 U.S. 696, 711 (1974); Yakim v. Califano, 587 F.2d 149, 150 (3d Cir. 1978).

[58] *See In re* Acushnet River & New Bedford Harbor re: Alleged PCB Pollution, 772 F. Supp. 888, 891 (D. Mass. 1989); United States v. Seymour Recycling Corp., 679 F. Supp. 859, 861–62 (S.D. Ind. 1987); United States v. Rohm & Haas Co., 669 F. Supp. 672, 677 (D.N.J. 1987); United States v. Nicolet, Inc., 14 Chemical Waste Litigation Rep. 130 (E.D. Pa. 1987), *aff'd,* 857 F.2d 202 (3d Cir. 1988) (Nicolet I).

[59] Bradley v. School Bd., 416 U.S. at 711.

SARA, PRPs can argue that, because they have been preparing for a full evidentiary hearing, an eleventh-hour switch to administrative record review would be manifestly unjust. Although not expressly making a determination about manifest injustice, at least two courts have refused to apply SARA's record review provisions to cases that were pending as of the Act's effective date.[60] The strength of such an argument depends greatly on the age of the case as of SARA's effective date and the degree of preparation in reliance upon a de novo judicial determination.

Two courts, after analyzing the issue, have explicitly decided that no manifest injustice would result from applying SARA § 113(j) retroactively.[61] According to *Seymour Recycling Corp.,* the PRPs' expectations of a full trial were not "matured and unconditional rights" sufficient to invoke the manifest injustice exception.[62] The *Rohm & Haas* court held that no manifest injustice existed because SARA does not affect vested substantive rights but only modifies the PRPs' procedural rights and legal remedies.[63]

As the time from the effective date of SARA lengthens, the issue of retroactivity will fade in importance as the cases that predate the Act are resolved.

§ 25.8 NCP Requirements for Public Involvement in Development of Administrative Record

Both SARA § 113(k) and the 1990 NCP set out the procedures the EPA must follow in developing the administrative record. These provisions are intended to ensure that interested parties, including PRPs, have the opportunity to participate in the process of selecting a response action.

SARA requires the president and, through him, the EPA, to establish procedures for the participation of the public and directly affected parties

---

[60] *See* United States v. Ottati & Goss, Inc., 900 F.2d 429, 435 (1st Cir. 1990) (upholding lower court's determination that "the case was so long underway when SARA became law, and the parties had relied so heavily upon independent court-record-based remedial determinations, that . . . application of the new law would prove fundamentally unfair"); United States v. Hardage, 663 F. Supp. 1280, 1283 (W.D. Okla. 1987) ("[t]he Court believes retroactive application of such section is improper"); *see also* United States v. Conservation Chem. Co., 661 F. Supp. 1416, 1424 n.10, 1429 (W.D. Mo. 1987) (finding that it would be inequitable to limit the court's ability to determine the appropriate remedy in a late stage of litigation).

[61] United States v. Seymour Recycling Corp., 679 F. Supp. 859 (S.D. Ind. 1987); United States v. Rohm & Haas Co., 669 F. Supp. 672 (D.N.J. 1987). *See also* United States v. Allied Signal Corp., 30 Env't Rep. Cas. (BNA) 2129 (N.D. Cal. 1990); *In re* Acushnet River & New Bedford Harbor, 722 F. Supp. 888, 891 (D. Mass. 1989).

[62] 679 F. Supp. at 862.

[63] 669 F. Supp. at 677.

in the development of the administrative record. Section 113(k)(2)(B) specifies the minimum procedures required under SARA:

1. Notice of the EPA's preferred remedy and any alternative plans must be given to the public and other parties who might be affected
2. The EPA must provide a reasonable period of time in which to comment on the information
3. There must be an opportunity for a public meeting
4. The EPA must respond to each significant comment or criticism
5. Upon selection of a remedy, the EPA must make a statement of the basis and purpose of the selected action.[64]

Until the necessary regulations were promulgated, the EPA was authorized to follow the procedures for response selection and public participation in use at the time SARA became effective.[65] However, as there were no statutory or administrative requirements regarding public participation in effect at the time,[66] the use of "current procedures" generally fell far short of the § 113(k) requirements.[67] A number of pre-SARA decisions reflected judicial discomfort with limitations on the scope of their review of EPA's choice of remedy when "the administrative record [had] been created almost entirely by EPA. It therefore contain[ed] virtually no evidence that might exculpate" the defendant-PRPs.[68] After SARA was enacted, the EPA added certain public notice and comment provisions to the NCP, but, until 1990, there were no regulations adopted pursuant to the mandate of § 113(k).

In March 1990, the EPA promulgated the revised NCP containing the regulations governing the development of the administrative record. These procedures are expressly limited to remedial actions in which the remedial investigation commenced after April 9, 1990, the effective date of the regulations.[69] If remedial actions have already taken place or are

---

[64] 42 U.S.C. § 9613(k)(2)(B).

[65] *Id.* § 9613(k)(2)(C).

[66] *See* United States v. Rohm & Haas Co., 669 F. Supp. 672, 678 (D.N.J. 1987).

[67] Courts responded by holding that the minimum requirements set forth in SARA § 113(k) were to be used to evaluate the pre-SARA procedures used by EPA. *See* In re Acushnet River & New Bedford Harbor, 722 F. Supp. 888, 892–93 (D. Mass. 1989); United States v. Rohm & Haas, 669 F. Supp. at 682–83 (procedures used to allow interested parties to participate in the selection of a response were so inadequate as to make the administrative record incomplete).

[68] Wagner Elec. Corp. v. Thomas, 612 F. Supp. 736, 747 (D. Kan. 1985).

[69] 40 C.F.R. § 300.800(d)(1). As for removal actions, the procedural regulations are only applicable if the action memorandum is signed after April 9, 1990. 40 C.F.R. § 300.800(d)(2).

being undertaken, the EPA is required to comply with the public participation procedures "to the extent practicable."[70] The 1988 NCP, which is presumably applicable to those cases in which investigation began after the 1988 revisions and before April 9, 1990, provides that the EPA must publish remedial alternatives for public comment. During the 21-day comment period, public meetings "shall, in most circumstances," be held, and the public may comment on any of the proposed alternatives.[71] Major issues raised during this time must be summarized and included in the EPA's documents, along with a description of the EPA's response to these issues.[72]

The 1990 NCP lengthens the comment period and elaborates the procedure that EPA must follow in developing the administrative record. Based upon the results of the RI/FS, the EPA is required to issue a proposed response plan that summarizes remedial alternatives that were analyzed by the EPA, identifies the alternative the EPA prefers, and recites the information relied upon to select the preferred action.[73] Notice of the availability of this proposed plan must then be given through a major local newspaper. The EPA must allow the public a reasonable opportunity, not less than 30 days, in which to respond to and comment on the proposed plan. Upon request, the EPA must extend the public comment period for another 30 days. During this period, the EPA must provide an opportunity for a public hearing. If such a hearing is held, a transcript of the meeting must be created and made available to the public. Finally, the EPA must respond to any "significant comments, criticisms, and new relevant information" which arise during the public comment period.[74]

In the final steps of the remedy selection process, the EPA must reevaluate its preferred remedial plan in light of any new information or points of view offered by the public. Upon choosing a final remedial plan, the EPA must document its decision, and all of the facts, analyses of facts, and site-specific policy determinations that served as the basis of that decision, in a Record of Decision (ROD).[75] In this way, the general public and the PRPs are kept apprised of the EPA's proposed actions at a site and can become involved in the selection of a remedy. As of this writing, there is no case law evaluating the consistency of the new NCP regulations with the requirements of SARA. However, as the EPA incorporated all of the key phrases of § 113(k) into the NCP, the new procedures for developing the administrative record will likely be found to satisfy the statutory requirements.

---

[70] 40 C.F.R. § 300.800(e).

[71] Hazardous Substance Response, 40 C.F.R. § 300.67(d) (1988).

[72] *Id.* § 300.67(e).

[73] 40 C.F.R. § 300.430(f)(2) (1990).

[74] *Id.* § 300.430(3).

[75] *Id.* § 300.430(5).

DEFENDING COST RECOVERY ACTIONS

§ 25.9   Influencing the Administrative Record

The preceding discussion regarding the limitations of judicial review in § 106(a) enforcement proceedings and § 107(a) cost recovery actions underscores the need for PRPs to utilize their limited opportunities to mold the administrative record. Favorable judicial review requires a continuous and diligent effort to monitor EPA response activities and to submit appropriate information for inclusion in the record, at the earliest stages of the site investigation.

The administrative record will consist, at a minimum, of the results of the preliminary site assessment, the RI/FS, factual findings made by the EPA, any public comments and EPA's responses to them, and the ROD. The 1990 NCP requires that the ROD must describe how the remedial option chosen:

1. Protects human health and the environment
2. Compares to the federal and state requirements
3. Is cost effective
4. Utilizes permanent solutions and alternative treatment technologies
5. Satisfies the preference for a remedy which reduces toxicity, mobility, or volume of pollutants.[76]

Because these documents constitute the administrative record on which a judge must base a determination of arbitrariness or capriciousness, the PRP must attempt both to influence their contents and to supplement them with submissions setting forth the PRP's position and/or impeaching EPA's position. Failure to do so when the opportunity exists is likely to preclude any meaningful court challenge to EPA's remedy for lack of evidence in the administrative record that contradicts the EPA's assumptions, data, or reasoning.

§ 25.10   —Preliminary Assessment and NPL Listing

The ultimate fate of a site is often strongly influenced by the results of an early preliminary assessment/site investigation (PA/SI). When the EPA is notified of a possible hazardous waste site, it typically has very little

---

[76] *Id.* § 300.430(f)(5)(ii).

information about the site. Nevertheless, inflexible and, to the PRPs, detrimental conclusions are often drawn at that stage regarding the significance of certain contaminants detected at the site, the level of endangerment posed by the site, or the unwillingness of PRPs to assume cleanup responsibility. PRPs are well advised to bring site-specific data to the EPA's attention and into the administrative record at the preliminary assessment stage, in order to stave off ill-considered judgments about a site that may otherwise lead inexorably to placement of the site on the National Priorities List (NPL). Unfortunately, PRPs, particularly non-owner/operator PRPs, seldom get involved at this stage because the EPA does not encourage such involvement and may not even issue notice letters to PRPs until much later in the remedy selection process.[77] In the absence of a notice letter, one may still learn that a site that the company formerly owned or operated or to which it sent waste is the subject of EPA assessment through periodic review of EPA's computer printout of identified sites, known as *CERCLIS*.

To avoid being disadvantaged through lack of notice, PRPs should make every attempt to inform themselves about activities at sites at which they may have future CERCLA liability. Once the EPA has become involved at a site, PRPs should utilize the Freedom of Information Act[78] to obtain EPA records, including PA/SI reports and any factual findings made by the EPA. If appropriate, any detrimental conclusions drawn by the EPA should be rebutted with factually supported statements and comments.

At the preliminary investigation stage, the PRP should consider whether to seek information that refutes the EPA's assertions that a hazardous substance has been released or that federal response activity is necessary. Interested parties might consider conducting their own study, which could include independent field samples to demonstrate low soil contamination levels or basic hydrogeology, in order to rebut EPA findings or assumptions.

Another avenue for PRP involvement is to follow the Federal Register notices of sites that EPA has proposed for inclusion on the NPL. The EPA periodically updates its proposals for NPL listing. In order to insure public involvement, these proposals follow agency rulemaking procedures, which means that any proposed listing is subject to a public comment period and that the EPA must respond to all significant comments and new data introduced during that period.[79] The EPA often takes up to one year or more between the proposed and final inclusion of a site on the NPL. In the interim, preliminary studies and/or removal actions may be conducted. Therefore, keeping abreast of the NPL listings may provide

---

[77] See § **25.19**.

[78] 5 U.S.C.A. § 552 (West 1977 & Supp. 1990).

[79] 40 C.F.R. § 300.425(d)(5).

advance warning of EPA activities to PRPs who may be connected to the site. Commenting on the initial ranking offers the PRP another opportunity to shape the record on which the court reviewing EPA's remedy selection must make its determination. However, EPA generally considers the documents involved in a proposed NPL listing to be a separate package from those relating to the selection of a final remedy. Thus, the EPA may not include any comments made concerning the NPL in the administrative record. For this reason, it is advisable to submit another copy of relevant NPL comments, with the EPA's documents attached, during the official comment period regarding selection of remedy.

§ 25.11 —RI/FS and Record of Decision

The decision by the EPA to engage in extensive remedial activities is based, in large part, on the results of the RI/FS. From them, the EPA determines the geographical scope of any environmental damage, the particular chemicals present and the dangers they pose, the ARARs to be used, and the universe of possible remedial alternatives. Although it is extremely useful to be involved at the preliminary assessment stage, it is often crucial to be involved in and, if possible, to perform the RI/FS.

EPA, however, often prefers to have government contractors perform the RI/FS before serious PRP negotiations begin.[80] In order to maximize the opportunity for PRP involvement, the PRP should, at some point before the government contractor submits a scope of work and work plan for the site, express in writing the desire to perform the RI/FS. In cases in which this is infeasible or impractical, a PRP should engage a consultant to monitor and critique the activities of the EPA's contractor. Oversight is particularly important with respect to the risk assessment portion of the RI/FS. In August 1990, the EPA announced that it would no longer allow PRPs to carry out such studies in lieu of EPA.[81] Thus, PRPs will be deprived of the opportunity to build a favorable record in this regard unless they comprehensively critique EPA's study, a task that is likely to entail the performance of an independent risk assessment.

Interested parties should obtain a copy of the contractor's work plans and make comments before the plans are implemented. The PRP should

---

[80] The process through which the EPA employs its contractors has come under scrutiny recently. Congressional committees like the Office of Technology Assessment and the General Accounting Office have noted that the lack of supervision provided by the EPA has prompted allegations of waste and excessive profits. *See EPA Response Action: Contracting and Cost Recovery Under CERCLA,* 4 Toxics L. Rep. (BNA) No. 8, at 216 (July 26, 1989).

[81] *See* EPA OSWER Directive No. 9835.15 (Aug. 28, 1990).

closely monitor the remedial investigation and the feasibility study. If possible, the party should comment on the draft feasibility study and the EPA's initial screening of the remedial alternatives proposed in the study.[82]

At a minimum, interested parties should engage a consultant to do an in-depth review and detailed critique of the government's final RI/FS and proposed remedial plan, including the risk assessment. Once the RI/FS begins, there is no official public comment period until after the EPA has screened proposed remedial alternatives and selected a plan for implementation. Upon selection, the EPA must present its plan to the public for a period of not less than 30 days. A PRP would be well advised to engage a consultant before the final remedial plan is issued for comment in order to allow adequate time to develop a sound rebuttal to EPA's position before the comment deadline.[83]

The draft of the Record of Decision (ROD) embodies the EPA's proposed decision on the final remedy and should be closely and completely critiqued. The EPA is required to reevaluate its choice of remedy in light of any comments and data offered during the public comment period before making its final decision. Although the EPA is free to depart from the ROD, provided it articulates the basis for its departure, such as newly discovered data, the ROD is ordinarily the EPA's final statement on the matter of remedy selection. Therefore, well-supported criticisms of the proposed ROD represent the PRP's last clear, legally assured opportunity to influence the EPA's choice of a final remedy. Even if it appears certain that the EPA is committed to finalize its proposed ROD, PRPs should nevertheless continue to challenge the conclusions and assumptions on which the EPA relied in formulating its plan, by appropriate submissions to the administrative record. Valid criticisms of the ROD made before it is issued go into the administrative record as facts considered by the EPA before making its selection.

During this public comment period, the EPA has no latitude to ignore or exclude information put before it. PRPs should use this opportunity to criticize any technical or procedural deficiencies in the remedy selection process. Independent evidence that shows that the EPA's position is unsubstantiated or mistaken is very valuable. In addition, any inconsistencies with SARA § 113 or the NCP should be noted at the public meetings

---

[82] EPA must make whatever exists of the administrative record available to the public as early as the RI stage. The EPA is "encouraged" to respond to any significant comments made during these early stages concerning the RI/FS. Once the remedial plan has been selected by the EPA, an official comment period begins. Any significant comments made during that period must receive a written response from the EPA. *See* 40 C.F.R. § 300.815.

[83] The EPA generally limits the comment period to the required 30 days. Should an interested party make a timely request to extend the period, however, the EPA must do so by a minimum of 30 additional days. 40 C.F.R. § 300.430(f)(3)(i)(C).

or in written comments so as to form the basis of a challenge to the remedy during the cost recovery or enforcement proceeding. If procedural errors are raised by the PRP, their materiality to the remedy selection must be shown in order for relief to be granted.[84] Therefore, a PRP should, wherever possible, particularize and quantify the harm caused by EPA's procedural errors.

Because EPA is only required to respond to public comments at discrete times during the remedy selection process, it is important to document, throughout the process, any instance in which the EPA has disregarded valid information that was placed before it in a timely manner. All comments and criticisms made during informal meetings with the EPA should be restated at the public meetings. In addition to, or in lieu of, presentations at public meetings, the PRP should make a written submission of its position, with appropriate technical support and expert opinion. Besides making the case that the EPA's proposed remedy is ill-chosen in comparison to alternatives (including no action, when applicable), the PRP's comments should lend themselves to being used to demonstrate that the EPA's proposed remedy is arbitrary and capricious or otherwise not in accordance with law.[85] If the EPA fails to include submitted material in its record, or fails to respond to significant comments, such instances will assist a PRP's argument that the administrative record is incomplete and must be supplemented.[86]

§ 25.12 Supplementing the Administrative Record

In situations in which the PRP has failed to or been prevented from building an effective or complete administrative record, the PRP's ability to mount a challenge to the remedy will depend on whether the PRP can supplement the record during litigation. Under certain limited circumstances, PRPs may introduce data or expert opinions not of record and may conduct discovery to probe EPA's remedy selection process.

Although SARA § 113(j)(1) limits a reviewing court to the administrative record, it also provides that "[o]therwise applicable principles of administrative law shall govern whether any supplemental materials may be considered by the court."[87] Administrative law recognizes four exceptions

---

[84] 42 U.S.C. § 9613(j)(4).

[85] See § 25.17.

[86] See In re Acushnet River & New Bedford Harbor, 722 F. Supp. 888, 893 (D. Mass. 1989) ("The Court assumes that the EPA will accept, consider, and make part of the record written submissions from the defendants' experts.").

[87] 42 U.S.C. § 9613(j)(1).

to the rule precluding non-record evidence. A judge may allow non-record evidence if:

1. There is a showing that the agency's record is incomplete
2. Outside materials are necessary to show that the agency failed to consider all of the relevant factors in making its decision (see § 25.13)
3. Explanatory or background information is necessary
4. The agency's decision was demonstrably tainted by bad faith (see § 25.15)

If a defendant in an enforcement or cost recovery proceeding can show that the administrative record is defective, limited supplementation of the record may be permitted.

In *Citizens to Preserve Overton Park, Inc. v. Volpe,*[88] the Supreme Court established the principle that judicial review must be based "on the full administrative record that was before the [Agency] at the time [it] made [its] decision."[89] Upon a showing that the record produced by the EPA is incomplete, a court may allow some discovery in order to insure that all of the relevant information has been presented. It is not clear, however, how much of a showing is necessary or how much discovery will be allowed. The D.C. Circuit required a party to make a "substantial showing" of the record's incompleteness before the party was entitled to limited discovery to determine whether other documents were withheld from the record.[90]

A "Catch-22" situation may arise because PRPs may not have had sufficient access to the decision-making process to determine whether the administrative record proffered by EPA is complete. Yet the PRP may be denied the discovery necessary to enable this determination.

The government routinely opposes discovery in cost recovery actions. Courts have generally sided with EPA if a PRP cannot provide a specific basis for asserting that the record is incomplete. For example, in *United States v. Mattiance Trucking Industry, Inc.,*[91] the PRP's argument that discovery was necessary in order to evaluate the record's completeness, considering its late entry into the proceeding, was rebuffed because there was no adequate showing that the record was incomplete. Likewise, in *Nicolet I,*[92] "vague assertions" that the administrative record was incomplete were

---

[88] 401 U.S. 402 (1971).

[89] *Id.* at 420.

[90] Natural Resources Defense Council v. Train, 519 F.2d 287, 290–91 (D.C. Cir. 1975).

[91] No. CV-86-1792 (E.D.N.Y. Sept. 24, 1987).

[92] United States v. Nicolet, Inc., 14 Chemical Waste Litig. Rep. (Computer L. Rep., Inc.) 130 (E.D. Pa. 1987), *aff'd,* 857 F.2d 202 (3d Cir. 1988).

insufficient to justify discovery. In contrast, the court in *United States v. Bell Petroleum Services, Inc.*[93] stated that

> the discovery process is meant to give litigants an opportunity to leave no stone unturned and, in order to do so, they must be allowed to uncover evidence which may or may not be admissible at trial. In order for the Defendants to determine whether the administrative record is complete, some evidence as to the documents, etc. considered by the EPA is relevant.[94]

Another defense strategy to pursue if an incomplete record can be demonstrated is a de novo hearing. The legislative history reflects Congressional intent that a de novo proceeding might be warranted in such instances. "If major deficiencies are shown to exist in the administrative record that has been assembled, judicial review of the response in an enforcement or cost recovery action may be de novo, *i.e.*, open to the introduction of evidence by all parties."[95] Thus far, courts have been unwilling to order such a hearing. However, several cases have resulted in a remand to EPA for supplementation of the record. In *United States v. Charles George Trucking Co.*,[96] the court ordered EPA to submit all correspondence, memoranda, reports, and data in its possession, and to accept additional PRP comments into the record.[97]

§ 25.13   Consideration of Relevant Factors

Both SARA and the NCP require the EPA to consider specific enumerated factors before choosing a removal or remedial action.[98] If the EPA fails to take these factors into account, the court should find that the remedy chosen was arbitrary and capricious.[99] The EPA may not rely on

---

[93] 718 F. Supp. 588 (W.D. Tex. 1989) (*Bell Petroleum I*).

[94] *Id.* at 591.

[95] S. Rep. No. 11, 99th Cong., 1st Sess. 57 (1985).

[96] No. 85-2463-WD, 19 Chemical Waste Litig. Rep. (Computer L. Rep., Inc.) 1300 (D. Mass. filed Feb. 20, 1990).

[97] *See also* United States v. Rohm & Haas Co., 669 F. Supp. 672 (D.N.J. 1987).

[98] 42 U.S.C. § 9621(b)(1)(A)–(G); 40 C.F.R. §§ 300.430(e)(9), 300.430(f)(1).

[99] *See* Natural Resources Defense Council v. EPA, 790 F.2d at 297–98 (citing Motor Vehicles Mfrs. Assn. v. State Farm Mut. Auto. Ins. Co., 463 U.S. 29, 43 (1983) (in deciding whether the EPA had acted in an arbitrary and capricious manner, it was necessary to determine whether the EPA had considered all of the relevant factors); Asarco, Inc. v. EPA, 616 F.2d 1153, 1158 (9th Cir. 1980) (citing *Citizens to Preserve Overton Park, Inc. v. Volpe,* 401 U.S. 402, 415 (1971)) ("[T]o determine whether the decision was arbitrary or capricious, the court must consider whether the decision was 'based on a consideration of the relevant factors.'").

claims that it has considered a certain factor if the record contains no such indication.[100] The preferred remedy for failure to consider relevant factors seems to be a remand to the EPA "for appropriate consideration of the factors originally not included by the Agency."[101]

The practical benefits of a remand to the agency are questionable, particularly in cost recovery actions in which the EPA has already implemented its remedial plan. EPA is more likely to rationalize its choice than to alter a ROD in light of overlooked data or factors. A court, however, may be persuaded to subject EPA's rationalization of its choice on remand to closer-than-customary scrutiny, recognizing EPA's nearly irresistible temptation to defend an already implemented plan. A compromise position between remand and de novo review is for the district court to supplement the record in any manner it deems necessary, including allowing discovery on particular issues.[102]

§ 25.14   Explanatory or Background Information

Courts have held that the administrative record may be supplemented with outside materials when such materials will serve an explanatory function, as opposed to an argumentative function. "[I]n the often difficult task of reviewing administrative regulations, the courts are not straightjacketed to the original record in trying to make sense of complex technical testimony, which is often presented in administrative proceedings without ultimate review by nonexpert judges in mind."[103] The court may request supplemental briefs from the parties in order to clarify the technical issues, or require in-court testimony from the administrative officials who participated in the decision in order to determine its basis.[104]

It is clear, however, that these exceptions to the prohibition on non-record evidence do not require a de novo hearing. Administrative law principles allow the court to seek out explanatory and background information,

---

[100] The Third Circuit in American Iron & Steel, 568 F.2d at 301–02, found that, although the EPA asserted otherwise, the record showed no evidence that it had taken certain relevant factors into account. The court remanded the case to the EPA for further consideration.

[101] *American Iron & Steel Inst. v. EPA,* 568 F.2d 284, 302 (3d Cir. 1977) *See also* United States v. Rohm & Haas Co., 669 F. Supp. 672, 683–84 (D.N.J. 1987).

[102] *See* United States v. Wastecontrol of Fla., Inc., 730 F. Supp. 401, 405 (M.D. Fla. 1989).

[103] Bunker Hill Co. v. EPA, 572 F.2d 1286, 1292 (9th Cir. 1977) (remanded EPA finding of technical feasibility for further proceedings).

[104] *Id.* at 1292; Asarco Inc. v. EPA, 616 F.2d 1153, 1159 (9th Cir. 1980).

but they do not necessarily authorize the creation of a new evidentiary record in the district court superseding the administrative record. This limitation was reinforced in *Asarco, Inc. v. EPA,*[105] in which the Ninth Circuit held that the district court's de facto trial of four days in length, which involved numerous exhibits and witnesses, exceeded the proper consideration of non-record evidence. In addition, the appellate court found that expert technical testimony was improperly considered for the purpose of judging the wisdom of the EPA's actions.

§ 25.15   Bad Faith

A court may require the EPA to supplement its administrative record if procedural inadequacies occurred as a result of bad faith by the agency.[106] In *United States v. Charles George Trucking Co,*[107] the court suggested that the EPA may have acted in bad faith by failing to provide adequate notice to the PRPs regarding their possible liability. The EPA had posted notice of the remedy selection process in the local newspapers and government building but had not issued notice letters to all suspected PRPs prior to issuance of a ROD. The court was not, therefore, convinced that the EPA had made a conscientious effort to solicit the defendants' input in the process.[108] However, as with explanatory or background material, an inference of bad faith does not necessarily warrant a de novo hearing. More often than not, the EPA will simply be invited to offer supplemental materials to rebut any inference of bad faith raised by the PRP.[109] The court in *Charles George Trucking,* however, awarded more meaningful relief by opening the record to any submissions that the defendants wished to make, at the same time limiting EPA's record to information in its possession at the time the ROD was issued.[110]

---

[105] 616 F.2d at 1160.

[106] *See* Citizens to Preserve Overton Park, Inc. v. Volpe, 401 U.S. 402, 420 (1971); United States v. Wastecontrol of Fla., Inc., 730 F. Supp. 401, 404 (M.D. Fla. 1989); United States v. Seymour Recycling Corp., 679 F. Supp. 859, 866 (S.D. Ind. 1987). *See also* Bethlehem Steel Corp. v. EPA, 638 F.2d 994, 1000 (7th Cir. 1980) (a mere assertion of EPA's bad faith was enough to warrant supplementation of the record).

[107] No. 85-2463-WD, 19 Chemical Waste Litig. Rep. (Computer L. Rep., Inc.) 1300 (D. Mass. 1990).

[108] *Id.* at 1213 (transcript location) (recounting information).

[109] *See* United States v. Wastecontrol of Fla., Inc., 730 F. Supp. at 405.

[110] United States v. Charles George Trucking Co., No. 85-2463-WD, 19 Chemical Waste Litig. Rep. at 1300–01.

§ 25.16   Due Process Challenges

Although the scope and standard of judicial review have been strictly limited by SARA, the constitutionality of the administrative record review scheme created by § 113 is itself reviewable.[111] The constitutional argument, in a nutshell, is that PRPs have procedural rights that are protected by the due process clause of the Fifth Amendment. A fundamental requirement of due process is that no person may be deprived of life, liberty, or property at the hands of the government without notice and an opportunity to be heard.[112] Although that opportunity does not necessarily have to be given before the deprivation takes place, the aggrieved individual must be heard "at a meaningful time, in a meaningful manner."[113] The deferral of review of remedy selection until after the remedy is implemented and cost recovery litigation has been initiated may fail the constitutional test.[114]

§ 25.17   —The *Mathews* Test

Determining the amount of process required by the Constitution in a particular factual situation requires the court to apply a balancing test. In

---

[111] A challenge to the constitutionality of the statutory scheme is a separate and distinct claim from a challenge to the particular remedial decision reached by the EPA. United States v. Bell Petroleum Servs., Inc., 718 F. Supp. 588, 590 (W.D. Tex.), *reconsideration denied,* 31 Env't Rep. Cas. (BNA) 1365 (W.D. Tex. 1989). Such challenges are subject to the jurisdictional limitations of § 113(h) and cannot be brought before an enforcement or cost recovery proceeding has been initiated. *See* Barmet Aluminum Corp. v. Thomas, No. 88-0173-0 (W.D. Ky. Feb. 20, 1990) (pre-enforcement constitutional challenges to EPA cleanup action are prohibited by § 113(h)).

[112] *See generally* Marbury v. Madison, 5 U.S. (Cranch) 137, 176 (1803) ("It is a proposition too plain to be contested, that the constitution controls any legislative act repugnant to it; or that the legislature may alter the constitution by an ordinary act."); *see also* New Jersey Speech-Language-Hearing v. Prudential Ins. Co., 724 F.2d 383, 387 (3d. Cir. 1983) ("We recognize that there are due process limitations on congressional power to preclude affected parties from seeking review of agency actions.").

[113] *See* Parrat v. Taylor, 451 U.S. 527, 540 (1981).

[114] *Id.; see also* West Penn Power Co. v. Train, 522 F.2d 302, 312 (3d Cir. 1975), *cert. denied,* 426 U.S. 947 (1976), *reh'g denied,* 429 U.S. 873 (1976); Southern Ohio Coal Co. v. Donovan, 593 F. Supp. 1014, 1022 (S.D. Ohio 1984), *aff'd,* 774 F.2d 693 (6th Cir. 1985). *Cf.* Industrial Park Dev. Co. v. EPA, 604 F. Supp. 1136, 1141 (E.D. Pa. 1985) (although questioning other pre-SARA decisions that strictly limited the availability of judicial review, the court stated, "This court has grave doubts about the constitutionality of delegating to a variety of administrative officials statutory authorization for deprivation of property without prior notice and hearing or prompt subsequent administrative or judicial review.").

Mathews v. Eldridge,[115] the Supreme Court found that three factors must be weighed in order to make this determination:

1. The nature of the private interest at stake
2. The risk of erroneous deprivation through the procedures used and the probable value, if any, of additional safeguards
3. The government's interest, including the burdens that additional procedural requirements would entail.

In applying this test to administrative record review under SARA § 113, the first factor, the nature of the private interest, suggests that substantial procedural safeguards are required to satisfy due process requirements. Many remedial actions have astronomical price tags,[116] which the PRPs will be expected to pay. Even when the response costs are limited, as in a removal action, there is a private interest in not being compelled to implement or pay for a remedy chosen by the government in which one has had no fair say.

According to one court, the risk of erroneous deprivation from the § 113 procedures and the value of additional procedural safeguards, which are the second factor in the *Mathews* test, suggest that a "scope of review less than *de novo* would be grossly unfair."[117] Administrative record review offers the defendant no right to cross-examine EPA witnesses on their selection of a particular remedy. EPA's remedy selection is often based on legitimately disputed facts, such as baseline human health risk in the absence of remediation or the feasibility of cross-effective containment and on-site treatment technologies. In such cases, the right to cross-examine key government witnesses may be of vital importance.[118] A

---

[115] 424 U.S. 319, 335 (1976).

[116] See § **25.3**.

[117] United States v. Hardage, 663 F. Supp. 1280, 1290 (W.D. Okla. 1987) ("the *Mathews* three prong test weighs in favor of *de novo* review of EPA's preferred remedy."). *But see In re* Acushnet River & New Bedford Harbor, 722 F. Supp. 888, 893 (D. Mass. 1989) (in a pretrial ruling on the scope and standard of review in a § 107(a) suit, court found that the PRPs' ability to influence the record, judged "under an arbitrary and capricious standard, coupled with trial on the liability issue, and this Court's review of the administrative record generated by the EPA's procedure, suffice to satisfy due process."); United States v. Seymour Recycling Corp., 679 F. Supp. 859, 864–65 (S.D. Ind. 1987) (in a § 106(a) suit for injunctive relief, de novo determinations of liability and the court's searching and in-depth review of the administrative record provide sufficient protection against erroneous deprivation of property).

[118] Goldberg v. Kelly, 397 U.S. 254, 269–70 (1970) ("In almost every setting where important decisions turn on questions of fact, due process requires an opportunity to confront and cross-examine witnesses.").

recent case, however, has suggested that a "paper hearing" may be sufficient if the disputed issues revolve around expert opinion and data.[119]

A striking feature of the administrative record review scheme erected in SARA is that the same EPA staff that selected the remedy then judges the merits of the criticisms and data raised in opposition to the plan and prosecutes liable parties to enforce the EPA's implementation order or to recover the costs incurred under the plan. Allowing the EPA to act as the decision maker, the judge, and the prosecutor in enforcement and cost recovery actions has been called the "most flagrant denial of due process."[120] This procedure greatly increases the risk of erroneous deprivation because there are no external checks on the EPA's discretion until the judicial review stage. And at that stage, SARA so confines the scope of the court's reviewing function as to call into question whether judicial review truly serves a deterrent or corrective function.

As for the third prong of the *Mathews* test, which is the government/public interest in streamlining the judicial review process, it has been said in defense of § 113 that its intent is to prevent parties from delaying the abatement of environmental hazards while they haggle or joust over the "correct" remedy.[121] Such court battles would undoubtedly delay the implementation of the EPA's chosen response plan.[122] However, it is debatable whether the interest in expeditious environmental cleanups justifies trimming due process in either § 106(a) enforcement proceedings or § 107(a) cost recovery actions.

If the PRP is faced with a cost recovery suit, the remedial plan has already been implemented and the need for emergency action has passed. Therefore, the public's interest in limiting a defendant's due process rights is minimal. The choice of remedy affects public health and welfare more than deciding who will pay for the cleanup. Moreover, the magnitude of cost expenditure may materially impact numerous PRPs. Why then, does liability determination get a full evidentiary hearing while remedy selection is limited to a paper trial? The answer may be that the government wants to limit the PRP's ability to prove arbitrariness and, thereby, restrict recovery of remedial expenditure by EPA. Although protection of the financial integrity of the Superfund is an important goal, one cannot help but question the one-sided nature of CERCLA judicial review.

---

[119] United States v. Rohm & Haas Co., 669 F. Supp. 672, 681 (D.N.J. 1987) (holding that if the issue to be decided depends less on fact finding and more on an evaluation of expert reports and technical data, due process is satisfied by a limited, paper hearing in which affected parties have a meaningful opportunity to participate).

[120] United States v. Hardage, 663 F. Supp. at 1290.

[121] See § **25.3**.

[122] *See* Voluntary Purchasing Groups, Inc. v. Reilly, 889 F.2d 1380, 1386–87 (5th Cir. 1989); United States v. Seymour Recycling Corp., 679 F. Supp. at 865.

Nevertheless, judicial empathy for this dilemma may be scarce. De novo review of the EPA's selection of a response action would not interfere with any legitimate government interest. One court even found that limited judicial review would result in fairness by producing national uniformity.[123]

§ 25.18 —At a Meaningful Time, in a Meaningful Manner

A PRP could also bring a facial challenge to the administrative record review process by asserting that the process does not come at a meaningful time or in a meaningful manner. The denial of a predeprivation hearing[124] is justifiable only if meaningful review is available at some stage of the proceedings. Section 113(k) forbids the EPA from holding an adjudicatory hearing in order to select a response action.[125] EPA would argue that this omission is justified because the PRP who will be asked to pay for the selected action will be given an opportunity to challenge the EPA's selection during the enforcement or cost recovery proceeding.[126] Instead of a judicial hearing on the overarching issue of remedy selection, however, the statute allows a full judicial hearing on the issue of liability only. Given the near absolute liability standard erected by § 107(a), however, the opportunity to meaningfully litigate what is typically a nonlitigable issue is due process of a hollow sort. The PRP is never given the opportunity to bring all of its evidence regarding the soundness of the EPA's remedial selection before the court.

Another rationale offered by courts for upholding the administrative record review process is that the interested parties are given ample opportunity to develop the administrative record and influence the EPA's choice

---

[123] *But see* United States v. Seymour Recycling Corp., 679 F. Supp. at 865 (government has an interest in "more uniform and consistent remedial action decisions for hazardous waste sites throughout the country, which ultimately will provide more fairness to the process").

[124] Note that there is a question concerning when the deprivation actually occurs. PRPs allege that they are deprived of property as soon as the EPA incurs costs, that is, as soon as the response plan is implemented. The EPA and some of the courts, however, maintain that there is no possible deprivation until the EPA brings a cost recovery suit. *See* Lone Pine Steering Comm. v. EPA, 777 F.2d 882, 887 (3rd Cir.), *cert. denied,* 476 U.S. 1115 (1985); J.V. Peters v. Ruckelshaus, 584 F. Supp. 1005 (N.D. Ohio 1984). If a court adopts the latter view, the cost recovery suit provides predeprivation process. The PRP must then rely on arguments that such process is so limited by § 113(j) that it is not constitutionally adequate.

[125] 42 U.S.C. § 9613(k)(2)(C).

[126] *See* Wagner Elec. Corp. v. Thomas, 612 F. Supp. 736, 748 (D. Kan. 1985) (pre-enforcement review of an administrative order disallowed on the express assumption that judicial review would not be limited to administrative record).

of remedy.[127] The statute and the NCP may theoretically allow for such participation but, as applied, the process often hinders the participation of interested parties.[128] Although Congress encourages the EPA to notify potentially responsible parties that they may be liable at a site and that they may wish to take an early interest in the activities at that site, there is no requirement that the EPA do so.[129]

In practice, the chances of being identified and notified early in the process depend upon the nature and extent of owner/operator records and the aggressiveness of EPA in issuing information requests to likely PRPs. At sites that EPA identifies early on as "Fund-lead," PRP identification may receive a low priority until the RI/FS process is well underway. In some cases, key PRPs may not be notified until a ROD is issued. For example, at the Bridgeport Rental and Oil Services (BROS) site in New Jersey, a ROD was issued in 1985, but notice letters to most PRPs were first issued in 1988.

Without timely notice, the opportunity for participation is altogether illusory. PRPs who are not notified of the administrative proceedings until after the record has been compiled and a remedy selected should arguably be entitled to de novo review because the justification for limited review, the opportunity to participate in the development of the record, does not apply to them.[130] The recent cases of *United States v. Charles George*

---

[127] *See* Lone Pine Steering Comm. v. EPA, 777 F.2d at 887.

[128] Note that challenging the constitutionality of § 113 along these lines is not necessarily a facial challenge to the statute but is a challenge to the manner in which the statute was applied. Such an argument should be offered in the alternative in case the judge finds that § 113 is constitutional. A statute that satisfies the Constitution on its face can be applied in a manner that violates the defendant-PRP's right to due process.

[129] 42 U.S.C. § 9613(k)(2)(D) ("The President shall make reasonable efforts to identify and notify potentially responsible parties as early as possible before selection of a response action. *Nothing in this paragraph shall be construed to be a defense to liability.*") (emphasis added). *But see* 40 C.F.R. § 300.825(c).

[130] *See* United States v. Rohm & Haas Co., 669 F. Supp. 672, 684 (D.N.J. 1987) ("[A] potential constitutional question [is raised] concerning the adequacy of SARA's judicial review procedures as applied to parties who had no opportunity to participate in the process before the agency."). *But see* General Elec. Co. v. Litton Business Sys., Inc., 715 F. Supp. 949, 961 (W.D. Mo. 1989) (one private party, GE, could sue another private party for cost recovery even though NCP public involvement requirements were not met; court stated that "no public hearing was required due to the fact that GE was complying with legally applicable or relevant and appropriate state requirements that the waste be removed."). Whereas *General Electric* requires almost no process, Bethlehem Steel v. EPA, 638 F.2d 994, 1004 (7th Cir. 1980), indicates that even those PRPs who have been involved in the remedy selection process may be able to challenge the constitutionality of § 113 as applied.

> [I]f the requirements of due process are to be met and adequate judicial review is to be obtained, the agency must provide a written decision that clearly sets out the grounds which form the basis of its action. Secrecy, whether intentional or

Trucking Co.[131] and *United States v. Kramer*[132] indicate that courts and possibly even the government have begun to recognize that PRPs may not lawfully be excluded from participation in the building of the administrative record. In *Kramer,* EPA took the position that defendants who were not identified at the time of the remedy selection, and who therefore did not participate in that process, should be given the opportunity to comment on the remedy selected.[133] These comments, and any EPA responses thereto, would be accepted pursuant to the criteria set forth in the NCP for such late submissions.[134] In *Charles George Trucking,* the tardiness of notice to PRPs was deemed to reflect negatively on the extent of good faith efforts made by EPA to elicit PRP participation in the remedy selection. The court therefore required EPA to produce additional documents and allow PRP submissions to the record.

It is noteworthy that the above cases, although supporting the notions that the record should be complete and that all PRPs should have the opportunity to participate in its creation, do not show a willingness to allow or undertake de novo review. Thus, EPA is still, presumably, entitled to judicial deference under an arbitrary and capricious standard.

Finally, due process generally requires that the party being deprived of his life, liberty, or property be given the opportunity to be heard by an impartial decision maker. In the administrative scheme set forth under § 113, the opinions, criticisms, and suggestions of the PRPs are judged by the EPA, an entity which is clearly not impartial because it has selected the remedy and its own funds are at stake regarding the issue of NCP consistency. When the EPA seeks to recover costs, the PRP may challenge the EPA's selection before a federal court judge. However, the judge's decision must be made on the basis of a record that was compiled by an interested actor, the EPA. And the judge's narrow scope and standard of review

---

otherwise, is inconsistent 'with fundamental notions of fairness implicit in due process and with the ideals of reasoned decision making on the merits which undergirds all our administrative law.'

[131] No. 85-2463-WD, 19 Chemical Waste Litig. Rep. (Computer L. Rep., Inc.) 1300 (D. Mass. 1990).

[132] United States v. Kramer, No. 89-4340 (D.N.J. Oct. 16, 1989).

[133] *See* Letter from Bernard P. Bell, Assistant Attorney General of the Environment and Natural Resources Division, to the Honorable Jerome B. Simandle, Magistrate *in* United States v. Kramer, (July 26, 1990); *see also* United States v. Charles George Trucking Co., No. 85-2463-WD, 19 Chemical Waste Litig. Reporter at 1300 (upon an inference that the EPA did not make a good faith effort to solicit PRP participation in the remedy selection process, court ordered EPA to supplement the record with current submissions from parties affected by EPA action).

[134] 40 C.F.R. § 300.825(c).

preclude a comprehensive evaluation, by the only impartial decision-maker in the process, of a critical EPA decision.

§ 25.19   PRP Strategy

The statutory and regulatory scheme created through SARA and the NCP strictly limits the PRP's ability to challenge the EPA's choice of remedial action. Under existing case law, pre-enforcement judicial review of any aspect of the response activity is next to impossible to obtain. Thus, PRPs are well advised to develop a defense strategy to prepare for the inevitable cost recovery suit:

1. During the remedial selection process, PRPs should introduce as much evidence into the record as possible and rebut unfavorable government data or conclusions
2. During litigation, PRPs should seek discovery to confirm the completeness of and clarify the record
3. PRPs should seek the opportunity to introduce data and experts and to examine government experts
4. To the extent PRPs are notified late in the process, or EPA excludes critical information from the record, PRPs should seek, at minimum, a remand of the record to EPA for supplementation.

CHALLENGING EPA'S EXPENDITURE
OF FUNDS

§ 25.20   EPA's Cost Billings to PRPs

The previous portion of this chapter focused upon challenging the substantive remedy selection decision and the administrative process which led thereto. The following sections will address issues pertaining to the actual expenditure of funds by the government and the documentation of such expenditures. EPA's contracting and accounting procedures will be reviewed and strategies for attacking government costs at trial will be discussed.

In the process of any cleanup, the government incurs costs that it will attempt to recover from the PRPs. These government costs include investigations of the site and evaluation of various remedies, oversight of PRP cleanup activities, and execution of any government cleanup action, if necessary.

By law, the EPA is entitled to recover its incurred cleanup costs from responsible parties. The NCP states that "Responsible parties shall be liable for all response costs incurred by the United States government or a State or an Indian tribe not inconsistent with the [NCP]."[135] CERCLA provides that when a release or threatened release "causes the incurrence of response costs responsible parties are liable for all costs of removal or remedial action incurred by the United States Government . . . not inconsistent with the [NCP]."[136]

The government incurs many types of costs in a response action. A determination of which costs should be recoverable from the PRPs is governed by the NCP and definitions used in CERCLA and SARA, by the Federal Acquisition Regulations (FAR), and by emerging case law.

Because CERCLA states that PRPs are "liable for all costs of removal or remedial action incurred," it is important to understand how the regulations define these terms. CERCLA classifies any removal (off-site disposal) or remedy (on-site neutralization) as a *response*. Removal and remedy are defined by CERCLA as follows:

> Removal . . . means the cleanup or removal of released hazardous waste . . . such actions as may be necessary to monitor, assess, and evaluate the release, . . . the disposal of removed material, or the taking of such actions . . . to prevent, minimize or mitigate the damage. . . . The term includes fencing . . . provision for alternate water supplies, temporary evacuation and housing.[137]

> Remedy . . . means those actions consistent with the permanent remedy. . . . The term includes . . . storage, confinement, perimeter protection, clay cover, neutralization, cleanup of released hazardous substances or contaminated materials, recycling or reuse . . . on-site treatment or incineration . . . and any monitoring reasonably required.[138]

SARA did not drastically alter these definitions. It clarified one area of contention by adding "related enforcement activities" to the definition of response activities.[139]

The FAR apply to government activities in general but were not written specifically to address environmental or EPA matters. The EPA has drafted its own regulations, Environmental Protection Agency Acquisition Regulations (EPAAR), to deal with certain specifications applicable only to environmental issues. The FAR establish basic rules for verifying what are proper and reasonable costs.

---

[135] 40 C.F.R. § 300.700(c)(1).

[136] CERCLA § 107(a), 42 U.S.C. § 9607(a).

[137] 42 U.S.C. § 9601(23).

[138] *Id.* § 9601(24).

[139] SARA § 101(25).

Actual costs are defined by the FAR as "amounts determined based on the basis of costs incurred, as distinguished from forecasted costs."[140] This concept sounds straightforward but becomes very complex in practice. For example, the government allows a *cost of facilities capital,* which is interest on the physical plant the contractor has dedicated to the project. A contractor who has no debt does not actually incur this cost, yet it is allowable. The government may include a market level charge for government-owned facilities such as office space. When the government's cost basis is substantially below these market level charges, the PRPs may dispute that these artificial charges were incurred.

The FAR also deals with the allocability or reasonableness of selected costs.[141] These regulations were established to standardize those costs that should be reimbursed by the government under a multitude of contract types. Items like first class airfare and lavish entertainment are examples of costs disallowed by the FAR.

In addition to reasonableness, the FAR deals with whether certain costs are allocable to specific activities.[142] These regulations were written by the government to establish what constitutes a proper allocation of costs to a site and which costs, although not incurred directly at the site, could be allocated or associated with that particular activity.

Allocability of various government indirect costs becomes a major issue when the PRPs begin to understand the source and magnitude of these indirect cost charges relative to the overall bill from the government. Government indirect cost rates can be as high as 300 percent of direct labor dollars.

---

[140] Federal Acquisition Regulations, 48 C.F.R. § 31.001 (1989).

[141] *Id.* § 31.205. *Selected costs* include detailed discussions of public relations and advertising costs; data processing equipment leasing costs; bad debts; bonding costs; civil defense costs; appropriate compensation for personal services; contributions or donations; contingencies; cost of money (interest); depreciation; economic planning costs; employee morale, health, and welfare; food service planning costs; dormitory costs; entertainment costs; fines and penalties; gains and losses on disposition of depreciable personal property or other capital assets; idle facilities and idle capacity costs; R&D and bid and proposal costs; insurance costs; interest and other financial costs; labor relations costs; legislative lobbying costs; losses on other contracts; maintenance and repair costs; manufacturing and production engineering costs; materials costs; organization and other business costs; plant protection costs; patent costs; plant reconversion costs; precontract costs; professional and consultant service costs; recruitment costs; relocation costs; rental costs; royalties and other costs for the use of patents; selling costs; special tooling and special test equipment costs; taxes; trade, business, technical, and professional activity costs; training and education costs; transportation costs; travel costs; defense of fraud proceedings; deferred R&D costs; goodwill; executive lobbying costs; and costs of alcoholic beverages.

[142] 48 C.F.R. §§ 31.201-4, 31.203.

§ 25.21   Challenging EPA's Incurred Cost Claim

In challenging the government's incurred cost claim, several important steps should be considered:

Adequacy of EPA's Documentation

EPA and its contractors are required to maintain certain minimum levels of documentation[143] for costs incurred at the site. Because of the complexity and size of our government, its various accounting systems, and the number of contractors involved, the quality of the cost documentation submitted by EPA can vary.

The government's controls and accounting systems have been repeatedly criticized by the GAO and other oversight and audit agencies. In an attempt to patch this weakness, the EPA has retained outside consulting services to manage the documentation of these incurred costs claims for each site.

EPA's Compliance with Government Contracting Rules

The government is not always proficient in following its own rules and regulations to insure that all of its costs incurred and submitted to PRPs meet government standards. The EPA's own Inspector General found that "about 30 percent of the contractor costs were questionable because they might be unallowable under provisions of applicable laws, regulations, or policies or were unacceptable without additional information or evaluations and approvals by responsible EPA officials."[144]

Prior to the commencement of a cleanup action, EPA normally establishes a budget for each element of the cleanup work. As the work progresses, EPA may approve substantial budget overruns on a site. Many times the EPA approves the cost increase after the fact. This situation was discussed by the GAO in their report: "In essence, the contractor rather than the EPA has decided how the funds should be spent. Since EPA is not controlling these increases, the government's risk of inefficient and ineffective use of contract resources is increased."[145]

The PRP should perform a detailed review to ensure that EPA is following appropriate contracting procedures and is properly accumulating incurred costs in accordance with the relevant rules and regulations.

---

[143] *Financial Management of the Superfund Program,* EPA Manual 2550D (Oct. 1, 1987).

[144] Office of Technology Assessment (OTA) Report, Assessing Contractor Use in Superfund (Jan. 1989).

[145] *EPA Needs to Control Contractor Costs,* Superfund Contracts (July 1988).

Evaluation of EPA Contractor's Performance

By the government's own admission, there are significant problems in the work that outside contractors perform for EPA at various cleanup sites. A government report stated,

> Redundant contractor work, poorly defined work by the government, greater use of less experienced people, poorly supervised work that leads to late recognition of problems, greater concerns about being criticized which lead to unnecessary, defensive work, and changing agency policies and personnel all probably contribute to high government cleanup costs. From looking at actual costs and speaking to contractors and PRPs, we find it plausible that the government may spend from 100 to 500 percent more than a private client would spend to accomplish essentially the same site study or cleanup.[146]

Another government report stated that

> challenging questionable contractor costs and hours is important because the challenge itself influences the contractor to be more economical. Conversely, failure to pursue actions where warranted could convey a message to the contractors—and may have already done so—that EPA is willing to accept cost increases no matter what level of performance is provided.[147]

PRPs may consider retaining outside engineering and financial analysis experts to evaluate the EPA contractor's performance and costs. An investigation should also be performed to determine if rates being paid are "market" rates. Additional investigation should be performed into the degree of subcontracting employed. If there are excessive layers of subcontractors, the overall cost of cleanup can become inflated by virtue of the multiple subcontract markups being paid.

The opinion in *United States v. Bell Petroleum Services Inc.* recently recognized that EPA's expenses are unreasonably excessive. Unfortunately, the court chose to rationalize the situation as inevitable and predictable:

> the Court keeps in mind the fact the wrongdoers . . . had the option of taking responsibility for their own actions at the outset, which, had they done so, would have limited certain costs. Our Government, God bless her, is a bureaucratic monster which, by definition, runs inefficiently. . . . Many, many costs would have been unnecessary had the Defendants shouldered the burden and sought to quickly and efficiently clean up the mess they made. Instead, their free ride expenses of a typical government, costs of discovery and trial, Court costs . . . the list is unending. For the

---

[146] OTA Report, Assessing Contractor Use in Superfund (Jan. 1989).
[147] *EPA Needs to Control Contractor Costs,* Superfund Contracts (July 1988).

Defendants to come to the Court now with white gloves and complain of dust is, in the Court's opinion, unbecoming to any member of society.[148]

Evaluation of Indirect Cost Charges

EPA has taken the position that it is entitled to recover costs incurred at the response site as well as costs incurred in support of the activities at that site. Costs incurred at the cleanup site are generally referred to as *direct costs*. These costs would include preliminary studies, planning costs, cleanup or removal costs, as well as most other on-site or site-specific costs. Costs that are incurred off-site and are not site-specific but can be causally linked as being necessary to support the cleanup site are referred to as *indirect costs*. These costs include many headquarters and regional EPA office costs as well as selected Department of Justice (DOJ) costs incurred in enforcement. These costs include indirect labor and related fringe benefits, office space and utilities, training, printing, supplies, travel not specific to the site, and freight.

The issues of allowability (reasonableness) and allocability discussed in the FAR may have a substantial impact on the nature and amount of charges the government may successfully bill to a PRP group.

According to Office of Management and Budget (OMB) Circular No. A-87, it is not appropriate for the government to bill the PRPs for the general cost of government. These costs are part of running the overall government bureaucracy and are usually not causally linked with a specific site. The general costs of government should instead be covered by tax revenues and not supplemented by government recoveries from PRPs.

Each of the ten EPA regions has a different indirect cost rate. These rates are audited by the government. The government audit causes significant delays in the final determination of the rates, so they usually are not finalized until years after the fact. The 1987 regional EPA indirect cost rates varied from a low of $47 per regional program hour in Region IV to a high of $62 per regional program hour in Region VIII.

The EPA includes an EPA headquarters charge in each region's rate. In 1986 the headquarters rate was $25 per regional program hour. Approximately half of the region's indirect cost charges, therefore, comes from EPA headquarters in Washington, D.C., a fact that does not bide well with most PRPs.

The DOJ may charge hours to a specific site. For every direct DOJ hour there is a corresponding indirect cost charge in excess of 200 percent of the direct DOJ labor dollars.

Due to these various rates, the indirect cost portion of an EPA incurred cost billing may be very substantial. These charges should be examined

---

[148] United States v. Bell Petroleum Servs. Inc., 734 F. Supp. 771, 781 (W.D. Tex. 1990).

carefully. The involvement of an expert familiar with these complex issues may be appropriate to investigate the costs and methodologies employed by the EPA and DOJ.

Because the indirect cost rates being used by EPA, DOJ, and some contractors may not be finalized until years later, any settlement with EPA should include a provision that any costs determined on the basis of tentative indirect cost rates will be modified if the audited rate turns out to be lower than the tentative rate.

CHAPTER 26

SETTLING CERCLA ACTIONS

Philip L. Hinerman
John L. Taft*

Philip L. Hinerman is an attorney with the Environmental Practice Group of the Philadelphia, Pennsylvania, office of the law firm of Pepper, Hamilton & Scheetz. Previously he served as corporate counsel for Leaseway Transportation Corp., where he focused on environmental issues affecting the transportation industry. Mr. Hinerman has represented generators and transporters in numerous federal Superfund and similar state matters in twelve states and four EPA regions. He also has an active practice providing advice in corporate acquisitions, loans, compliance, and auditing.

John L. Taft is partner in charge of the Business Investigation Services Group in the Los Angeles, California, office of Coopers & Lybrand, where he is actively involved in both the litigation services and business reorganization services practices. Mr. Taft is a CPA and graduated from the University of Nevada-Reno. He is a member of the American Institute of Certified Public Accountants, the California Society of Certified Public Accountants, the National Association of Real Estate Investment Trusts, the Real Estate Investment Association, the American Electronics Association, and the Semiconductor Industry Association.

*The authors gratefully acknowledge the assistance of Thomas M. Neches, formerly of Coopers & Lybrand's Dallas, Texas office, in preparing this chapter.

§ 26.1   Introduction

Hazardous waste is produced in the United States at a rate of 700,000 tons per day, or approximately one ton per year for each person in the United States. As a result of disposal practices which adversely affected public health, Congress enacted in 1980 the Comprehensive Environmental Response, Compensation and Liability Act (CERCLA) commonly known as Superfund. The Superfund is a fund of money for cleanup of sites managed by the Environmental Protection Agency. The CERCLA program achieved few successful cleanups in its first years of existence.

Congress sensed that private cleanups of sites were not being performed as frequently as initially hoped and enacted the Superfund Amendments and Reauthorization Act of 1986 (SARA), giving EPA additional authority to compel potential responsible parties (PRPs) to clean up sites and giving added incentives for private cleanups. SARA expanded the program and authorized $10.1 billion for federal cleanup when willing and able PRPs could not be found. Following SARA's enactment, the average cleanup cost of a facility rose to in excess of $25 million.[1] EPA estimates that total cleanup costs for the current 1,200 Superfund sites will total $30 billion.[2] The Office of Technology Assessment estimates that spending for cleanups at toxic waste sites could eventually reach $500 billion.[3]

Given the enormous costs involved in cleanups, both PRPs and the government realize benefits when CERCLA enforcement actions are settled rather than litigated in court. Settlements save litigation costs for all parties. Cleanups of settled sites need not await the ultimate resolution of a trial. Also, cleanups performed by PRPs generally cost less than those performed by the EPA's contractors. Finally, settlement allows the government to focus on cleaning up the most significant waste sites and allows the PRPs to focus their energies and finances on other matters.

This chapter addresses settlements with EPA and other parties and discusses many of the issues that commonly arise in the process of settling CERCLA cleanup actions. An overview of settlement and enforcement alternatives is followed by a discussion of liability issues that should be addressed when preparing settlement strategies.

§ 26.2 Overview of Settlement and Enforcement Alternatives

EPA's enforcement process begins with a search for PRPs. Once they are identified, EPA may offer to negotiate a settlement with the PRPs for the conduct of a Remedial Investigation and Feasibility Study (RI/FS) identifying conditions at a site and analyzing alternatives for cleanup,[4] for reimbursement of EPA costs incurred responding to the site, or for conduct of the Remedial Design and Remedial Action (RD/RA), which addresses remediation of the site.

Generally, settlements with EPA are of three types. First, PRPs agree to fund and perform a substantial portion, often 100 percent, of the cleanup and to conduct the RD/RA. These settlements often reimburse

---

[1] EPA, Unfinished Business: A Comparative Assessment of Environmental Problems (Feb. 1987).

[2] U.S. General Accounting Office, Superfund—A More Vigorous and Better Managed Enforcement Program is Needed, Report to the Chairman, Subcommittee on Superfund, Ocean and Water Protection, U.S. Senate Committee on Environmental and Public Works (Dec. 1989) [hereinafter GAO Superfund Report].

[3] Office of Technology Assessment, U.S. Congress, Coming Clean: Superfund Problems Can Be Solved (Oct. 1989).

[4] The EPA has issued a guidance document which removes the risk assessment component from PRP's conduct of the RI/FS. This Guidance is currently the subject of litigation, on the grounds that the Guidance is a rule, subject to rule making proceedings.

EPA for its incurred costs and costs needed to conduct future oversight of remediation.

Second, EPA and PRPs may enter into mixed funding agreements. Mixed funding uses monies from both the Superfund and the PRPs for remediation. Mixed funding is most likely to be accepted by EPA when some, but not all, of the PRPs are willing to perform the cleanup, and when there are financially viable nonsettlors from whom EPA can recover Superfund's share of the mixed funding agreement.

Third, de minimis and landowner settlements may be entered into by parties who contributed very small amounts of hazardous waste with low toxicity. A de minimis settlement may eliminate numerous small volume contributors from the negotiation and litigation process, which can save all parties time and money. Most frequently, these settlements provide for premiums exceeding the normal share of the settlor's costs in exchange for releases of liability.

Generally, EPA will only consider a settlement proposal from a PRP if the initial offer from the PRP constitutes a substantial portion of the cost of cleanup or the remedial action.[5] EPA may enter into negotiations with PRPs even when the offers from the PRPs do not represent a substantial portion of the cost of cleanup if the proposal is related to an administrative settlement of a cost recovery action in which total cleanup costs are less than $200,000 or involve a bankrupt PRP.

Pursuant to its 1985 Interim Settlement Policy,[6] EPA will analyze settlement proposals using the following criteria:

1. Volume of waste contributed to site by each PRP
2. Nature of wastes contributed
3. Strength of evidence tracing the wastes at the site to the settling parties
4. Ability of the settling parties to pay
5. Litigative risks in proceeding to trial
6. Public interest considerations
7. Precedential value
8. Value of obtaining a present sum certain
9. Inequities and aggravating factors
10. Nature of the case that remains after settlement.

Mixed funding and de minimis settlements are seldom implemented. During the three years following the enactment of SARA, EPA reached

---

[5] See EPA Memorandum, Interim Settlement Policy (Dec. 5, 1984).

[6] 50 Fed. Reg. 5,034 (Feb. 5, 1985).

RD/RA settlements at 78 sites. Of these settlements, EPA reported nine mixed funding and 18 de minimis settlements. The reasons for the limited use of mixed funding and de minimis settlements include: 1) limited EPA staff trained and experienced in these types of settlements; 2) limited EPA staff and financial resources to address issues other than actual cleanup of sites; and 3) lower priority at EPA for settlements that do not address the remediation of the site.

When EPA is unable to reach a negotiated agreement, it has two options under CERCLA to achieve cleanup or PRP response. First, under § 106 of CERCLA, the EPA can issue an administrative order to compel PRPs to clean up the site. Second, EPA can remediate the site using Superfund monies under § 104 and then seek recovery of its cleanup costs from PRPs under § 107.

The EPA has a number of additional investigatory and enforcement tools aside from the negotiated or ordered response. Among other things, it can issue subpoenas to obtain information, file liens against property to recover its cleanup costs, and issue nonbinding preliminary allocations of responsibility calculating each PRP's share of a site cleanup cost.

§ 26.3   Potential Liabilities

Following the passage of CERCLA in 1980, EPA experienced the growing pains normally associated with the start-up of a major program. The courts cooperated in this start-up in an effort to speed cleanups at hazardous waste sites. The courts broadly construed CERCLA liability provisions and deferred judgment on issues of allocation among the parties. Almost every person or entity involved in commerce using or producing hazardous substances or disposing of these substances was said to be subject to strict liability (without fault) and joint and several liability providing that one or all parties were liable for the full amount of remediation costs.

The case law was not instructive on ways to allocate this liability among the various parties. Therefore, settlement theories and strategies are of prime importance. To evaluate settlement theories and strategies, one must first be knowledgeable about the grounds of potential liabilities.

Under § 107 of CERCLA, parties in the chain of treatment, disposal, and storage of hazardous substances[7] may be liable for cleanup costs and penalties. The four classes of liable parties are: (1) owners and operators of

---

[7] The term *hazardous substance* covers virtually every chemical compound known to man. For example, one judge has held that asbestos lying on the ground constitutes a release or threat of a release, as it may be blown by the wind. *See* United States v. Metate Asbestos Corp., 584 F. Supp. 1143, 1149 (D. Ariz. 1984).

facilities where hazardous substances are present; (2) persons who arranged to treat, store, or dispose of hazardous substances; (3) persons who operated disposal sites at the time of the hazardous substance's disposal; and (4) persons who transported hazardous substances to sites they selected. Of the four classes of responsible parties, the generators are the class of parties who most frequently participate in the settlement of CERCLA claims.

The statutory defenses to liability under CERCLA are that: 1) the contamination was caused by act of God or act of war; 2) the problem was solely caused by a third party; and 3) the potential defendant "exercised due care" and "took precautions against foreseeable acts or omissions" of third parties.[8] Additionally, owners of property have a defense if they acquired the property after reasonable precautions were taken to determine the presence or absence of hazardous substances, or if the acquisition was by bequest.[9]

§ 26.4 —Cost Recovery Claims

CERCLA § 104 allows EPA to use Superfund monies for initial response. Subsequently, § 109 allows the EPA to seek the recovery of these monies from PRPs. Under § 113 of CERCLA, parties may be jointly and severally liable for response costs incurred by EPA in connection with a site from which there is a release or a potential release of hazardous substances. Furthermore, CERCLA § 109 allows EPA to assert administrative penalties which, in certain situations, allow assessments of up to $75,000 per day in penalties.

EPA asserts its cost recovery claim against PRPs either by sending a demand letter or by issuing an order. Frequently, EPA asserts the claim at the onset of a remedial action because it is attempting to obtain PRP participation for future actions so that EPA need not commit Superfund moneys for sites at which the PRPs will respond.

PRPs often seek to participate in the performance of a remedy and avoid a more costly recovery action, because EPA's costs of remedy typically exceed those costs which may be incurred by private parties. Also, through negotiation, PRPs may have input on the planned remedy that the EPA selects in its Record of Decision (ROD).

---

[8] CERCLA § 107(b).

[9] A lender has an additional defense if its interest in the property was merely to protect its security. At the time of publication, the EPA has proposed rules defining lender liability and several legislative initiatives are pending.

§ 26.5   —Administrative Orders

EPA has increased its use of administrative orders under § 106 of CERCLA, responding to congressional complaints that it was not aggressive in its pursuit of private party cleanups. Under § 106, EPA can order one or more PRPs to undertake a response action to prevent or cease a release from a site at which hazardous substances are located. If a PRP is named in an EPA order and that party fails to undertake the ordered action without "sufficient cause," a court may impose a civil penalty of up to $25,000 per day in civil penalties for the period of non-compliance and also award EPA treble the cost of any response incurred by the Superfund.

CERCLA does not define "sufficient cause." Civil cases have addressed the issue and defined sufficient cause to include the financial inability to perform the order,[10] the lack of a threatened or actual release of hazardous substances,[11] and the failure of a party to be a liable party under CERCLA.[12] In the 1980 debate on CERCLA, Senator Stafford provided the genesis of these defenses by stating that the sufficient cause language was intended to:

> encompass defenses such as the defense that the person who was the subject of the [EPA] order was not the party responsible under the act for the release of hazardous substances. It would certainly be unfair to assess punitive damages against the party, who for a good reason, believed himself not to be the responsible party. For example, if there were, at the time of the order, substantial facts in question, or if the party subject to the order was not a substantial contributor to the release or threatened release, putative damages should either not be assessed or should be reduced in the interest of equity. There could also be 'sufficient cause' for not complying with an order if the party . . . did not at the time have the financial or technical resources to comply or if no technological means for complying was available. We also intend that the [EPA's] order, and the expenditures for which a person might be liable for punitive damages, must be valid.[13]

EPA has issued memoranda on the use and issuance of administrative orders. A September 1983 *Guidance Memorandum on Use and Issuance of Administrative Orders Under § 106(a) of CERCLA* focused on the four factors EPA evaluates in deciding whether or not to issue an administrative order:

---

[10] United States v. Reilly Tar, 546 F. Supp. 1100 (D. Minn. 1982).

[11] Solid State Circuits v. EPA, 812 F.2d 383 (8th Cir. 1987).

[12] Wagner Elec. Corp. v. Thomas, 612 F. Supp. 736 (D. Kan. 1985).

[13] 126 Cong. Rec. 30986 (daily ed. Nov. 24, 1980).

1. Financial status of the parties
2. Number of parties
3. Certainty of the needed response
4. EPA's readiness to litigate the merits of the order.

In its February 1989 *Guidance on CERCLA Section 106 Judicial Actions,* EPA refined these points and stated its preference to use orders if relatively few PRPs are available. Also, EPA stated it would consider "carving out" settlements by issuing orders requiring performance of some part of the response work by nonsettling parties.

Section 106 does provide for an opportunity to confer with EPA following receipt of an order. Given the potential exposure for treble damages under § 106 of CERCLA and the lack of clarity in the sufficient cause defenses to the order, there is much incentive for PRPs to attempt to negotiate a settlement of a § 106 order.

Section 106(b)(2) allows a PRP to comply with orders and make a later claim against EPA for reimbursement if it can show that the order was arbitrary or if the party was not responsible under § 107. PRPs with substantial resources may consider this option, although no claim under this section has been allowed by the EPA to date.

§ 26.6 Settlements

After a sufficient number of PRPs have decided that the benefits of a settlement outweigh the costs and risks of litigation, the focus becomes what companies are PRPs, what each PRP contributed, how much each contributed, and how the settlement will be funded by each PRP.

§ 26.7 —Chronology of Settlement

Settlements with the EPA are frequently entered into at the early stages of site cleanup. At the later stages of a cleanup or prior to an offer to EPA to perform the cleanup, PRPs usually attempt settlement among each other. Private party settlements present unique issues. EPA settlements typically focus on total cost recovery and the liability of parties for performance of the remedial work at the site. Private party settlements, however, normally involve establishing mechanisms for technical review of EPA's suggested remediation, assessing monetary shares for expenses, and establishing mutual defense groups.

Prior to settling with either the EPA or other PRPs, the parties typically review the number and alleged involvement of all PRPs at the site. In order to assess individual exposure at a site, PRPs need to know the relationship of their alleged contributions to the contributions of other viable PRPs. EPA normally has taken the first step to determine who the initial PRPs are at a site. EPA's investigation often starts with the business records of site operators. These records may contain customer lists, shipping documents, and invoices. To identify other possible generators and transporters, EPA (or its contractor) may have conducted interviews with employees at the waste disposal site, waste transporters, and persons who live in the vicinity of the site. This information may be compiled by EPA into a so-called *waste-in list,* which is often an inaccurate and incomplete first cut of PRPs.[14]

EPA typically follows up this list with a questionnaire to the identified parties. This questionnaire, issued under the investigatory authority of CERCLA § 104, is broad in scope and is similar to interrogatories that might be filed in a lawsuit. EPA also has subpoena authority under CERCLA § 122(e)(3)(B) but does not normally utilize that authority.

At most sites, the PRPs interested in settlement gather additional information on other PRPs. Often working with government information obtained from a Freedom of Information Act request, the parties may retain an outside consultant or common counsel to prepare a waste-in list of PRPs at the site. That list includes volume and/or toxicity information about the parties. PRPs perform this task routinely, even if the EPA has previously compiled a list, because PRP-prepared lists are usually more accurate and more inclusive of new potential parties.

CPAs and other financial experts who specialize in environmental litigation consulting often perform these information gathering activities. The experts may perform the following procedures:

1. Collect and review government business records
2. Interview government and business personnel
3. Conduct historical research of site operations
4. Reconstruct chain of title
5. Update PRP names and addresses
6. Conduct PRP corporate historical research
7. Assess PRP ability to pay for the cleanup
8. Consolidate and organize records.

Often, the information gathering continues throughout the negotiation or litigation period. In fact, given the often incomplete records at sites,

---

[14] One-half of EPA's project managers and attorneys surveyed by the United States General Accounting Office indicated dissatisfaction with EPA's waste-in lists. *See* GAO Superfund Report.

information gathering is seldom finished to the complete satisfaction of all PRPs.

§ 26.8 —Defenses to Liability
Impacting Settlement

Two defenses to liability are frequently asserted at Superfund sites to reduce potential settlement shares: the transporter defense and the innocent landowner defense. Under § 107(a)(4) of CERCLA, transporters are only liable for transportation of hazardous substances to disposal sites they have selected. Transporters asserting this defense often locate bills of lading showing direction by shippers. Landowners often assert that they are entitled to the innocent purchaser defense of § 101(35). To establish this defense, the landowner must provide evidence that it acquired the property without reason to know that hazardous substances were disposed of on it.

Although CERCLA § 107(b) provides a defense if releases are caused by acts of God, war, or third parties, no party has been released by EPA from a CERCLA suit on these grounds.[15]

§ 26.9 —Allocations of Liability

The most divisive problem among PRPs is the method of allocating monetary shares for settlement. Section 113(f)(1) of CERCLA provides for allocation based on equitable factors: "In resolving contribution claims, the court may allocate response costs among liable parties using such equitable factors as the court determines are appropriate."[16]

Several cases have set out these equitable factors to be considered in allocations. These factors are based on criteria proposed for CERCLA by Senator Gore in 1980, even though the criteria were not adopted in the original Superfund bill.[17] The Fifth Circuit stated in *Amoco Oil Co. v. Borden, Inc.*[18] that the relevant factors include:

---

[15] The third party defense, which holds the most promise to defendants, has been narrowly construed. In United States v. Ward, 618 F. Supp. 884 (D.C.N.C. 1985), the defense was held not to apply if the third party was an agent, employee, or had a contractual relationship to the defendant. In the lower court decision of New York v. Shore Realty Corp., 759 F.2d 1045, 1048–9 (3rd Cir. 1984), the court held that the defense was not applicable to the owner of a site where leakage had occurred during its ownership, even though disposal activities predated its ownership.

[16] CERCLA § 113(f)(1), 42 U.S.C. § 9613(f)(1).

[17] See United States v. A&F Materials Co., 578 F. Supp. 1249, 1256 (S.D. Ill. 1984) (indicating Gore amendment criteria would be considered in an apportionment).

[18] 889 F.2d 664 (5th Cir. 1989).

The amount of hazardous substances involved; the degree of toxicity or hazard of the materials involved; the degree of involvement by parties in the generation, transportation, treatment, storage or disposal of the substances; the degree of care exercised by the parties with respect to the substances involved; and the degree of cooperation of the parties with government officials to prevent any harm to public health or the environment.[19]

Courts have also considered other factors with regard to landowner liability, such as the circumstances surrounding the conveyance of property, the price paid, and any discounts granted. Because allocations vary on case-by-case basis for similarly situated parties, past precedence gives little guidance as to the proper method of allocating liability among PRPs in order to aid in establishing settlement shares.[20]

Settlement allocations are most often based on waste-in lists consisting solely of volumes. Volume allocations are the easiest of the allocation formulas. Toxicity of waste streams is considered at sites at which toxicity of the waste varies and significantly affects the proposed remedy. Toxicity does inject a degree of subjectivity to the list that makes this type of allocation difficult to calculate.

Independent experts can be of great assistance in determining PRP waste contributions and cleanup cost allocations. Technical experts may characterize waste types and quantify the volumes associated with each PRP based upon available records. CPAs may also assist by determining the costs to implement remediation and by allocating the costs among the PRPs based upon a comprehensive cost allocation model. These calculations may assist the PRPs and the government in reaching a settlement acceptable to the largest number of parties.

§ 26.10   —Settlements by Use of Notice Letters

In the 1986 SARA amendments, Congress gave EPA several settlement tools to encourage PRP participation in the remedy at a Superfund site. Section 122 of CERCLA provides opportunities for PRPs to organize and to take over the performance of the cleanup. The EPA may, at its option, initially notify PRPs that it is considering action by sending a *general notice letter* stating that a remedy is being proposed. It provides PRPs with

---

[19] *Id.* at 672–73.

[20] *See* United States v. Tyson, 19 Chem. Waste Litig. Rep. (Computer L. Rep., Inc.) 1310, 1324 (E.D.P.A. 1980) (50 percent liability assessed on landowner and operator); *see* United States v. Northernaire Plating Co., 17 Chem. Waste Litig. Rep. (Computer L. Rep., Inc.) 1130, 1131 (W.D. Mich. 1989) (assessed two-thirds of liability on operator and one-third on owner).

time to organize and develop an offer to conduct or finance the selected response or comment on the appropriateness of that response.

Following the general notice letter, EPA may issue a *special notice letter,* which allows selected PRPs a period of time in which to negotiate with EPA to perform the response action. This special notice letter must provide each PRP with the names and addresses of all known PRPs, the volume and nature of substances contributed by each PRP, if available, and a ranking by volume of substances found at the facility, if known. CERCLA § 122(e)(1) also provides that the agency must make this information available in advance of the special notice letter upon a PRP's request. With that information, PRPs may consider the viability of privately funding an RI/FS, determine the likelihood of de minimis cash settlements, and develop an overall settlement strategy.

After the issuance of a special notice letter, EPA may not undertake cleanup or remedial actions at the site for 120 days nor initiate an RI/FS for 90 days. EPA may, however, conduct other studies, including remedial designs, in this moratorium period. If the PRPs have not submitted a good faith proposal to the EPA within 60 days of receipt of the special notice letter, the moratorium period ends and EPA may commence response actions or initiate an RI/FS.

If § 122 settlement procedures are used, the EPA must also notify state and natural resource trustees of any pending settlement negotiations. States have the opportunity to participate in those negotiations, subject to the right to intervene in § 106 actions to secure compliance with any more restrictive state cleanup standards.

PRPs agreeing to perform the remedial action then enter into a consent decree with the government pursuant to § 122(d)(1)(A). The decree is open for public comment, as discussed in **§ 26.13**. If EPA determines not to use the § 122 settlement process, the only statutorily mandated PRP notice is provided in § 113(k)(2)(D), which states that PRPs will be identified and notified "as early as possible" before EPA's selection of a response action.

§ 26.11 —EPA De Minimis Settlements

The EPA is encouraged by CERCLA § 122(g) to enter into prompt settlements with de minimis waste contributors. On June 19, 1987, EPA issued its *Interim Guidance on Settlements with De Minimis Waste Contributors under Section 122(a) of SARA,*[21] at 54 Fed. Reg. 34235. This EPA policy encourages de minimis parties to present group settlement offers. To be eligible for a de minimis waste contributor settlement with EPA, a party must have contributed no more than a minimal amount of hazardous

---

[21] 54 Fed. Reg. 34235.

substances to a facility, and the substances contributed must not be significantly more toxic than other hazardous substances found at the site. These settlements allocate to PRPs their percentage share of liability and normally add a premium payment, to cover cost overruns and future response costs, in exchange for a covenant not to sue.

Prior to determining whether it will entertain de minimis settlements, the EPA obtains an estimate of the cost of cleaning up the contamination. As a general rule, EPA will not consider de minimis settlements until the completion of a PRP search or until the EPA believes that it has adequate information about each settling party's waste contributions.

The first de minimis settlement proposal drafted by EPA under § 122(g) involved the Cannons Engineering site in Bridgewater, Massachusetts. The EPA stated that parties are eligible for early settlement if their "volumetric contribution . . . does not exceed 1% of the total waste volume listed for that site."[22] A settlement premium of 60 percent was added to the volumetric share to reimburse cost overruns incurred following settlement. De minimis settlors paid 100 percent of their volumetric share, plus 60 percent of their volumetric share for unexpected costs, plus an additional 100 percent premium, for a total 260 percent share. Subsequent de minimis settlement proposals at other sites have ranged across the spectrum and vary from site to site.

§ 26.12 —Landowner's Settlement

The landowner faces unique settlement issues in determining whether it can assert the innocent landowner defense. That defense must meet several threshold tests to establish that the landowner is, in fact, innocent. Under CERCLA §§ 101(35) and 107(b)(3), the landowner must have acquired the property by bequest or without knowledge or reason to know of the disposal of hazardous substances.

Technically, the party who has satisfied the statutory burden is innocent and is not liable for any costs.[23] To be innocent, however, the landowner must provide some showing of the exercise of due care at the time it acquired the property. Information is seldom available regarding the condition of the property at the time of purchase. Additionally, the party claiming innocent landowner status should provide documentation and evidence of representations made by the seller at the time of sale. Because the evidence to support the defense is rarely available, the landowner often participates in settlement.

---

[22] EPA, *Cannons Engineering* Case *De Minimis* Settlement Offer Draft at 2 (Mar. 4, 1987), United States v. Commons Eng'g Corp., 720 F. Supp. 1027 (D. Mass. 1989).

[23] *See* EPA Interim Settlement Policy, 50 Fed. Reg. 5034 (Feb. 5, 1985).

In 1989, EPA issued its *De minimis Landowner's Settlement Policy.*[24] The policy focuses on the amount of evidence a party needs to produce to establish its innocent landowner defense. The policy requires that, to be innocent, a purchaser must obtain property without "actual or constructive knowledge" of its use for disposal of hazardous substances. If the property is acquired by inheritance or bequest, the policy also imposes a standard that the landowner must have conducted "all appropriate inquiry," although the statute does not expressly impose this requirement.[25]

§ 26.13   Negotiating Consent Decrees with EPA

There are the two types of consent agreements that PRPs may negotiate with EPA. The first is a *cash out settlement,* which involves an agreement to pay all or a portion of the costs of the response action the government has determined to be appropriate for the facility. This type of agreement does not require court approval, although it is often obtained.[26]

The second type of consent agreement provides for performance of the remedial work by the PRPs. These agreements typically are more difficult to negotiate. Because future performance by PRPs is mandated, additional provisions are required to address dispute resolution during performance, changed conditions at the site, and failure to perform in accordance with deadlines because of force majeure events. Additionally, these agreements contain stipulated penalties for failure of the settling parties to comply with the terms of the agreement.[27]

Negotiated settlements between PRPs and the EPA for performance of the work and settlement of claims are incorporated into either a consent order or a consent decree. A *consent order* is an administrative order issued by EPA and agreed to by the PRPs. These orders normally involve the PRP's payment of costs incurred by EPA under CERCLA § 107 and performance of work by PRPs. The orders must be published in the *Federal Register* for comment at least 30 days before they become final. The

---

[24] 54 Fed. Reg. 32235 (Aug. 18, 1989).

[25] *Id.* at 34238.

[26] A court-issued consent decree often allows the court to retain jurisdiction over future disputes and carries the legal authority of a final judgment. Disputes not resolved by dispute resolution clauses are submitted to the court for a status conference or similar motion. EPA-issued administrative orders lack the authority of final federal judgments. Disputes arising under these orders must be resolved informally with EPA and, if necessary, appealed to the EPA administrator.

[27] Courts reviewing the proposed settlement focus on the impact settlement has on non-settlors. In one case, New York v. Shore Realty Corp., 759 F.2d 1032 (2nd Cir. 1985), the trial court, in fact, rejected a proposed settlement agreement after it determined that the settlement failed to protect the rights of third-party defendants.

EPA then reviews comments prior to the final acceptance of the order. Nonsettlors may mount a challenge to the EPA's selected remedy set out in the order by filing suit in the federal court pursuant to § 113 of CERCLA. Any challenges to the other terms of the administrative settlement must be brought under the citizens' suit provisions of CERCLA § 310.

Consent decrees normally are sought if PRPs and EPA agree either to settle § 106 orders for response actions or to perform major response actions that will lead to private party cost recovery actions. Pursuant to § 122(d) of CERCLA, the decrees are entered in the United States District Court in which the site is located. Prior to entry, the Department of Justice must review whether the decree is appropriate, proper, and adequate. There is no explicit judicial review mechanism for that determination set out in CERCLA. The final consent decree is then lodged with the court for 30 days prior to final judgment, for public comment.

The parties choosing to settle with EPA must focus on negotiating the terms of the consent decree in a form proposed initially by EPA. The high rate of EPA employee turnover provides an interesting aspect to negotiating the terms of these decrees. The EPA teams may lack negotiation experience, and some PRPs may attempt to use this lack of experience to their clients' advantage. The EPA team, however, may also resist innovative proposals for settlement in order to avoid potential criticism from the EPA hierarchy.

The 1986 SARA amendments required that consent decrees contain several provisions. EPA drafted a Model Administrative Order on Consent for CERCLA Remedial Investigation/Feasibility Study, which was made public on January 30, 1990, incorporating these and other general provisions. The model order has been roundly criticized by the defense bar as being a "wish list" containing all items EPA would like to have in an order, not items reasonably agreeable to PRPs in a final order. These provisions and other typical provisions that may arise are discussed below.

§ 26.14   —Covenants Not to Sue

Whether settling past costs or agreeing to future performance, the settling parties should always insist on a covenant not to sue from the EPA pursuant to CERCLA § 122(c) and (f). The covenant should state that the EPA will not sue settling parties for expenses incurred by the government to date and for those incurred for future activities performed by EPA which may result in statutory liability to the settling parties. As to costs incurred by EPA to the date of the decree, the covenant is effective as of the date the decree is entered. The covenant not to sue for future costs is not effective until EPA "certifies" that remediation has been "completed."

Generally, the scope of the covenant not to sue depends on the nature of the remedy. Typically there will be a more complete release if a more permanent remedy will be instituted. Settling parties should focus on foreclosing all governmental liability by including all relevant federal and state government agencies including natural resource trustees (such as the U.S. Department of the Interior and similar state agencies).

EPA's *Interim Guidance on Covenants Not to Sue*[28] and § 122(f) of CERCLA contemplate two types of covenants not to sue. *Discretionary covenants* provide for a reopener and reserve the right of the EPA to sue for unknown future conditions after it certifies completion of the remedial action. The EPA provides a discretionary covenant if it determines that the covenant is in the public interest, that it would expedite response actions consistent with the National Contingency Plan, that the settling party is in full compliance with the terms of the consent decree, and that a response action has been approved by EPA.

Special covenants typically contain no reopener and will be granted in either of two events. First, EPA will grant a special covenant if it has required PRPs to dispose of hazardous substances off-site despite an offer from PRPs for on-site treatment consistent with the National Contingency Plan. Second, EPA will grant this covenant if the response action will destroy, eliminate, or permanently immobilize waste at the site so that no current or foreseeable future health or environmental risks exist. Special covenants are also appropriate for de minimis settlements or for "extraordinary circumstances" to be determined by the EPA.

In EPA's *Interim CERCLA Settlement Policy* and in its guidance entitled *Drafting Consent Decrees in Hazardous Waste Imminent Hazard Cases (May 1, 1985),* it indicated that covenants will be limited to remedial work actually performed. This interpretation would provide very limited protection to PRPs, if agreed to, and will not extend the covenant to liabilities associated with off-site disposal of waste. In its *Interim Guidance on Covenants Not to Sue,* EPA stated that it will seek to include a reopener to cover situations in which new information reveals that the earlier remedy no longer protects human health or the environment. EPA agreed, however, that it must demonstrate that the additional remedial action required results from conditions not known at the time the decree was entered.

§ 26.15   —Contribution Protection

If fewer than all PRPs settle, those settlors are exposed to possible action by later sued parties for contribution. Contribution claims are based on

---

[28] 52 Fed. Reg. 28,039 (July 27, 1987).

the theory that the initial settling parties must ultimately pay their appropriate percentage of any costs for which the nonsettling parties may be held liable. Settling parties would point to CERCLA § 122(h)(4), which states that any party resolving its liability to the United States is not liable for claims of contribution "regarding matters addressed in the settlement." This section potentially provides broad protection for settlors from actions brought by the nonsettling parties. The section also benefits nonsettlors because it provides for a reduction in potential liability of nonsettlors if an administrative or judicially approved settlement is entered.

Pursuant to § 122, contribution protection extends only to matters addressed in the settlement. There has been controversy as to whether or not the contribution protection provisions extend to causes of action from private parties incurring response costs. In EPA's *Guidance on Covenants Not to Sue,* the EPA suggests that contribution protection for settlors should correspond to the items covered in EPA's covenant not to sue (that is, EPA's expenses).

To qualify for contribution protection, the consent decree must be "judicially approved."[29] The court approval may be as little as a review of the decree and supporting affidavits to as much as a full evidentiary hearing.[30]

§ 26.16   —Remedy Selection

The consent decree formalizes the remedy selected by the ROD if settling parties will be performing work. CERCLA § 117(c) requires that the EPA explain any significant difference between the ROD and the work to be performed as set out in the consent decree.

The selected remedy is often referred to as the *remedial action plan* (RAP). In negotiating compliance with the RAP, consideration should be given to the possibility that the actual conditions at the site may differ from that set out in the RAP. Parties should provide in the agreement with the EPA for independent negotiation of changes to the RAP required by these changed conditions. That negotiation provision should provide for input from technical experts in order to maximize the likelihood that technical solutions will be reasonable and cost effective.

Under § 121(d) of CERCLA, the remedial action must comply with applicable, relevant, and appropriate requirements (ARARs) of federal law

---

[29] CERCLA § 113(f)(2).

[30] *Compare* United States v. Hooker Chem. & Plastics Corp., 607 F. Supp. 1052, 1056–57 (W.D.N.Y. 1985) (formal judicial opinion was issued after four days of hearings) *with* United States v. Westinghouse, IP 81-488C, IP 83-9-C (S.D. Ind., Aug. 22, 1985) (technical affidavits sufficient to support entry of decree).

and more stringent state law. The EPA has issued its interpretation of the meaning of ARARs in its *Interim Guidance on Compliance with Applicable State and Federal CERCLA Requirements for Remedial Actions,*[31] and in its *Memorandum on CERCLA Compliance With Other Environmental Statutes.*[32] It is EPA's position that *applicable requirements* are cleanup, control, and other environmental protection requirements promulgated under federal or state law that specifically address a similar hazardous substance problem for which those standards are legally required. *Relevant and appropriate requirements* are criteria which may not be legally applicable to the specific circumstances at the site but which address similar problems at other sites. ARARs may be set for levels of chemicals (such as those set by the Safe Drinking Water Act) or levels of action or cleanup (such as those set by RCRA closure regulations). Additionally, local requirements such as siting laws for hazardous waste facilities may be applicable. Federal or state guidance documents are not ARARs, but they may be considered for cleanup levels, particularly if no specific ARARs exist.

During the consent decree negotiation, the EPA may actively seek comments on its proposed ARARs. The parties should be prepared to propose and negotiate the ARARs, because the EPA recognizes that they are set on a site-by-site basis. Also, negotiations should address whether ARARs must be met at all points inside the site or only at the boundaries of the site. Significant savings can result if the ARARs standards need only apply to the area in which waste was disposed.[33]

CERCLA § 121(d) provides some flexibility in the designation of ARARs and allows PRPs to propose alternative concentration limits (ACLs). ACLs are a way to obtain an extra degree of cost effectiveness by setting more relaxed cleanup standards. ACLs have been most effectively used in groundwater cleanups.

EPA typically seeks to require compliance with ARARs at the earliest practical time. It may also require that ARARs' compliance be met for a significant period before allowing the shutdown of other remediation at the site. The costs of continued operations can be expensive. A reasonable time frame for ARAR compliance should be negotiated, because CERCLA does not specifically speak to this issue.

The EPA also may attempt to establish cleanup targets or goals instead of using statutorily required standards. EPA's cleanup goals often focus on improving the quality of the site, rather than removing the contamination. PRPs should resist this, because the remedy should only be what is needed to eliminate the spread of contamination onto adjoining sites.

---

[31] 50 Fed. Reg. 32496 (Aug. 27, 1987).

[32] 52 Fed. Reg. 47946 (Aug. 8, 1988).

[33] The ROD often specifies where compliance will be measured.

EPA provides certifications when construction is completed and before commencement of maintenance activities. This certification period allows EPA to determine that the remedy is achieving the requirements set forth in the RD and ROD. EPA typically does not alter the ROD or impose additional cleanup requirements in the period following completion of the remedy unless a previously unknown condition has been discovered. The settling parties should be careful, however, to ensure that the certification decision does not allow the EPA to have an increased time to require additional work without having to use any negotiated reopener provision. EPA has indicated in the past that it would include a limitation on certification decisions, upon request.

Other suggestions for dealing with remedy selection and completion in consent decrees include the following:

1. State a preference for effective cleanups, not a requirement to complete remediation by a set date.
2. Avoid over-committing to the extent of making the required cleanup if it exceeds the levels set out in an ARAR.
3. As much as possible, avoid an unlimited time period for operation of a specific treatment component.
4. Specify that the PRPs' cleanup, if conducted in compliance with the EPA's design, be *cost effective.* The language in the decree can be helpful in any later private cost recovery action in which the PRP must prove its costs were reasonable and cost effective. Cost effective means that the remedy implemented should be efficient and achieve the appropriate level of health and environmental protection.[34]
5. Keep in mind that, although a complete release of liability may be obtained for the total destruction of hazardous substances, this may necessitate a more extensive cleanup. The legal benefits of a complete release should be balanced against the cost of achieving that result.

§ 26.17   —Incurred and Future EPA Costs

Pursuant to CERCLA § 107(a), EPA is authorized to recover, among other things, previously incurred response costs and future oversight costs. Significant savings can result from using technical consultants to analyze EPA's claim of past and future costs.

---

[34] *See* definition in H.R. Conf. Rep. No. 962, 99th Cong., 2d Sess. 245 (1986).

The EPA has taken the position that personnel and program overhead costs necessary to support the Superfund operations are recoverable. These expenses include Superfund's share of rent, utilities, telephones, administrative support, program management, and fringe benefits.[35] In connection with PRP performance of the RI/FS, § 104(a)(1) of CERCLA, however, only requires that settlors reimburse the Superfund for "any costs incurred . . . under, or in connection with, the oversight contract or arrangement (for the cleanup)." As to cleanups conducted by the government, § 107(a)(4)(A), (B), and (D) only provide recovery of removal, response, or remedial costs and health assessment costs. PRPs often argue that the statutory language does not contemplate recovery of indirect costs.

The settling parties should attempt to limit future EPA costs to a fixed dollar amount, to require strict accounting of these costs, to retain the right to challenge the appropriateness of the costs, and to limit recovery of state oversight costs above and beyond the federal oversight costs.

Technical experts should review the EPA's government cost accounting and procurement methods. The cost claim should not include costs that have been excessive, duplicative, unnecessary, or inadequately documented.[36] Additionally, settling parties should evaluate whether government expenditures resulting from technical foul-ups have increased the overall cost of government activities. PRPs at several sites have avoided paying some indirect costs, such as duplicative EPA office rent already recovered at other sites, excessive technical services, and undocumented contractor charges, which were initially included in EPA's cost claim. EPA's lack of accounting for payment of outside contractor costs is also a fertile ground for reduction. Sometimes these costs are attributable to contracts at other sites that are not properly chargeable to the site in question.

Expert assistance is essential to analyze the costs incurred by the EPA, Department of Justice, contractors, and other claimants. Furthermore, the government may delay filing claims until millions of dollars have been expended at a particular facility, and it is wise to retain an expert to monitor and control costs as soon as significant expenses are incurred by the government. In addition, experts should be retained to analyze the cost allocation methodologies used by the government, which may yield unfair costs charged to PRPs.

---

[35] *See* Financial Management Division, EPA, Memorandum: Recovering Indirect Costs Related to Superfund Site Clean Up (Dec. 12, 1985).

[36] *See* General Accounting Office, EPA Needs to Control Contractor Costs (July 1988); EPA Memorandum: CERCLA Response Claims (undated 1988). *See also* EPA Memorandum from V. Goeri, Recovering Indirect Costs Related to Superfund Site Cleanup (Dec. 12, 1985).

Numerous procedures can be undertaken by CPAs and other experts to analyze incurred costs and cost allocations. Settlors should consider retaining experts to perform tasks such as the following:

1. Compute the cost of government response actions determined to be inconsistent with the National Contingency Plan
2. Identify and challenge unnecessary, duplicative, excessive, or improperly performed work
3. Challenge indirect costs allocated inappropriately to the facility by EPA and other federal government agencies
4. Review the adequacy of incurred cost documentation
5. Identify and challenge excess costs resulting from multiple layers of contractors and subcontractors
6. Determine appropriate contractor costs and indirect cost rates
7. Analyze the propriety of contractor allocations to sites
8. Compare contractor costs to market rates
9. Evaluate compliance with government contracting requirements
10. Compare actual incurred costs to budgeted costs
11. Determine the costs applicable to individual PRPs.

§ 26.18   —Dispute Resolution Provisions

CERCLA § 121(e) requires that consent decrees contain some dispute resolution mechanism. These clauses are important because modifications to the RD and RA arise frequently during cleanup and should be expeditiously resolved.

The burden of proof established by these clauses is significant. In the 1985 consent decree guidance memorandum, the EPA took the position that the invocation of dispute resolution should not stay the obligation of settling parties to perform work required under the order. Additionally, the guidance placed the burden of proof in dispute resolution on settling parties to demonstrate that their position is correct and that EPA's position is arbitrary and capricious.

PRPs should consider the scope of the review and argue that limited review using the arbitrary and capricious standard should not apply. At a minimum, parties should exempt those issues that are not related to the adequacy of the remedy, such as oversight cost and adequacy of reports, from the arbitrary and capricious standard. To the extent the review of the EPA's administrative record is provided for in the decree under the arbitrary and capricious standard, the parties should preserve their right to supplement the record with other materials.

§ 26.19   —Stipulated Penalties

Section 121(c) of CERCLA requires that stipulated penalties be included in consent decrees. These penalties may be provided in lieu of possible civil, administrative, and judicial penalties that may be assessed pursuant to § 109 of CERCLA. Stipulated penalty amounts are usually in the $1,000 to $5,000 range and seldomly reach the § 109 penalty maximum of $25,000 daily for the initial violation and $75,000 for second and subsequent violations. Although actual penalties vary significantly from site to site, one clear principal, set out in EPA's January 24, 1990 *Memorandum on the Use of Stipulated Penalties in Settlement Agreements,*[37] is that penalties will be set higher after the initial penalty, because the party is a "repeat offender."

These penalties are especially significant if imposed during any period of dispute resolution. If EPA refuses to stay obligations to perform the disputed activity under the order, penalties could be assessed in the absence of a stay. However, EPA is often unwilling to forego stipulated penalties unless there are legitimate disputes related to modifications of the work. EPA's concern that dispute resolution may be invoked frivolously has often lead to EPA's waiving penalties only if the PRPs prevail in dispute resolutions. This risk of PRPs' losing dispute resolution and facing significant penalties, however, may deter the settling parties from presenting valid disputes.

Settling parties often request provisions allowing a chance to "cure" a failure to perform prior to the imposition of stipulated penalties. This type of provision can help parties avoid costly fines if they fail to meet one deadline and that failure pushes back other deadlines, triggering cascading penalties. Also, language in EPA's model consent order provides that if EPA extends one deadline, that extension does not also extend later deadlines. Stipulated penalties should not accrue for missing the later deadlines if the delay is directly related to a previously extended deadline. Parties should also not be responsible for penalties for insubstantial requirements, such as reporting and record keeping obligations, and for delays caused by EPA's actions in reviewing and evaluating material.

In 1987, EPA retained Clean Sites, Inc. (see **Chapter 24**) to conduct an analysis of stipulated penalties with input from various groups in the environmental bar. On May 4, 1988, Clean Sites issued its *Agreements in Principle on Stipulated Penalties,* which should be consulted in crafting a stipulated penalty provision. This report developed a consensus on 11 principles that should guide parties in developing stipulated penalty provisions. These principles include a forgiveness of penalties during certain force majeure events.

---

[37] 1 Federal Laws, 41 Env't Rep. (BNA) 3581.

The analysis of stipulated penalties is another area in which CPAs and other financial experts may provide useful assistance to PRPs. CPAs may provide documentation and expert support to challenge the appropriateness of EPA's determination of penalties. CPAs can analyze the appropriateness of the underlying assumptions in EPA's penalty determination models. They can calculate the economic benefits that may be derived due to the failure of the PRP to comply and test the sensitivity of the economic benefit to changes in assumptions used in the penalty determination model. CPAs can also analyze the impact of additional factors on penalty calculations, including the significance of violations, the extent of health and environmental harm, the number of violations, the duration of noncompliance, the history of recalcitrance, and the PRP's ability to pay.

§ 26.20   —Mixed Funding

Settling parties often attempt to obtain a *mixed funding agreement* with EPA. CERCLA § 122(b) allows Superfund moneys to be used in connection with private response dollars, provided the EPA "pre-authorizes" the use of fund money. Typically, the preauthorization is triggered by the PRPs' filing of a formal request for mixed funding.

Reimbursement from the Superfund is limited to amounts that should have been the responsibility of any unidentified or nonsettling parties. This includes "orphan shares" for parties who are "unknown, insolvent, similarly unavailable or (who) refuse to settle."[38] EPA typically attempts to obtain reimbursement of Superfund expenditures from these nonparticipating parties by way of a § 107 cost recovery action. EPA may require settlors to waive or assign their claims against those nonsettlors in exchange for the mixed funding. Alternatively, EPA has, at some sites, agreed to assert a claim against nonsettlors and for a fixed period of time attempt settlements with those nonparticipating parties. Failing settlement or judgment, EPA then may obtain reimbursement of the mixed funding portion from the initial settlors.[39]

EPA may agree to provide mixed funding for additional remediation or actions required due to changed conditions, in proportion to the amount provided by the original mixed funding agreement, under § 122(b)(4).

United States v. General Motors Corp.[40] was one of the first mixed funding agreements reached under CERCLA. That agreement required

---

[38] H.R. Conf. Rep. No. 962, 99th Cong., 2d Sess. 252 (1986).

[39] *See, e.g.,* United States v. Air Prods. & Chems., Civ. Action No. 87-7352 (E.D. Pa. Nov. 17, 1987).

[40] No. 87-464 (D. Del. 1987).

General Motors to conduct a cleanup estimated to cost over $9 million. General Motors obtained one-third of its costs from the Superfund. EPA has typically refused to consider mixed funding proposals in which the government component exceeds the percentage agreed to in the GM cleanup.

§ 26.21   —Miscellaneous Provisions

A number of other issues typically arise based on the particular facts of each settlement. These miscellaneous issues include the following.

Disclaimer of Liability.   The parties should include a disclaimer of liability. This disclaimer should state explicitly that participation in the consent agreement is not admission of liability for any purpose. CERCLA § 122(d)(1) contemplates that no admissions of liability need to be obtained by EPA. The disclaimer is especially important in settlement of claims which will be later asserted against non-settling parties.

Site Access.   If the PRPs do not own the site, EPA will require that the parties use their "best efforts" to obtain access to the site. The decree should specify that, if these efforts fail, EPA will secure site access under statutory authority at CERCLA § 104(e)(j).

Financial Security.   Consent decrees often include requirements to provide financial security, such as bonds. If a participating company is in a strong financial position, the parties may be able to avoid the cost of these security mechanisms by providing financial information. CPAs may assist PRPs by performing audits or other procedures that help document the financial position of the company.

EPA Indemnity.   EPA may seek to require that settlors indemnify EPA against liability related to remedial work, without regard to fault. The government, however, is unwilling to provide a similar indemnification for its actions. The indemnification obligation should relate only to liability that arises from the acts of the settlors and their contractors. Additionally, it should be worded to encompass claims for which the parties may obtain insurance.

Parties Bound.   EPA's standard form consent order includes language that binds "officers, directors and principals" of settling companies. This language should be avoided because the corporate fiduciary duties of officers and directors do not include being personally liable under a consent order with EPA.

Findings of Fact. The EPA's draft order also includes a section on findings of facts. In order not to be bound in subsequent proceedings, parties should suggest that the findings be denominated as EPA's findings, without an admission by the settling party.

§ 26.22 —Benefits to Settling Parties

EPA always has the option of cleaning up a Superfund site without involving PRPs. Most experienced parties know that it is best to become involved in site assessment and participate in the RI/FS early in the process in order to influence the selection of the remedy, thereby reducing future liability and costs.

It is also in EPA's best interests to maximize the use of the private sector's technical resources and financial contributions through settlement. From a technical standpoint, the private sector typically has greater technical expertise than EPA and can provide valuable input.[41] The private sector also has more incentive to design an effective remedy in order to minimize future liability. If the EPA elects to perform the cleanup itself, past experience shows that the cleanup will be more costly than if the PRPs perform the work. Estimates indicated that the EPA's costs are 30 to 40 percent higher than equivalent private cleanups.[42]

Retaining CPAs and other financial experts to perform economic analyses of remedial alternatives may both increase the likelihood of settlement and reduce the settlement amount. Technical experts can review the appropriateness of cleanup criteria. For example, experts can determine whether appropriate concentration limits have been set. Experts can analyze underlying assumptions for reasonableness and consistency among alternative remedies. CPAs can verify the accuracy of calculations and test the sensitivity of a proposed remedy's cost estimates to changes in key assumptions. CPAs may also compare site cost estimates to a variety of standards, including industry standard costs, quotes obtained independently from contractors, costs estimated for similar remedial solutions at other sites, and actual costs incurred for remedial solutions at other sites.

---

[41] *See Lautenberg Criticizes Lack of Progress in Superfund Program, Cites Turnover Rate,* 18 Env't Rep. (BNA) 918–19 (July 31, 1987).

[42] Anderson, *Negotiation Ends In Formal Agency Action; The Case of Superfund,* 2 Duke L.J. 261, 301–02 (1985).

§ 26.23   —Failure of Settlement

If settlements fail, it is often EPA's practice to sue some, not all, of the PRPs.[43] Target defendants typically are large generators and financially solvent companies. These companies therefore have additional incentive to settle.

The sued parties have limited success in arguing that the action should be dismissed due to the government's failure to join indispensable parties.[44] Typically, third parties are brought in by the initial defendants pursuant to Rule 14 of the Federal Rules of Civil Procedure, which provides the basis for defendants to add third parties in a contribution action.

Adding additional PRPs may facilitate settlement in some cases and lead to confusion and administrative problems in others. Typically, PRPs only add other "deep pockets" because the cost of assembling PRPs without financial resources increases the transaction costs and may delay final settlement. Also, parties should consider whether addition of other parties will affect their position regarding joint and several liability. If this liability is imposed, a Superfund defendant may be required to pay more than its proportional share. Addition of parties is also warranted if PRPs may wrongfully conclude that they are not potentially responsible because they are not named in the lawsuit.

Superfund cases are among the most complex, costly, and time-consuming of all litigations. Therefore, the use of case management orders and bifurcation of issues has assisted in the prompt resolution of these cases. Discovery is often staged so that the initial discovery issues address the links between generators and hazardous substances found at sites. Counsel for the private litigant should rely upon partial motions for summary judgment to attempt to resolve as many liability issues as possible within the scope of this stage of discovery. Even if these motions are not granted, they provide an opportunity for the government or the private litigant to make its best case.

Settlements are frequently not obtained in appropriate cases due to the inexperience of counsel and corporations in this complex area. Parties often miss crucial opportunities to resolve issues short of trial. Because Superfund liability is increasingly costly, parties should commit to promptly assessing exposure and defining their desired course of defense.

By utilizing the technical and legal resources available, PRPs may avoid long-term financial drain by settling liability at reasonable dollar amounts at early stages in the proceedings.

---

[43] Typically, the landowner is named a party in order to facilitate access to the site.

[44] *See* United States v. A&F Materials Co., 578 F. Supp. 1249, 1260–61 (S.D. Ill. 1984); United States v. Conservation Chem. Corp., 14 Envtl. L. Rep. (Envtl. L. Inst.) 20,207, 20,209 (W.D. Mo. 1984).

TABLE OF CASES

Case	*Book §*
Ayers v. Jackson Township, No. L-5808 (N.J. Super. Ct. Law Div. Nov. 22, 1983), *rev'd in part,* No. A-2103-83T3, slip op. at 25, *reprinted in* 1986 Hazardous Waste Litig. Rep. (Andrews) 7569 (App. Div. June 4, 1986), *rev'd in part,* No. A83/84, slip op. at 12-16, *reprinted in* 1987 Hazardous Waste Litig. Rep. (Andrews) 10,909 (N.J. Sup. Ct. May 1987)	§ 5.12
Ayers v. Township of Jackson, 189 N.J. Super. 561, 461 A.2d 184 (Law Div. 1983), *aff'd in part, rev'd in part,* 106 N.J. 557, 525 A.2d 287 (1987)	§§ 4.7, 4.9, 4.12, 15.12
Babash v. Philadelphia Elec. Co., 717 F. Supp. 297 (M.D. Pa. 1989)	§ 15.12
Baggio v. Lombardi, 726 F. Supp. 922 (E.D.N.Y. 1989)	§ 14.10
Bagley v. Controlled Env't Corp., 127 N.H. 556, 503 A.2d 823 (1986)	§§ 17.7, 17.8
Baim & Blank, Inc. v. Philco Corp., 148 F. Supp. 541 (E.D.N.Y. 1957)	§ 6.14
Baltimore & Ohio Chicago Terminal R.R. v. Soo Line R.R., 646 F. Supp. 327 (N.D. Ill. 1986)	§ 5.18
Barker v. Lull Eng'g. Co., 20 Cal. 3d 413, 573 P.2d 433, 143 Cal. Rptr. 225 (1978)	§ 7.2
Barmet Aluminum Corp. v. Thomas, No. 88-0173-0 (W.D. Ky. Feb. 20, 1990)	§ 25.16
Barr v. Matteo, 360 U.S. 654 (1959)	§ 14.10
Barracuda Tanker Corp., *In re,* 281 F. Supp. 228 (S.D.N.Y. 1968)	§ 15.9
Barth v. B.F. Goodrich Tire Co., 265 Cal. App. 2d 228, 71 Cal. Rptr. 306 (1968)	§ 7.8
Barton v. Firestone Tire & Rubber Co., 673 F. Supp. 1466 (N.D. Cal. 1987)	§ 15.12
Bateman v. Johns-Manville Sales Corp., 781 F.2d 1132 (5th Cir. 1986)	§ 22.13
BCW Assocs. v. Occidental Chem. Corp., 1988 U.S. Dist. LEXIS 11275 (E.D. Pa. 1988)	§§ 12.2, 13.14
BCW Assocs., Ltd, v. Occidental Chem. Corp., No. 86-5947, slip op. (E.D. Pa. Sept. 29, 1988) (1988 WESTLAW 102,641)	§ 22.8
Bergsoe Metal Corp., *In re,* No. 89-35397, slip op. (9th Cir. Aug. 9, 1990)	§§ 9.6, 12.3, 13.4, 13.5, 13.6
Berkey v. Third Ave. Ry., 244 N.Y. 84, 155 N.E. 58 (1926)	§ 6.10
Beryllium Corp. v. American Mut. Liab. Ins. Co., 223 F.2d 71 (3d Cir. 1955)	§ 15.10
Bethlehem Steel Corp. v. EPA, 651 F.2d 877 (3d Cir. 1981), *cert. denied,* 457 U.S. 1105 (1982)	§§ 25.5, 25.15
B.F. Goodrich Co. v. Murtha, 697 F. Supp. 89 (D. Conn. 1988)	§ 10.4

Case	*Book §*
Citizens to Preserve Overton Park, Inc. v. Volpe, 401 U.S. 402 (1971)	§§ 20.2, 25.4, 25.12, 25.13, 25.15
Claussen v. Aetna Casualty & Sur. Co., 259 Ga. 333, 380 S.E.2d 686 (1989)	§ 11.15
Clay v. Union Carbide Corp., 828 F.2d 1103 (5th Cir. 1987)	§ 4.9
Cline v. Watkins, 66 Cal. App. 3d 174, 135 Cal. Rptr. 838 (1977)	§ 18.2
Cloud v. Olin Corp., 552 F. Supp. 528 (N.D. Ala. 1982)	§ 4.5
Coburn v. San Chem. Corp., 19 Envtl. L. Rep. (Envtl. L. Inst.) 20,256 (E.D. Pa. 1989)	§ 21.2
Coburn v. Sun Chem. Corp., 17 Chem. Waste Litig. Rptr. (Computer L. Rep., Inc.) 106 (E.D. Pa. 1988)	§ 20.4
Colorado v. Cotter Corp., No. 83-C-2389 (signed Apr. 4, 1988)	§ 24.11
Colorado v. Gulf & W. Indus., Inc., No. 83-C-2387 (signed June 24, 1988)	§ 24.11
Colorado v. Idarado Mining Co., 707 F. Supp. 1227 (D. Colo. 1989)	§ 20.2
Colorado v. Union Carbide Corp., No. 83-C-2384 (signed Feb. 23, 1987)	§ 24.11
Colorado v. United States Dep't of the Army, 707 F. Supp. 1562 (D. Colo. 1989)	§ 14.5
Colorado Dep't of Health v. Martin Marietta Corp., No. 86-CV-2034 (signed May 7, 1986)	§ 24.11
Columbus, City of v. Clark-Dietz & Assocs. Eng'rs, 550 F. Supp. 610 (N.D. Miss. 1982)	§ 17.5
Commonwealth v. Prince Mfg. Co., 56 Pa. D.& C.2d 69 (1971)	§ 3.3
Commonwealth v. Scantena, 508 Pa. 512, 498 A.2d 1314 (1985)	§ 3.8
Commonwealth Dep't of Envtl. Resources v. Locust Point Quarries, Inc., 483 Pa. 350, 396 A.2d 1205 (1979)	§ 3.3
Commonwealth Dep't of Envtl. Resources v. PBS Coals, Inc., 112 Pa. Commw. 1, 534 A.2d 1130, *appeal dismissed,* 520 Pa. 591, 551 A.2d 217 (1987)	§ 3.8
Commonwealth Dep't of Envtl. Resources v. Peggs Run Coal Co., 55 Pa. Commw. 312, 423 A.2d 765 (1980)	§ 3.8
Connolly v. Pension Benefit Guar. Corp., 475 U.S. 211 (1986)	§ 14.11
Consolidated Rail Corp. v. City of Bayonne, 724 F. Supp. 320 (D.N.J. 1989)	§ 8.7
Continental Ins. v. Northeastern Pharmaceutical & Chem. Co., 842 F.2d 977 (8th Cir.), *cert. denied,* 484 U.S. 1008 (1988)	§§ 11.15, 15.11, 15.15
Cook, Flanagan & Berst v. Clausing, 73 Wash. 2d 393, 438 P.2d 865 (1986)	§ 18.2
Coombs v. Beeds, 89 Me. 187, 36 A. 104 (1896)	§ 17.5

Case	*Book §*
Matthews v. Eldridge, 424 U.S. 319 (1976)	§ 25.17
Mauro v. Raymark Indus., Inc., 116 N.J. 126, 561 A.2d 257 (1989)	§§ 4.9, 15.12
Max Daetwyler Corp. v. R. Meyer, 762 F.2d 290 (3d Cir.), *cert. denied,* 474 U.S. 980 (1985)	§ 5.17
Mazetti v. Armour & Co., 75 Wash. 622, 135 p.633 (1913)	§ 7.5
McClanahan v. California Spray Chem. Corp., 194 Va. 842, 75 S.E.2d 712 (1953)	§ 7.3
McClellan Ecological Seepage Situation (MESS) v. Weinberger, 655 F. Supp. 601 (E.D. Cal. 1988)	§§ 14.3, 14.6, 14.7
McGee v. International Life Ins. Co., 355 U.S. 220 (1957)	§ 5.16
Melendrez v. Soales, 105 Mich. App. 73, 306 N.W.2d 399 (1981)	§ 4.6
Melo v. Hafer, 912 F.2d 628 (3d Cir. 1990)	§ 14.10
Menne v. Celotex Corp., 861 F.2d 1453 (10th Cir. 1988)	§ 22.13
Merry v. Westinghouse Elec. Corp., 684 F. Supp. 847 (M.D. Pa. 1988)	§ 4.12
Mesiti v. Microdot, Inc., 1990 Westlaw 78,124, Civ. No. 89-321-D (D.N.H. June 8, 1990)	§§ 5.18, 21.2
Meyer v. United States Coast Guard, 644 F. Supp. 221 (E.D.N.C. 1986)	§§ 14.5, 14.6
Mianus River Preservation Comm. v. EPA, 541 F.2d 899 (2d Cir. 1976)	§ 3.6
Michigan Chem. Corp. v. Midland Ins. Co., 728 F.2d 374 (6th Cir. 1984)	§ 15.13
Middlesex County Sewerage Auth. v. National Sea Clammers Ass'n, 453 U.S. 1 (1981)	§ 14.9
Midlantic Nat'l Bank v. New Jersey Dep't of Envtl. Protection, 474 U.S. 494, *reh'g denied,* 106 S. Ct. 1482 (1986)	§§ 5.13, 24.21
Miller v. DeWitt, 59 Ill. App. 2d 38, 208 N.E.2d 249 (1965), *aff'd in part, rev'd in part on other grounds,* 37 Ill. 2d 273, 226 N.E.2d 630 (1967)	§§ 17.2, 17.3
Milwaukee v. Illinois, 451 U.S. 304 (1981)	§ 14.9
Mississippi Meadows, Inc. v. Hodson, 13 Ill. App. 3d 24, 299 N.E.2d 359 (1973), *appeal denied,* 54 Ill. 2d 597 (1973)	§ 17.3
Missouri v. Bliss, 23 Env't Rep. Cas. (BNA) 1978 (E.D. Mo. 1985)	§ 5.18
Missouri Pac. R.R. v. Ault, 256 U.S. 554 (1921)	§ 14.3
Mitchell v. United States, 709 F. Supp. 767 (W.D. Tex. 1989), *rev'd on other grounds sub nom.,* Mitchell v. Carlson, 896 F.2d 128 (5th Cir. 1990)	§ 14.10
Mitzelfelt v. Department of Air Force, 903 F.2d 1293 (10th Cir. 1990)	§ 14.6
Mizerak v. Adams, 682 F.2d 374 (2d Cir. 1982)	§ 25.5
Montgomery v. Jack, 556 So. 2d 267 (La. Ct. App. 1990)	§ 18.2
Montijo v. Swift, 219 Cal. App. 2d 351, 33 Cal. Rptr. 133 (1963)	§ 17.2

Case	*Book §*
Quadion Corp. v. Mache, 738 F. Supp. 270 (N.D. Ill. 1990)	§ 9.6
Quarles v. Fugua Indus., 504 F.2d 1358 (10th Cir. 1974)	§ 5.17
Quasha v. Shale Dev. Corp., 667 F.2d 483 (5th Cir. 1982)	§ 5.17
Queensbury Union Free School Dist. v. Jim Walter Corp., 91 Misc. 2d 804, 398 N.Y.S.2d 832 (1977)	§ 17.9
Raffaele v. Compagnie Generale Maritime, 707 F.2d 395 (9th Cir. 1983)	§ 5.17
Ray Indus., Inc. v. Liberty Mut. Ins. Co., 728 F. Supp. 1310 (E.D. Mich. 1989)	§ 15.10
Reardon v. United States, 731 F. Supp. 558 (D. Mass. 1990)	§§ 14.11, 16.9
Regan v. Cherry Corp., 706 F. Supp. 145 (D.R.I. 1989)	§ 20.4
Remon v. Sooter, 1 Ill. App. 3d 406, 274 N.E.2d 200 (1971)	§ 4.9
Reyno v. Piper Aircraft Co., 479 F. Supp. 727 (M.D. Pa. 1979)	§ 5.32
Reynolds Metals Co. v. Yturbide, 258 F.2d 321 (9th Cir. 1958), *cert. denied,* 358 U.S. 840 (1958)	§ 17.12
Ridgefield Bourough v. New York Susquehanna & W.R., 632 F. Supp. 582 (D.N.J. 1986), *aff'd,* 801 F.2d 57 (3d Cir. 1987)	§ 8.7
Roanoke Hosp. Assoc. v. Doyle & Russell, Inc., 215 Va. 796, 214 S.E.2d 155 (1975)	§ 17.13
Roberts v. Ball, Hunt, Hart, Brown & Baerwitz, 57 Cal. App. 3d 104, 128 Cal. Rptr. 901 (1976)	§ 18.4
Robertson v. Allied-Signal, No. 89-2123 (3d Cir. Aug. 2, 1990), 18 Prod. Safety & Liab. Rep. (BNA) 1000	§ 4.8
Robertson Lumber Co. v. Stephen Farmers Coop. Elevator Co., 274 Minn. 17, 143 N.W.2d 622 (1966)	§ 17.4
Robins Dry Dock v. Flint, 275 U.S. 303 (1927)	§ 21.2
Rockwell Int'l Corp. v. IU Int'l Corp., 702 F. Supp. 1384 (N.D. Ill. 1988)	§§ 6.4, 6.5, 6.7, 9.6, 9.9
Rollins Envtl. Servs., Inc. v. Logan Township, 209 N.J. Super. 556, 508 A.2d 271, *cert. denied,* 523 A.2d 157 (App. Div. 1986)	§ 3.12
Romero-Barcelo v. Brown, 643 F.2d 835 (1st Cir. 1981)	§ 14.5
Rose v. A.C.&S., Inc., 796 F.2d 294 (9th Cir. 1986)	§ 4.9
Rosos Litho Supply Corp. v. Hansen, 123 Ill. App. 3d 290, 462 N.E.2d 566 (1984)	§ 17.5
Ruckelshaus v. Sierra Club, 463 U.S. 680 (1983)	§ 14.3
Rusch Factors, Inc. v. Levin, 284 F. Supp. 85 (D.R.I. 1968)	§ 18.4
Ruston Mining Co. v. Commonwealth, 16 Pa. Commw. 135, 328 A.2d 185 (1974)	§ 3.3
Ryan v. Progressive Grocery Stores, 255 N.Y. 388, 175 N.E. 105 (1931)	§ 7.5
Rylands v. Fletcher, L.R. 1 Exc. 265 (1866), *aff'd,* L.R. 3 H.L. 330 (1868)	§§ 1.4, 4.3, 17.7, 17.8

TABLE OF
UNITED STATES
CODE CITATIONS

TABLE OF
CODE OF FEDERAL
REGULATIONS CITATIONS

INDEX